BOWDITCH FOR YACHTSMEN:

Piloting

BOWDITCH FOR YACHTSMEN: *PILOTING*

Selected from AMERICAN PRACTICAL NAVIGATOR

NATHANIEL BOWDITCH

DAVID McKAY COMPANY, INC.

New York

BOWDITCH FOR YACHTSMEN:
Piloting
Selected from AMERICAN PRACTICAL NAVIGATOR

Published by
David McKay Company, Inc.
2 Park Avenue
New York, N.Y.
10016

ISBN: 0-679-50930-5

MANUFACTURED IN THE UNITED STATES OF AMERICA
Designed by Bernard Schliefer

About the Book

American Practical Navigator: An Epitome of Navigation has lived up to its title for over a century and a half. "Bowditch," as it is called, has been the navigator's bible and a primary source for the yachtsman ever since its first publication in 1802.

Because of its size, however, and because it covers so many topics that are only peripheral to the needs of the coastal pilot, many boat owners hesitate to keep it aboard for lack of space.

Bowditch for Yachtsmen: Piloting extracts those portions of Bowditch that are of interest and use to the coastal pilot—the skipper who wants to guide his craft safely and intelligently to his destination but who doesn't necessarily need to refer to a chapter on submarine or polar navigation this trip (he hopes).

In this book the reader will find a short history of navigation, definitions of important terms, a detailed explanation of chart projections and nautical charts, sources of charts and publications, explanation of compass error and its causes, piloting equipment and instruments, and the basics of piloting and dead reckoning, including information on tides, tidal currents, and weather.

Bowditch for Yachtsmen: Piloting is designed to be taken aboard. Like the original, it is practical, and like the original, it also includes background in history and theory that can provide interesting and informative reading on rainy days and leisurely passages.

Last painting by Gilbert Stuart (1828). Considered by the family of Bowditch to be the best of various paintings made, although it was unfinished when the artist died.

Nathaniel Bowditch
(1773-1838)

NATHANIEL BOWDITCH was born on March 26, 1773, at Salem, Mass., fourth of the seven children of shipmaster Habakkuk Bowditch and his wife, Mary. Since the seventeenth century, the family had resided at Salem. Most of its sons, like those of other families in this New England seaport, had gone to sea, and many of them became shipmasters.

It is reported that Nathaniel Bowditch's father lost two ships at sea, and by late Revolutionary days he returned to his previous trade of cooper. This provided insufficient income to supply the needs of his growing family, and for many years they received an annual grant from the Salem Marine Society. By the time Nathaniel had reached the age of ten, poverty necessitated his leaving school and joining his father's trade.

Nathaniel was unsuccessful as a cooper, and at about twelve he entered a ship-chandlery firm. During this time his great mind first attracted public attention. Bowditch had developed an all-consuming interest in learning, particularly mathematics. By his middle teens he was recognized in Salem as an authority on that subject, and certain learned men who were impressed by his desire to educate himself supplied him with books. Since many of the best books were written by Europeans, Bowditch first taught himself French, Spanish, Latin, Greek, and German, among other languages. At sixteen he began the study of Newton's *Principia*, translating parts of it from the Latin. He even found an error, and, though lacking the confidence to announce it at the time, later published his findings and had them accepted.

During the Revolutionary War a privateer out of a neighboring town had taken an English vessel which was carrying the philosophical library of a famed Irish scholar. The books were bought by a group of educated Salem men who used them to found the Philosophical Library Company, reputed to have been the best library north of Philadelphia at the time. In 1791, when Bowditch was eighteen, the Company was persuaded to allow Bowditch the use of its library. Encouraged by several scholarly mentors from Harvard, Bowditch studied the works, especially those of mathematicians and astronomers. By the time he came of age, young Bowditch was the outstanding mathematician in the Commonwealth, and perhaps in the country.

Bowditch was drawn to navigation early, learning the subject at the age of thirteen from an old British sailor. A year later he began studying surveying, and in 1794 he assisted in a survey of the town. At fifteen he devised an almanac reputed to have been of great accuracy. His other youthful accomplishments included the construction of a crude barometer and a sundial.

When Bowditch went to sea at the age of twenty-one, it was as captain's writer and nominal second mate on the ship *Henry*, the officer's berth being offered him because of his reputation as a scholar. In those days accurate time was not available to the average naval or merchant ship. A reliable marine chronometer had been invented some sixty years before, but the prohibitive cost, plus the long voyages without opportunity to check the error of the timepiece, made the large investment impractical. A known system of determining longitude by "lunar distance" did not require an accurate timepiece but was so involved as to be beyond the capabilities of the uneducated seamen of that day. Consequently, ships navigated by a combination of dead reckoning and parallel sailing (a system of sailing north or south to the latitude of the destination and then east or west to the destination).

To Bowditch, the mathematical genius, computation of lunar distances was no mystery, of course, but he recognized the need for an easier method of working them. Through analysis and observation, he derived a new and simplified formula which was to open the book of celestial navigation to all seamen.

John Hamilton Moore's *The Practical Navigator* was the leading navigational text at the time, and had been for many years. Bowditch, however, began turning up errors in Moore's book, and before long he found it necessary to recompute some of the tables he most often used in working his sights. Bowditch recorded the errors he found, and by the end of his second voyage, made in the higher capacity of supercargo, the news of his findings had reached a publisher at Newburyport, Mass. At the publisher's request, Bowditch agreed to correct Moore's book. The first edition of *The New Practical Navigator* was published in 1799, with correction of the errors and some additional information. The following year a second edition was published with additional corrections. Bowditch eventually found more than 8,000 errors in the work, however, and it was finally decided to rewrite the book completely and publish it under his own name. In 1802 the first edition of *The New American Practical Navigator* by Nathaniel Bowditch was published, and his vow to put nothing in the book he could not teach every member of his crew served to keep the work within the understanding of the average seaman. His simplified methods, easily grasped by the intelligent seaman willing to learn, paved the way for "Yankee" supremacy of the seas during the clipper ship era. He revised the book several times.

Two months before sailing for Cadiz on his third voyage, in 1798, Bowditch married Elizabeth Boardman, daughter of a shipmaster. While he was away, his wife died at the age of eighteen. Two years later, he married his cousin, Mary Ingersoll—she, too, the daughter of a shipmaster. They had eight children.

Bowditch made a total of five trips to sea over a period of about nine years, his last as master and part owner of the three-masted *Putnam*. Homeward bound from a thirteen-month voyage, the *Putnam* approached Salem harbor on December 25, 1803, during a thick fog without having had a celestial observation since noon on the twenty-fourth. Relying on his dead reckoning, Bowditch conned his wooden-hulled ship to the entrance of the rocky harbor, where he had the good fortune to get a momentary glimpse of land that confirmed his position. The *Putnam* proceeded in, past such hazards as "Bowditch's Ledge" (named after a great-grandfather who had wrecked his ship on the rock more than a century before) and anchored safely at 1900 that evening. Word of the daring feat, performed when other masters were hove-to outside the harbor, spread along the coast and added greatly to Bowditch's reputation.

His standing as a mathematician and successful shipmaster earned him a lucrative position ashore within weeks after his last voyage. He was installed as president of a Salem fire and marine insurance company at the age of thirty, and during the twenty years he held that position the company prospered. In 1823 he left Salem to take a similar position with a Boston insurance firm, serving that company with equal success until his death.

Bowditch continued his mathematical and scientific pursuits and in 1814 turned to what he considered the greatest work of his life, the translation into English of *Mécanique Céleste*, by Pierre Laplace. *Mécanique Céleste* was a summary of all the then known facts about the workings of the heavens. Bowditch translated four of the five volumes before his death and published them at his own expense. He added formula derivations and included recent discoveries. His work made this information available to American astronomers and enabled them to pursue their studies on the basis of what was already known.

Among Bowditch's many honors were master of arts and doctor of laws degrees from Harvard University. From the time the Harvard graduates of Salem first assisted him in his studies, Bowditch had a great interest in that college. At one time he was offered a professorship in mathematics there, but this, as well as similar offers from West Point and the University of Virginia, he declined. In all his life he was never known to have made a public speech or to have addressed any large group of people.

Other honors included membership in the American Academy of Arts and Sciences, the East India Marine Society, the Royal Academy of Edinburgh, the Royal Society of London, the Royal Irish Academy, the American Philosophical Society, the Connecticut Academy of Arts and Sciences, the Boston Marine Society, the Royal Astronomical Society, the Palermo Academy of Science, and the Royal Academy of Berlin.

Nathaniel Bowditch outlived all his brothers and sisters by nearly thirty years. He died on March 16, 1838, at sixty-four. The following portion of the eulogy by the Salem Marine Society indicates the regard in which this distinguished American was held by his contemporaries:

". . . as long as ships shall sail, the needle point to the north, and the stars go through their wonted courses in the heavens, the name of Dr. Bowditch will be revered as of one who helped his fellow-men in a time of need, who was and is a guide to them over the pathless ocean, and of one who forwarded the great interests of mankind."

After Bowditch's death, Jonathan Ingersoll Bowditch, a son who made several voyages, took up the work and his name appeared on the title page until the thirty-fifth edition, in 1867. In 1868 the newly organized U.S. Navy Hydrographic Office (now the Naval Oceanographic Office) bought the copyright and has published the book since that time, revisions being made from time to time to keep the work in step with navigational improvements. The name has been altered to the *American Practical Navigator*, but the book is still commonly known as "Bowditch." A total of more than 700,000 copies has been printed in about 70 editions. It has lived since 1802 because it has combined the best thoughts of each generation of navigators, who have looked to it as their authority.

THE NEW AMERICAN

PRACTICAL NAVIGATOR;

BEING AN

EPITOME of NAVIGATION;

CONTAINING ALL THE TABLES NECESSARY TO BE USED WITH THE

NAUTICAL ALMANAC,

IN DETERMINING THE

L A T I T U D E;

AND THE

LONGITUDE BY LUNAR OBSERVATIONS;

AND

KEEPING A COMPLETE RECKONING AT SEA:

ILLUSTRATED BY

PROPER RULES AND EXAMPLES:

THE WHOLE EXEMPLIFIED IN A

J O U R N A L,

KEPT FROM

BOSTON TO MADEIRA,

IN WHICH ALL THE RULES OF NAVIGATION ARE INTRODUCED:

A L S O

The Demonstration of the most useful Rules of TRIGONOMETRY: With many useful Problems in MENSURATION, SURVEYING, and GAUGING: And a Dictionary of SEA-TERMS; with the Manner of performing the most common Evolutions at Sea.

TO WHICH ARE ADDED,

Some GENERAL INSTRUCTIONS and INFORMATION to MERCANTS, MASTERS of VESSELS, and others concerned in NAVIGATION, relative to MARITIME LAWS and MERCANTILE CUSTOMS.

FROM THE BEST AUTHORITIES.

ENRICHED WITH A NUMBER OF

NEW TABLES,

WITH ORIGINAL IMPROVEMENTS AND ADDITIONS, AND A LARGE VARIETY OF NEW AND IMPORTANT MATTER:

A L S O,

MANY THOUSAND ERRORS ARE CORRECTED,

WHICH HAVE APPEARED IN THE BEST SYSTEMS OF NAVIGATION YET PUBLISHED.

BY NATHANIEL BOWDITCH,

FELLOW OF THE AMERICAN ACADEMY OF ARTS AND SCIENCES.

ILLUSTRATED WITH COPPERPLATES.

First Edition.

PRINTED AT NEWBURYPORT, (MASS.) 1802,

BY

EDMUND M. BLUNT, (Proprietor)

FOR CUSHING & APPLETON, SALEM.

SOLD BY EVERY BOOK-SELLER, SHIP-CHANDLER, AND MATHEMATICAL INSTRUMENT MAKER, IN THE UNITED STATES AND WEST-INDIES.

Original title page of The New American Practical Navigator, *written by Nathaniel Bowditch and published in 1802.*

Contents

[1]

A Brief History of Navigation

Background • Navigation began with the first man. One of his first conscious acts probably was to home on some object that caught his eye, and thus **land navigation** was undoubtedly the earliest form. His first venture upon the waters may have come shortly after he observed that some objects float, and through curiosity or an attempt at self-preservation he learned that a larger object, perhaps a log, would support him. **Marine navigation** was born when he attempted to guide his craft.

The earliest marine navigation was a form of **piloting,** which came into being as man became familiar with landmarks and used them as guides. **Dead reckoning** probably came next as he sought to predict his future positions, or perhaps as he bravely ventured farther from landmarks. **Celestial navigation,** as it is known today, had to await acquisition of information regarding the motions of the heavenly bodies, although these bodies were used to steer by almost from the beginning. **Electronic navigation** is the modern application of a different form of energy to solve an old problem, its principal use being to extend the range of piloting.

From art to science • Navigation is the process of directing the movements of a craft from one point to another. To do this safely is an *art*. In perhaps 6,000 years—some writers make it 8,000—man has transformed this art almost into a *science*, and navigation today is so nearly a science that the inclination is to forget that it was ever anything else. It is commonly thought that to navigate a ship one must have a chart to determine the course and distance, a compass to steer by, and a means of determining the positions of the ship during the passage. *Must* have? The word *must* betrays how dependent the modern navigator has become upon the tools now in his hands. Many of the great voyages of history—voyages that made known much of the world—were made without one or more of these "essentials."

Epic voyages • History records a number of great voyages of varying navigational significance. Little or nothing is known of the navigational accomplishments of the ancient mariners, but the record of the knowledge and equipment used during later voyages serves to illustrate periodic developments in the field.

Pre-Christian navigation • Down through the stream of time a number of voyages have occurred without navigational significance. Noah's experience in the ark is of little interest navigationally, except for his use of a dove to locate land. There is evidence that at least some American Indians reached these shores by sea as early as about 2200 B.C., the approximate time that a general exodus seems to have occurred from a center in southwestern Asia. This is about the time the Tower of Babel is believed to have been built. It is noteworthy that almost every land reached by the great European explorers was already inhabited.

It is not difficult to understand how a people not accustomed to the sea might make a single great voyage without contributing anything of significance to the advancement of navigation. Not so clear, however, is the fact that the Norsemen and the Polynesians, great seafaring people, left nothing more than conflicting traditions of their methods. The reputed length of the voyages made by these people suggests more advanced navigational methods than their records indicate, although the explanation may be that they left few written accounts of any kind. Or perhaps they developed their powers of perception to such an extent that navigation, to them, was a highly advanced art. In this respect their navigation may not have differed greatly from that of some birds, insects, fishes, and animals.

One of the earliest well-recorded voyages is known today through the book of observations written by Pytheas of Massalia, a Greek astronomer and navigator. Sometime between 350 B.C. and 300 B.C. he sailed from a Mediterranean port and followed an established trade route to England. From there he ventured north to Scotland and Thule, the legendary land of the midnight sun. He went on to explore Norwegian fiords and rivers in northwest Germany. He may have made his way into the Baltic.

Pytheas' voyage, and others of his time, were significant in that they were the work of men who had no compasses, no sextants, no chronometers, no electronic devices such as are commonplace today. Some historians have said that before seafaring men had adequate equipment they hugged the shore and sailed only by daylight in fair weather. Many undoubtedly did use this practice, but the more intrepid did not creep along the coast. They were often out of sight of land, and yet knew sufficiently well where they were and how to get home again. They were able to use the sun, the stars, and the winds without the aid of mechanical devices.

Although Pytheas had none of the equipment considered essential today, he must have known what the mariners of his time, Phoenician and Greek, knew about navigation. There was a fair store of knowledge about the movements of the stars, for example, which all seafaring men shared. They had a practical grasp of some part of what is now called celestial navigation, for the moving celestial bodies were their compasses. Pytheas may not have been acquainted with the *Periplus* of Scylax, the earliest known sailing directions, but it is reasonable to suppose that he had similar information. There may well have been charts of a sort, even though no record of them exists.

These early seamen knew direction by day or night if the sky was clear, and they could judge it reasonably well when the sky was overcast, using the wind and the sea. They knew the hot Libyan wind from the desert—today called the **sirocco**—and the northern wind, the **mistral.** They could estimate distance. Their ships must have carried some means of measuring time—the sand glass was known to the ancients—and they could estimate speed by counting the strokes of the oars, a common practice from galley to modern college racing shell. Mariners who spent their lives traveling the Mediterranean knew what their ships could do, even if today it is not known what they meant by "a day's sail"—whether 35 miles, or 50, or 100.

Sixteenth century navigation • Progress in the art of navigation came slowly during the early centuries of the Christian era, all but stopped during the Dark Ages, and then spurted forward when Europe entered a golden age of discovery. The circumnavigation of the globe by the expedition organized by Ferdinand Magellan illustrates the advances made during the 1,800 years following Pytheas.

Magellan was able first to draw on a good deal of existing nautical knowledge. When he sailed in 1519, his equipment included sea charts, parchment skins to be made into charts en route, a terrestrial globe, wooden and metal theodolites, wooden and wood-and-bronze quadrants, compasses, magnetic needles, hour glasses and "timepieces," and a log to be towed astern. So the sixteenth century navigator had crude charts of the known world, a compass to steer by, instruments with which he could determine his latitude, a log to estimate speed, certain sailing directions, and solar and traverse tables. The huge obstacle yet to be overcome was an accurate method of determining longitude.

Eighteenth century navigation • Little is known today of the "timepieces" carried by Magellan, but surely they were not used to determine longitude. Two hundred years later, however, the chronometer began to emerge.

With it, the navigator for the first time was able to determine his longitude accurately and fix his position at sea.

The three voyages of discovery made by James Cook of the Royal Navy in the Pacific Ocean between 1768 and 1779 may be said to mark the dawn of modern navigation. Cook's expedition had the full backing of England's scientific organizations, and he was the first captain to undertake extended explorations at sea with navigational equipment, techniques, and knowledge that might be considered modern.

On his first voyage Cook was provided with an astronomical clock, a "journeyman" clock, and a watch lent by the Astronomer Royal. With these he could determine longitude, using the long and tedious lunar distance method. On his second voyage four chronometers were provided. These instruments, added to those already possessed by the mariner, enabled Cook to navigate his vessels with a precision undreamed of by Pytheas and Magellan.

By the time Cook began his explorations, the acceptance of the heliocentric theory of the universe had led to the publication of the first official nautical almanac. Charts had progressed steadily, and adequate projections were available. With increased understanding of variation, the compass had become reliable. Good schools of navigation existed, and textbooks which reduced the mathematics of navigation to the essentials had been published. Speed through the water could be determined with reasonable accuracy by the logs then in use. Most important, the first chronometers were being produced.

Twentieth century navigation • The maiden voyage of the SS *United States* in July, 1952 served to illustrate the progress made in navigation during the 175 years since Cook's voyages. Outstanding because of its record trans-Atlantic passage, the vessel is of interest navigationally in that it carried the most modern equipment available and exemplified the fact that navigation had become nearly a science.

Each of the deck officers owned a sextant with which he could make observations more accurately than did Cook. Reliable chronometers, the product of hundreds of years of experimental work, were available to determine the time of each observation. The gyro compass indicated true north regardless of variation and deviation.

Modern, convenient almanacs were used to obtain the coordinates of various celestial bodies, to an accuracy greater than needed. Easily used altitude and azimuth tables gave the navigator data for determining his Sumner (celestial) line of position by the method of Marcq St.-Hilaire. Accurate charts were available for the waters plied, sailing directions for coasts and ports visited, light lists giving the characteristics of the various aids to navigation along these coasts, and pilot charts and navigational texts for reference purposes.

Electronics served the navigator in a number of ways. Radio time signals and weather reports enabled him to check his chronometers and avoid foul weather. A radio direction finder was available to obtain bearings, and a radiotelephone was used to communicate with persons on land and sea. The electrically operated echo sounder indicated the depth of water under the keel, radar the distances and bearings of objects within range, even in the densest fog. Using loran, the navigator could fix the position of his ship a thousand miles and more from transmitting stations.

Piloting and Dead Reckoning

Background •, The history of piloting and dead reckoning extends from man's earliest use of landmarks to the latest model of the gyro compass. In the thousands of years between, navigation by these methods has progressed from short passages along known coast lines to transoceanic voyages during which celestial observations cannot be, or are not, made.

Charts • A form of sailing directions was written several hundred years before Christ. Although charts cannot be traced back that far, they may have existed during the same time. From earliest times men have undoubtedly known that it is more difficult to explain how to get to a place than it is to draw a diagram, and since the first charts known are comparatively accurate and cover large areas, it seems logical that earlier charts served as guides for the cartographers.

Undoubtedly, the first charts were not made on any "projection" but were simple diagrams which took no notice of the shape of the earth. In fact, these "plane" charts were used for many centuries after chart projections were available.

The **gnomonic projection** (see Chapter 3) is believed to have been developed by Thales of Miletus (640–546 B.C.), who was chief of the Seven Wise Men of ancient Greece; founder of Greek geometry, astronomy, and philosophy, and a navigator and cartographer.

The size of the earth was measured with some accuracy at least as early as the third century B.C. by Eratosthenes. Eratosthenes is also believed to have been the first person to measure latitude, using the degree for this purpose. He constructed a 16-point wind rose, prepared a table of winds, and recognized local and prevailing winds. From his own discoveries and from information gleaned from the manuscripts of mariners, explorers, land travelers, historians, and philosophers, he wrote an outstanding description of the known world, which helped elevate geography to the status of a science.

Stereographic and **orthographic projections** (see Chapter 3) were originated by Hipparchus in the second century B.C.

Ptolemy's World Map. The Egyptian Claudius Ptolemy was a second century A.D. astronomer, writer, geographer, and mathematician who had no equal in astronomy until the arrival of Copernicus in the sixteenth century. An outstanding cartographer, for his time, Ptolemy constructed many charts and listed the latitudes and longitudes, as determined by celestial observations, of the places shown. As a geographer, however, he made his most serious mistake, taking an estimate that the earth was 18,000 miles in circumference. The result was that those who accepted his work—and for many hundreds of years few thought to question it—had to deal with a concept that was far too small. One of them was Columbus. Not until 1669, when Jean Picard computed the circumference of the earth to be 24,500 miles, was a more accurate figure generally used.

Ptolemy's map of the world (fig. 1.1) was a great achievement, however. It was the original conic projection, and on it he located some 8,000 places by latitude and longitude. It was he who fixed the convention that the top of the map is north.

Asian Charts. Through the Dark Ages some progress was made. Moslem cartographers as well as astronomers took inspiration from Ptolemy. However, they knew that Ptolemy had overestimated the length of the Mediterranean by some 20°. Charts of the Indian Ocean, bearing horizontal lines indicating parallels of latitude, and vertical lines dividing the seas according to the direction of the wind, were drawn by Persian and Arabian navigators. The prime meridian separated a windward from a leeward region and other meridians were drawn at intervals indicating "three hours sail." This information, though far from exact, was helpful to the sailing ship masters.

Portolan Charts. The mariners of Venice, Leghorn, and Genoa must have had charts when they competed for Mediterranean trade before, during, and after the Crusades. Venice at one time had 300 ships, a navy of 45 galleys, and 11,000 men engaged in her maritime industry. But perhaps the rivalry was too keen for masters carelessly to leave charts lying about. At any rate, the earliest useful charts of the Middle Ages that are known today were drawn by seamen of Catalonia (now part of Spain).

The Portolan charts were constructed from the knowledge acquired by seamen during their voyages about the Mediterranean. The actual courses and dead reckoning distances between land points were used as a skeleton for the charts, and the coasts between were usually filled in from data obtained in land surveys. After the compass came into use, these charts became quite accurate.

These charts were distinguished by a group of long rhumb lines intersecting at a common point, surrounded by eight or sixteen similar groups of shorter lines. Later *Portolanis* had a *rose dei venti* (rose of the winds), the forerunner of the compass rose, superimposed over the center (fig. 1.2). They carried a scale of miles, located nearly all the known hazards

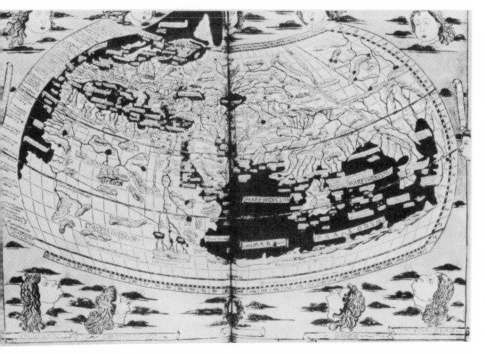

Courtesy of the Map Division of the Library of Congress.

Fig. 1.1. The world, as envisioned by Ptolemy about 150 A.D. This chart was prepared in 1482 by Nicolaus Germanus for a translation of Ptolemy's Cosmographia.

Courtesy of the Map Division of the Library of Congress.

Fig. 1.2. A fourteenth-century Portolan chart.

to navigation, and had numerous notes of interest to the pilot. They were not marked with parallels of latitude or meridians of longitude, but present-day harbor and coastal charts trace their ancestry directly to them.

Padrón Real. The growing habit of assembling information for charts took concrete form in the *Padrón Real.* This was the pattern, or master, map kept after 1508 by the *Casa de Contratación* at Seville. It was intended to contain everything known about the world, and it was constructed from facts brought back by mariners from voyages to newly discovered lands. From it were drawn the charts upon which the explorers of the Age of Discovery most depended.

World maps of the Middle Ages. In 1515 Leonardo de Vinci drew his famous map of the world. On it, America is represented as extending more to the east and west than to the north and south, with only a chain of islands, the largest named Florida, between it and South America. A wide stretch of ocean is shown between South America and *Terra Australis Nondum Cognita,* the mythical south-seas continent whose existence in the position shown was not disproved until 250 years later.

Ortelius' atlas *Theatrum Orbis Terra* was published at Antwerp in 1570. One of the most magnificent ever produced, it illustrates Europe, Africa, and Asia with comparative accuracy. North and South America are poorly depicted, but Magellan's Strait is shown. All land to the south

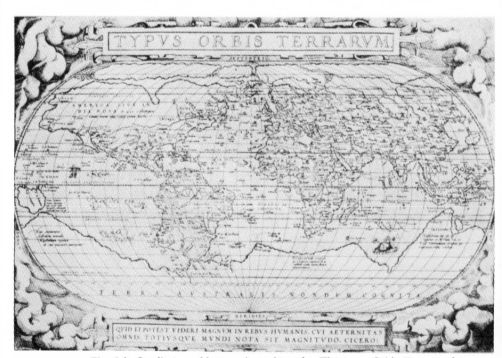

Fig. 1.3. Ortelius' world map, from his atlas Theatrum Orbis Terra, *published at Antwerp in 1570.*

of it, as well as Australia, is considered part of *Terra Australis Nondum Cognita* (fig. 1.3).

The Mercator projection (see Chapter 3). For hundreds, perhaps thousands, of years cartographers drew their charts as "plane" projections, making no use of the discoveries of Ptolemy and Hipparchus. As the area of the known world increased, however, the attempt to depict that larger area on the flat surface of the plane chart brought map makers to the realization that allowance would have to be made for the curvature of the earth.

Gerardus Mercator (Latinized form of Gerhard Kremer) was a brilliant Flemish geographer who recognized the need for a better method of chart projection. In 1569 he published a world chart which he had constructed on the principle since known by his name. The theory of his work was correct, but Mercator made errors in his computation, and because he never published a complete description of the mathematics involved, mariners were deprived of the full advantages of the projection for another 30 years.

Then Edward Wright published the results of his own independent study in the matter, explaining the Mercator projection fully and providing the table of meridional parts which enabled all cartographers to make use of the principle.

The Lambert projections. Johann Heinrich Lambert, 1728–1777, self-educated son of an Alsace tailor, designed a number of map projections. Some of these are still widely used, the most renowned being the **Lambert conformal** (see Chapter 3).

Sailing directions • The *Periplus* of Scylax, written sometime between the sixth and fourth centuries B.C., is the earliest known book that approximates sailing directions. Surprisingly similar to modern sailing directions, it provided the mariner with information on distances between ports, aids and dangers, port facilities, and other pertinent matters.

Parts Around the World, Pytheas' book of observations made during his epic voyage in the fourth century B.C., was another early volume of sailing directions. His rough estimates of distances and descriptions of coast lines would be considered crude today, but they served as an invaluable aid to navigators who followed him into these otherwise unknown waters.

Sailing directions during the Renaissance. No particularly noteworthy improvements were made in sailing directions during the Middle Ages, but several were published—the *Portolano Rizo* in 1490; the French "routiers"—the **rutters** of the English sailor; and in 1557 the Italian pilot Battista Testa Rossa's *Brieve Compendio del Arte del Navigar*, which was designed to serve the mariner on soundings and off. It forecast the single, all-inclusive volume that was soon to come, the **Waggoner.**

About 1584 the Dutch pilot Lucas Jans Zoon Waghenaer published a volume of navigational principles, tables, charts, and sailing directions which served as a guide for such books for the next 200 years. In *Spieghel der Zeevaerdt* (*The Mariner's Mirror*), Waghenaer gave directions and charts for sailing the waters of the Low Countries and later a second volume was published covering waters of the North and Baltic seas.

These "Waggoners" met with great success and during the next 30 years, 24 editions were published in Dutch, German, Latin, and English. The success of these books and the subsequent competition among authors were responsible for their eventual discontinuance, for each writer attempted to make his work more inclusive than any other and the result was a tremendous book difficult to handle.

Modern sailing directions. The publication of modern sailing directions by the U.S. Navy Hydrographic Office (now the Naval Oceanographic Office) is one of the achievements properly attributed to Matthew Fontaine Maury. During the two decades he headed the institution, Maury gathered data that led directly to the publication of eight volumes of sailing directions. Today there are more than 65 volumes providing the mariner with detailed information on almost all foreign coasts, in addition to **coast pilots** of the United States and its possessions, published by the National Ocean Survey.

The compass • Early in the history of navigation man noted that the pole star remained close to one point in the northern sky. This served as his compass. When it was not visible, he used other stars, the sun and moon, winds, clouds, and waves. The development of the magnetic compass, perhaps a thousand years ago, and the twentieth century development of the gyro compass offer today's navigator a method of steering his course with an accuracy as great as he is capable of using.

The **magnetic compass** (see Chapter 6) is one of the oldest of the navigator's instruments. Its origin is not known. Probably it was known first in the west. The Norsemen of the eleventh century were familiar with it, and about 1200 a compass used by mariners when the pole star was hidden was described by a French poet, Guyot de Provins. A needle thrust through a straw and floated in water in a container comprised the earliest compass known, and the reliability of the magnetic compass of today is a comparatively recent achievement. Some 75 years ago, Lord Kelvin developed the Admiralty type compass used today.

The **compass card,** according to tradition, originated about the beginning of the fourteenth century, when Flavio Gioja of Amalfi attached a sliver of lodestone or a magnetized needle to a card. But the rose on the compass card is probably older than the needle. It is the wind rose of the ancients. Primitive man naturally named directions by the winds. The

Latin rose of 12 points was common on most compasses used in the Middle Ages.

Variation (see Chapter 7) was well understood 200 years ago, and navigators made allowance for it, but earliest recognition of its existence is not known. Columbus and even the eleventh century Chinese have been given credit for its discovery, but little proof can be offered for either claim.

The secular change in variation was determined by a series of magnetic observations made at Limehouse, England. In 1580 William Borough fixed the variation in that area at approximately 11°25′ east. Thirty-two years later Edmund Gunter determined it to be 6°13′ east. At first it was believed that Borough had made an error in his work, but in 1633 a further decrease was found, and the earth's changing magnetic field was established.

A South Atlantic expedition was led by Edmond Halley at the close of the seventeenth century to gather data and to map, for the first time, lines of variation. In 1724 George Graham published his observations in proof of the diurnal change in variation. Canton determined that the change was considerably less in winter than in summer, and about 1785 the strength of the magnetic force was shown by Paul de Lamanon to vary in different places.

The existence of **deviation** (see Chapter 7) was known to John Smith in 1627 when he wrote of the "bittacle" as being a "square box nailed together with wooden pinnes, because iron nails would attract the Compasse." But no one knew how to correct a compass for deviation until Captain Matthew Flinders discovered a method of doing so. Flinders did not understand deviation completely, but the vertical bar he erected to correct for it was part of the solution, and the **Flinders bar** used today is a memorial to its discoverer.

The gyro compass. The age of iron ships demanded a compass which could be relied upon to indicate true north at all times, free from disturbing forces of variation and deviation.

In 1851 Leon Foucault performed his famous pendulum experiment to demonstrate the rotation of the earth. Foucault's realization that the swinging pendulum would maintain the plane of its motion led him, the following year, to develop and name the first gyroscope, using the principle of a common toy called a "rotascope." Handicapped by the lack of a source of power to maintain the spin of his gyroscope, Foucault used a microscope to observe the indication of the earth's rotation during the short period in which his manually operated gyroscope remained in rotation. A gyro compass was not practical until electric power became available, more than 50 years later, to maintain the spin of the gyroscope.

Elmer A. Sperry, an American, and Anschutz-Kampfe, a German, independently invented gyro compasses during the first decade of the twentieth century.

The log • Since virtually the beginning of navigation, the mariner has attempted to determine his speed in traveling from one point to another. The earliest method was probably by estimate.

The oldest speed measuring device known is the **Dutchman's log.** Originally, any object which would float was thrown overboard on the lee side, from a point well forward, and the time required for it to pass between two points on the deck was noted. The time, as determined by sand glass, was compared with the known distance along the deck between the two points to determine the speed.

Near the end of the sixteenth century a line was attached to the log, and as the line was paid out a sailor recited certain sentences. The length of line which was paid out during the recitation was used to determine the speed. There is record of this method having been used as recently as the early seventeenth century. In its final form this **chip log, ship log,** or **common log** consisted of the *log chip* (or *log ship*), *log line, log reel,* and *log glass.* The chip was a quadrant-shaped piece of wood weighted along its circumference to keep it upright in the water. The log line was made fast to the log chip by means of a bridle, in such manner that a sharp pull on the log line dislodged a wooden peg and permitted the log chip to be towed horizontally through the water and hauled aboard. Sometimes a *stray line* was attached to the log to veer it clear of the ship's wake. In determining speed, the observer counted the knots in the log line which was paid out during a certain time. The length of line between knots and the number of seconds required for the sand to run out were changed from time to time as the accepted length of the mile was altered.

The chip log has been superseded by patent logs that register on dials. However, the common log has left its mark on modern navigation, as the use of the term **knot** to indicate a speed of one nautical mile per hour dates from this device.

Mechanical logs first appeared about the middle of the seventeenth century. By the beginning of the nineteenth century, the forerunners of modern mechanical logs were used by some navigators, although many years were to pass before they became generally accepted.

In 1773 logs on which the distance run was recorded on dials secured to the taffrail were tested on board a British warship and found reasonably adequate, although the comparative delicateness of the mechanism led to speculation about their long-term worth. Another type of existence at the time consisted of a wheel arrangement made fast on the underside of the keel, which transmitted readings to a dial inside the vessel as the wheel rotated.

An improved log was introduced by Edward Massey in 1802. This log gave considerably greater accuracy by means of a more sensitive rotator attached by a short length of line to a geared recording instrument. The difficulty with this log was that it had to be hauled aboard to take each reading. Various improvements were made, but it was not until 1878 that a log was developed in which the rotator could be used in conjunction with a dial secured to the after rail of the ship. Although refinements and improvements have been made, the patent log used today is essentially the same as that developed in 1878.

Engine revolution counters (see Chapter 6) had their origin with the observations of the captains of the first paddle steamers, who discovered that by counting the paddle revolutions, they could, with practice, estimate their runs in thick weather as accurately as they could by streaming the log. Later developments led to the modern revolution counter on screw-type vessels, which can be used with reasonable accuracy if the propeller is submerged and an accurate estimate of slip is made.

Pitot-static and impeller-type logs (see Chapter 6) are recent mechanical developments in the field of speed measurement.

Units of distance and depth • The modern navigator is concerned principally with three units of linear measure: the **nautical mile,** the **fathom,** and the **foot** (sometimes also the **meter**). Primitive man, however, used such natural units as the width of a finger, the **span** of his hand, the length of his **foot,** the distance from elbow to the tip of the middle finger (the **cubit** of biblical renown), or the **pace** (sometimes one but usually a double step) to measure short distances.

These ancient measurements varied from place to place, and from person to person. One of the first recorded attempts to establish a tangible standard length was made by the Greeks, who used the length of the Olympic stadium as a unit called a **stadium.** This was set at 600 Greek feet (607.9 modern U.S. feet), or almost exactly one-tenth of a modern nautical mile. The Romans adopted this unit and extended its use to nautical and even astronomical measurements. The Roman stadium was 625 Roman feet, or 606.3 U.S. feet, in length. This approximates the modern British Navy **cable** of 608 feet. The U.S. Navy cable is 720 feet.

The origin of the **Mediterranean mile** of 4,035.43 U.S. feet is attributed to the Greeks. The **Roman mile** of 4,858.60 U.S. feet gradually replaced the shorter Greek unit.

The **nautical mile** bears little relation to these land measures, which were not associated with the size of the earth. With the emergence of the nautical chart, it became customary to show a scale of miles on the chart, and the accepted value of this unit varied over the centuries with the changing estimates of the size of the earth. These estimates varied widely, ranging from about 44.5 to 87.5 modern nautical miles per degree of latitude, although generally they were too small. The *Almagest* of Ptolemy considered 62 Roman miles equivalent to one degree, but a 1466 edition of this book contained a chart on which 60 miles were shown to a degree. Whether the change was considered a correction or an adaptation to provide a more convenient relationship between the mile and the degree is not clear, but this is the earliest known use of this ratio.

Later, when the size of the earth was determined by measurement, the relationship of 60 Roman miles of 4,858.60 U.S. feet to a degree of latitude was seen to be in error. Both possible solutions to the problem— changing the ratio of miles to a degree, or changing the length of the mile—had their supporters, and neither group was able to convince the other. As a result, the shorter mile remained as the **land** or **statute mile** (now established as 5,280 U.S. feet), and the longer **nautical mile** gradually became established at sea. The earliest known reference to it by this name occurred in 1730, but it was not standardized until much later (see Chapter 2).

The **fathom** as a unit of length or depth is of obscure origin, but primitive man considered it a measure of the outstretched arms, and the modern seaman still estimates the length of a line in this manner. That the unit was used in early times is indicated by reference to it in the New Testament, but how old the unit was at that time is unknown.

Soundings • Probably the most dangerous phase of navigation occurs when the vessel is "on soundings." Since man first began navigating the waters, the possibility of grounding his vessel has been a major concern, and frequent soundings have been the most highly valued safeguard against that experience. Undoubtedly used long before the Christian era, the lead line is perhaps the oldest instrument of navigation.

The lead line. The **hand lead** (see Chapter 6), consisting of a lead weight attached to a line usually marked in fathoms, has been known since antiquity and, with the exception of the markings, is probably the same today as it was 2,000 or more years ago. The **deep sea lead,** a heavier weight with a longer line, was a natural outgrowth of the hand lead. Matthew Fontaine Maury made his deep sea soundings by securing a cannon shot to a ball of strong twine. The heavy weight caused the twine to run out rapidly, and when bottom was reached, the twine was cut and the depth deduced from the amount remaining on the ball.

The sounding machine. The biggest disadvantage of the deep sea lead is that the vessel must be stopped if depths are to be measured accurately. This led to the development of the sounding machine.

Early in the nineteenth century a sounding machine similar to one of the earlier patent logs was invented. A wheel was secured just above the lead and the cast made in such a way that all the line required ran out freely and the lead sank directly to the bottom. The motion through the water during the descent set the wheel revolving, and this in turn caused the depth to be indicated on a dial. A somewhat similar device was the **buoy sounder.** The lead was passed through a buoy in which a spring catch was fitted and both were cast over the side. The lead ran freely until bottom was reached, when the catch locked, preventing further running out of the line. The whole assembly was then brought on board, the depth from the buoy to the lead being read.

The first use of the pressure principle to determine the depth of water occurred early in the nineteenth century when the "Self-acting Sounder" was introduced. A hollow glass tube open at its lower end contained an index which moved up in the tube as greater water pressure compressed the air inside. The index retained its highest position when hauled aboard the vessel, and its height was proportional to the depth of the water.

The British scientist William Thomson (Lord Kelvin) in 1878 perfected the sounding machine after repeated tests at sea. Prior to his invention, fibre line was used exclusively in soundings. His introduction of piano wire solved the problem of rapid descent of the lead and also that of hauling it back aboard quickly. The chemically coated glass tube which he used to determine depth was an improvement of earlier methods, and the worth of the entire machine is evidenced by the fact that it is still used in essentially the same form.

Echo sounding. Based upon the principle that sound travels through sea water at a nearly uniform rate, automatic depth-registering devices have been invented to indicate the depth of water under a vessel, regardless of its speed. The first practical echo sounder was developed by the United States Navy in 1922.

The actual time between emission of a sonic or ultrasonic signal and return of its echo from the bottom, the angle at which the signal is beamed downward in order that its echo will be received at another part of the vessel, and the phase difference between signal and echo have all been used in the development of the modern echo sounder.

Aids to navigation • The Cushites and Libyans constructed towers along the Mediterranean coast of Egypt, and priests maintained beacon fires in them. These were the earliest known lighthouses. At Sigeum in the Troad (part of Troy) a lighthouse was built before 660 B.C. One of the seven wonders of the ancient world was the lighthouse called the Pharos of Alexandria, which may have been more than 200 feet tall. It was built by Sostratus of Cnidus (Asia Minor) in the third century B.C., during the reign of Ptolemy Philadelphus. The word "pharos" has since been a general term for lighthouses. Some time between 1584 and 1611 the light of Cordouan, the earliest wave-swept lighthouse, was erected at the entrance to the Gironde river in western France. An oak log fire illuminated this structure until the eighteenth century.

Wood or coal fires were used in the many lighthouses built along the European and British coasts in the seventeenth and eighteenth centuries.

In England such structures were privately maintained by interested organizations. One of the most famous of these groups, popularly known as "Trinity House," was organized in the sixteenth century, perhaps earlier, when a "beaconage and buoyage" fee was levied on English vessels. This prompted the establishment of Trinity House "to make, erect, and set up beacons, marks, and signs for the sea" and to provide vessels with pilots. The organization is now in its fifth century of operation, and its chief duties are to serve as a general lighthouse and pilotage authority, and to supply pilots.

The first lightship was a small vessel with lanterns hung from its yardarms. It was stationed at the Nore, an estuary in the Thames River, England, in 1732.

Seafaring people of the United States had erected lighthouses and buoys before the Revolutionary War, and in 1789 Congress passed legislation providing for federal expansion of the work. About 1767 the first buoys were placed in the Delaware River. These were logs or barrels, but about 1820 they were replaced with spar buoys. In that same year, the first lightship was established in Chesapeake Bay.

As the maritime interests of various countries grew, more and better aids to navigation were made available. In 1850 Congress prescribed the present system of coloring and numbering United States buoys. Conformity as to shape resulted from the recommendations of the International Marine Conference of 1889. The second half of the nineteenth century saw the development of bell, whistle, and lighted buoys, and in 1910 the first lighted buoy in the United States utilizing high pressure acetylene apparatus was placed in service. Stationed at the entrance to Ambrose Channel in New York, it provided the basis for the high degree of perfection which has been achieved in the lighted buoy since that time. The complete buoyage system maintained by the U.S. Coast Guard today is chiefly a product of the twentieth century. In 1900 there were approximately 5,000 buoys of all types in use in the United States, while today there are more than 20,000.

The sailings • The various methods of mathematically determining course, distance, and position have a history almost as old as mathematics itself.

Plane sailing. Based upon the assumption that the surface of the earth is plane, or flat; this method was used by navigators for many centuries. The navigator solved problems by laying down his course relative to his meridian, and stepping off the distance run to the new position. This system is used with accuracy today in measuring short runs on a Mercator chart, which compensates for the convergence of the meridians, but on the plane chart, serious errors resulted. Early navigators might have obtained mathematical solutions to this problem, with no greater accuracy, but the graphical method was commonly used.

Traverse sailing. Because sailing vessels were subject to the winds, navigators of old were seldom able to sail one course for great distances, and consequently a series of small triangles had to be solved. Equipment was designed to help seamen in maintaining their dead reckoning positions. The modern **rough log** evolved from the *log board*, hinged wooden boards that folded like a book and on which courses and distances were marked in chalk. Each day the position was determined from this data and entered in the ship's journal, today's **smooth log.**

The log board was succeeded by the **travas,** a board with lines radiating from the center in 32 compass directions. Regularly spaced along the lines were small holes into which pegs were fitted to indicate time run on the particular course.

These devices were of great value to the navigator in keeping a record of the courses and distances sailed, but still left him the long mathematical solutions necessary to determine the new position. In 1436 what appears to have been the first **traverse table** was prepared by Andrea Biancho. Using this table of solutions of right-angled plane triangles, the navigator was able to determine his course and distance made good after sailing a number of distances in different directions.

Parallel sailing was an outgrowth of the navigator's inability to determine his longitude. Not a mathematical solution in the sense that the other sailings are, it involved converting the distance sailed along a parallel (departure), as determined by dead reckoning, into longitude.

Middle-latitude sailing. The inaccuracies involved in plane sailing led to the improved method of middle-latitude sailing early in the seventeenth century. Middle-latitude sailing is based upon the assumption that the use of a parallel midway between those of departure and arrival will eliminate the errors inherent in plane sailing due to the convergence of the meridians. The assumption is reasonably accurate and although the use of Mercator sailing usually results in greater accuracy, middle-latitude sailing still serves a useful purpose.

Mercator sailing. Edward Wright's published table of meridional parts provided the basis for the most accurate of rhumb line sailings—Mercator sailing.

Great-circle sailing. For many hundreds of years mathematicians have known that a great circle is the shortest distance between two points on the surface of a sphere, but it was not until the nineteenth century that navigators began to make use of this information regularly.

The gradual accumulation of knowledge concerning seasonal and prevailing winds, weather conditions, and ocean currents eventually made it possible for the navigator to plan his voyage with more assurance. Nineteenth century writers of navigational texts recommended the use of great-circle sailing, and toward the close of that century such sailing became increasingly popular, particularly in the Pacific.

The mathematics involved in great-circle sailing may be tedious, but the use of the gnomonic projection in locating points along the great-circle track has simplified the method.

Hydrographic offices • The practice of recording hydrographic data was centuries old before the establishment of the first official hydrographic office in 1720 in France. The Hydrographic-Department of the British Admiralty, though not established until 1795, has played a major part in European hydrographic work.

The **U.S. Coast and Geodetic Survey** was originally founded when Congress, in 1807, passed a resolution authorizing a survey of the coast, harbors, outlying islands, and fishing banks of the United States. The approaches to New York were the first sections of the coast charted by the new Coast Survey, and from there the work spread northward and southward along the eastern seaboard. In 1844 the work was expanded and arrangements made to chart simultaneously the Gulf and East Coasts. Investigation of tidal conditions began, and in 1855 the first tables of tide predictions were published. The California gold rush gave impetus to the survey of the West Coast, which began in 1850, the year California became a state. Coast pilots, or sailing directions, for the Atlantic coast were privately published in the first half of the nineteenth century, but about 1850 the Survey began accumulating data that led to federally pro-duced coast pilots. The 1889 *Pacific Coast Pilot* was an outstanding con-tribution to the safety of West Coast shipping.

Today the U.S. Coast and Geodetic Survey is known as the National Ocean Survey and provides the mariner with the charts and coast pilots of all waters of the United States and its possessions, and tide and tidal current tables for much of the world.

U.S. Naval Oceanographic Office. In 1830 the U.S. Navy established a "Depot of Charts and Instruments" in Washington, D.C. Primarily, it was to serve as a storehouse where such charts and sailing directions as were available, together with navigational instruments, could be assembled for issue to Navy ships which required them. Two men constituted the entire staff.

From 1842 until 1861 Lieutenant Matthew Fontaine Maury served as officer-in-charge. Under his command the office rose to international prominence. Maury decided upon an ambitious plan to increase the mariner's knowledge of existing winds, weather, and currents. He began by making a detailed record of pertinent matter included in old log books stored at the depot. He then inaugurated a hydrographic reporting pro-gram among shipmasters, and the thousands of answers received, along with the log book data, were first utilized to publish the *Wind and Current Chart of the North Atlantic* of 1847. The United States instigated an international conference in 1853 to interest other nations in a system of exchanging nautical information. The plan, which was Maury's, was enthusiastically adopted by other maritime nations, and is the basis upon which hydrographic offices operate today.

In 1854 the depot was redesignated the "U.S. Naval Observatory and Hydrographical Office," and in 1866 Congress separated the two, broadly increasing the functions of the latter, which was to become the Oceanographic Office. The office was authorized to carry out surveys, collect information, and print every kind of nautical chart and publication, all "for the benefit and use of navigators generally."

One of the first acts of the new office was to purchase the copyright of *The New American Practical Navigator*. Several volumes of sailing directions had already been published. The first *Notice to Mariners* appeared in 1869. Daily broadcast of navigational warnings was inaugurated in 1907, and in 1912, following the sinking of the SS *Titanic*, Hydrographic Office action led to the establishment of the International Ice Patrol.

The development by the U.S. Navy of an improved depth finder in 1922 and the use of aerial photography and electronic equipment have all contributed to the improvement and extension of the surveys.

Navigation manuals • Although navigation is as old as man himself, navigation textbooks, as they are thought of today, are a product of the last several centuries. Until the end of the Dark Ages such books, or manuscripts, as were available were written by astronomers for other astronomers. The navigator was forced to make use of these, gleaning what little was directly applicable to his profession. After 1500, however, the need for books on navigation resulted in the publication of a series of manuals of increasing value to the mariner. "Bowditch," coming much later, has gained a reputation as one of the best.

Conclusion • **Navigation** has come a long way, but there is no evidence that it is nearing the end of its development. Progress will continue as long as man remains unsatisfied with the means at his disposal.

Perhaps the best guides to the future are the desires of the present, for a want usually precedes an acquisition. Pytheas and his contemporaries undoubtedly dreamed of devices to indicate direction and distance. The sixteenth century navigator had these, and wanted a method of determining longitude at sea. The eighteenth century navigator could determine longitude, but found the task a tedious one, and perhaps longed to be freed from the *drudgery* of navigation. The modern navigator is still seeking further release from the *work* of navigation, and now wants to be freed from the limitations of weather.

Further release from the work of navigation is more likely to come through another approach—*automation*. This process might be said to have started with the application of electronics to computation. The direct use of electronics in navigation is more spectacular, but in this it is vulnerable to jamming, intentional or accidental mechanical damage, natural failure, propagation limitations in certain areas and at certain times, and accuracy limitations at long ranges.

In the future, it is likely that electronics will be applied increasingly as an additional source of energy to extend the range of usefulness of other methods, rather than to replace them. To date electronics has been related primarily to piloting, extending its range far to sea, and permitting its use in periods of foul weather. In the future it can be expected to play an increasingly important role in the field of dead reckoning and celestial navigation.

It is not inconceivable that a fix may someday be automatically and continuously available, perhaps on latitude and longitude dials. However, when this is accomplished, by one or a combination of systems, it will be but a short additional step to feed this information electronically to a pen which will automatically trace the path of the vessel across a chart. Another short step would be to feed the information electrically to a device to control the movements of the vessel, so that it would automatically follow a predetermined track.

When this has been accomplished, new problems will undoubtedly arise, for it is not likely that the time will ever come when there will be no problems to be solved.

The navigator • It might seem that when complete automation has been achieved, all of the work of the navigator will have been eliminated. However, advance planning of route and schedule will undoubtedly require human intelligence. So will the interpretation of results en route, and the alteration of schedule when circumstances render this desirable. Unless the automatic system can be made 100 percent reliable—a remote prospect for the foreseeable future—it will need checking from time to time, and provision will have to be made for other, perhaps cruder, methods in the event of failure.

Until such time as mechanization may become complete and perfect, the prudent navigator will not permit himself to become wholly dependent upon "black boxes" which may fail at crucial moments, or ready-made solutions that may not be available when most needed. Today and in the future, as in the past, a knowledge of fundamental principles is essential to adequate navigation. If the navigator contents himself with the ability to read dials or look up answers in a book, he will be of questionable value. His future, if he has one, will be in jeopardy.

Human beings who entrust their lives to the skill and knowledge of a navigator are entitled to expect him to be capable of handling any reasonable emergency. When his customary tools or methods are denied him, they have a right to expect him to have the necessary ability to take them safely to their destination, however elementary the knowledge and means available to him.

The wise navigator uses all reliable aids available to him, and seeks to understand their uses and limitations. He learns to evaluate his various aids when he has means for checking their accuracy and reliability, so that he can adequately interpret their indications when his resources are limited. He stores in his mind the fundamental knowledge that may be needed in an emergency. Machines may reflect much of the *science* of navigation, but only a competent human can practice the *art* of navigation.

[2]

Basic Definitions

Navigation • Navigation is the process of directing the movements of a craft from one point to another. The word *navigate* is from the Latin *navigatus*, the past participle of the verb *navigere*, which is derived from the words *navis*, meaning "ship," and *agere*, meaning "to move" or "to direct." Navigation of water craft is called **marine navigation** to distinguish it from navigation of aircraft, called **air navigation.** Navigation of a vessel on the surface is sometimes called **surface navigation** to distinguish it from **underwater navigation** of a submerged vessel. The expression **submarine navigation** is applicable to a submarine, whether submerged or on the surface. Navigation of vehicles across land or ice is called **land navigation.** The expression **lifeboat navigation** is used to refer to navigation of lifeboats or life rafts, generally involving rather crude methods. The expression **polar navigation** refers to navigation in the regions near the geographical poles of the earth, where special techniques are employed.

The principal divisions of navigation are as follows:

Dead reckoning is the determination of position by advancing a known position for courses and distances. A position so determined is called a **dead reckoning position.** It is generally accepted that the course *steered* and the speed *through the water* should be used, but the expression is also used to refer to the determination of position by use of the course and speed expected to be made good over the ground, thus making an estimated allowance for disturbing elements such as current and wind. A position so determined is better called an **estimated position.** The expression "dead reckoning" probably originated from use of the Dutchman's log, a buoyant object thrown overboard to determine the speed of the vessel relative to the object, which was assumed to be *dead* in the water.

Apparently, the expression **deduced reckoning** was used when allowance was made for current and wind. It was often shortened to *ded reckoning* and the similarity of this expression to *dead reckoning* was undoubtedly the source of the confusion that is still associated with these expressions.

Piloting (or **pilotage**) is navigation involving frequent or continuous determination of position or a line of position relative to geographic points, to a high order of accuracy. It is practiced in the vicinity of land, dangers, aids to navigation, etc., and requires good judgment and almost constant attention and alertness on the part of the navigator.

Electronic navigation involves the use of electronic equipment in any way. It may be called **radio navigation** if any form of radio is used. **Sonic navigation,** involving the use of sound waves, becomes part of electronic navigation when electronic equipment is used in the control, production, transmission, reception, or amplification of sound signals. Electronic navigation overlaps piloting.

Celestial navigation is navigation using information obtained from celestial bodies.

The earth • The earth is approximately an **oblate spheroid** (a sphere flattened at the poles). Its dimensions and the amount of flattening are not known exactly, but the values determined by the English geodesist A. R. Clarke in 1866, as defined by the U.S. Coast and Geodetic Survey in 1880, are used for charts of North America. According to these dimensions the longer or equatorial radius, a, is 3,443.96 nautical, or 3,963.23 statute, miles and the shorter or polar radius, b, is 3,432.28 nautical, or 3,949.80 statute, miles. The mean radius $\left(\dfrac{2a+b}{3}\right)$ is 3,440.07 nautical, or 3,958.76 statute, miles. The "oblateness" or amount of. flattening is $\dfrac{a-b}{a} = \dfrac{11.68}{3443.96} = \dfrac{1}{295}$, or $\dfrac{1}{294.98}$ if a and b are computed to additional decimal places. For many navigational purposes the earth is assumed to be a sphere, without intolerable error.

The **axis of rotation** or **polar axis** of the earth is the line connecting the **north pole** and the **south pole.**

Circles of the earth • A **great circle** is the line of intersection of a sphere and a plane through the center of the sphere. This is the largest circle that can be drawn on a sphere. The shortest line on the surface of a sphere between two points on that surface is part of a great circle. On the spheroidal earth the shortest line is called a **geodesic.** A great circle is a near enough approximation of a geodesic for most problems of navigation.

A **small circle** is the line of intersection of a sphere and a plane which does not pass through the center of the sphere.

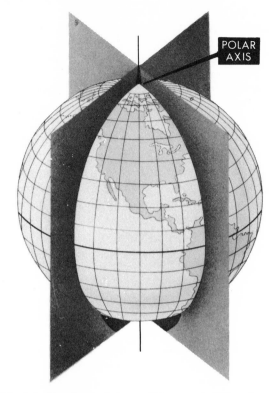

Fig. 2.1. The planes of the meridians meet at the polar axis.

A **meridian** is a great circle through the geographical poles of the earth. Hence, all meridians meet at the poles, and their planes intersect each other in a line, the **polar axis** (fig. 2.1). The term *meridian* is usually applied to the **upper branch** only, that half from pole to pole which passes through a given point. The other half is called the **lower branch.**

The **prime meridian** is that meridian used as the origin for measurement of longitude (fig. 2.2). The prime meridian used almost universally is that through the original position of the British Royal Observatory at Greenwich, near London.

The **equator** is the terrestrial great circle whose plane is perpendicular to the polar axis. It is midway between the poles.

A **parallel** or **parallel of latitude** is a circle on the surface of the earth, parallel to the plane of the equator (fig. 2.3). It connects all points of equal latitude. The equator, a great circle, is a limiting case connecting points of 0° latitude. The poles, single points at latitude 90°, are the other limiting case. All other parallels are small circles.

Position on the earth • A position on the surface of the earth (except at either of the poles) may be defined by two magnitudes called **coordinates.**

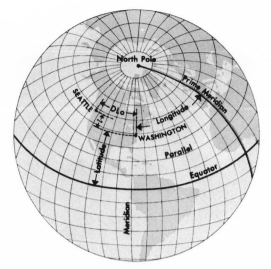

*Fig. 2.2. Circles and coordinates of the earth. All parallels except the equator
are small circles; the equator and meridians are great circles.*

Those customarily used are *latitude* and *longitude*. A position may also
be expressed in relation to known geographical positions.

Latitude (L, lat.) is angular distance from the equator, measured northward or southward along a meridian from 0° at the equator to 90° at the
poles (fig. 2.2). It is designated *north* (N) or *south* (S) to indicate the
direction of measurement.

The **difference of latitude** (*l*) between two places is the angular length
of arc of any meridian between their parallels (fig. 2.2). It is the numerical
difference of the latitudes if the places are on the same side of the equator,
and the sum if they are on opposite sides. It may be designated *north* (N)
or *south* (S) when appropriate.

The **middle** or **mid latitude (Lm)** between two places on the same side
of the equator is half the sum of their latitudes. Mid latitude is labeled
N or S to indicate whether it is north or south of the equator. The
expression is occasionally used with reference to two places on opposite
sides of the equator, when it is equal to half the *difference* between the
two latitudes and takes the name of the place farthest from the equator.
However, this usage is misleading, as it lacks the significance usually associated with the expression. When the places are on opposite sides of the
equator, two mid latitudes are generally used, the average of each latitude
and 0°.

Longitude (λ, **long.**) is the arc of a parallel or the angle at the pole
between the prime meridian and the meridian of a point on the earth,
measured eastward or westward from the prime meridian through 180°
(fig. 2.2). It is designated *east* (E) or *west* (W) to indicate the direction
of measurement.

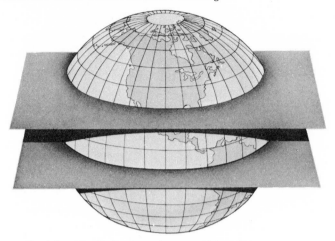

Fig. 2.3. A parallel of latitude is parallel to the equator.

The **difference of longitude (DLo)** between two places is the shorter arc of the parallel or the smaller angle at the pole between the meridians of the two places (fig. 2.2). If both places are on the same side (east or west) of Greenwich, DLo is the numerical difference of the longitudes of the two places; if on opposite sides, DLo is the numerical sum unless this exceeds 180°, when it is 360° minus the sum. The distance between two meridians at any parallel of latitude, expressed in distance units, usually nautical miles, is called **departure (p).** It represents the distance made good to the east or west as a craft proceeds from one point to another. Its numerical value between any two meridians decreases with increased latitude, while DLo is numerically the same at any latitude. Either DLo or p may be designated *east* (E) or *west* (W) when appropriate.

Distance on the earth • Distance (D, dist.) is the spatial separation of two points, and is expressed as the length of a line joining them. On the surface of the earth it is usually stated in miles. Navigators customarily use the **nautical mile (mi., M)** of 1852 meters exactly. This is the value suggested by the International Hydrographic Bureau in 1929, and since adopted by most maritime nations. It is often called the **international nautical mile** to distinguish it from slightly different values used by some countries. On July 1, 1959, the United States adopted the exact relationship of 1 yard = 0.9144 meter. The length of the international nautical mile is consequently equal to 6,076.11549 U.S. feet (approximately).

For most navigational purposes the nautical mile is considered the length of one minute of latitude, or of any great circle of the earth, regardless of location. On the Clarke spheroid of 1866, used for mapping North America, the length of one minute of latitude varies from about 6,046 feet at the equator to approximately 6,108 feet at the poles. The length of one minute of a great circle of a sphere having an area equal to that of the earth, as represented by this spheroid, is 6,080.2 U.S. feet. This was the standard value of the nautical mile in the United States prior to adoption of the international value. A **geographical mile** is the length of one minute of the equator, or about 6,087 feet.

The **land** or **statute mile (mi., m)** or 5,280 feet is commonly used for navigation on rivers and lakes, notably the Great Lakes of North America. The nautical mile is about 38/33 or approximately 1.15 statute miles.

Distance, as customarily used by the navigator, refers to the length of the **rhumb line** connecting two places. This is a line making the same oblique angle with all meridians. Meridians and parallels (including the equator), which also maintain constant true directions, may be considered special cases of the rhumb line. Any other rhumb line spirals toward the pole, forming a **loxodromic curve** or **loxodrome** (fig. 2.4). Distance along the great circle connecting two points is customarily designated **great-circle distance.**

Speed • **Speed (S)** is rate of motion, or distance per unit of time.

A **knot (kn.)**, the unit of speed commonly used in navigation, is a rate of one nautical mile per hour. The expression "knots per hour" refers to acceleration, not speed.

Sometimes the expression **speed of advance (SOA)** is used to indicate

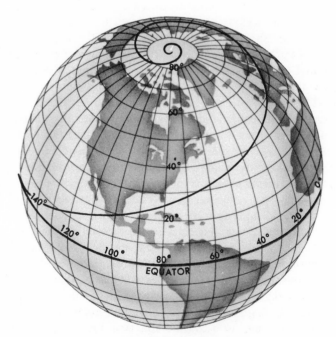

Fig. 2.4. A rhumb line or loxodrome.

the speed expected to be made good over the ground, and **speed over ground (SOG)** the actual speed made good over the ground.

Direction on the earth • Direction is the position of one point relative to another, without reference to the distance between them. In navigation, direction is customarily expressed as the angular difference in degrees from a reference direction, usually north or the ship's head. Compass directions (east, south by west, etc.) or points (of $11\frac{1}{4}°$ or $\frac{1}{32}$ of a circle) are seldom used by modern navigators for precise directions.

Course (C, Cn) is the intended horizontal direction of travel, expressed as angular distance from north, usually from 000° at north, clockwise through 360°. Strictly, the term applies to direction *through the water*, not the direction intended to be made good *over the ground*, but in common American usage it is applied to either. **Course made good** is the single course from the point of departure to point of arrival at any given time. Sometimes the expression **course of advance** (**COA**) is used to indicate the direction expected to be made good over the ground, and **course over ground (COG)** the actual direction made good over the ground. **Course line** is a line extending in the direction of a course.

In making computations it is sometimes convenient to express a course as an angle from *either* north or south, through 90° or 180°. In this case it is designated **course angle** (**C**) and should be properly labeled to indicate the origin (prefix) and direction of measurement (suffix). Thus, C N 35° E = Cn 035° (000°+35°), C N 155° W = Cn 205° (360°—155°), C S 47° E = Cn 133° (180°—47°). But Cn 260° may be either C N 100° W or C S 80° W, depending upon the conditions of the problem.

The symbol C is always used for *course angle*, and is usually used for *course* where there is little or no possibility of confusion.

Track (TR) is the path actually followed by a vessel, or the path of proposed travel. It differs from *course* and *course made good* by including the element of distance as well as direction, although the term is occasionally used to refer to direction only. However, the path actually followed is usually a somewhat irregular line. The path of proposed travel consists of one or a series of course lines from the point of departure to the destination, along which it is intended the vessel will proceed. A great circle which a vessel intends to follow approximately is called a **great-circle track.**

Heading (Hdg., SH) is the direction in which a vessel is pointed, expressed as angular distance from north, usually from 000° at north, clockwise through 360°. *Heading* should not be confused with *course*. *Heading* is a constantly changing value as a vessel oscillates or yaws back and forth across the course or as the direction of motion is temporarily changed, as in avoiding an obstacle. *Course* is a predetermined value and usually remains constant for a considerable time (fig. 2.5).

Bearing (B, Bn) is the direction of one terrestrial point from another,

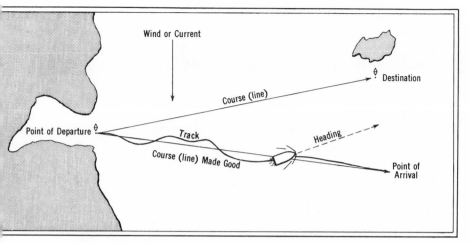

Fig. 2.5. Course (line), course (line) made good, track, and heading.

expressed as angular distance from a reference direction, usually from 000° at the reference direction, clockwise through 360°. When measured through 90° or 180° from *either* north or south, it is called **bearing angle** (**B**), which bears the same relationship to bearing as *course angle* does to *course*. *Bearing* and *azimuth* are sometimes used interchangeably, but the latter is better reserved exclusively for reference to horizontal direction of a point on the celestial sphere from a point on the earth.

A **relative bearing** (**RB**) is one relative to the heading, or to the vessel itself. It is usually measured from 000° at the heading, clockwise through 360°. However, it is sometimes conveniently measured right or left from

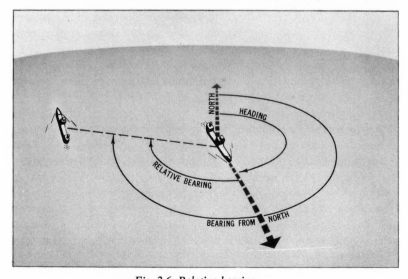

Fig. 2.6. Relative bearing.

0° at the ship's head through 180°. Older methods, such as indicating the number of degrees or points from some part of the vessel (10° forward of the starboard beam, two points on the port quarter, etc.), are seldom used by modern navigators to indicate precise directions, except for bearings dead ahead or astern, or broad on the bow, beam, or quarter.

To convert a relative bearing to a bearing from north (fig. 2.6), express the relative bearing in terms of the 0°–360° system and add the heading: Bn=RB+SH. Thus, if another vessel bears 127° relative from a ship whose heading is 150°, the bearing from north is 127°+150°=277°. If the total exceeds 360°, subtract this amount. To convert a bearing from north to a relative bearing, subtract the heading. RB=Bn—SH. Thus, a lightship which bears 241° from north bears 241°—137°=104° relative from a ship whose heading is 137°. If SH is larger than Bn, add 360° to Bn before subtracting.

[3]

Chart Projections

The navigator's chart • A **map** is a conventional representation, usually on a plane surface, of all or part of the physical features of the earth's surface or any part of it. A **chart** is such a representation intended primarily for navigation. A **nautical** or **marine chart** is one intended primarily for marine navigation. It generally shows depths of water (by soundings and sometimes also by depth curves), aids to navigation, dangers, and the outline of adjacent land and such land features as are useful to the navigator.

Chart making presents the problem of representing the surface of a spheroid upon a plane surface. The surface of a sphere or spheroid is said to be **undevelopable** because no part of it can be flattened without distortion. A **map projection** or **chart projection** is a method of representing all or part of the surface of a sphere or spheroid upon a plane surface. The process is one of transferring points on the surface of the sphere or spheroid onto a plane, or onto a **developable** surface (one that can be flattened to form a plane) such as a cylinder or cone. If points on the surface of the sphere or spheroid are projected from a single point (including infinity), the projection is said to be **perspective** or **geometric.** Most map projections are not perspective.

Selecting a projection • Each projection has distinctive features which make it preferable for certain uses, no one projection being best for all conditions. These distinctive features are most apparent on charts of large areas. As the area becomes smaller, the differences between various projections become less noticeable until on the largest scale chart, such as of a harbor, all projections become practically identical. Some of the desirable properties are:

1. *True shape* of physical features.
2. *Correct angular relationship.* A projection with this characteristic is said to be **conformal** or **orthomorphic.**
3. *Equal area*, or the representation of areas in their correct relative proportions.
4. *Constant scale* values for measuring distances.
5. *Great circles* represented as straight lines.
6. *Rhumb lines* represented as straight lines.

It is possible to preserve any one and sometimes more than one property in any one projection, but it is impossible to preserve all of them. For instance, a projection cannot be both conformal and equal area, nor can both great circles and rhumb lines be represented as straight lines.

Types of projection • Projections are usually classified primarily as to the type of developable surface to which the spherical or spheroidal surface is transferred. They are sometimes further classified as to whether the projection (but not necessarily the charts made by it) is centered on the equator (**equatorial**), a pole (**polar**), or some point or line between (**oblique**). The name of a projection often indicates its type and sometimes, in addition, its principal feature.

The projection used most frequently by mariners is commonly called **Mercator,** after its inventor. Classified according to type this is an **equatorial cylindrical orthomorphic** projection, the cylinder conceived as being tangent along the equator. A similar projection based upon a cylinder tangent along a meridian is called **transverse Mercator** or **transverse cylindrical orthomorphic.** It is sometimes called **inverse Mercator** or **inverse cylindrical orthomorphic.** If the cylinder is tangent along a great circle other than the equator or a meridian, the projection is called **oblique Mercator** or **oblique cylindrical orthomorphic.**

In a **simple conic** projection points on the surface of the earth are conceived as transferred to a tangent cone. In a **Lambert conformal** projection the cone intersects the earth (a **secant** cone) at two small circles. In a **polyconic** projection, a series of tangent cones is used.

An **azimuthal** or **zenithal** projection is one in which points on the earth are transferred directly to a plane. If the origin of the projecting rays is the center of the earth, a **gnomonic** projection results; if it is the point opposite the plane's point of tangency, a **stereographic** projection; and if at infinity (the projecting lines being parallel to each other), an **orthographic** projection (fig. 3.1). The gnomonic, stereographic, and orthographic are perspective projections. In an **azimuthal equidistant** projection, which is not perspective, the scale of distances is constant along any radial line from the point of tangency.

Cylindrical and plane projections can be considered special cases of conical projections with the heights infinity and zero, respectively.

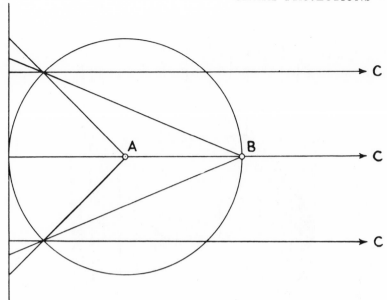

Fig. 3.1. Azimuthal projections: A, *gnomonic;* B, *stereographic;* C *(at infinity),*
orthographic.

A **graticule** is the network of latitude and longitude lines laid out in accordance with the principles of any projection.

Cylindrical Projections

Features • If a cylinder is placed around the earth, tangent along the equator, and the planes of the meridians are extended, they intersect the cylinder in a number of vertical lines (fig. 3.2). These lines, all being vertical, are parallel, or everywhere equidistant from each other, unlike the terrestrial meridians, which become closer together as the latitude increases. On the earth the parallels of latitude are perpendicular to the meridians, forming circles of progressively smaller diameter as the latitude increases. On the cylinder they are shown perpendicular to the projected meridians, but because a cylinder is everywhere of the same diameter, the projected parallels are all the same size.

If the cylinder is cut along a vertical line (a meridian) and spread out flat, the meridians appear as equally spaced, vertical lines, and the parallels as horizontal lines. The spacing of the parallels relative to each other differs in the various types of cylindrical projections.

The cylinder may be tangent along some great circle other than the equator, forming an oblique or transverse cylindrical projection, on which the pattern of latitude and longitude lines appears quite different, since the line of tangency and the equator no longer coincide.

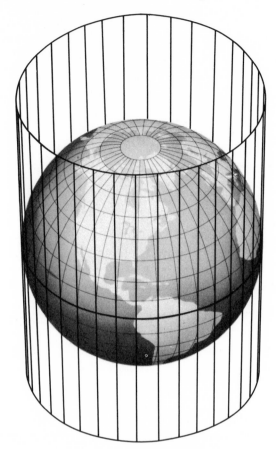

Fig. 3.2. A cylindrical projection.

Mercator projection • The only cylindrical projection widely used for navigation is the **Mercator** or **equatorial cylindrical orthomorphic.** It is not perspective and the parallels cannot be located by geometrical projection, the spacing being derived mathematically. The use of a tangent cylinder to explain the development of the projection has been used, but the relationship of the terrestrial latitude and longitude lines to those on the cylinder is often carried beyond justification, resulting in misleading statements and illustrations.

The distinguishing feature of the Mercator projection (fig. 3.3) among cylindrical projections is that both the meridians and parallels are expanded at the same ratio with increased latitude. The expansion is equal to the secant of the latitude, with a small correction for the ellipticity of the earth. Since the secant of 90° is infinity, the projection cannot include the poles. Expansion is the same in all directions and angles are correctly shown, the projection being conformal. Rhumb lines appear as straight lines, the

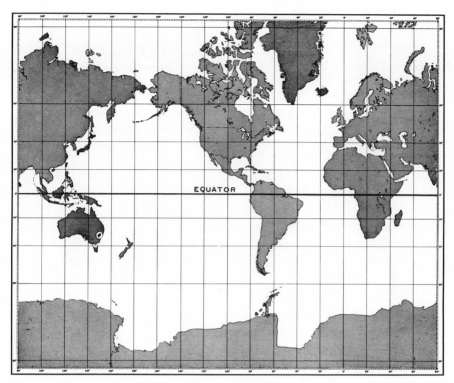

Fig. 3.3. A Mercator map of the world.

directions of which can be measured directly on the chart. Distances can also be measured directly, to practical accuracy, but not by a single distance scale over the entire chart, unless the spread of latitude is small. The latitude scale is customarily used for measuring distances, the expansion of the scale being the same as that of distances at the same latitude. Great circles, except meridians and the equator, appear as curved lines concave to the equator (fig. 3.8). Small areas appear in their correct shape but of increased size unless they are near the equator. Plotting of positions by latitude and longitude is done by means of rectangular coordinates, as on any cylindrical projection.

Meridional parts • At the equator a degree of longitude is approximately equal in length to a degree of latitude. As the distance from the equator increases, degrees of latitude remain approximately the same (not exactly because the earth is not quite a sphere), while degrees of longitude become progressively shorter. Since degrees of longitude appear everywhere the same length in the Mercator projection, it is necessary to increase the length of the meridians if the expansion is to be equal in all directions. Thus, to maintain the correct proportions between degrees of latitude and degrees of longitude, the former are shown progressively longer as the distance from the equator increases (fig. 3.3).

The length of the meridian, as thus increased between the equator and any given latitude, expressed in minutes of the equator as a unit, constitutes the number of **meridional parts** (M) corresponding to that latitude. Meridional parts, given in Table 1 for every minute of latitude from the equator to the pole, afford facilities for constructing a Mercator chart. These values are for the Clarke spheroid of 1866. By means of Table 2 they can be converted to the values for certain other spheroids and the sphere.

Mercator chart construction • To construct a Mercator chart, first select the scale and then proceed as follows:

Draw a series of vertical lines to represent the meridians, spacing them in accordance with the scale selected. If the chart is to include the equator, the distances of the various parallels from the equator are given directly in Table 1, although it may be desirable to convert the tabulated values to more convenient units. Thus, if $1°(60')$ of longitude is to be shown as one inch, each meridional part will be $\frac{1}{60}$ or 0.01667 inch in length. The distance, in inches, of any parallel from the equator is then determined by dividing its meridional parts by 60 or multiplying them by 0.01667.

If the equator is not to be included, the **meridional difference** (m) is used. This is the difference between the meridional parts of the various latitudes and that of the lowest parallel (the one nearest the equator) to be shown. Distances so determined are measured from the lowest parallel.

It is often desired to show a minimum area on a chart of limited size, to the largest possible scale. The scale is then dictated by the limitations.

When the graticule has been completed, the features to be shown are located by means of the latitude and longitude scales.

Example. A Mercator chart is to be constructed at the maximum scale on a sheet of paper 35 × 46 inches, with a minimum two-inch margin outside the **neat line** limiting the charted area. The minimum area to be covered is lat. 44°–50° north and long. 56°–68° west.

Solution. Step one: Determine which dimension to place horizontal. From Table 1 the meridional difference is:

$$M_{50°} \quad 3456.6$$
$$M_{44°} \quad 2929.6$$
$$m \qquad \ \ 527.0$$

The chart is to cover at least $12°$ $(68°—56°)$ of longitude. The longitude is therefore to cover a distance of $12 \times 60 = 720$ meridional parts. Since there is a great number of meridional parts of longitude to be shown than of latitude, the long dimension is placed horizontal.

TABLE 1
Meridional Parts

Lat.	0°	1°	2°	3°	4°	5°	6°	7°	8°	9°	Lat.
0	0.0	59.6	119.2	178.9	238.6	298.4	358.2	418.2	478.3	538.6	0
1	1.0	60.6	20.2	79.9	39.6	299.4	59.2	19.2	79.3	39.6	1
2	2.0	61.6	21.2	80.9	40.6	300.3	60.2	20.2	80.3	40.6	2
3	3.0	62.6	22.2	81.8	41.6	01.3	61.2	21.2	81.3	41.6	3
4	4.0	63.6	23.2	82.8	42.6	02.3	62.2	22.2	82.3	42.6	4
5	5.0	64.6	124.2	183.8	243.6	303.3	363.2	423.2	483.3	543.6	5
6	6.0	65.6	25.2	84.8	44.5	04.3	64.2	24.2	84.3	44.6	6
7	7.0	66.6	26.2	85.8	45.5	05.3	65.2	25.2	85.4	45.6	7
8	7.9	67.5	27.2	86.8	46.5	06.3	66.2	26.2	86.4	46.6	8
9	8.9	68.5	28.2	87.8	47.5	07.3	67.2	27.2	87.4	47.6	9
10	9.9	69.5	129.2	188.8	248.5	308.3	368.2	428.2	488.4	548.7	10
11	10.9	70.5	30.1	89.8	49.5	09.3	69.2	29.2	89.4	49.7	11
12	11.9	71.5	31.1	90.8	50.5	10.3	70.2	30.2	90.4	50.7	12
13	12.9	72.5	32.1	91.8	51.5	11.3	71.2	31.2	91.4	51.7	13
14	13.9	73.5	33.1	92.8	52.5	12.3	72.2	32.2	92.4	52.7	14
15	14.9	74.5	134.1	193.8	253.5	313.3	373.2	433.2	493.4	553.7	15
16	15.9	75.5	35.1	94.8	54.5	14.3	74.2	34.2	94.4	54.7	16
17	16.9	76.5	36.1	95.8	55.5	15.3	75.2	35.2	95.4	55.7	17
18	17.9	77.5	37.1	96.8	56.5	16.3	76.2	36.2	96.4	56.7	18
19	18.9	78.5	38.1	97.8	57.5	17.3	77.2	37.2	97.4	57.7	19
20	19.9	79.5	139.1	198.8	258.5	318.3	378.2	438.2	498.4	558.7	20
21	20.9	80.5	40.1	199.8	59.5	19.3	79.2	39.2	499.4	59.7	21
22	21.9	81.5	41.1	200.7	60.5	20.3	80.2	40.2	500.4	60.7	22
23	22.8	82.4	42.1	01.7	61.5	21.3	81.2	41.2	01.4	61.7	23
24	23.8	83.4	43.1	02.7	62.5	22.3	82.2	42.2	02.4	62.7	24
25	24.8	84.4	144.1	203.7	263.5	323.3	383.2	443.2	503.4	563.8	25
26	25.8	85.4	45.1	04.7	64.5	24.3	84.2	44.2	04.4	64.8	26
27	26.8	86.4	46.1	05.7	65.5	25.3	85.2	45.2	05.4	65.8	27
28	27.8	87.4	47.0	06.7	66.5	26.3	86.2	46.2	06.4	66.8	28
29	28.8	88.4	48.0	07.7	67.5	27.3	87.2	47.3	07.4	67.8	29
30	29.8	89.4	149.0	208.7	268.5	328.3	388.2	448.3	508.4	568.8	30
31	30.8	90.4	50.0	09.7	69.4	29.3	89.2	49.3	09.4	69.8	31
32	31.8	91.4	51.0	10.7	70.4	30.3	90.2	50.3	10.5	70.8	32
33	32.8	92.4	52.0	11.7	71.4	31.3	91.2	51.3	11.5	71.8	33
34	33.8	93.4	53.0	12.7	72.4	32.3	92.2	52.3	12.5	72.8	34
35	34.8	94.4	154.0	213.7	273.4	333.3	393.2	453.3	513.5	573.8	35
36	35.8	95.4	55.0	14.7	74.4	34.3	94.2	54.3	14.5	74.8	36
37	36.8	96.4	56.0	15.7	75.4	35.3	95.2	55.3	15.5	75.8	37
38	37.7	97.4	57.0	16.7	76.4	36.3	96.2	56.3	16.5	76.8	38
39	38.7	98.3	58.0	17.7	77.4	37.3	97.2	57.3	17.5	77.9	39
40	39.7	99.3	159.0	218.7	278.4	338.3	398.2	458.3	518.5	578.9	40
41	40.7	100.3	60.0	19.7	79.4	39.3	399.2	59.3	19.5	79.9	41
42	41.7	01.3	61.0	20.7	80.4	40.3	400.2	60.3	20.5	80.9	42
43	42.7	02.3	62.0	21.6	81.4	41.3	01.2	61.3	21.5	81.9	43
44	43.7	03.3	63.0	22.6	82.4	42.3	02.2	62.3	22.5	82.9	44
45	44.7	104.3	163.9	223.6	283.4	343.2	403.2	463.3	523.5	583.9	45
46	45.7	05.3	64.9	24.6	84.4	44.2	04.2	64.3	24.5	84.9	46
47	46.7	06.3	65.9	25.6	85.4	45.2	05.2	65.3	25.5	85.9	47
48	47.7	07.3	66.9	26.6	86.4	46.2	06.2	66.3	26.5	86.9	48
49	48.7	08.3	67.9	27.6	87.4	47.2	07.2	67.3	27.5	87.9	49
50	49.7	109.3	168.9	228.6	288.4	348.2	408.2	468.3	528.5	588.9	50
51	50.7	10.3	69.9	29.6	89.4	49.2	09.2	69.3	29.5	90.0	51
52	51.7	11.3	70.9	30.6	90.4	50.2	10.2	70.3	30.5	91.0	52
53	52.6	12.3	71.9	31.6	91.4	51.2	11.2	71.3	31.6	92.0	53
54	53.6	13.2	72.9	32.6	92.4	52.2	12.2	72.3	32.6	93.0	54
55	54.6	114.2	173.9	233.6	293.4	353.2	413.2	473.3	533.6	594.0	55
56	55.6	15.2	74.9	34.6	94.4	54.2	14.2	74.3	34.6	95.0	56
57	56.6	16.2	75.9	35.6	95.4	55.2	15.2	75.3	35.6	96.0	57
58	57.6	17.2	76.9	36.6	96.4	56.2	16.2	76.3	36.6	97.0	58
59	58.6	18.2	77.9	37.6	97.4	57.2	17.2	77.3	37.6	98.0	59
60	59.6	119.2	178.9	238.6	298.4	358.2	418.2	478.3	538.6	599.0	60
Lat.	0°	1°	2°	3°	4°	5°	6°	7°	8°	9°	Lat.

TABLE 1

Meridional Parts

Lat.	10°	11°	12°	13°	14°	15°	16°	17°	18°	19°	Lat.
0	599. 0	659. 7	720. 5	781. 5	842. 9	904. 4	966. 3	1028. 5	1091. 0	1153. 9	0
1	600. 0	60. 7	21. 5	82. 6	43. 9	05. 5	67. 3	29. 5	92. 1	55. 0	1
2	01. 0	61. 7	22. 5	83. 6	44. 9	06. 5	68. 4	30. 6	93. 1	56. 0	2
3	02. 1	62. 7	23. 5	84. 6	45. 9	07. 5	69. 4	31. 6	94. 2	57. 1	3
4	03. 1	63. 7	24. 5	85. 6	47. 0	08. 6	70. 4	32. 7	95. 2	58. 1	4
5	604. 1	664. 7	725. 6	786. 6	848. 0	909. 6	971. 5	1033. 7	1096. 3	1159. 2	5
6	05. 1	65. 7	26. 6	87. 7	49. 0	10. 6	72. 5	34. 7	97. 3	60. 2	6
7	06. 1	66. 7	27. 6	88. 7	50. 0	11. 6	73. 5	35. 8	98. 3	61. 3	7
8	07. 1	67. 8	28. 6	89. 7	51. 1	12. 7	74. 6	36. 8	1099. 4	62. 3	8
9	08. 1	68. 8	29. 6	90. 7	52. 1	13. 7	75. 6	37. 9	1100. 4	63. 4	9
10	609. 1	669. 8	730. 6	791. 7	853. 1	914. 7	976. 7	1038. 9	1101. 5	1164. 4	10
11	10. 1	70. 8	31. 7	92. 8	54. 1	15. 8	77. 7	39. 9	02. 5	65. 5	11
12	11. 1	71. 8	32. 7	93. 8	55. 1	16. 8	78. 7	41. 0	03. 6	66. 5	12
13	12. 1	72. 8	33. 7	94. 8	56. 2	17. 8	79. 8	42. 0	04. 6	67. 6	13
14	13. 2	73. 8	34. 7	95. 8	57. 2	18. 8	80. 8	43. 1	05. 7	68. 6	14
15	614. 2	674. 8	735. 7	796. 8	858. 2	919. 9	981. 8	1044. 1	1106. 7	1169. 7	15
16	15. 2	75. 9	36. 7	97. 9	59. 3	20. 9	82. 9	45. 1	07. 8	70. 7	16
17	16. 2	76. 9	37. 8	98. 9	60. 3	21. 9	83. 9	46. 2	08. 8	71. 8	17
18	17. 2	77. 9	38. 8	799. 9	61. 3	23. 0	84. 9	47. 2	09. 9	72. 8	18
19	18. 2	78. 9	39. 8	800. 9	62. 3	24. 0	86. 0	48. 3	10. 9	73. 9	19
20	619. 2	679. 9	740. 8	802. 0	863. 4	925. 0	987. 0	1049. 3	1111. 9	1175. 0	20
21	20. 2	80. 9	41. 8	03. 0	64. 4	26. 1	88. 0	50. 3	13. 0	76. 0	21
22	21. 2	81. 9	42. 8	04. 0	65. 4	27. 1	89. 1	51. 4	14. 0	77. 1	22
23	22. 2	82. 9	43. 9	05. 0	66. 4	28. 1	90. 1	52. 4	15. 1	78. 1	23
24	23. 3	84. 0	44. 9	06. 0	67. 5	29. 2	91. 1	53. 5	16. 1	79. 2	24
25	624. 3	685. 0	745. 9	807. 1	868. 5	930. 2	992. 2	1054. 5	1117. 2	1180. 2	25
26	25. 3	86. 0	46. 9	08. 1	69. 5	31. 2	93. 2	55. 6	18. 2	81. 3	26
27	26. 3	87. 0	47. 9	09. 1	70. 5	32. 2	94. 3	56. 6	19. 3	82. 3	27
28	27. 3	88. 0	48. 9	10. 1	71. 6	33. 3	95. 3	57. 6	20. 3	83. 4	28
29	28. 3	89. 0	50. 0	11. 1	72. 6	34. 3	96. 3	58. 7	21. 4	84. 4	29
30	629. 3	690. 0	751. 0	812. 2	873. 6	935. 3	997. 4	1059. 7	1122. 4	1185. 5	30
31	30. 3	91. 1	52. 0	13. 2	74. 6	36. 4	98. 4	60. 8	23. 5	86. 5	31
32	31. 3	92. 1	53. 0	14. 2	75. 7	37. 4	999. 4	61. 8	24. 5	87. 6	32
33	32. 3	93. 1	54. 0	15. 2	76. 7	38. 4	1000. 5	62. 8	25. 6	88. 7	33
34	33. 4	94. 1	55. 1	16. 3	77. 7	39. 5	01. 5	63. 9	26. 6	89. 7	34
35	634. 4	695. 1	756. 1	817. 3	878. 7	940. 5	1002. 5	1064. 9	1127. 7	1190. 8	35
36	35. 4	96. 1	57. 1	18. 3	79. 8	41. 5	03. 6	66. 0	28. 7	91. 8	36
37	36. 4	97. 1	58. 1	19. 3	80. 8	42. 6	04. 6	67. 0	29. 8	92. 9	37
38	37. 4	98. 2	59. 1	20. 3	81. 8	43. 6	05. 7	68. 1	30. 8	93. 9	38
39	38. 4	699. 2	60. 1	21. 4	82. 9	44. 6	06. 7	69. 1	31. 9	95. 0	39
40	639. 4	700. 2	761. 2	822. 4	883. 9	945. 7	1007. 7	1070. 1	1132. 9	1196. 0	40
41	40. 4	01. 2	62. 2	23. 4	84. 9	46. 7	08. 8	71. 2	34. 0	97. 1	41
42	41. 4	02. 2	63. 2	24. 4	85. 9	47. 7	09. 8	72. 2	35. 0	98. 2	42
43	42. 5	03. 2	64. 2	25. 5	87. 0	48. 7	10. 8	73. 3	36. 1	1199. 2	43
44	43. 5	04. 2	65. 2	26. 5	88. 0	49. 8	11. 9	74. 3	37. 1	1200. 3	44
45	644. 5	705. 3	766. 3	827. 5	889. 0	950. 8	1012. 9	1075. 4	1138. 2	1201. 3	45
46	45. 5	06. 3	67. 3	28. 5	90. 0	51. 8	14. 0	76. 4	39. 2	02. 4	46
47	46. 5	07. 3	68. 3	29. 5	91. 1	52. 9	15. 0	77. 4	40. 3	03. 4	47
48	47. 5	08. 3	69. 3	30. 6	92. 1	53. 9	16. 0	78. 5	41. 3	04. 5	48
49	48. 5	09. 3	70. 3	31. 6	93. 1	54. 9	17. 1	79. 6	42. 4	05. 5	49
50	649. 5	710. 3	771. 4	832. 6	894. 2	956. 0	1018. 1	1080. 6	1143. 4	1206. 6	50
51	50. 5	11. 3	72. 4	33. 6	95. 2	57. 0	19. 2	81. 6	44. 5	07. 7	51
52	51. 6	12. 4	73. 4	34. 7	96. 2	58. 0	20. 2	82. 7	45. 5	08. 7	52
53	52. 6	13. 4	74. 4	35. 7	97. 2	59. 1	21. 2	83. 7	46. 6	09. 8	53
54	53. 6	14. 4	75. 4	36. 7	98. 3	60. 1	22. 3	84. 8	47. 6	10. 8	54
55	654. 6	715. 4	776. 4	837. 7	899. 3	961. 1	1023. 3	1085. 8	1148. 7	1211. 9	55
56	55. 6	16. 4	77. 5	38. 8	900. 3	62. 2	24. 3	86. 8	49. 7	12. 9	56
57	56. 6	17. 4	78. 5	39. 8	01. 4	63. 2	25. 4	87. 9	50. 8	14. 0	57
58	57. 6	18. 5	79. 5	40. 8	02. 4	64. 2	26. 4	88. 9	51. 8	15. 1	58
59	58. 6	19. 5	80. 5	41. 8	03. 4	65. 3	27. 5	90. 0	52. 9	16. 1	59
60	659. 7	720. 5	781. 5	842. 9	904. 4	966. 3	1028. 5	1091. 0	1153. 9	1217. 2	60
Lat.	10°	11°	12°	13°	14°	15°	16°	17°	18°	19°	Lat.

TABLE 1
Meridional Parts

Lat.	20°	21°	22°	23°	24°	25°	26°	27°	28°	29°	Lat.
0	1217.2	1280.9	1345.0	1409.5	1474.6	1540.2	1606.3	1672.9	1740.2	1808.1	0
1	18.2	81.9	46.0	10.6	75.7	41.3	07.4	74.1	41.4	09.3	1
2	19.3	83.0	47.1	11.7	76.8	42.4	08.5	75.2	42.5	10.4	2
3	20.4	84.1	48.2	12.8	77.9	43.4	09.6	76.3	43.6	11.6	3
4	21.4	85.1	49.3	13.9	78.9	44.5	10.7	77.4	44.7	12.7	4
5	1222.5	1286.2	1350.3	1414.9	1480.0	1545.6	1611.8	1678.5	1745.9	1813.8	5
6	23.5	87.2	51.4	16.0	81.1	46.7	12.9	79.6	47.0	15.0	6
7	24.6	88.3	52.5	17.1	82.2	47.8	14.0	80.8	48.1	16.1	7
8	25.6	89.4	53.5	18.2	83.3	48.9	15.1	81.9	49.3	17.3	8
9	26.7	90.4	54.6	19.3	84.4	50.0	16.2	83.0	50.4	18.4	9
10	1227.8	1291.5	1355.7	1420.3	1485.5	1551.1	1617.3	1684.1	1751.5	1819.5	10
11	28.8	92.6	56.8	21.4	86.6	52.2	18.4	85.2	52.6	20.7	11
12	29.9	93.6	57.8	22.5	87.7	53.3	19.6	86.4	53.8	21.8	12
13	30.9	94.7	58.9	23.6	88.8	54.4	20.7	87.5	54.9	23.0	13
14	32.0	95.8	60.0	24.7	89.8	55.5	21.8	88.6	56.0	24.1	14
15	1233.1	1296.8	1361.1	1425.8	1490.9	1556.6	1622.9	1689.7	1757.2	1825.2	15
16	34.1	97.9	62.1	26.8	92.0	57.7	24.0	90.8	58.3	26.4	16
17	35.2	1299.0	63.2	27.9	93.1	58.8	25.1	91.9	59.4	27.5	17
18	36.2	1300.0	64.3	29.0	94.2	59.9	26.2	93.1	60.5	28.7	18
19	37.3	01.1	65.4	30.1	95.3	61.0	27.3	94.2	61.7	29.8	19
20	1238.4	1302.2	1366.4	1431.2	1496.4	1562.1	1628.4	1695.3	1762.8	1830.9	20
21	39.4	03.2	67.5	32.2	97.5	63.2	29.5	96.4	63.9	32.1	21
22	40.5	04.3	68.6	33.3	98.6	64.3	30.6	97.5	65.1	33.2	22
23	41.5	05.4	69.7	34.4	1499.7	65.4	31.8	98.7	66.2	34.4	23
24	42.6	06.4	70.7	35.5	1500.8	66.5	32.9	1699.8	67.3	35.5	24
25	1243.7	1307.5	1371.8	1436.6	1501.8	1567.6	1634.0	1700.9	1768.5	1836.6	25
26	44.7	08.6	72.9	37.7	02.9	68.7	35.1	02.0	69.6	37.8	26
27	45.8	09.6	74.0	38.7	04.0	69.8	36.2	03.1	70.7	38.9	27
28	46.8	10.7	75.0	39.8	05.1	70.9	37.3	04.3	71.8	40.1	28
29	47.9	11.8	76.1	40.9	06.2	72.0	38.4	05.4	73.0	41.2	29
30	1249.0	1312.9	1377.2	1442.0	1507.3	1573.1	1639.5	1706.5	1774.1	1842.4	30
31	50.0	13.9	78.3	43.1	08.4	74.2	40.6	07.6	75.2	43.5	31
32	51.1	15.0	79.3	44.2	09.5	75.3	41.8	08.8	76.4	44.6	32
33	52.1	16.1	80.4	45.3	10.6	76.4	42.9	09.9	77.5	45.8	33
34	53.2	17.1	81.5	46.3	11.7	77.6	44.0	11.0	78.6	46.9	34
35	1254.3	1318.2	1382.6	1447.4	1512.8	1578.7	1645.1	1712.1	1779.8	1848.1	35
36	55.3	19.3	83.7	48.5	13.9	79.8	46.2	13.2	80.9	49.2	36
37	56.4	20.3	84.7	49.6	15.0	80.9	47.3	14.4	82.0	50.4	37
38	57.5	21.4	85.8	50.7	16.1	82.0	48.4	15.5	83.2	51.5	38
39	58.5	22.5	86.9	51.8	17.1	83.1	49.5	16.6	84.3	52.7	39
40	1259.6	1323.5	1388.0	1452.8	1518.2	1584.2	1650.7	1717.7	1785.4	1853.8	40
41	60.6	24.6	89.0	53.9	19.3	85.3	51.8	18.9	86.6	54.9	41
42	61.7	25.7	90.1	55.0	20.4	86.4	52.9	20.0	87.7	56.1	42
43	62.8	26.8	91.2	56.1	21.5	87.5	54.0	21.1	88.8	57.2	43
44	63.8	27.8	92.3	57.2	22.6	88.6	55.1	22.2	90.0	58.4	44
45	1264.9	1328.9	1393.3	1458.3	1523.7	1589.7	1656.2	1723.4	1791.1	1859.5	45
46	66.0	30.0	94.4	59.4	24.8	90.8	57.3	24.5	92.2	60.7	46
47	67.0	31.0	95.5	60.5	25.9	91.9	58.5	25.6	93.4	61.8	47
48	68.1	32.1	96.6	61.5	27.0	93.0	59.6	26.7	94.5	63.0	48
49	69.1	33.2	97.7	62.6	28.1	94.1	60.7	27.9	95.6	64.1	49
50	1270.2	1334.2	1398.7	1463.7	1529.2	1595.2	1661.8	1729.0	1796.8	1865.3	50
51	71.3	35.3	1399.8	64.8	30.3	96.3	62.9	30.1	97.9	66.4	51
52	72.3	36.4	1400.9	65.9	31.4	97.4	64.0	31.2	1799.1	67.5	52
53	73.4	37.5	02.0	67.0	32.5	98.5	65.1	32.4	1800.2	68.7	53
54	74.5	38.5	03.1	68.1	33.6	1599.6	66.3	33.5	01.3	69.8	54
55	1275.5	1339.6	1404.1	1469.1	1534.7	1600.7	1667.4	1734.6	1802.5	1871.0	55
56	76.6	40.7	05.2	70.2	35.8	01.8	68.5	35.7	03.6	72.1	56
57	77.7	41.7	06.3	71.3	36.9	02.9	69.6	36.9	04.7	73.3	57
58	78.7	42.8	07.4	72.4	38.0	04.1	70.7	38.0	05.9	74.4	58
59	79.8	43.9	08.5	73.5	39.1	05.2	71.8	39.1	07.0	75.6	59
60	1280.9	1345.0	1409.5	1474.6	1540.2	1606.3	1672.9	1740.2	1808.1	1876.7	60
Lat.	20°	21°	22°	23°	24°	25°	26°	27°	28°	29°	Lat.

TABLE 1
Meridional Parts

Lat.	30°	31°	32°	33°	34°	35°	36°	37°	38°	39°	Lat.
0	1876.7	1946.0	2016.0	2086.8	2158.5	2230.9	2304.3	2378.6	2453.9	2530.3	0
1	77.9	47.2	17.2	88.0	59.7	32.1	05.5	79.9	55.2	31.6	1
2	79.0	48.3	18.4	89.2	60.9	33.4	06.8	81.1	56.5	32.8	2
3	80.2	49.5	19.6	90.4	62.1	34.6	08.0	82.4	57.7	34.1	3
4	81.3	50.7	20.7	91.6	63.3	35.8	09.2	83.6	59.0	35.4	4
5	1882.5	1951.8	2021.9	2092.8	2164.5	2237.0	2310.5	2384.9	2460.2	2536.7	5
6	83.6	53.0	23.1	94.0	65.7	38.2	11.7	86.1	61.5	38.0	6
7	84.8	54.2	24.3	95.2	66.9	39.4	12.9	87.3	62.8	39.3	7
8	85.9	55.3	25.4	96.3	68.1	40.7	14.2	88.6	64.0	40.5	8
9	87.1	56.5	26.6	97.5	69.3	41.9	15.4	89.8	65.3	41.8	9
10	1888.2	1957.6	2027.8	2098.7	2170.5	2243.1	2316.6	2391.1	2466.6	2543.1	10
11	89.4	58.8	29.0	2099.9	71.7	44.3	17.9	92.3	67.8	44.4	11
12	90.5	60.0	30.1	2101.1	72.9	45.5	19.1	93.6	69.1	45.7	12
13	91.7	61.1	31.3	02.3	74.1	46.7	20.3	94.8	70.4	47.0	13
14	92.8	62.3	32.5	03.5	75.3	48.0	21.6	96.1	71.6	48.2	14
15	1894.0	1963.5	2033.7	2104.7	2176.5	2249.2	2322.8	2397.3	2472.9	2549.5	15
16	95.1	64.6	34.8	05.9	77.7	50.4	24.0	98.6	74.2	50.8	16
17	96.3	65.8	36.0	07.1	78.9	51.6	25.3	2399.8	75.4	52.1	17
18	97.4	66.9	37.2	08.2	80.1	52.8	26.5	2401.1	76.7	53.4	18
19	98.6	68.1	38.4	09.4	81.3	54.1	27.7	02.4	78.0	54.7	19
20	1899.8	1969.3	2039.6	2110.6	2182.5	2255.3	2329.0	2403.6	2479.3	2556.0	20
21	1900.9	70.4	40.7	11.8	83.7	56.5	30.2	04.9	80.5	57.3	21
22	02.1	71.6	41.9	13.0	84.9	57.7	31.4	06.1	81.8	58.5	22
23	03.2	72.8	43.1	14.2	86.1	58.9	32.7	07.4	83.1	59.8	23
24	04.4	73.9	44.3	15.4	87.3	60.2	33.9	08.6	84.3	61.1	24
25	1905.5	1975.1	2045.4	2116.6	2188.5	2261.4	2335.1	2409.9	2485.6	2562.4	25
26	06.7	76.3	46.6	17.8	89.8	62.6	36.4	11.1	86.9	63.7	26
27	07.8	77.4	47.8	19.0	91.0	63.8	37.6	12.4	88.1	65.0	27
28	09.0	78.6	49.0	20.2	92.2	65.1	38.9	13.6	89.4	66.3	28
29	10.1	79.8	50.2	21.4	93.4	66.3	40.1	14.9	90.7	67.6	29
30	1911.3	1980.9	2051.3	2122.5	2194.6	2267.5	2341.3	2416.1	2492.0	2568.9	30
31	12.4	82.1	52.5	23.7	95.8	68.7	42.6	17.4	93.2	70.1	31
32	13.6	83.3	53.7	24.9	97.0	69.9	43.8	18.7	94.5	71.4	32
33	14.8	84.4	54.9	26.1	98.2	71.2	45.1	19.9	95.8	72.7	33
34	15.9	85.6	56.1	27.3	2199.4	72.4	46.3	21.2	97.1	74.0	34
35	1917.1	1986.8	2057.2	2128.5	2200.6	2273.6	2347.5	2422.4	2498.3	2575.3	35
36	18.2	87.9	58.4	29.7	01.8	74.8	48.8	23.7	2499.6	76.6	36
37	19.4	89.1	59.6	30.9	03.0	76.1	50.0	24.9	2500.9	77.9	37
38	20.5	90.3	60.8	32.1	04.3	77.3	51.3	26.2	02.2	79.2	38
39	21.7	91.5	62.0	33.3	05.5	78.5	52.5	27.4	03.4	80.5	39
40	1922.8	1992.6	2063.2	2134.5	2206.7	2279.7	2353.7	2428.7	2504.7	2581.8	40
41	24.0	93.8	64.3	35.7	07.9	81.0	55.0	30.0	06.0	83.1	41
42	25.2	95.0	65.5	36.9	09.1	82.2	56.2	31.2	07.3	84.4	42
43	26.3	96.1	66.7	38.1	10.3	83.4	57.5	32.5	08.5	85.7	43
44	27.5	97.3	67.9	39.3	11.5	84.6	58.7	33.7	09.8	87.0	44
45	1928.6	1998.5	2069.1	2140.5	2212.7	2285.9	2359.9	2435.0	2511.1	2588.3	45
46	29.8	1999.6	70.3	41.7	13.9	87.1	61.2	36.3	12.4	89.5	46
47	30.9	2000.8	71.4	42.9	15.2	88.3	62.4	37.5	13.6	90.8	47
48	32.1	02.0	72.6	44.1	16.4	89.6	63.7	38.8	14.9	92.1	48
49	33.3	03.2	73.8	45.3	17.6	90.8	64.9	40.0	16.2	93.4	49
50	1934.4	2004.3	2075.0	2146.5	2218.8	2292.0	2366.2	2441.3	2517.5	2594.7	50
51	35.6	05.5	76.2	47.7	20.0	93.2	67.4	42.6	18.8	96.0	51
52	36.7	06.7	77.4	48.9	21.2	94.5	68.7	43.8	20.0	97.3	52
53	37.9	07.8	78.5	50.1	22.4	95.7	69.9	45.1	21.3	98.6	53
54	39.1	09.0	79.7	51.3	23.6	96.9	71.1	46.3	22.6	2599.9	54
55	1940.2	2010.2	2080.9	2152.5	2224.9	2298.2	2372.4	2447.6	2523.9	2601.2	55
56	41.4	11.4	82.1	53.7	26.1	2299.4	73.6	48.9	25.1	02.5	56
57	42.5	12.5	83.3	54.9	27.3	2300.6	74.9	50.1	26.4	03.8	57
58	43.7	13.7	84.5	56.1	28.5	01.8	76.1	51.4	27.7	05.1	58
59	44.9	14.9	85.7	57.3	29.7	03.1	77.4	52.7	29.0	06.4	59
60	1946.0	2016.0	2086.8	2158.5	2230.9	2304.3	2378.6	2453.9	2530.3	2607.7	60
Lat.	30°	31°	32°	33°	34°	35°	36°	37°	38°	39°	Lat.

TABLE 1
Meridional Parts

Lat.	40°	41°	42°	43°	44°	45°	46°	47°	48°	49°	Lat.
0	2607.7	2686.3	2766.1	2847.2	2929.6	3013.5	3098.8	3185.7	3274.2	3364.5	0
1	09.0	87.6	67.5	48.6	31.0	14.9	3100.2	87.1	75.7	66.0	1
2	10.3	89.0	68.8	49.9	32.4	16.3	01.7	88.6	77.2	67.5	2
3	11.6	90.3	70.1	51.3	33.8	17.7	03.1	90.1	78.7	69.1	3
4	12.9	91.6	71.5	52.7	35.2	19.1	04.5	91.5	80.2	70.6	4
5	2614.2	2692.9	2772.8	2854.0	2936.6	3020.5	3106.0	3193.0	3281.7	3372.1	5
6	15.5	94.2	74.2	55.4	38.0	21.9	07.4	94.5	83.2	73.6	6
7	16.8	95.6	75.5	56.8	39.3	23.3	08.8	95.9	84.7	75.1	7
8	18.1	96.9	76.9	58.1	40.7	24.8	10.3	97.4	86.1	76.7	8
9	19.4	98.2	78.2	59.5	42.1	26.2	11.7	3198.8	87.6	78.2	9
10	2620.7	2699.5	2779.5	2860.9	2943.5	3027.6	3113.2	3200.3	3289.1	3379.7	10
11	22.0	2700.9	80.9	62.2	44.9	29.0	14.6	01.8	90.6	81.2	11
12	23.3	02.2	82.2	63.6	46.3	30.4	16.0	03.2	92.1	82.8	12
13	24.6	03.5	83.6	65.0	47.7	31.8	17.5	04.7	93.6	84.3	13
14	26.0	04.8	84.9	66.3	49.1	33.2	18.9	06.2	95.1	85.8	14
15	2627.3	2706.2	2786.3	2867.7	2950.5	3034.7	3120.4	3207.7	3296.6	3387.4	15
16	28.6	07.5	87.6	69.1	51.8	36.1	21.8	09.1	98.1	88.9	16
17	29.9	08.8	89.0	70.4	53.2	37.5	23.2	10.6	3299.6	90.4	17
18	31.2	10.1	90.3	71.8	54.6	38.9	24.7	12.1	3301.1	91.9	18
19	32.5	11.5	91.7	73.2	56.0	40.3	26.1	13.5	02.6	93.5	19
20	2633.8	2712.8	2793.0	2874.5	2957.4	3041.7	3127.6	3215.0	3304.1	3395.0	20
21	35.1	14.1	94.4	75.9	58.8	43.2	29.0	16.5	05.6	96.5	21
22	36.4	15.4	95.7	77.3	60.2	44.6	30.5	17.9	07.1	98.1	22
23	37.7	16.8	97.1	78.6	61.6	46.0	31.9	19.4	08.6	3399.6	23
24	39.0	18.1	98.4	80.0	63.0	47.4	33.4	20.9	10.1	3401.1	24
25	2640.3	2719.4	2799.8	2881.4	2964.4	3048.8	3134.8	3222.4	3311.6	3402.7	25
26	41.6	20.7	2801.1	82.8	65.8	50.3	36.2	23.8	13.1	04.2	26
27	42.9	22.1	02.5	84.1	67.2	51.7	37.7	25.3	14.6	05.7	27
28	44.3	23.4	03.8	85.5	68.6	53.1	39.1	26.8	16.1	07.3	28
29	45.6	24.7	05.2	86.9	70.0	54.5	40.6	28.3	17.6	08.8	29
30	2646.9	2726.1	2806.5	2888.2	2971.4	3055.9	3142.0	3229.7	3319.1	3410.3	30
31	48.2	27.4	07.9	89.6	72.8	57.4	43.5	31.2	20.6	11.9	31
32	49.5	28.7	09.2	91.0	74.2	58.8	44.9	32.7	22.1	13.4	32
33	50.8	30.1	10.6	92.4	75.6	60.2	46.4	34.2	23.6	14.9	33
34	52.1	31.4	11.9	93.7	77.0	61.6	47.8	35.6	25.2	16.5	34
35	2653.4	2732.7	2813.3	2895.1	2978.4	3063.1	3149.3	3237.1	3326.7	3418.0	35
36	54.7	34.1	14.6	96.5	79.8	64.5	50.7	38.6	28.2	19.5	36
37	56.0	35.4	16.0	97.9	81.2	65.9	52.2	40.1	29.7	21.1	37
38	57.4	36.7	17.3	2899.3	82.6	67.3	53.6	41.6	31.2	22.6	38
39	58.7	38.1	18.7	2900.6	84.0	68.8	55.1	43.0	32.7	24.2	39
40	2660.0	2739.4	2820.0	2902.0	2985.4	3070.2	3156.5	3244.5	3334.2	3425.7	40
41	61.3	40.7	21.4	03.4	86.8	71.6	58.0	46.0	35.7	27.2	41
42	62.6	42.1	22.7	04.8	88.2	73.0	59.4	47.5	37.2	28.8	42
43	63.9	43.4	24.1	06.1	89.6	74.5	60.9	49.0	38.7	30.3	43
44	65.2	44.7	25.5	07.5	91.0	75.9	62.3	50.4	40.2	31.9	44
45	2666.6	2746.1	2826.8	2908.9	2992.4	3077.3	3163.8	3251.9	3341.8	3433.4	45
46	67.9	47.4	28.2	10.3	93.8	78.7	65.3	53.4	43.3	35.0	46
47	69.2	48.7	29.5	11.7	95.2	80.2	66.7	54.9	44.8	36.5	47
48	70.5	50.1	30.9	13.0	96.6	81.6	68.2	56.4	46.3	38.0	48
49	71.8	51.4	32.2	14.4	98.0	83.0	69.6	57.9	47.8	39.6	49
50	2673.1	2752.7	2833.6	2915.8	2999.4	3084.5	3171.1	3259.3	3349.3	3441.1	50
51	74.5	54.1	35.0	17.2	3000.8	85.9	72.5	60.8	50.8	42.7	51
52	75.8	55.4	36.3	18.6	02.2	87.3	74.0	62.3	52.4	44.2	52
53	77.1	56.8	37.7	19.9	03.6	88.8	75.5	63.8	53.9	45.8	53
54	78.4	58.1	39.0	21.3	05.0	90.2	76.9	65.3	55.4	47.3	54
55	2679.7	2759.4	2840.4	2922.7	3006.4	3091.6	3178.4	3266.8	3356.9	3448.9	55
56	81.0	60.8	41.8	24.1	07.8	93.1	79.8	68.3	58.4	50.4	56
57	82.4	62.1	43.1	25.5	09.2	94.5	81.3	69.7	59.9	52.0	57
58	83.7	63.4	44.5	26.9	10.6	95.9	82.8	71.2	61.5	53.5	58
59	85.0	64.8	45.8	28.2	12.1	97.4	84.2	72.7	63.0	55.1	59
60	2686.3	2766.1	2847.2	2929.6	3013.5	3098.8	3185.7	3274.2	3364.5	3456.6	60
Lat.	40°	41°	42°	43°	44°	45°	46°	47°	48°	49°	Lat.

TABLE 1

Meridional Parts

Lat.	50°	51°	52°	53°	54°	55°	56°	57°	58°	59°	Lat.
0	3456. 6	3550. 7	3646. 8	3745. 2	3845. 8	3948. 9	4054. 6	4163. 1	4274. 5	4389. 2	0
1	58. 2	52. 3	48. 5	46. 8	47. 5	50. 6	56. 4	64. 9	76. 4	91. 1	1
2	59. 7	53. 9	50. 1	48. 5	49. 2	52. 4	58. 2	66. 7	78. 3	93. 0	2
3	61. 3	55. 5	51. 7	50. 1	50. 9	54. 1	59. 9	68. 6	80. 2	95. 0	3
4	62. 8	57. 0	53. 3	51. 8	52. 6	55. 8	61. 7	70. 4	82. 1	96. 9	4
5	3464. 4	3558. 6	3654. 9	3753. 4	3854. 3	3957. 6	4063. 5	4172. 2	4284. 0	4398. 9	5
6	65. 9	60. 2	56. 6	55. 1	56. 0	59. 3	65. 3	74. 1	85. 8	4400. 8	6
7	67. 5	61. 8	58. 2	56. 8	57. 7	61. 1	67. 1	75. 9	87. 7	02. 8	7
8	69. 1	63. 4	59. 8	58. 4	59. 4	62. 8	68. 9	77. 8	89. 6	04. 7	8
9	70. 6	65. 0	61. 4	60. 1	61. 1	64. 6	70. 7	79. 6	91. 5	06. 6	9
10	3472. 2	3566. 6	3663. 1	3761. 8	3862. 8	3966. 3	4072. 5	4181. 4	4293. 4	4408. 6	10
11	73. 7	68. 2	64. 7	63. 4	64. 5	68. 1	74. 3	83. 3	95. 3	10. 5	11
12	75. 3	69. 8	66. 3	65. 1	66. 2	69. 8	76. 1	85. 1	97. 2	12. 5	12
13	76. 8	71. 3	67. 9	66. 8	67. 9	71. 6	77. 8	87. 0	4299. 1	14. 4	13
14	78. 4	72. 9	69. 6	68. 4	69. 6	73. 3	79. 6	88. 8	4301. 0	16. 4	14
15	3480. 0	3574. 5	3671. 2	3770. 1	3871. 3	3975. 1	4081. 4	4190. 7	4302. 9	4418. 3	15
16	81. 5	76. 1	72. 8	71. 8	73. 0	76. 8	83. 2	92. 5	04. 8	20. 3	16
17	83. 1	77. 7	74. 5	73. 4	74. 7	78. 6	85. 0	94. 3	06. 7	22. 2	17
18	84. 6	79. 3	76. 1	75. 1	76. 4	80. 3	86. 8	96. 2	08. 6	24. 2	18
19	86. 2	80. 9	77. 7	76. 8	78. 2	82. 1	88. 6	98. 0	10. 5	26. 2	19
20	3487. 8	3582. 5	3679. 4	3778. 4	3879. 9	3983. 8	4090. 4	4199. 9	4312. 4	4428. 1	20
21	89. 3	84. 1	81. 0	80. 1	81. 6	85. 6	92. 2	4201. 7	14. 3	30. 1	21
22	90. 9	85. 7	82. 6	81. 8	83. 3	87. 3	94. 0	03. 6	16. 2	32. 0	22
23	92. 4	87. 3	84. 3	83. 4	85. 0	89. 1	95. 8	05. 4	18. 1	34. 0	23
24	94. 0	88. 9	85. 9	85. 1	86. 7	90. 8	97. 6	07. 3	20. 0	35. 9	24
25	3495. 6	3590. 5	3687. 5	3786. 8	3888. 4	3992. 6	4099. 4	4209. 1	4321. 9	4437. 9	25
26	97. 1	92. 1	89. 2	88. 5	90. 1	94. 4	4101. 2	11. 0	23. 8	39. 9	26
27	3498. 7	93. 7	90. 8	90. 1	91. 9	96. 1	03. 0	12. 9	25. 7	41. 8	27
28	3500. 3	95. 3	92. 4	91. 8	93. 6	97. 9	04. 9	14. 7	27. 6	43. 8	28
29	01. 8	96. 9	94. 1	93. 5	95. 3	3999. 6	06. 7	16. 6	29. 5	45. 8	29
30	3503. 4	3598. 5	3695. 7	3795. 2	3897. 0	4001. 4	4108. 5	4218. 4	4331. 4	4447. 7	30
31	05. 0	3600. 1	97. 3	96. 8	3898. 7	03. 2	10. 3	20. 3	33. 3	49. 7	31
32	06. 5	01. 7	3699. 0	3798. 5	3900. 5	04. 9	12. 1	22. 1	35. 3	51. 7	32
33	08. 1	03. 3	3700. 6	3800. 2	02. 2	06. 7	13. 9	24. 0	37. 2	53. 6	33
34	09. 7	04. 9	02. 3	01. 9	03. 9	08. 4	15. 7	25. 9	39. 1	55. 6	34
35	3511. 3	3606. 5	3703. 9	3803. 6	3905. 6	4010. 2	4117. 5	4227. 7	4341. 0	4457. 6	35
36	12. 8	08. 1	05. 6	05. 2	07. 3	12. 0	19. 3	29. 6	42. 9	59. 6	36
37	14. 4	09. 7	07. 2	06. 9	09. 1	13. 7	21. 1	31. 4	44. 8	61. 5	37
38	16. 0	11. 3	08. 8	08. 6	10. 8	15. 5	23. 0	33. 3	46. 7	63. 5	38
39	17. 5	12. 9	10. 5	10. 3	12. 5	17. 3	24. 8	35. 2	48. 7	65. 5	39
40	3519. 1	3614. 6	3712. 1	3812. 0	3914. 2	4019. 0	4126. 6	4237. 0	4350. 6	4467. 5	40
41	20. 7	16. 2	13. 8	13. 7	16. 0	20. 8	28. 4	38. 9	52. 5	69. 4	41
42	22. 3	17. 8	15. 4	15. 3	17. 7	22. 6	30. 2	40. 8	54. 4	71. 4	42
43	23. 8	19. 4	17. 1	17. 0	19. 4	24. 4	32. 0	42. 6	56. 3	73. 4	43
44	25. 4	21. 0	18. 7	18. 7	21. 1	26. 1	33. 9	44. 5	58. 3	75. 4	44
45	3527. 0	3622. 6	3720. 4	3820. 4	3922. 9	4027. 9	4135. 7	4246. 4	4360. 2	4477. 3	45
46	28. 6	24. 2	22. 0	22. 1	24. 6	29. 7	37. 5	48. 2	62. 1	79. 3	46
47	30. 1	25. 8	23. 7	23. 8	26. 3	31. 5	39. 3	50. 1	64. 0	81. 3	47
48	31. 7	27. 4	25. 3	25. 5	28. 1	33. 2	41. 1	52. 0	66. 0	83. 3	48
49	33. 3	29. 0	27. 0	27. 2	29. 8	35. 0	43. 0	53. 9	67. 9	85. 3	49
50	3534. 9	3630. 7	3728. 6	3828. 8	3931. 5	4036. 8	4144. 8	4255. 7	4369. 8	4487. 3	50
51	36. 5	32. 3	30. 3	30. 5	33. 2	38. 6	46. 6	57. 6	71. 8	89. 3	51
52	38. 0	33. 9	31. 9	32. 2	35. 0	40. 3	48. 4	59. 5	73. 7	91. 2	52
53	39. 6	35. 5	33. 6	33. 9	36. 7	42. 1	50. 3	61. 4	75. 6	93. 2	53
54	41. 2	37. 1	35. 2	35. 6	38. 5	43. 9	52. 1	63. 2	77. 5	95. 2	54
55	3542. 8	3638. 7	3736. 9	3837. 3	3940. 2	4045. 7	4153. 9	4265. 1	4379. 5	4497. 2	55
56	44. 4	40. 4	38. 5	39. 0	41. 9	47. 5	55. 8	67. 0	81. 4	4499. 2	56
57	45. 9	42. 0	40. 2	40. 7	43. 7	49. 2	57. 6	68. 9	83. 4	4501. 2	57
58	47. 5	43. 6	41. 8	42. 4	45. 4	51. 0	59. 4	70. 8	85. 3	03. 2	58
59	49. 1	45. 2	43. 5	44. 1	47. 1	52. 8	61. 2	72. 6	87. 2	05. 2	59
60	3550. 7	3646. 8	3745. 2	3845. 8	3948. 9	4054. 6	4163. 1	4274. 5	4389. 2	4507. 2	60
Lat.	50°	51°	52°	53°	54°	55°	56°	57°	58°	59°	Lat.

TABLE 1
Meridional Parts

Lat.	60°	61°	62°	63°	64°	65°	66°	67°	68°	69°	Lat.
0	4507.2	4628.8	4754.4	4884.2	5018.5	5157.7	5302.2	5452.5	5609.2	5772.8	0
1	09.2	30.9	56.5	86.4	20.7	60.0	04.7	55.1	11.9	75.6	1
2	11.2	33.0	58.7	88.6	23.0	62.4	07.1	57.7	14.5	78.4	2
3	13.2	35.0	60.8	90.8	25.3	64.8	09.6	60.2	17.2	81.2	3
4	15.2	37.1	62.9	93.0	27.6	67.1	12.1	62.8	19.9	84.0	4
5	4517.2	4639.1	4765.0	4895.2	5029.9	5169.5	5314.5	5465.4	5622.6	5786.8	5
6	19.2	41.2	67.2	97.4	32.2	71.9	17.0	67.9	25.2	89.6	6
7	21.2	43.3	69.3	4899.6	34.5	74.3	19.4	70.5	27.9	92.4	7
8	23.2	45.3	71.5	4901.8	36.7	76.6	21.9	73.1	30.6	95.2	8
9	25.2	47.4	73.6	04.0	39.0	79.0	24.4	75.6	33.3	5798.0	9
10	4527.2	4649.5	4775.7	4906.2	5041.3	5181.4	5326.9	5478.2	5636.0	5800.8	10
11	29.2	51.6	77.9	08.4	43.6	83.8	29.3	80.8	38.7	03.6	11
12	31.2	53.6	80.0	10.7	45.9	86.1	31.8	83.4	41.3	06.4	12
13	33.2	55.7	82.1	12.9	48.2	88.5	34.3	85.9	44.0	09.2	13
14	35.2	57.8	84.3	15.1	50.5	90.9	36.8	88.5	46.7	12.0	14
15	4537.2	4659.9	4786.4	4917.3	5052.8	5193.3	5339.2	5491.1	5649.4	5814.9	15
16	39.3	61.9	88.6	19.5	55.1	95.7	41.7	93.7	52.1	17.7	16
17	41.3	64.0	90.7	21.7	57.4	5198.1	44.2	96.3	54.8	20.5	17
18	43.3	66.1	92.9	24.0	59.7	5200.5	46.7	5498.9	57.5	23.3	18
19	45.3	68.2	95.0	26.2	62.0	02.9	49.2	5501.4	60.2	26.1	19
20	4547.3	4670.2	4797.2	4928.4	5064.3	5205.2	5351.7	5504.0	5662.9	5829.0	20
21	49.3	72.3	4799.3	30.6	66.6	07.6	54.1	06.6	65.6	31.8	21
22	51.4	74.4	4801.5	32.9	68.9	10.0	56.6	09.2	68.3	34.6	22
23	53.4	76.5	03.6	35.1	71.2	12.4	59.1	11.8	71.1	37.5	23
24	55.4	78.6	05.8	37.3	73.5	14.8	61.6	14.4	73.8	40.3	24
25	4557.4	4680.7	4807.9	4939.6	5075.9	5217.2	5364.1	5517.0	5676.5	5843.2	25
26	59.4	82.8	10.1	41.8	78.2	19.6	66.6	19.6	79.2	46.0	26
27	61.5	84.8	12.3	44.0	80.5	22.0	69.1	22.2	81.9	48.8	27
28	63.5	86.9	14.4	46.3	82.8	24.4	71.6	24.8	84.6	51.7	28
29	65.5	89.0	16.6	48.5	85.1	26.8	74.1	27.4	87.4	54.5	29
30	4567.5	4691.1	4818.7	4950.7	5087.4	5229.3	5376.6	5530.0	5690.1	5857.4	30
31	69.6	93.2	20.9	53.0	89.8	31.7	79.1	32.7	92.8	60.3	31
32	71.6	95.3	23.1	55.2	92.1	34.1	81.6	35.3	95.5	63.1	32
33	73.6	97.4	25.2	57.4	94.4	36.5	84.1	37.9	5698.3	66.0	33
34	75.7	4699.5	27.4	59.7	96.7	38.9	86.7	40.5	5701.0	68.8	34
35	4577.7	4701.6	4829.6	4961.9	5099.1	5241.3	5389.2	5543.1	5703.7	5871.7	35
36	79.7	03.7	31.7	64.2	5101.4	43.7	91.7	45.7	06.5	74.6	36
37	81.8	05.8	33.9	66.4	03.7	46.2	94.2	48.4	09.2	77.4	37
38	83.8	07.9	36.1	68.7	06.0	48.6	96.7	51.0	12.0	80.3	38
39	85.8	10.0	38.3	70.9	08.4	51.0	5399.2	53.6	14.7	83.2	39
40	4587.9	4712.1	4840.4	4973.2	5110.7	5253.4	5401.8	5556.2	5717.5	5886.0	40
41	89.9	14.2	42.6	75.4	13.0	55.8	04.3	58.9	20.2	88.9	41
42	91.9	16.3	44.8	77.7	15.4	58.3	06.8	61.5	22.9	91.8	42
43	94.0	18.4	47.0	79.9	17.7	60.7	09.3	64.1	25.7	94.7	43
44	96.0	20.5	49.1	82.2	20.1	63.1	11.9	66.8	28.5	5897.6	44
45	4598.1	4722.6	4851.3	4984.4	5122.4	5265.6	5414.4	5569.4	5731.2	5900.4	45
46	4600.1	24.7	53.5	86.7	24.7	68.0	16.9	72.1	34.0	03.3	46
47	02.2	26.8	55.7	89.0	27.1	70.4	19.5	74.7	36.7	06.2	47
48	04.2	29.0	57.9	91.2	29.4	72.9	22.0	77.3	39.5	09.1	48
49	06.3	31.1	60.0	93.5	31.8	75.3	24.5	80.0	42.3	12.0	49
50	4608.3	4733.2	4862.2	4995.8	5134.1	5277.7	5427.1	5582.6	5745.0	5914.9	50
51	10.3	35.3	64.4	4998.0	36.5	80.2	29.6	85.3	47.8	17.8	51
52	12.4	37.4	66.6	5000.3	38.8	82.6	32.1	87.9	50.6	20.7	52
53	14.4	39.5	68.8	02.6	41.2	85.1	34.7	90.6	53.3	23.6	53
54	16.5	41.7	71.0	04.8	43.5	87.5	37.2	93.2	56.1	26.5	54
55	4618.6	4743.8	4873.2	5007.1	5145.9	5290.0	5439.8	5595.9	5758.9	5929.4	55
56	20.6	45.9	75.4	09.4	48.2	92.4	42.3	98.5	61.7	32.3	56
57	22.7	48.0	77.6	11.6	50.6	94.9	44.9	5601.2	64.4	35.3	57
58	24.7	50.1	79.8	13.9	53.0	97.3	47.4	03.9	67.2	38.2	58
59	26.8	52.3	82.0	16.2	55.3	5299.8	50.0	06.5	70.0	41.1	59
60	4628.8	4754.4	4884.2	5018.5	5157.7	5302.2	5452.5	5609.2	5772.8	5944.0	60
Lat.	60°	61°	62°	63°	64°	65°	66°	67°	68°	69°	Lat.

TABLE 1
Meridional Parts

Lat.	70°	71°	72°	73°	74°	75°	76°	77°	78°	79°	Lat.
0	5944.0	6123.7	6312.7	6512.1	6723.3	6947.8	7187.4	7444.5	7721.8	8022.8	0
1	46.9	26.7	15.9	15.5	27.0	51.7	91.6	48.9	26.6	28.1	1
2	49.9	29.8	19.1	19.0	30.6	55.5	95.7	53.4	31.4	33.3	2
3	52.8	32.9	22.4	22.4	34.2	59.4	7199.9	57.8	36.2	38.6	3
4	55.7	36.0	25.6	25.8	37.9	63.3	7204.0	62.3	41.0	43.8	4
5	5958.6	6139.0	6328.9	6529.3	6741.5	6967.2	7208.2	7466.8	7745.9	8049.1	5
6	61.6	42.1	32.1	32.7	45.2	71.1	12.3	71.2	50.7	54.4	6
7	64.5	45.2	35.4	36.1	48.8	75.0	16.5	75.7	55.6	59.7	7
8	67.5	48.3	38.6	39.6	52.5	78.8	20.7	80.2	60.4	65.0	8
9	70.4	51.4	41.9	43.0	56.1	82.7	24.8	84.7	65.3	70.3	9
10	5973.3	6154.5	6345.1	6546.5	6759.8	6986.6	7229.0	7489.2	7770.2	8075.6	10
11	76.3	57.6	48.4	49.9	63.4	90.6	33.2	93.7	75.0	80.9	11
12	79.2	60.7	51.7	53.4	67.1	94.5	37.4	7498.2	79.9	86.3	12
13	82.2	63.8	55.0	56.8	70.8	6998.4	41.6	7502.7	84.8	91.6	13
14	85.1	66.9	58.2	60.3	74.5	7002.3	45.8	07.3	89.7	8096.9	14
15	5988.1	6170.0	6361.5	6563.8	6778.1	7006.2	7250.0	7511.8	7794.6	8102.3	15
16	91.1	73.1	64.8	67.2	81.8	10.2	54.2	16.3	7799.5	07.7	16
17	94.0	76.2	68.1	70.7	85.5	14.1	58.4	20.9	7804.5	13.0	17
18	97.0	79.3	71.4	74.2	89.2	18.0	62.6	25.4	09.4	18.4	18
19	5999.9	82.4	74.6	77.7	92.9	22.0	66.8	29.9	14.3	23.8	19
20	6002.9	6185.6	6377.9	6581.2	6796.6	7025.9	7271.1	7534.5	7819.3	8129.2	20
21	05.9	88.7	81.2	84.6	6800.3	29.9	75.3	39.1	24.2	34.6	21
22	08.9	91.8	84.5	88.1	04.0	33.8	79.5	43.6	29.2	40.0	22
23	11.8	94.9	87.8	91.6	07.7	37.8	83.8	48.2	34.1	45.4	23
24	14.8	6198.1	91.1	95.1	11.4	41.7	88.0	52.8	39.1	50.9	24
25	6017.8	6201.2	6394.4	6598.6	6815.2	7045.7	7292.3	7557.4	7844.1	8156.3	25
26	20.8	04.3	6397.7	6602.1	18.9	49.7	7296.5	62.0	49.1	61.8	26
27	23.8	07.5	6401.1	05.6	22.6	53.6	7300.8	66.6	54.0	67.2	27
28	26.7	10.6	04.4	09.1	26.3	57.6	05.1	71.2	59.0	72.7	28
29	29.7	13.8	07.7	12.7	30.1	61.6	09.3	75.8	64.0	78.2	29
30	6032.7	6216.9	6411.0	6616.2	6833.8	7065.6	7313.6	7580.4	7869.1	8183.6	30
31	35.7	20.1	14.3	19.7	37.5	69.6	17.9	85.0	74.1	89.1	31
32	38.7	23.2	17.7	23.2	41.3	73.6	22.2	89.6	79.1	8194.6	32
33	41.7	26.4	21.0	26.7	45.0	77.6	26.5	94.3	84.1	8200.1	33
34	44.7	29.5	24.3	30.3	48.8	81.6	30.8	7598.9	89.2	05.7	34
35	6047.7	6232.7	6427.7	6633.8	6852.6	7085.6	7335.1	7603.6	7894.2	8211.2	35
36	50.7	35.9	31.0	37.3	56.3	89.6	39.4	08.2	7899.3	16.7	36
37	53.7	39.0	34.4	40.9	60.1	93.7	43.7	12.9	7904.3	22.3	37
38	56.8	42.2	37.7	44.4	63.9	7097.7	48.0	17.5	09.4	27.8	38
39	59.8	45.4	41.0	48.0	67.6	7101.7	52.4	22.2	14.5	33.4	39
40	6062.8	6248.6	6444.4	6651.5	6871.4	7105.8	7356.7	7626.9	7919.6	8238.9	40
41	65.8	51.7	47.8	55.1	75.2	09.8	61.0	31.6	24.7	44.5	41
42	68.8	54.9	51.1	58.6	79.0	13.8	65.4	36.3	29.7	50.1	42
43	71.8	58.1	54.5	62.2	82.8	17.9	69.7	41.0	34.9	55.7	43
44	74.9	61.3	57.8	65.8	86.6	21.9	74.1	45.7	40.0	61.3	44
45	6077.9	6264.5	6461.2	6669.3	6890.4	7126.0	7378.4	7650.4	7945.1	8266.9	45
46	80.9	67.7	64.6	72.9	94.2	30.1	82.8	55.1	50.2	72.5	46
47	84.0	70.9	68.0	76.5	6898.0	34.1	87.2	59.8	55.4	78.2	47
48	87.0	74.1	71.3	80.1	6901.8	38.2	91.6	64.5	60.5	83.8	48
49	90.0	77.3	74.7	83.7	05.6	42.3	7395.9	69.3	65.6	89.5	49
50	6093.1	6280.5	6478.1	6687.3	6909.4	7146.4	7400.3	7674.0	7970.8	8295.1	50
51	96.1	83.7	81.5	90.8	13.2	50.4	04.7	78.7	76.0	8300.8	51
52	6099.2	86.9	84.9	94.4	17.1	54.5	09.1	83.5	81.1	06.5	52
53	6102.2	90.1	88.3	6698.0	20.9	58.6	13.5	88.3	86.3	12.2	53
54	05.3	93.3	91.7	6701.6	24.7	62.7	17.9	93.0	91.5	17.9	54
55	6108.3	6296.5	6495.1	6705.2	6928.6	7166.8	7422.3	7697.8	7996.7	8323.6	55
56	11.4	6299.8	6498.5	08.9	32.4	71.0	26.8	7702.6	8001.9	29.3	56
57	14.5	6303.0	6501.9	12.5	36.2	75.1	31.2	07.4	07.1	35.0	57
58	17.5	06.2	05.3	16.1	40.1	79.2	35.6	12.2	12.4	40.7	58
59	20.6	09.4	08.7	19.7	44.0	83.3	40.0	17.0	17.6	46.5	59
60	6123.7	6312.7	6512.1	6723.3	6947.8	7187.4	7444.5	7721.8	8022.8	8352.2	60
Lat.	70°	71°	72°	73°	74°	75°	76°	77°	78°	79°	Lat.

TABLE 1

Meridional Parts

Lat.	80°	81°	82°	83°	84°	85°	86°	87°	88°	89°	Lat.
0	8352. 2	8716. 0	9122. 4	9582. 7	10113. 7	10741. 4	11509. 3	12498. 8	13893. 1	16276. 2	0
1	58. 0	22. 4	29. 6	90. 9	123. 3	752. 9	523. 6	518. 0	921. 9	334. 0	1
2	63. 8	28. 8	36. 8	9599. 1	132. 9	764. 4	538. 0	537. 2	950. 9	392. 8	2
3	69. 5	35. 3	44. 0	9607. 4	142. 5	776. 0	552. 5	556. 6	13980. 2	452. 6	3
4	75. 3	41. 7	51. 2	15. 6	152. 2	787. 6	567. 1	576. 1	14009. 7	513. 4	4
5	8381. 1	8748. 1	9158. 5	9623. 9	10161. 9	10799. 2	11581. 7	12595. 7	14039. 5	16575. 4	5
6	86. 9	54. 6	65. 7	32. 3	171. 6	810. 9	596. 4	615. 4	069. 5	638. 5	6
7	92. 8	61. 1	73. 0	40. 6	181. 3	822. 6	611. 1	635. 2	099. 8	702. 7	7
8	8398. 6	67. 5	80. 3	48. 9	191. 1	834. 4	625. 9	655. 2	130. 3	768. 2	8
9	8404. 4	74. 0	87. 6	57. 3	200. 9	846. 2	640. 7	675. 2	161. 2	835. 0	9
10	8410. 3	8780. 5	9195. 0	9665. 7	10210. 7	10858. 1	11655. 7	12695. 4	14192. 3	16903. 0	10
11	16. 1	87. 1	9202. 3	74. 1	220. 6	870. 0	670. 7	715. 7	223. 7	16972. 5	11
12	22. 0	8793. 6	09. 7	82. 6	230. 4	881. 9	685. 7	736. 1	255. 4	17043. 4	12
13	27. 9	8800. 1	17. 0	91. 0	240. 3	893. 9	700. 8	756. 6	287. 4	115. 8	13
14	33. 8	06. 7	24. 4	9699. 5	250. 3	905. 9	716. 0	777. 3	319. 7	189. 7	14
15	8439. 7	8813. 2	9231. 8	9708. 0	10260. 2	10917. 9	11731. 3	12798. 1	14352. 2	17265. 3	15
16	45. 6	19. 8	39. 3	16. 5	270. 2	930. 0	746. 6	819. 0	385. 2	342. 5	16
17	51. 5	26. 4	46. 7	25. 0	280. 3	942. 2	762. 0	840. 0	418. 4	421. 5	17
18	57. 4	33. 0	54. 2	33. 6	290. 3	954. 3	777. 5	861. 2	451. 9	502. 4	18
19	63. 4	39. 6	61. 6	42. 2	300. 4	966. 6	793. 0	882. 5	485. 8	585. 3	19
20	8469. 3	8846. 3	9269. 1	9750. 8	10310. 5	10978. 8	11808. 6	12903. 9	14520. 0	17670. 2	20
21	75. 3	52. 9	76. 6	59. 4	320. 7	10991. 2	824. 3	925. 4	554. 6	757. 2	21
22	81. 3	59. 6	84. 1	68. 0	330. 8	11003. 5	840. 0	947. 1	589. 5	846. 5	22
23	87. 2	66. 2	91. 7	76. 7	341. 0	015. 9	855. 8	969. 0	624. 7	17938. 2	23
24	93. 2	72. 9	9299. 2	85. 4	351. 3	028. 4	871. 7	12990. 9	660. 4	18032. 4	24
25	8499. 2	8879. 6	9306. 8	9794. 1	10361. 5	11040. 8	11887. 7	13013. 1	14696. 4	18129. 2	25
26	8505. 2	86. 3	14. 4	9802. 8	371. 8	053. 4	903. 7	035. 3	732. 7	228. 9	26
27	11. 3	93. 0	22. 0	11. 6	382. 1	066. 0	919. 8	057. 7	769. 5	331. 5	27
28	17. 3	8899. 8	29. 6	20. 4	392. 5	078. 6	936. 0	080. 3	806. 7	437. 3	28
29	23. 3	8906. 5	37. 2	29. 2	402. 9	091. 3	952. 3	103. 0	844. 3	546. 4	29
30	8529. 4	8913. 3	9344. 9	9838. 0	10413. 3	11104. 0	11968. 6	13125. 8	14882. 2	18659. 2	30
31	35. 4	20. 0	52. 6	46. 8	423. 7	116. 8	11985. 0	148. 8	920. 7	775. 7	31
32	41. 5	26. 8	60. 2	55. 7	434. 2	129. 6	12001. 5	172. 0	959. 5	18896. 3	32
33	47. 6	33. 6	67. 9	64. 6	444. 7	142. 4	018. 1	195. 3	14998. 8	19021. 4	33
34	53. 7	40. 4	75. 7	73. 5	455. 3	155. 3	034. 8	218. 8	15038. 6	151. 1	34
35	8559. 8	8947. 2	9383. 4	9882. 4	10465. 9	11168. 3	12051. 5	13242. 4	15078. 8	19285. 9	35
36	65. 9	54. 1	91. 2	9891. 4	476. 5	181. 3	068. 3	266. 2	119. 5	426. 3	36
37	72. 0	60. 9	9398. 9	9900. 4	487. 1	194. 4	085. 2	290. 2	160. 6	572. 6	37
38	78. 2	67. 8	9406. 7	09. 4	497. 8	207. 5	102. 2	314. 3	202. 3	725. 4	38
39	84. 3	74. 7	14. 5	18. 4	508. 5	220. 6	119. 3	338. 6	244. 5	19885. 3	39
40	8590. 5	8981. 6	9422. 3	9927. 5	10519. 2	11233. 9	12136. 4	13363. 1	15287. 2	20053. 1	40
41	8596. 7	88. 5	30. 2	36. 6	530. 0	247. 1	153. 7	387. 7	330. 4	229. 4	41
42	8602. 8	8995. 4	38. 0	45. 7	540. 8	260. 4	171. 0	412. 5	374. 2	415. 3	42
43	09. 0	9002. 3	45. 9	54. 8	551. 7	273. 8	188. 4	437. 6	418. 6	611. 8	43
44	15. 2	09. 3	53. 8	63. 9	562. 5	287. 2	205. 9	462. 7	463. 5	20820. 2	44
45	8621. 5	9016. 2	9461. 7	9973. 1	10573. 4	11300. 7	12223. 5	13488. 1	15509. 1	21042. 0	45
46	27. 7	23. 2	69. 7	82. 3	584. 4	314. 2	241. 2	513. 7	555. 2	279. 2	46
47	33. 9	30. 2	77. 6	9991. 5	595. 4	327. 8	259. 0	539. 4	602. 0	534. 0	47
48	40. 2	37. 2	85. 6	10000. 8	606. 4	341. 4	276. 8	565. 4	649. 4	21800. 2	48
49	46. 4	44. 2	9493. 6	010. 0	617. 4	355. 1	294. 8	591. 5	697. 5	22108. 3	49
50	8652. 7	9051. 3	9501. 6	10019. 3	10628. 5	11368. 8	12312. 9	13617. 9	15746. 3	22435. 9	50
51	59. 0	58. 3	09. 6	028. 7	639. 6	382. 6	331. 0	644. 5	795. 7	22798. 1	51
52	65. 3	65. 4	17. 6	038. 0	650. 8	396. 4	349. 3	671. 2	845. 9	23203. 1	52
53	71. 6	72. 4	25. 7	047. 4	662. 0	410. 3	367. 6	698. 2	896. 9	23662. 1	53
54	77. 9	79. 5	33. 8	056. 8	673. 2	424. 3	386. 0	725. 4	15948. 6	24192. 0	54
55	8684. 2	9086. 6	9541. 9	10066. 2	10684. 5	11438. 3	12404. 6	13752. 8	16001. 1	24818. 8	55
56	90. 6	9093. 7	50. 0	075. 6	695. 8	452. 4	423. 2	780. 4	054. 4	25585. 9	56
57	8696. 9	9100. 9	58. 1	085. 1	707. 1	466. 5	442. 0	808. 2	108. 5	26574. 9	57
58	8703. 3	08. 0	66. 3	094. 6	718. 5	480. 7	460. 8	836. 3	163. 5	27968. 9	58
59	09. 6	15. 2	74. 5	104. 1	729. 9	494. 9	479. 8	864. 6	219. 4	30351. 9	59
60	8716. 0	9122. 4	9582. 7	10113. 7	10741. 4	11509. 3	12498. 8	13893. 1	16276. 2	—	60
Lat.	80°	81°	82°	83°	84°	85°	86°	87°	88°	89°	Lat.

TABLE 2

Conversion Table for Meridional Parts

Latitude	Inter-national	Clarke (1880)	Sphere	Latitude	Inter-national	Clarke (1880)	Sphere	Latitude	Inter-national	Clarke (1880)	Sphere
° ′				° ′				° ′			
0 00	0.00	0.00	0.00	30 00	+0.08	−0.06	+11.64	60 00	+0.14	−0.10	+20.19
0 30	0.00	0.00	+0.20	30 30	+0.08	−0.06	+11.82	60 30	+0.14	−0.10	+20.29
1 00	0.00	0.00	+0.41	31 00	+0.08	−0.06	+11.99	61 00	+0.14	−0.11	+20.39
1 30	0.00	0.00	+0.61	31 30	+0.08	−0.06	+12.17	61 30	+0.14	−0.11	+20.48
2 00	+0.01	0.00	+0.81	32 00	+0.08	−0.06	+12.34	62 00	+0.14	−0.11	+20.58
2 30	+0.01	−0.01	+1.02	32 30	+0.09	−0.06	+12.51	62 30	+0.14	−0.11	+20.68
3 00	+0.01	−0.01	+1.22	33 00	+0.09	−0.07	+12.68	63 00	+0.14	−0.11	+20.77
3 30	+0.01	−0.01	+1.42	33 30	+0.09	−0.07	+12.85	63 30	+0.14	−0.11	+20.86
4 00	+0.01	−0.01	+1.62	34 00	+0.09	−0.07	+13.02	64 00	+0.14	−0.11	+20.95
4 30	+0.01	−0.01	+1.83	34 30	+0.09	−0.07	+13.19	64 30	+0.14	−0.11	+21.04
5 00	+0.01	−0.01	+2.03	35 00	+0.09	−0.07	+13.36	65 00	+0.14	−0.11	+21.13
5 30	+0.02	−0.01	+2.23	35 30	+0.09	−0.07	+13.52	65 30	+0.14	−0.11	+21.21
6 00	+0.02	−0.01	+2.43	36 00	+0.09	−0.07	+13.69	66 00	+0.14	−0.11	+21.30
6 30	+0.02	−0.01	+2.63	36 30	+0.09	−0.07	+13.85	66 30	+0.15	−0.11	+21.38
7 00	+0.02	−0.01	+2.84	37 00	+0.10	−0.07	+14.01	67 00	+0.15	−0.11	+21.46
7 30	+0.02	−0.02	+3.04	37 30	+0.10	−0.07	+14.18	67 30	+0.15	−0.11	+21.54
8 00	+0.02	−0.02	+3.24	38 00	+0.10	−0.07	+14.34	68 00	+0.15	−0.11	+21.62
8 30	+0.02	−0.02	+3.44	38 30	+0.10	−0.07	+14.50	68 30	+0.15	−0.11	+21.69
9 00	+0.02	−0.02	+3.64	39 00	+0.10	−0.08	+14.66	69 00	+0.15	−0.11	+21.77
9 30	+0.03	−0.02	+3.84	39 30	+0.10	−0.08	+14.81	69 30	+0.15	−0.11	+21.84
10 00	+0.03	−0.02	+4.04	40 00	+0.10	−0.08	+14.97	70 00	+0.15	−0.11	+21.91
10 30	+0.03	−0.02	+4.24	40 30	+0.10	−0.08	+15.13	70 30	+0.15	−0.11	+21.98
11 00	+0.03	−0.02	+4.44	41 00	+0.10	−0.08	+15.28	71 00	+0.15	−0.11	+22.05
11 30	+0.03	−0.02	+4.64	41 30	+0.10	−0.08	+15.43	71 30	+0.15	−0.11	+22.11
12 00	+0.03	−0.02	+4.84	42 00	+0.11	−0.08	+15.59	72 00	+0.15	−0.11	+22.18
12 30	+0.03	−0.03	+5.04	42 30	+0.11	−0.08	+15.74	72 30	+0.15	−0.11	+22.24
13 00	+0.04	−0.03	+5.23	43 00	+0.11	−0.08	+15.89	73 00	+0.15	−0.12	+22.30
13 30	+0.04	−0.03	+5.43	43 30	+0.11	−0.08	+16.03	73 30	+0.15	−0.12	+22.36
14 00	+0.04	−0.03	+5.63	44 00	+0.11	−0.08	+16.18	74 00	+0.15	−0.12	+22.41
14 30	+0.04	−0.03	+5.83	44 30	+0.11	−0.08	+16.33	74 30	+0.15	−0.12	+22.47
15 00	+0.04	−0.03	+6.02	45 00	+0.11	−0.08	+16.47	75 00	+0.15	−0.12	+22.52
15 30	+0.04	−0.03	+6.22	45 30	+0.11	−0.09	+16.62	75 30	+0.15	−0.12	+22.58
16 00	+0.04	−0.03	+6.41	46 00	+0.11	−0.09	+16.76	76 00	+0.15	−0.12	+22.63
16 30	+0.04	−0.03	+6.61	46 30	+0.11	−0.09	+16.90	76 30	+0.15	−0.12	+22.67
17 00	+0.05	−0.04	+6.80	47 00	+0.12	−0.09	+17.04	77 00	+0.15	−0.12	+22.72
17 30	+0.05	−0.04	+7.00	47 30	+0.12	−0.09	+17.18	77 30	+0.16	−0.12	+22.77
18 00	+0.05	−0.04	+7.19	48 00	+0.12	−0.09	+17.31	78 00	+0.16	−0.12	+22.81
18 30	+0.05	−0.04	+7.38	48 30	+0.12	−0.09	+17.45	78 30	+0.16	−0.12	+22.85
19 00	+0.05	−0.04	+7.58	49 00	+0.12	−0.09	+17.58	79 00	+0.16	−0.12	+22.89
19 30	+0.05	−0.04	+7.77	49 30	+0.12	−0.09	+17.72	79 30	+0.16	−0.12	+22.93
20 00	+0.05	−0.04	+7.96	50 00	+0.12	−0.09	+17.85	80 00	+0.16	−0.12	+22.97
20 30	+0.06	−0.04	+8.15	50 30	+0.12	−0.09	+17.98	80 30	+0.16	−0.12	+23.00
21 00	+0.06	−0.04	+8.34	51 00	+0.12	−0.09	+18.11	81 00	+0.16	−0.12	+23.03
21 30	+0.06	−0.04	+8.53	51 30	+0.12	−0.09	+18.24	81 30	+0.16	−0.12	+23.06
22 00	+0.06	−0.04	+8.72	52 00	+0.12	−0.09	+18.36	82 00	+0.16	−0.12	+23.09
22 30	+0.06	−0.05	+8.91	52 30	+0.13	−0.10	+18.49	82 30	+0.16	−0.12	+23.12
23 00	+0.06	−0.05	+9.10	53 00	+0.13	−0.10	+18.61	83 00	+0.16	−0.12	+23.15
23 30	+0.06	−0.05	+9.28	53 30	+0.13	−0.10	+18.73	83 30	+0.16	−0.12	+23.17
24 00	+0.06	−0.05	+9.47	54 00	+0.13	−0.10	+18.85	84 00	+0.16	−0.12	+23.19
24 30	+0.07	−0.05	+9.65	54 30	+0.13	−0.10	+18.97	84 30	+0.16	−0.12	+23.21
25 00	+0.07	−0.05	+9.84	55 00	+0.13	−0.10	+19.09	85 00	+0.16	−0.12	+23.23
25 30	+0.07	−0.05	+10.02	55 30	+0.13	−0.10	+19.21	85 30	+0.16	−0.12	+23.25
26 00	+0.07	−0.05	+10.21	56 00	+0.13	−0.10	+19.32	86 00	+0.16	−0.12	+23.26
26 30	+0.07	−0.05	+10.39	56 30	+0.13	−0.10	+19.43	86 30	+0.16	−0.12	+23.28
27 00	+0.07	−0.05	+10.57	57 00	+0.13	−0.10	+19.55	87 00	+0.16	−0.12	+23.29
27 30	+0.07	−0.06	+10.75	57 30	+0.13	−0.10	+19.66	87 30	+0.16	−0.12	+23.30
28 00	+0.07	−0.06	+10.93	58 00	+0.13	−0.10	+19.77	88 00	+0.16	−0.12	+23.31
28 30	+0.08	−0.06	+11.11	58 30	+0.14	−0.10	+19.87	88 30	+0.16	−0.12	+23.31
29 00	+0.08	−0.06	+11.29	59 00	+0.14	−0.10	+19.98	89 00	+0.16	−0.12	+23.32
29 30	+0.08	−0.06	+11.46	59 30	+0.14	−0.10	+20.08	89 30	+0.16	−0.12	+23.32
30 00	+0.08	−0.06	+11.64	60 00	+0.14	−0.10	+20.19	90 00	—	—	—

Step two: Determine whether the latitude or longitude is the limiting scale factor. The number of inches available for latitude coverage is 31 (35 inches minus a two-inch margin top and bottom). If 527 meridional parts are to be shown in 31 inches, each meridional part will be $\frac{31}{527}=$ 0.05882 inch. There are 46—4=42 inches available for longitude, and therefore the length of each meridional part will be $\frac{42}{720}=$0.05833 inch. Thus, the longitude is the limiting scale factor, for all of the desired area could not be shown in the available space if the larger scale were to be used. Using the smaller scale, it is found that 30.74 inches (0.05833×527) will be needed to show the desired latitude coverage. The top and bottom margins can be increased slightly, or additional latitude coverage can be shown. If it is desired to include the additional coverage, the amount can be determined by dividing the available space, 31 inches, by the scale, 0.05833. This is 531.5 meridional parts, or 4.5 more than the minimum. By inspection of Table 1, it is seen that the latitude can be extended either 3′.3 below 44° or 2′.9 above 50°. Suppose it is decided that the margin will be increased slightly and only the desired minimum coverage shown.

Step three: Determine the spacing of the meridians and parallels. Meridians 1° or 60′ apart will be placed 60 × 0.05833=3.50 inches apart. Next, determine each degree of latitude separately. First, compute the meridional difference between the lowest parallel and the various parallels to be shown:

$M_{45°}$ 3013.5	$M_{46°}$ 3098.8	$M_{47°}$ 3185.7	$M_{48°}$ 3274.2	$M_{49°}$ 3364.5	$M_{50°}$ 3456.6
$M_{44°}$ 2929.6	$M_{44°}$ 2929.6	$M_{44°}$ 2929.6	$M_{44°}$ 2929.6	$M_{44°}$ 2929.6	$M_{44°}$ 2929.6
m 83.9	m 169.2	m 256.1	m 344.6	m 434.9	m 527.0

Next, determine the distance of each parallel from that of L 44° N by multiplying its meridional difference by the scale, 0.05833:

L 44° to L 45°=0.05833× 83.9= 4.89 in.
L 44° to L 46°=0.05833×169.2= 9.87 in.
L 44° to L 47°=0.05833×256.1=14.94 in.
L 44° to L 48°=0.05833×344.6=20.10 in.
L 44° to L 49°=0.05833×434.9=25.37 in.
L 44° to L 50°=0.05833×527.0=30.74 in.

Step four: Draw the graticule. Draw a horizontal line 2.13 inches $\left(\frac{35-30.74}{2}\right)$ from the bottom. This is the lower neat line. Label it "44° N." Draw the right-hand neat line two inches from the edge. Label it "56° W." Along the lower parallel measure off distances in units of 3.50 inches from λ 56° W at the right to λ 68° W at the left. Through the points thus located draw vertical lines to represent the meridians. Along any meridian measure upward from the horizontal line a series of distances as determined by the calculations above. Through these points draw horizontal lines to represent the parallels. Label the meridians and parallels as shown in figure 3.4.

Step five: Mark off the latitude and longitude scales around the neat line. The scales can be graduated in units as small as desired. Determine the longitude scale by dividing the degrees into equal parts. Establish the latitude scale by computing each subdivision of a degree in the same manner as described above for whole degrees. In low latitudes degrees of latitude can be divided into equal parts without serious loss of accuracy.

Step six: Fill in the desired detail.

In *south* latitude the distance between consecutive parallels increases toward the *south.* The top parallel is drawn first and distances measured downward from it. Latitude labels increase toward the *south* (down).

In *east* longitude the longitude labels increase toward the *east* (right).

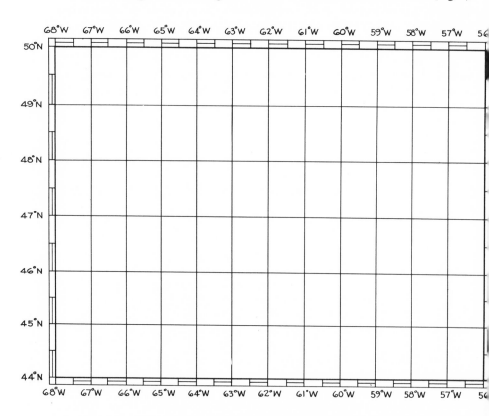

Fig. 3.4. The graticule of a Mercator chart from L 44° N to L 50° N and from λ 56° W to λ 68° W.

Transverse and oblique Mercator projections • If a Mercator chart is constructed with the cylinder tangent along a meridian instead of the equator, a **transverse Mercator** or **transverse cylindrical orthomorphic** projection results. The word "inverse" is sometimes used in place of "transverse" with the same meaning. If the cylinder is tangent at some great circle other than the equator or a meridian (fig. 3.5), the projection is called **oblique Mercator** or **oblique cylindrical orthomorphic.** These projections utilize a **fictitious graticule** similar to but offset from the familiar network of meridians and parallels (fig. 3.6). The tangent great circle is the **fictitious equator.** Ninety degrees from it are two **fictitious poles.** A group of great circles through these poles and perpendicular to the tangent great circle are the **fictitious meridians,** while a series of circles parallel to the plane of the tangent great circle form the **fictitious parallels.**

The actual meridians and parallels appear as curved lines (figs. 3.7 and 3.9).

A straight line on the transverse or oblique Mercator projection makes the same angle with all fictitious meridians, but not with the terrestrial meridians. It is therefore a **fictitious rhumb line.** Near the tangent great circle a straight line closely approximates a great circle. It is in this area that the chart is most useful.

The **Universal Transverse Mercator (UTM) grid** is a military grid superimposed upon a transverse Mercator graticule, or the representation of these grid lines upon any graticule.

This grid system and these projections are often used for large-scale (harbor) nautical charts and military charts.

Transverse Mercator projection • Since the area of minimum distortion in a **transverse (inverse) Mercator** or **transverse (inverse) cylindrical orthomorphic** projection is near a meridian, this projection is useful for charts covering a large band of latitude and extending a relatively short distance on each side of the tangent meridian (fig. 3.7) or for charts of the polar regions.

Oblique Mercator projection • The **oblique Mercator** or **oblique cylindrical orthomorphic** projection is used principally where it is desired to depict an area in the near vicinity of an oblique great circle, as, for instance, along the great-circle route between two important, widely separated centers. Figure 3.8 is a Mercator map showing Washington and Moscow and the great circle joining them. Figure 3.9 is an oblique Mercator map with the great circle between these two centers as the tangent great circle or fictitious equator (as in fig. 3.6). The limits of the chart of figure 3.9 are indicated in figure 3.8. Note the large variation in scale as the latitude changes.

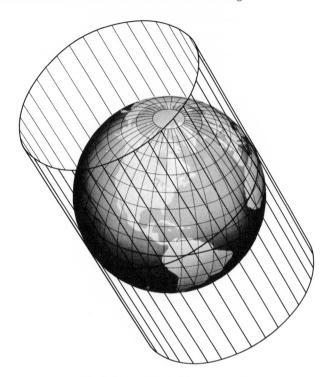

Fig. 3.5. An oblique Mercator projection.

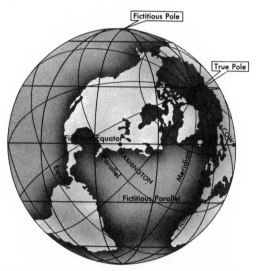

Fig. 3.6. The fictitious graticule of an oblique Mercator projection.

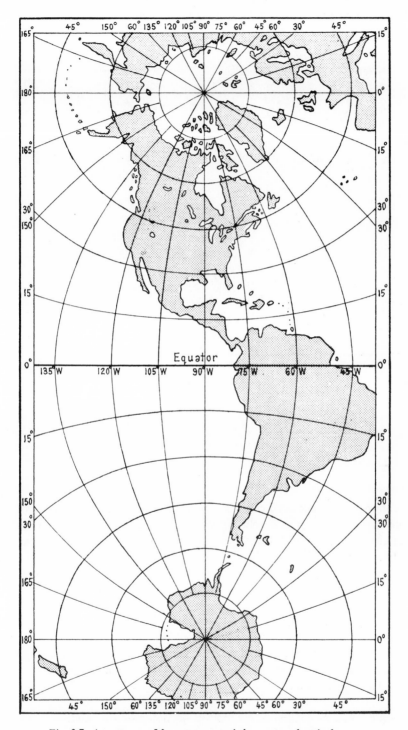

Fig. 3.7. *A transverse Mercator map of the western hemisphere.*

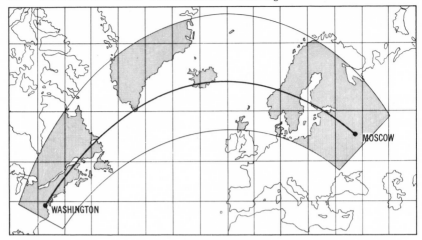

Fig. 3.8. The great circle between Washington and Moscow as it appears on a Mercator map. See figures 3.6 and 3.9.

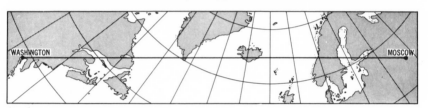

Fig. 3.9. An oblique Mercator map based upon a cylinder tangent along the great circle through Washington and Moscow. The map includes an area 500 miles on each side of the great circle. The limits of this map are indicated on the Mercator map of figure 3.8.

Conic Projections

Features • A conic projection is produced by transferring points from the surface of the earth to a cone or series of cones which are then cut along an element and spread out flat to form the chart. If the axis of the cone coincides with the axis of the earth, the usual situation, the parallels appear as arcs of circles and the meridians as either straight or curved lines converging toward the nearer pole. Excessive distortion is usually avoided by limiting the area covered to that part of the cone near the surface of the earth. A parallel along which there is no distortion is called a **standard parallel.**

The appearance and features of conic projections are varied by using cones tangent at various parallels, using a secant (intersecting) cone, or by using a series of cones.

Simple conic projection • A conic projection using a single tangent cone is called a **simple conic** projection (fig. 3.10). The height of the cone increases as the latitude of the tangent parallel decreases. At the equator

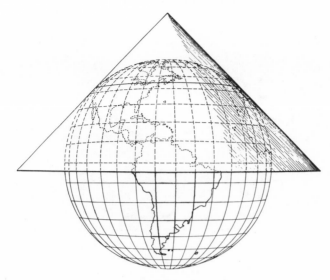

Fig. 3.10. A simple conic projection.

the height reaches infinity and the cone becomes a cylinder. At the pole its height is zero and it becomes a plane. As in the Mercator projection, the simple conic projection is not perspective, as only the meridians are projected geometrically, each becoming an element of the cone. When this is spread out flat to form a map, the meridians appear as straight lines converging at the apex of the cone. The standard parallel, or that at which the cone is tangent to the earth, appears as the arc of a circle with its center at the apex of the cone, or the common point of intersection of all the meridians. The other parallels are concentric circles, the distance along any meridian between consecutive parallels being in correct relation to the distance on the earth, and hence derived mathematically. The pole is represented by a circle (fig. 3.11). The scale is correct along any meridian and along the standard parallel. All other parallels are too great in length, the error increasing with increased distance from the standard parallel. Since the scale is not the same in all directions about every point, the projection is not conformal, its principal disadvantage for navigation. Neither is it an equal-area projection.

Since the scale is correct along the standard parallel and varies uniformly on each side, with comparatively little distortion near the standard parallel, this projection is useful for mapping an area covering a large spread of longitude and a comparatively narrow band of latitude.

Lambert conformal projection • The useful latitude range of the simple conic projection can be increased by using a secant cone intersecting the earth at two standard parallels (fig. 3.12). The area between the two standard parallels is compressed, and that beyond is expanded. Such a

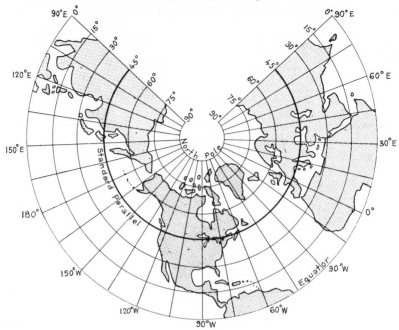

Fig. 3.11. A simple conic map of the northern hemisphere.

projection is called a **secant conic** or **conic projection with two standard parallels.**

If, in such a projection, the spacing of the parallels is altered so that the distortion is the same along them as along the meridians, the projection becomes conformal. This is known as the **Lambert conformal** projection. It is the most widely used conic projection for navigation, though its use is more common among aviators than mariners. Its appearance is very much the same as that of the simple conic projection. If the chart is not carried far beyond the standard parallels, and if these are not a great distance apart, the distortion over the entire chart is small. A straight line on this projection so nearly approximates a great circle that the two can be considered identical for many purposes of navigation. Radio bearings, from signals which are considered to travel great circles, can be plotted on this projection without the correction needed when they are plotted on a Mercator chart. This feature, gained without sacrificing conformality, has made this projection popular for aeronautical charts, since aircraft make wide use of radio aids to navigation. It has made little progress in replacing the Mercator projection for marine navigation, except in high latitudes.

Polyconic projection • The latitude limitations of the secant conic projection can be essentially eliminated by the use of a series of cones, resulting in a **polyconic** projection. In this projection each parallel is the base of a

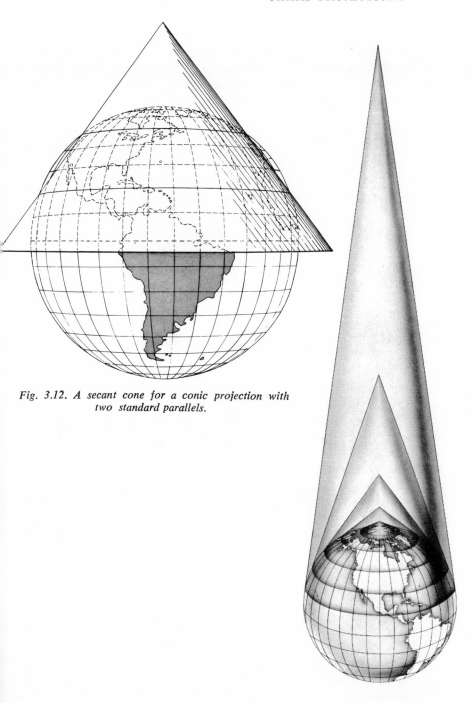

Fig. 3.12. A secant cone for a conic projection with two standard parallels.

Fig. 3.13. A polyconic projection.

tangent cone (fig. 3.13). At the edges of the chart the area between parallels is expanded to eliminate gaps. The scale is correct along any parallel and along the central meridian of the projection. Along other meridians the scale increases with increased difference of longitude from the central meridian. Parallels appear as nonconcentric circles and meridians as curved lines converging toward the pole and concave to the central meridian.

The polyconic projection is widely used in atlases, particularly for areas of large range in latitude and reasonably large range in longitude, as for a continent such as North America (fig. 3.14). However, since it is not conformal, this projection is not customarily used in navigation, except for **boat sheets** used in hydrographic surveying.

Azimuthal Projections

Features • If points on the earth are projected directly to a plane surface, a map is formed at once, without cutting and flattening, or "developing." This can be considered a special case of a conic projection in which the cone has zero height.

The simplest case of the azimuthal projection is one in which the plane is tangent at one of the poles. The meridians are straight lines intersecting at the pole, and the parallels are concentric circles with their common center at the pole. Their spacing depends upon the method of transferring points from the earth to the plane.

If the plane is tangent at some point other than a pole, straight lines through the point of tangency are great circles, and concentric circles with their common center at the point of tangency connect points of equal distance from that point. Distortion, which is zero at the point of tangency, increases along any great circle through this point. Along any circle whose center is the point of tangency, the distortion is constant. The bearing of any point from the point of tangency is correctly represented. It is for this reason that these projections are called **azimuthal.** They are also called **zenithal.** Several of the common azimuthal projections are perspective.

Gnomonic projection • If a plane is tangent to the earth, and points are projected geometrically from the center of the earth, the result is a **gnomonic** projection (fig. 3.15). This is probably the oldest of the projections. Since the projection is perspective, it can be demonstrated by placing a light at the center of a transparent terrestrial globe and holding a flat surface tangent to the sphere.

For the oblique case the meridians appear as straight lines converging toward the nearer pole. The parallels, except the equator, appear as curves (fig. 3.16). As in all azimuthal projections, bearings from the point of

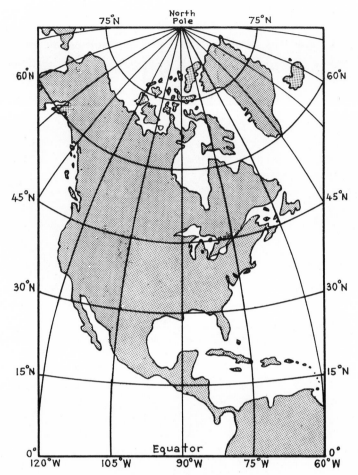

Fig. 3.14. A polyconic map of North America.

tangency are correctly represented. The distance scale, however, changes rapidly. The projection is neither conformal nor equal area. Distortion is so great that shapes, as well as distances and areas, are very poorly represented, except near the point of tangency.

The usefulness of the projection rests upon the one feature that *any* great circle appears on the map as a straight line. This is apparent when it is realized that a great circle is the line of intersection of a sphere and a plane through the center of the sphere, this center being the origin of the projecting rays for the map. This plane intersects any other nonparallel plane, including the tangent plane, in a straight line. It is this one useful feature that gives charts made on this projection the common name **great-circle charts.**

The principal navigational use of gnomonic charts is for plotting the

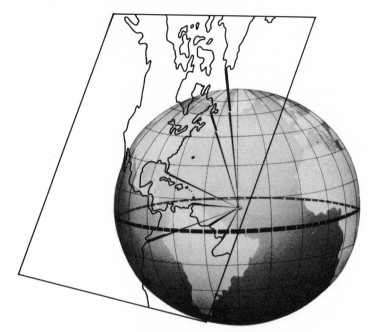

Fig. 3.15. An oblique gnomonic projection.

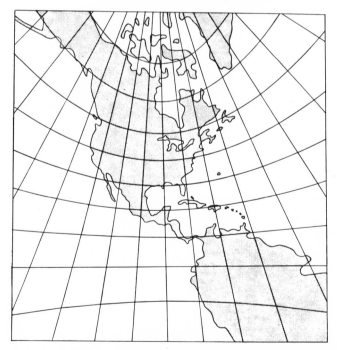

Fig. 3.16. A gnomonic map with point of tangency at latitude 30° N, longitude 90° W.

great-circle track between points, for planning purposes. Points along the track are then transferred, by latitude and longitude, to the navigational chart, usually one on the Mercator projection. The great circle is then followed approximately by following the rhumb line from one point to the next.

Stereographic projection • If points on the surface of the earth are projected geometrically onto a tangent plane, from a point on the surface of the earth opposite the point of tangency, a **stereographic** projection results. It is also called an **azimuthal orthomorphic** projection.

The scale of the stereographic projection increases with distance from the point of tangency, but more slowly than in the gnomonic projection. An entire hemisphere can be shown on the stereographic projection without excessive distortion (fig. 3.17). As in other azimuthal projections, great circles through the point of tangency appear as straight lines. All other circles, including meridians and parallels, appear as circles or arcs of circles.

The principal navigational use of the stereographic projection is for

Fig. 3.17. A stereographic map of the western hemisphere.

charts of the polar regions and devices for mechanical or graphical solution of the navigational triangle.

Orthographic projection • If terrestrial points are projected geometrically from infinity (projecting lines parallel) to a tangent plane, an **orthographic** projection results. This projection is neither conformal nor equal area and has no advantages as a map projection. Its principal navigational use is in the field of navigational astronomy.

Azimuthal equidistant projection • An azimuthal projection in which the distance scale along any great circle through the point of tangency is constant is called an **azimuthal equidistant** projection. If a pole is the point of tangency, the meridians appear as straight radial lines and the parallels as concentric circles, equally spaced. If the plane is tangent at some point other than a pole, the concentric circles represent distance from the point of tangency. In this case meridians and parallels appear as curves. The projection can be used to portray the entire earth, the point 180° from the point of tangency appearing as the largest of the concentric circles. The projection is neither conformal nor equal area, nor is it perspective. Near the point of tangency the distortion is small, but it increases with distance until shapes near the opposite side of the earth are unrecognizable (fig. 3.18).

The projection is useful because it combines the three features of being azimuthal, having a constant distance scale from the point of tangency, and permitting the entire earth to be shown on one map. Thus, if an important harbor or airport is selected as the point of tangency, the great-circle course, distance, and track from that point to any other point on the earth are quickly and accurately determined. For communication work at a fixed point, the point of tangency, the path of an incoming signal is at once apparent if the direction of arrival has been determined. The direction to train a directional antenna for desired results can be determined easily. The projection is also used for polar charts.

Polar Charts

Polar projections • Special consideration is given to the selection of projections for polar charts, principally because the familiar projections become special cases with unique features.

In the case of cylindrical projections in which the axis of the cylinder is parallel to the polar axis of the earth, distortion becomes excessive and the scale changes rapidly. Such projections cannot be carried to the poles. However, both the transverse and oblique Mercator projections are used.

Conic projections with their axes parallel to the earth's polar axis are limited in their usefulness for polar charts because parallels of latitude

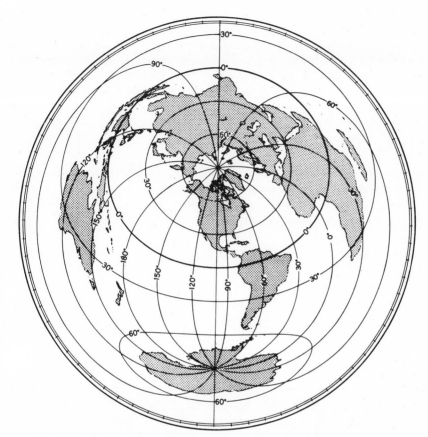

Fig. 3.18. An azimuthal equidistant map of the world with the point of tangency at latitude 40° N, longitude 100° W.

extending through a full 360° of longitude appear as arcs of circles rather than full circles. This is because a cone, when cut along an element and flattened, does not extend through a full 360° without stretching or resuming its former conical shape. The usefulness of such projections is also limited by the fact that the pole appears as an arc of a circle instead of a point. However, by using a parallel very near the pole as the higher standard parallel, a conic projection with two standard parallels can be made which requires little stretching to complete the circles of the parallels and eliminate that of the pole. Such a projection, called the **modified Lambert conformal** or **Ney's** projection, is useful for polar charts. It is particularly acceptable to those accustomed to using the ordinary Lambert conformal charts in lower latitudes.

Azimuthal projections are in their simplest form when tangent at a pole, since the meridians are straight lines intersecting at the pole, and parallels are concentric circles with their common center at the pole.

Within a few degrees of latitude of the pole they all look essentially alike, but as the distance becomes greater, the spacing of the parallels becomes distinctive in each projection. In the polar azimuthal equidistant it is uniform; in the polar stereographic it increases with distance from the pole until the equator is shown at a distance from the pole equal to twice the length of the radius of the earth, or about 27% too much; in the polar gnomonic the increase is considerably greater, becoming infinity at the equator; in the polar orthographic it decreases with distance from the pole (fig. 3.19). All of these but the last are used for polar charts.

Selection of a polar projection • The principal considerations in the choice of a suitable projection for polar navigation are:

1. *Conformality.* It is desirable that angles be correctly represented so that plotting can be done directly on the chart, without annoying corrections.

2. *Great-circle representation.* Since great circles are more useful than rhumb lines in high latitudes, it is desirable that great circles be represented by straight lines.

3. *Scale variation.* Constant scale over an entire chart is desirable.

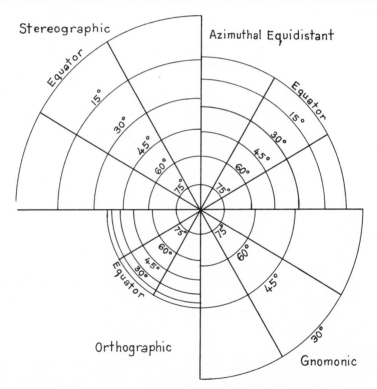

Fig. 3.19. Expansion of polar azimuthal projections.

4. *Meridian representation.* Straight meridians are desirable for convenience and accuracy of plotting, and for grid navigation.

5. *Limits of utility.* Wide limits are desirable to reduce to a minimum the number of projections needed. The ideal would be a single projection for world coverage.

The projections commonly used for polar charts are the transverse Mercator, modified Lambert conformal, gnomonic, stereographic, and azimuthal equidistant. Near the pole there is little to choose between them. Within the limits of practical navigation all are essentially conformal and on all a great circle is nearly a straight line. As the distance from the pole increases, however, the distinctive features of each projection become a consideration.*

Plotting Sheets

Definition and use • A **plotting sheet** is a blank or incomplete chart. It has the latitude and longitude lines, and it may have one or more *compass roses* (see Chapter 5) for measuring direction, but little or no additional information. The meridians are usually unlabeled by the publisher so the plotting sheet can be used for any longitude. If it is suitable for use in any latitude, the parallels, also, may be unlabeled.

Plotting sheets are less expensive to produce than charts and are equally suitable or superior for some purposes. They are used primarily for plotting lines of position from celestial observations and for dead reckoning, particularly when land, aids to navigation, and depth of water are not important.

Any projection can be used for constructing a plotting sheet, but that used for the navigator's charts is customarily employed also for his plotting sheets.

Small area plotting sheets • A Mercator plotting sheet can be constructed by the method explained earlier. For a relatively small area a good approximation can be more quickly constructed by the navigator by either of two alternative methods based upon a graphical solution of the secant of the latitude, which approximates the expansion.

First method (fig. 3.20). *Step one.* Draw a series of equally spaced, vertical lines at any spacing desired. These are the meridians; label them at any desired interval, as 1', 2', 5', 10', 30', 1°, etc.

Step two. Through the center of the sheet draw a horizontal line to represent the parallel of the mid latitude of the area to be covered, and label it.

* Ed. note: A detailed description of such features, however, is beyond the scope of this volume.

Fig. 3.20. Small area plotting sheet with selected longitude scale.

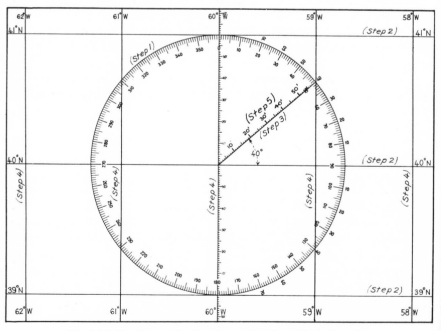

Fig. 3.21. Small area plotting sheet with selected latitude scale.

Step three. Through any convenient point, such as the intersection of the central meridian and the parallel of the mid latitude, draw a line making an angle with the *horizontal* equal to the mid latitude. In figure 3.20 this angle is 35°.

Step four. Draw in and label additional parallels. The length of the oblique line between consecutive meridians is the perpendicular distance between consecutive parallels, as shown by the dashed arc. The number of minutes of arc between consecutive parallels thus drawn is the same as that between the meridians shown.

Step five. Graduate the oblique line into convenient units. If 1′ is selected, this scale serves as both a latitude and mile scale. It can also be used as a longitude scale by measuring horizontally from a meridian instead of obliquely along the line.

Second method (fig. 3.21). *Step one.* At the center of the sheet draw a circle with a radius equal to 1° (or any other convenient unit) of latitude at the desired scale. If a sheet with a compass rose is available, as in figure 3.21, the compass rose can be used as the circle and will prove useful for measuring directions. It need not limit the scale of the chart, as an additional concentric circle can be drawn and desired graduations extended to it.

Step two. Draw horizontal lines through the center of the circle and tangent at the top and bottom. These are parallels of latitude; label them accordingly, at the selected interval (as every 1°, 30′, etc.).

Step three. Through the center of the circle draw a line making an angle with the *horizontal* equal to the mid latitude. In figure 3.21 this angle is 40°.

Step four. Draw in and label the meridians. The first is a vertical line through the center of the circle. The second is a vertical line through the intersection of the oblique line and the circle. Additional meridians are drawn the same distance apart as the first two.

Step five. Graduate the oblique line into convenient units. If 1′ is selected, this scale serves as a latitude and mile scale. It can also be used as a longitude scale by measuring horizontally from a meridian instead of obliquely along the line.

The same end result is produced by either method. The first method, starting with the selection of the longitude scale, is particularly useful when the longitude limits of the plotting sheet determine the scale. When the latitude coverage is more important, the second method may be preferable. If a standard size is desired, part of the sheet can be printed in advance. Such sheets are available from the Defense Mapping Agency Hydrographic Center. In either method a central compass rose might be printed. In the first method the meridians may be shown at the desired interval and the mid parallel may be printed and graduated in units of longitude. In using the sheet it is necessary only to label the meridians and draw the oblique line and from it determine the interval and draw in and label additional parallels. If the central meridian is graduated, the oblique line need not be. In the second method the parallels may be shown at the desired interval, and the central meridian may be printed and graduated in units of latitude. In using the sheet it is necessary only to label the parallels, draw the oblique line and from it determine the interval and draw in and label additional meridians. If the central meridian is graduated, as shown in figure 3.21, the oblique line need not be.

Both methods use a constant relationship of latitude to longitude over the entire sheet and both fail to allow for the ellipticity of the earth. For practical navigation these are not important considerations for a small area. If a larger area is to be shown or if more precise results are desired, the method for Mercator chart construction should be used.

Grids

Purpose and definition of grid • No system has been devised for showing the surface of the earth *on a flat surface*, without distortion. Moreover, the appearance of any portion of the surface varies with the projection and, in many cases, with the location of the portion with respect to the point or line of tangency. For some purposes (particularly military) it is desirable to be able to identify a location or area by rectangular coordinates, using numbers or letters, or a combination of numbers and letters, without the necessity of indicating the units used or assigning a name (north, south, east, or west), thus reducing the possibility of a mistake. This is accomplished by means of a **grid.** In its usual form this consists of two series of lines which are mutually perpendicular *on the chart*, with suitable designators. The grid used in **grid navigation** is a similar network, or a single series of parallel lines, used to provide a uniform directional reference, particularly in polar regions. In any system the difference in direction between true north at any point and grid north at that same point is called **grid declination.**

[4]

Charts and Publications

Introduction • Charts and publications are important navigational aids. It is desirable that the navigator have a knowledge of what is available in this field, how he can obtain the various items, how he can be sure they are accurate and up-to-date, and what information he can expect to get from each.

Sources of charts and publications • There is no central government office from which the navigator can satisfy all of his chart and publications requirements. The principal sources are the Defense Mapping Agency Hydrographic Center (which publishes much material based on data from the U.S. Naval Oceanographic Office), National Ocean Survey, and U.S. Coast Guard.

The U.S. Naval Oceanographic Office maintains liaison with foreign hydrographic departments; makes hydrographic, topographic, oceanographic, and geomagnetic surveys in international waters and along foreign coasts; conducts research in oceanography and in navigational methods (both marine and air); and systematically collects data in these fields from public and private institutions and persons in all parts of the world.

The products of the Defense Mapping Agency, based on such data, include nautical and aeronautical charts of the high seas and foreign waters, sailing directions for foreign shores, light lists, various navigational manuals and tables, weather summaries, various oceanographic charts and publications, pilot charts, loran and radar charts, plotting sheets, a number of special charts, and several periodical publications to notify navigators of changes to their charts and publications.

The National Ocean Survey, part of the National Oceanic and Atmospheric Administration of the Department of Commerce, conducts research in hydrography, cartography, tides, currents, geodesy, geomagnetism, and seismology. It publishes coast and harbor charts of the United States and its possessions and aeronautical charts of the United States, tide and tidal current tables for both United States and foreign waters, coast pilots (sailing directions) for coasts of the United States and its possessions (including the intracoastal waterway) and a number of special publications covering results of its research.

The U.S. Coast Guard has charge of the inspection of merchant marine vessels, licensing of merchant marine officers, and the installation and maintenance of aids to marine navigation (lighthouses, beacons, buoys, etc.). It publishes light lists for the waters of the United States and its possessions, and international and inland rules of the road and pilot rules.

Miscellaneous sources • The U.S. Geological Survey publishes topographic and geological maps of the United States and its possessions. The National Ocean Survey, Lake Survey Center, has charts of the Great Lakes, Lake Champlain, New York State Barge Canal System, Minnesota, and Ontario Border Lakes. The U.S. Army Corps of Engineers has the following charts: (Galveston, Texas) charts of the Gulf Intracoastal Waterway; (Missouri River Division) charts of the Missouri River; (Ohio River Division) charts of the Ohio River and tributaries; (St. Louis District) charts of the Illinois River; (Vicksburg District) charts of the Mississippi River and tributaries.

Obtaining charts and publications • Publications of the Defense Mapping Agency Hydrographic Center and the National Ocean Survey are available through authorized sales agents listed in the catalogs of these organizations or from the organizations themselves. To obtain a DMAHC catalog (Pub. No. 1-N-A), write to Defense Mapping Depot, 5801 Tabor Avenue, Philadelphia, Pa. 19120, or Defense Mapping Agency Depot, Clearfield, Utah 84016. To obtain a National Ocean Survey catalog, write to Distribution Division, C44, National Ocean Survey, Riverdale, Md. 20840. For a catalog from the National Oceanic and Atmospheric Administration, write to NOAA Public Affairs, 6010 Executive Boulevard, Rockville, Md. 20852. Publications of many other organizations, including the National Weather Service, are sold by the Superintendent of Public Documents, U.S. Government Printing Office. U.S. Coast Guard publications are distributed both by the Government Printing Office and by the Coast Guard. For a catalog, write to U.S. Coast Guard, G-BA-2, Washington, D.C. 20590.

Oceanographic and Meteorological Charts and Publications

Tide tables are published annually by the National Ocean Survey. In them are tabulated the predicted times and heights of high and low waters for every day in the year for a number of **reference stations,** and differences for obtaining similar predictions for numerous other places. They also give other useful information such as a method for obtaining the height of the tide at any time, local mean time of sunrise and sunset for various latitudes, reduction of local mean time to standard time, zone time of moonrise and moonset for certain ports, and other astronomical data. The use of some of these tables is explained in Chapter 9.

Tidal current tables, published annually by the National Ocean Survey, tabulate daily predictions of the times of slack water and the times and speeds of maximum flood and ebb currents for a number of waterways, together with differences for obtaining predictions at numerous other places. They also include other useful information on tidal currents, such as a method for obtaining the speed of current at any time and one for determining the duration of slack water, coastal tidal currents, the combination of currents, and current diagrams. The use of these tables is explained in Chapter 9.

Tidal current charts for various United States harbors are published by the National Ocean Survey. These publications consist of a set of 12 charts which depict the direction and speed of the tidal current for each hour of the tidal cycle, thus presenting a comprehensive view of the tidal current movement in the respective waterways as a whole, and supplying a means for readily determining for any time the direction and speed of the current at various localities throughout the areas covered. The charts are intended for use in connection with the tidal current tables for the same areas, except for Narragansett Bay and New York Harbor, where the tide tables are to be used.

Pilot charts are published by the Defense Mapping Agency Hydrographic Center for each month for (1) the North Atlantic Ocean, and (2) the North Pacific Ocean. Pilot charts are published in atlas form for (1) the Northern North Atlantic Ocean, (2) the South Atlantic Ocean and Central American Waters, and (3) the South Pacific and Indian Oceans.

These charts present in graphical form the available facts or conclusions obtained from many years of research in navigation, oceanography, and meteorology, to assist the mariner in selecting the safest and quickest routes and avoiding dangers. Their principal features are monthly averages for: prevailing winds and currents; percentage of gales, calms, and fog; lines of equal air and water temperature, and atmospheric pressure; and limits of the drift of both field ice and icebergs. Also presented are lines of equal magnetic variation, location of ocean station vessels, and recommended routes or steamer tracks. Timely articles are printed on the backs of many pilot charts.

Marine Weather Services Charts are prepared by the National Weather Service for 15 coastal areas of the United States, Alaska, Hawaii, and Puerto Rico. They list locations of weather warning facilities, local sources of marine weather information and broadcasts, and antenna coordinates of local radio stations for use with RDF. They are available through the National Ocean Survey Distribution Division.

Electronic Navigation Charts and Publications

Loran • Tables for plotting loran lines of position are published by the Defense Mapping Agency Hydrographic Center as Pub. No. 221, in a number of volumes. Loran lines of position are printed on certain nautical and aeronautical charts by DMAHC and National Ocean Survey. Information on loran charts and publications is contained in the catalogs of these organizations.

Radar • The National Ocean Survey publishes charts showing a great number of land contours for use with radar.

Miscellaneous • The Defense Mapping Agency Hydrographic Center publications entitled *Radio Navigational Aids* (Pubs. Nos. 117–A, Atlantic and Mediterranean Area and 117–B, Pacific and Indian Oceans Area) contain detailed information on radiobeacons and other aids to navigation. The light lists include some details of radiobeacons. *International Code of Signals* (Pub. No. 102) deals with radio communication.

Information by radio • Defense Mapping Agency Hydrographic Center Pubs. Nos. 117–A and 117–B, *Radio Navigational Aids*, contain complete lists of the radio stations that perform services of value to the mariner, and give general and detailed information concerning these services.

In addition to its information on radiobeacons and radio direction finder stations, Pub. No. 117 gives full information on time signals, navigational warnings, distress signals, medical advice, quarantine stations, long-range navigational aids, and radio regulations for territorial waters.

The National Weather Service prepares a book called *Worldwide Marine Weather Broadcasts* that lists U.S. and selected foreign radio stations that provide weather information, including Coast Guard, Navy, and commercial stations and National Oceanic and Atmospheric Administration continuous broadcast stations. The book is available from the Superintendent of Public Documents.

Navigational Publications

Sailing Directions or **pilots** are books containing descriptions of coast lines, harbors, dangers, aids to navigation, winds, currents, and tides; instructions for navigating narrow waterways and for approaching and entering harbors; information on port facilities, signal systems, and pilotage services; and other data that cannot be conveniently shown on charts. Those covering the coasts of the United States and its possessions, including the Intracoastal Waterway, are called **coast pilots,** and are published by the National Ocean Survey. Those covering foreign coasts, called **sailing directions,** are published in looseleaf form by the Defense Mapping Agency Hydrographic Center.

Supplements to coast pilots are published annually, and change pages to sailing directions are published periodically. The more important changes are published in *Notice to Mariners.*

Light lists for the United States and its possessions, including the Intracoastal Waterway, the Great Lakes, and the Mississippi River and its navigable tributaries, are published annually by the U.S. Coast Guard. Similar publications covering foreign coasts are published in looseleaf form by the Defense Mapping Agency Hydrographic Center in seven volumes (Pubs. Nos. 111–A, 111–B, and 112 through 116). "Changes" are published at appropriate intervals. Light lists give detailed information regarding navigational lights, light structures, radiobeacons, and fog signals. Corrections to both sets of light lists are published weekly in the *Notice to Mariners.* Coast Guard light lists also give unlighted buoys.

Navigational tables • Many types of navigational tables are published. While many of these appear as parts of other books, a number of separate books of tables are available. The ones of principal interest for piloting are:

Defense Mapping Agency Hydrographic Center Pub. No. 151, *Table of Distances between Ports,* tabulates about 40,000 distances between various ports throughout the world.

Distances between United States Ports, published by the National Ocean Survey, tabulates distances between 700 United States ports. It also includes conversion tables of nautical and statute miles.

The Defense Mapping Agency Hydrographic Center Pub. No. 221, *Loran Tables,* is discussed earlier.

Manuals • Reference or instruction books are published by many sources, both governmental and commercial. Some of these are general, and others are limited to particular aspects of the subject, such as DMAHC Pub. No. 1310, *Radar Navigation Manual,* Pub. No. 217, *Maneuvering Board Manual,* and Pub. No. 226, *Handbook of Magnetic Compass Adjustment* *and Compensation.* There are a great number and variety of such books. In general, they can be obtained from stores handling nautical publications, government agencies having cognizance over the subjects of the manuals, or instrument makers (in the case of manuals describing specific instruments). The U.S. Government Printing Office publishes lists of publications on a number of subjects and most other government agencies and commercial publishing companies have similar lists for distribution.

Periodical Publications and Broadcasts

Periodicals • *Notice to Mariners,* published weekly by the Defense Mapping Agency Hydrographic Center, lists changes in aids to navigation throughout the world, newly reported dangers such as wrecks, important new soundings, and official regulations affecting navigation. It is the official publication for the correction of charts, sailing directions, light lists, etc. It also carries announcements of new charts, new editions of charts, and new publications. *Notice to Mariners* is distributed without charge to qualified users. It can be consulted at offices of sales agents for products of the DMAHC and NOS.

Local Notice to Mariners, published by U.S. Coast Guard districts, contains information pertinent to the local area. It is available through district offices.

Radio broadcasts • Nearly all maritime nations broadcast radio navigational warnings. In general, such broadcasts contain information of importance to the safety of vessels at sea, such as the position of ice and derelicts, inadequacy and changes in aids to navigation, etc. Most of the information is furnished by cooperating observers at sea.

Miscellaneous Charts and Publications

Miscellaneous charts • Both the Defense Mapping Agency Hydrographic Center and the National Ocean Survey publish a number of special charts listed in their catalogs.

Miscellaneous publications • There are numerous other publications of greater or less interest to the coastal pilot. Among these are:

Chart No. 1, *Nautical Chart Symbols and Abbreviations.* A pamphlet showing the standard symbols in color and the various abbreviations which have been approved for use on nautical charts published by the United States of America.

Weather maps prepared by the National Weather Service, available from the Superintendent of Public Documents, Government Printing Office.

Rules of the Road. A pamphlet giving the international and inland rules of the road, published by the U.S. Coast Guard. Additional pamphlets or individual sheets published by the same agency give the specific rules applying to U.S. waterways.

Aids to Marine Navigation of the United States, published by the U.S. Coast Guard.

[5]

The Nautical Chart

Introduction • A nautical chart is a conventional graphic representation, on a plane surface, of a navigable portion of the surface of the earth. It shows the depth of water by numerous soundings, and sometimes by depth curves, the shore line of adjacent land, topographic features that may serve as landmarks, aids to navigation, dangers, and other information of interest to navigators. It is designed as a work sheet on which courses may be plotted, and positions ascertained. It assists the navigator in avoiding dangers and arriving safely at his destination. The nautical chart is one of the most essential and reliable aids available to the navigator.

Projections • Nearly all nautical charts used for ordinary purposes of navigation are constructed on the Mercator projection (see Chapter 3). Large-scale harbor charts on standard scales (1:12,500, 1:25,000, 1:50,000) are often constructed on the transverse Mercator projection. Charts for special purposes, such as great-circle sailing or polar navigation, often are on some other projection.

Scale • The *scale* of a chart is the ratio of a given distance on the chart to the actual distance which it represents on the earth. It may be expressed in various ways:

Natural scale is expressed as a simple ratio or fraction. For example, 1:80,000 or $\frac{1}{80,000}$ means that one unit (such as an inch) on the chart represents 80,000 of the same unit on the surface of the earth.

Numerical scale is a statement of that distance on the earth shown in one unit (usually an inch) on the chart, or vice versa. For example, "30 miles to the inch" means that one inch on the chart represents 30 miles of the earth's surface. Similarly, "2 inches to a mile" indicates that 2 inches on the chart represent 1 mile on the earth.

In **graphic scale,** a line or bar may be drawn at a convenient place on the chart and subdivided into nautical miles, yards, etc. All charts vary somewhat in scale from point to point, and in some projections the scale is not the same in all directions about a single point. A single subdivided line or bar for use over an entire chart is shown only when the chart is of such scale and projection that the scale varies a negligible amount over the chart, usually one of about 1:50,000 or larger. Since one minute of latitude is very nearly equal to one nautical mile, the latitude scale serves as an approximate graphical scale. On most nautical charts the east and west borders are subdivided to indicate the latitude scale.

On a Mercator chart the scale varies with the latitude. This is noticeable on a chart covering a relatively large distance in a north-south direction. On such a chart the scale at the latitude in question should be used for measuring distances.

Of the various methods of indicating scale, the graphical method is normally available in some form on the chart. In addition, the natural scale is customarily stated on charts on which the scale does not change appreciably over the chart.

The natural and numerical scales of a chart are readily interchangeable. For instance, in a nautical mile there are about 6,076.11549 feet or $6,076.11549 \times 12 = 72,913.39$ inches. If the natural scale of a chart is 1:80,000, one inch of the chart represents 80,000 inches of the earth, or a little more than a mile. To find the exact amount, divide the scale by the number of inches in a mile, or $\dfrac{80,000}{72,913.39} = 1.097$. Thus, a natural scale of 1:80,000 is the same as a numerical scale of 1.097 (or approximately 1.1) miles to an inch. Stated another way, there are $\dfrac{72,913.39}{80,000} = 0.911$ (approximately 0.9) inch to a mile. Similarly, if the numerical scale is 60 nautical miles to an inch, the natural scale is $1:(60 \times 72,913.39) = 1:4,374,803$.

It should be clearly understood that scale, as discussed above, refers to *distances*, not *areas*. If the area scale is desired, it is found by squaring the natural scale. Thus, if the natural scale of a chart is 1:50,000, the corresponding area scale is $1:(50,000 \times 50,000) = 1:2,500,000,000$ or one square inch on the chart represents 2,500,000,000 square inches on the earth, or a square 50,000 inches on a side.

A chart covering a relatively large area is called a *small-scale* chart and one covering a relatively small area is called a *large-scale* chart. Since the terms are relative, there is no sharp division between the two. Thus, a chart of scale 1:100,000 is large scale when compared with a chart of 1:1,000,000 but small scale when compared with one of 1:25,000.

Chart classification by scale • Charts are constructed on many different scales, ranging from about 1:2,500 to 1:14,000,000 (and even smaller for some world charts). Small-scale charts covering large areas are used for planning and for offshore navigation. Charts of larger scale, covering smaller areas, should be used as the vessel approaches pilot waters. Several methods of classifying charts according to scale are in use in various nations. The following classifications of nautical charts are those used by the National Ocean Survey:

Sailing charts are the smallest scale charts used for planning, fixing position at sea, and for plotting the dead reckoning while proceeding on a long voyage. The scale is generally 1:600,000 or smaller. The shore line and topography are generalized and only offshore soundings, the principal navigational lights, outer buoys, and landmarks visible at considerable distances are shown.

General charts are intended for coastwise navigation outside of outlying reefs and shoals. The scales range from about 1:150,000 to 1:600,000.

Coast charts are intended for inshore coastwise navigation where the course may lie inside outlying reefs and shoals, for entering or leaving bays and harbors of considerable width, and for navigating large inland waterways. The scales range from about 1:50,000 to 1:150,000.

Harbor charts are intended for navigation and anchorage in harbors and small waterways. The scale is generally larger than 1:50,000.

Accuracy • The accuracy of a chart depends upon:

1. *Thoroughness and up-to-dateness of the survey and other navigational information.* Some estimate of the accuracy of the survey can be formed by an examination of the source notes given in the title of the chart. If the chart is based upon very old surveys, it should be used with caution. Many of the earlier surveys were made under conditions that were not conducive to great accuracy. It is safest to question every chart based upon surveys of doubtful accuracy.

The number of soundings and their spacing is some indication of the completeness of the survey. Only a small fraction of the soundings taken in a thorough survey are shown on the chart, but sparse or unevenly distributed soundings indicate that the survey was probably not made in detail. Large or irregular blank areas, or absence of depth curves, generally indicate lack of soundings in the area. If the water surrounding such a blank area is deep, there is generally considerable depth in the blank; conversely, shallow water surrounding such an area indicates the strong possibility of shoal water. If neighboring areas abound in rocks or are particularly uneven, the blank area should be regarded with additional suspicion. However, it should be kept in mind that relatively few soundings are shown when there is a large number of depth curves or where

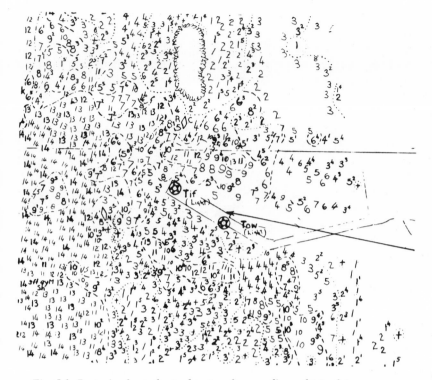

Fig. 5.1. Part of a boat sheet, showing the soundings obtained in a survey.

the bottom is flat or gently and evenly sloping. Additional soundings are shown when they are helpful in indicating the uneven character of a rough bottom (figs. 5.1 and 5.2).

Even a detailed survey may fail to locate every rock or pinnacle, and in waters where their existence is suspected, the best methods for determining their presence are wire drag surveys or use of electronic underwater obstacle detection gear. Areas that have been dragged may be indicated on the chart and a note added to show the effective depth at which the drag was operated.

Changes in the contour of the bottom are relatively rapid in areas where there are strong currents or heavy surf, particularly when the bottom is composed principally of soft mud or sand. The entrances to bar harbors are especially to be regarded with suspicion. Similarly, there is sometimes a strong tendency for dredged channels to shoal, especially if they are surrounded by sand or mud, and cross currents exist. Notes are sometimes shown on the chart when the bottom contours are known to change rapidly. However, the absence of such a note should not be regarded as evidence that rapid change does not occur.

Changes in aids to navigation, structures, etc., will render a chart

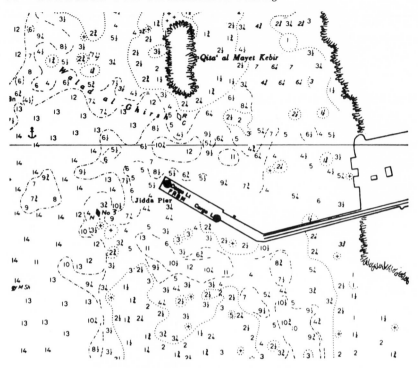

Fig. 5.2. Part of a nautical chart made from the boat sheet of figure 5.1. Compare the number of soundings in the two figures.

inadequate. All issues of *Notice to Mariners* and quarterly summaries of corrections printed after the date of publication should be checked to ensure accuracy in this respect.

2. *Suitability of the scale for the design and intended navigational use.* The same detail cannot be shown on a small-scale chart as on one of a larger scale. For this reason it is good practice to use the largest scale chart available when in the vicinity of shoals or other dangers.

3. *Presentation and adequacy of data.* The amount and kind of detail to be shown, and the method of presentation, are continually under study by charting agencies. Development of a new navigational aid may render many previous charts inadequate. An example is radar. Many of the charts produced before radar became available lack the detail needed for confident identification of targets.

Part of the responsibility for the continuing accuracy of charts lies with the user. If charts are to remain reliable, they must be corrected as indicated. In addition, the user's reports of errors and changes and his suggestions often are useful to the publishing agencies in correcting and improving their charts. Navigators and maritime activities have contributed much to the reliability and usefulness of the modern nautical chart.

Chart Reading

Chart symbols • Much of the information contained on charts is shown by conventional symbols which make no attempt at accuracy in scale or detail, but are shown at the correct location and make possible the showing of a large amount of information without congestion or confusion. The standard symbols and abbreviations which have been approved for use on regular nautical charts published by the United States of America are contained in Chart No. 1, which should be aboard every vessel.* A knowledge of the meanings of these symbols is essential to a full understanding of charts. Figure 5.3 is a sample chart showing a number of these symbols.

Most of the symbols and abbreviations are in agreement with those recommended by the International Hydrographic Organization. Where there is disagreement, Chart No. 1 indicates this fact. The symbols and abbreviations on any given chart may differ somewhat from those shown in Chart No. 1 because of a change in the standards since printing of the chart or because the chart was published by an agency having a different set of standards.

Lettering • Certain standards regarding lettering have been adopted, except on charts made from reproducibles furnished by foreign nations.

Vertical type is used for features which are dry at high water and not affected by movement of the water, except for heights above water.

Leaning type is used for water, underwater, and floating features, except soundings.

The type of lettering used may be the only means of determining whether a feature may be visible at high tide. For instance, a rock might bear the title "White Rock" whether or not it extends above the surface. If the name is given in vertical letters, the rock constitutes a small islet; if in leaning type, the rock constitutes a reef.

The shore line • The shore line shown on nautical charts is the boundary between water and land at high tide (usually mean high water). A broken line indicates that the charted position is approximate only. The nature of the shore may be indicated.

Where the low-water line differs considerably from the high-water line, the low-water line may be indicated by dots in the case of mud, sand, gravel, or stones, with the kind of material indicated, and by a characteristic symbol in the case of rock or coral. The area alternately covered and

* Ed. note: Changes in chart symbols occur often enough to make it advisable to keep the latest edition aboard.

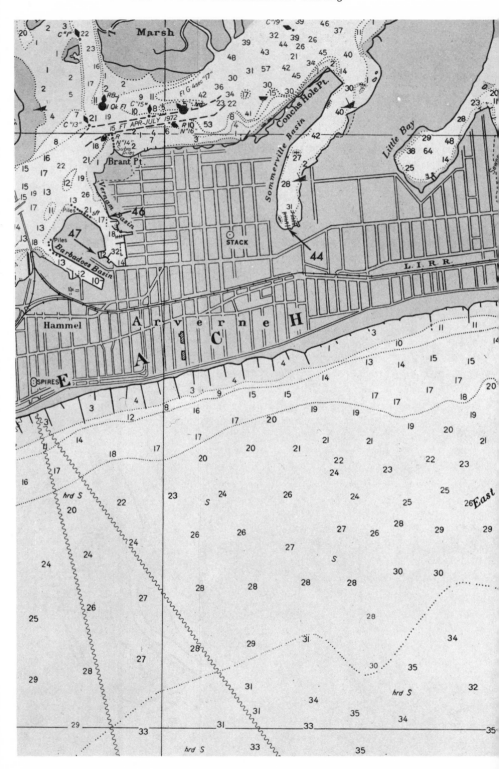

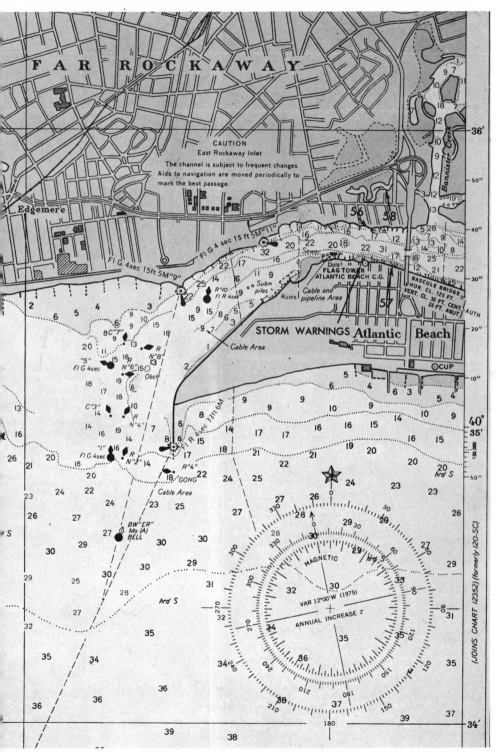

Fig. 5.3. A sample nautical chart.

uncovered may be shown by a tint which is a combination of the land tint and a blue water tint.

In marsh or mangrove areas, the outer edge of vegetation is used as the shore line. The inner edge is marked by a broken line when no other symbol (such as a cliff, levee, etc.) furnishes such a limit. The area between inner and outer limits may be given the combined land-water tint or the land tint.

Water areas • Soundings or depths of water are shown in several ways. Individual soundings are shown by numbers. These do not follow the general rule for lettering. They may be either vertical or leaning, or both may be used on the same chart to distinguish between the data based upon different surveys, different datums, or furnished by different authorities.

On all charts produced from surveys by United States vessels, soundings are shown in English units (feet or fathoms). The unit used is shown in the chart legend.

"No bottom" soundings are indicated by a number with a line over the top and a dot over the line, thus: $\dot{\overline{45}}$. This indicates that the spot was sounded to the depth indicated without reaching the bottom. Areas which have been wire dragged are shown by a limiting line, and the clear effective depth is indicated, with a characteristic symbol under the numbers, thus: $\llcorner 24 \lrcorner$.

The soundings are supplemented by a series of bottom contours or *depth curves* connecting points of equal depth. These lines present a graphic indication of the configuration of the bottom. On some of the recent charts of the National Ocean Survey an increased number of depth curves have been shown in solid blue or black lines, the depth represented by each being shown by numbers placed in breaks in the lines, as with land contours. This type chart, presenting a more detailed indication of the bottom configuration with fewer numerical soundings, is particularly useful to the vessel equipped with an echo sounder permitting continuous determination of a profile of the bottom. Such a chart, to be reliable, can be made only for areas which have been surveyed in great detail.

Areas which uncover at low tide are tinted as indicated earlier. Areas out to a given depth, usually one, two, or three fathoms, often are given a blue tint, and occasionally a lighter blue is carried to some greater depth, usually five fathoms. On older charts the one-, two-, and three-fathom curves have stippled edges. Charts designed to give maximum emphasis to the configuration of the bottom show depths over the entire chart by a series of blue gradient tints. These are called *bathymetric* charts.

The side limits of dredged channels are indicated by broken lines. The controlling depth and the date it was determined, if known, are shown by a statement in or along the channel. The *controlling* depth is not necessarily an indication of the *least* depth in the channel on the date of determination. For channels less than 100 feet in width, at least 80 percent at the center is clear to the charted (controlling) depth. For channels more than 100 feet in width, at least the 50 percent at the center is clear to the charted depth. The possibility of shoaling since the controlling depth was determined should be considered.

The chart scale is generally too small to permit all soundings to be shown. In the selection of soundings to be shown, *least* depths are generally chosen first and a sounding pattern worked out to provide safety, a practical presentation of the bottom configuration, and a neat appearance. Depths greater than those indicated may be found close to charted depths, but steep changes in depth are given every consideration in sounding selection. Also, the state of the tide affects the depth at any given moment. An isolation shoal sounding should be approached with caution, or avoided, unless it is known that the area has been wire dragged, for there is always the possibility that a depth less than the least shown may have escaped detection. Also, the shoal area near a coast little frequented by vessels is sometimes not surveyed with the same thoroughness as other areas. Such areas and those where rocks, coral, etc., are known to exist should be entered with caution or avoided. The substance forming the bottom is shown by abbreviations.

Chart datum • *Depths.* All depths indicated on charts are reckoned from some selected level of the water, called the *chart datum*. The various chart datums are explained in Chapter 10. On charts made from surveys conducted by the United States the chart datum is selected with regard to the tides of the region, so that depths might be shown in their least favorable aspect. On charts based upon those of other nations the datum is that of the original authority. When it is known, the datum used is stated on the chart. In some cases where the chart is based upon old surveys, particularly in areas where the range of tide is not great, the actual chart datum may not be known. The chart datum of the largest-scale charts of an area is generally the same as the reference level from which height of tide is tabulated in the tide tables.

The height of a chart datum is usually only an approximation of the actual mean value specified, for determination of the actual mean height usually requires a longer series of tidal observations than is available to the cartographer, and the height changes somewhat over a period of time.

Since the chart datum is generally a computed mean or average height at some state of the tide, the depth of water at any particular moment may be less than shown on the chart. For example, if the chart datum is *mean lower low water*, the depth of water at *lower low water* will be less than the charted depth about as often as it is greater. A lower depth is indicated in the tide tables by a minus sign (−).

Heights. The shore line shown on charts is the high-water line, generally the level of mean high water. The heights of lights, rocks, islets, etc., are generally reckoned from this level. However, heights of islands, especially those at some distance from the coast, are often taken from sources other than hydrographic surveys, and may be reckoned from some other level, often mean sea level. The plane of reference for topographic detail is frequently not stated on the chart.

Since heights are usually reckoned from high water and depths from some form of low water, the reference levels are seldom the same. This is generally of little practical significance, but it might be of interest under some conditions, particularly where the range of tide is large.

Dangers • Dangers are shown by appropriate symbols, as indicated in Chart No. 1.

A rock which is uncovered at mean high water is shown as an islet enclosed by a dotted line to make it more prominent. If an isolated, offlying rock is known to uncover at the chart datum but to be covered at high water, the appropriate symbol is shown and the height above the chart datum, if known, is usually given, either by statement such as "*Uncov 2 ft*" or by the figure indicating the number of feet above the chart datum underlined and usually enclosed in parentheses, thus: (2). A rock which does not uncover is shown by the appropriate symbol. If it is considered a danger to surface vessels, the symbol is enclosed by a dotted curve.

A distinctive symbol is used to show a detached coral reef which uncovers at the chart datum. For a coral or rocky reef which is submerged at chart datum, the sunken rock symbol or an appropriate statement is used, enclosed by a dotted or dashed line if the limits have been determined.

Several different symbols are used for wrecks, depending upon the nature of the wreck or scale of the chart. One standard symbol is used for a visible wreck. A sunken wreck with less than ten fathoms of water over it is considered dangerous and its symbol is surrounded by a dotted curve. The safe clearance depth found over a wreck is indicated by a standard sounding number placed at the wreck. If this depth is determined by a wire drag, the sounding is underscored by the wire drag symbol.

Tide rips, eddies, and kelp are shown by symbol or lettering.

Piles, dolphins (clusters of piles), snags, stumps, etc., are shown by small circles and a label identifying the type of obstruction. If such dangers are submerged, the letters "Subm" precede the label.

Aids to navigation • Aids to navigation are shown by symbol, usually supplemented by abbreviations and sometimes by additional descriptive text. In order to render the symbols conspicuous it is necessary to show them in greatly exaggerated size relative to the scale of the chart. It is therefore important that the navigator know which part of the symbol represents the actual position of the aid. For floating aids (lightships and buoys), the position part of the symbol marks the location of the anchor or sinker, the aid swinging in an orbit around this position.

The principal charted aids to navigation are lighthouses, beacons, lightships, radiobeacons, and buoys. The number of aids shown and the amount of information concerning them varies with the scale of the chart. Wherever distance of visibility is given, it is computed for a height of eye of the observer of 15 feet. Unless otherwise indicated, lights which do not alternate in color are white, and alternating lights are red and white. Light lists give complete navigational information concerning them.

Lighthouses and *lighted beacons* are shown as black dots surrounded by magenta disks or with magenta light symbols to the side. The center of the black dot is the position of the light. On older charts a six-pointed star symbol was used for primary lighthouses and a five-pointed star symbol for beacons. The center of the star symbol marks the position of the light.

On large-scale charts the characteristics of lights are shown in the following order:

Characteristic	Example	Meaning
1. Character	Gp. Fl.	group flashing
2. Color	R	red
3. Period	(2) 10 sec.	two flashes every 10 seconds
4. Height	160 ft.	160 feet
5. Visibility	19M	visible 19 nautical miles (15 ft. height of eye)
6. Number	"6"	light number 6

The legend for this light would appear on the chart:

Gp. Fl. R (2) 10 sec. 160 ft. 19 M "6"

On older charts this form is varied slightly. As the chart scale becomes smaller one or more of the six items listed above are omitted as necessary. Names of unnumbered lights are shown when space permits.

Daybeacons (unlighted beacons) are shown by small triangles, the center of the triangle marking the position of the aid. Except on Intracoastal Waterway charts the abbreviation Bn is shown beside the symbol, with the appropriate abbreviation for color. For black beacons the triangle is solid black and there is no color abbreviation. All beacon abbreviations are in vertical lettering, as appropriate for fixed aids.

Lightships are shown by ship symbol, the center of the small circle at the base of the symbol indicating the position of the lightship's anchor. On recent charts the circle is overprinted by a small magenta disk or the "ship" has a magenta light symbol at the masthead. As a floating aid, the light characteristics and the name of the lightship are given in leaning letters.

Radiobeacons are indicated on the chart by a small magenta circle, accompanied by the appropriate abbreviation to indicate whether an ordinary radiobeacon (R Bn) or a radar beacon (Racon). The same symbol is used for a radio direction finder station with the abbreviation "RDF" and a coast radar station with the abbreviation Ra. Other radio stations are indicated by a small black circle with a dot in the center, or a smaller circle without a dot, and the appropriate abbreviation. In every case the center of the circle marks the position of the aid.

Buoys, except mooring buoys, are shown by a diamond-shaped symbol and a small circle attached to one of its points or a dot outside the diamond and near one of its points (at one of its acute angles). The circle or dot indicates the position of the buoy's sinker. A mooring buoy is shown by a distinctive symbol as indicated on Chart No. 1.

A black buoy is shown by a solid black diamond symbol, without abbreviation. For all other buoys, color is indicated by an abbreviation, or in full by a note on the chart. In addition, the diamond shape of symbols of red buoys are colored magenta. A buoy symbol with a line connecting the side points (shorter axis), half of the symbol being magenta or open and the other half black, indicates horizontal bands. A line connecting the upper and lower points (longer axis) represents vertical stripes. Two lines connecting the opposite *sides* of the symbol indicate a checkered buoy.

There is no significance to the angle at which the diamond shape appears on the chart. The symbol is placed so as to avoid interference with other features of the chart.

Lighted buoys are indicated by a small magenta disk centered on the dot or small circle indicating the position of the buoy's sinker or by a magenta light symbol. On older charts a series of radiating lines representing light rays was drawn about the dot or circle, and no magenta disk was given.

Abbreviations for light characteristics, type and color of buoy, number of the buoy, and any other pertinent information given near the symbol are in leaning letters. The letter C, N, or S indicates a can, nun, or spar, respectively. The words "bell," "gong," and "whistle," are shown as BELL, GONG, and WHIS, respectively. The number or letter designation of the buoy is given in quotation marks on small-scale charts. On large-scale charts they are given without quotation marks or punctuation, thus: No 1, No 2, etc.

Station buoys are not shown on small-scale charts, but are given on some large-scale charts.

Aeronautical lights included in the light lists are shown by the lighthouse symbol, accompanied by the abbreviation "AERO." The completeness to which the characteristics are shown depends principally upon the effective range of other navigational lights in the vicinity, and the usefulness of the light for marine navigation.

Ranges are indicated by a dashed or solid line. If the direction is given, it is expressed in degrees clockwise from true north.

Fog signal apparatus is indicated by the appropriate word in capital letters (HORN, BELL, GONG, etc.) or an abbreviation indicating the type of sound. The letters "D.F.S." indicate a **distance finding station** having synchronized sound and radio signals. The location of a fog signal which does not accompany a visual aid, either lighted or unlighted, is shown by a small circle and the appropriate word in vertical block letters.

Private aids are not indicated on the chart except in special cases. When they are shown, they are marked "Privately maintained" or "Priv maintd."

Floats are indicated by the open buoy symbol accompanied by the word "FLOAT." Either the lighted or unlighted symbol is used, as appropriate, to indicate whether or not the float displays a light.

A *light sector* is the sector or area bounded by two radii and the arc of a circle in which a light is visible or in which it has a distinctive color different from that of adjoining sectors. The limiting radii are indicated on the chart by dotted lines.

Colors of the sectors are indicated by words spelled out if space permits, or by abbreviation (W, R, etc.) if it does not.

Limits of light sectors and arcs of visibility *as observed from a vessel* are given in the light lists, in clockwise order.

Land areas • The amount of detail shown on the land areas of nautical charts depends upon the scale, the intended purpose of the chart, and available information. Since the advent of radar, topographical details have increased and have been extended farther inland, where this information has been available.

Relief is shown by contours, form lines, hachures, or tint shading. Tint shading is used principally to stress those terrain features affecting surface radar returns. It may be shown with or without contours and spot elevations.

Contours are lines connecting points of equal elevation. The heights represented by the contours are indicated in leaning figures at suitable places along the lines. Heights are usually expressed in feet (or in meters with means for conversion to feet on certain special charts). The interval between contours is uniform over any one chart, except that certain intermediate contours are sometimes shown by dashed line. When contours are broken, their locations are approximate.

Form lines are approximations of contours used for the purpose of indicating relative elevations. They are used in areas where accurate information is not available in sufficient detail to permit exact location of contours. Elevations of individual form lines are not indicated on the chart.

Hachures are short lines, or groups of lines, indicating the direction and extent of steep slopes. The lines generally follow the direction of the slope, the length of the lines indicating the height of the slope. Distinctive symbols somewhat resembling hachures are used for cliffs or other steep slopes on or near the coast line, where contours or form lines, being virtually over each other, would be difficult to interpret or would fail to give a true indication of the nature of the terrain.

Spot elevations are generally given only for summits or for tops of conspicuous landmarks. The heights of spot elevations and contours are given with reference to mean high water when this information is available. When there is insufficient space to show the heights of islets or rocks, they are indicated by leaning figures enclosed in parentheses in the water area nearby.

Cities and roads. Except on the smaller scale charts, cities are usually represented by their street systems or a conventional system of intersecting lines. The symbol for large cities approximates their extent and shape. Street names are generally not charted except those along the waterfront on the largest scale charts. Only the more important streets are shown on smaller scale charts. In general, only the important through highways and roads leading from them to the waterfront are shown. Occasionally, highway numbers are given. When shown, trails are indicated by a light broken line. Buildings along the waterfront or individual ones back from the waterfront but of special interest to the mariner are shown on large-scale charts. Special symbols are used for certain kinds of buildings. Both single and double track railroads are indicated by a single line with cross marks. In general, city electric railways are not charted. A fence or sewer extending into the water is shown by a broken line, usually labeled. Airports are shown on small-scale charts by symbol and on large-scale charts by shape and extent of runways. Breakwaters and jetties are shown by single or double lines depending upon the scale of the chart. A submerged portion and the limits of the submerged base are shown by broken lines.

Landmarks • Landmarks are shown by symbols, as given in Chart No. 1. Some of the accompanying labels encountered on a chart are interpreted as follows:

Building or **house.** One of these terms, as appropriate, is used when the entire structure is the landmark, rather than an individual feature of it.

A **spire** is a slender pointed structure extending above a building. It is seldom less than two-thirds of the entire height of the structure, and its lines are rarely broken by stages or other features. The term is not applied to a short pyramid-shaped structure rising from a tower or belfry.

A **cupola** (kū'pô·là) is a small dome-shaped tower or turret rising from a building.

A **chimney** is a relatively small, upright structure projecting above a building for the conveyance of smoke.

A **stack** is a tall smokestack or chimney. The term is used when the stack is more prominent as a landmark than accompanying buildings.

A **flagpole** is a single staff from which flags are displayed. The term is used when the pole is not attached to a building.

The term **flagstaff** is used for a flagpole rising from a building.

A **flag tower** is a scaffold-like tower from which flags are displayed.

A **radio tower** is a tall pole or structure for elevating radio antennas.

A **radio mast** is a relatively short pole or slender structure for elevating radio antennas, usually found in groups.

A **tower** is any structure with its base on the ground and high in proportion to its base, or that part of a structure higher than the rest, but having essentially vertical sides for the greater part of its height.

A **lookout station** or **watch tower** is a tower surmounted by a small house from which a watch is kept regularly.

A **water tower** is a structure enclosing a tank or standpipe so that the presence of the tank or standpipe may not be apparent.

A **standpipe** is a tall cylindrical structure, in a waterworks system, the height of which is several times the diameter.

The term **tank** is used for a water tank elevated high above the ground by a tall skeleton framework.

The expression **gas tank** or **oil tank** is used for the distinctive structures described by these words.

Miscellaneous • *Measured mile.* A measured nautical mile indicated on a chart is accurate to within six feet of the correct length. Most measurements in the United States were made before 1959, when the United States adopted the international nautical mile. The new value is within six feet of the previous standard length of 6,080.20 feet, adjustments not having been made. If the measured distance differs from the standard value by more than six feet, the actual measured distance is stated and the words "measured mile" are omitted.

Periods after abbreviations in water areas are omitted, as these might be mistaken for rocks. However, a lower case *i* or *j* is dotted.

Courses shown on charts are given in true directions, to the nearest minute of arc.

Bearings shown are in true directions *toward* (not from) the objects.

Commercial radio broadcasting stations are shown on charts when they are of value to the mariner either for obtaining radio bearings or as landmarks.

Rules of the road. Lines of demarcation between the areas in which international and inland rules apply are shown only when they cannot be adequately described in notes on the chart.

Compass roses are placed at convenient locations on Mercator charts to facilitate the plotting of bearings and courses. The outer circle is graduated in degrees with zero at true north. The inner circle is graduated in points and degrees with the arrow indicating magnetic north.

Magnetic information. On many charts magnetic variation is given to the nearest 15′ by notes in the centers of compass roses. When this is done, the annual change is given to the nearest 1′ to permit correction of the given value at a later date. However, since the annual change is a variable quantity, and since the values given are rounded off, as well as for other reasons, it is wise to use a chart of recent date. On other charts the variation is given by a series of **isogonic lines** connecting points of equal variation, usually a separate line being given for each degree of variation. The line of zero variation is called the **agonic line.** Many plans and insets show neither compass roses nor isogonic lines, but indicate magnetic information by note. A local magnetic disturbance of sufficient force to cause noticeable deflection of the magnetic compass, called **local attraction,** is indicated by a note on the chart.

Currents are sometimes shown on charts by means of arrows giving the directions, and figures giving the speeds. The information thus given refers to the usual or average conditions, sometimes based upon very few observations. It is not safe to assume that conditions at any given time will not differ considerably from those shown.

Longitudes are reckoned eastward and westward from the meridian of Greenwich, England, unless otherwise stated. Nearly all modern charts use Greenwich.

Notes on charts should be read with care, as they may give important information not graphically presented. Several types of notes are used. First, those in the margin give such information as the chart number and (sometimes) price, publication and edition notes, identification of adjoining charts, etc. Second, notes in connection with the chart title include such information as scale, sources of charted data, tidal information, the unit in which soundings are given, cautions, etc. A third class of notes is that given in proximity to the detail to which it refers. Examples of this type of note are those referring to local magnetic disturbance, controlling depths of channels, measured miles, dangers, dumping grounds, anchorages, etc.

Title. The chart title may be at any convenient location, usually in some area not important to navigation. It is composed of several distinctive parts: the general geographic area, the specific locality, the source and date (or dates) of the survey, the chart datum, a legend, the projection, the horizontal datum, and the scale.

Use of Charts

Advance preparation • Before a chart is to be used, it should be studied carefully. All notes should be read and understood. There should be no question of the meanings of symbols or the unit in which depths are given, for there may not be time to determine such things when the ship is underway, particularly if an emergency should arise. Since the graduations of the latitude and longitude scales differ considerably on various charts, those of the chart to be used should be noted carefully. Dangers and abnormal conditions of any kind should be noted.

Particular attention should be given to soundings. It is good practice to select a realistic danger sounding (see Chapter 9) and mark this prominently with a colored pencil.

It may be desirable to place additional information on the chart. Arcs of circles might be drawn around navigational lights to indicate the limit of visibility at the height of eye of an observer on the bridge. Notes regarding the appearance of light structures, tidal information, prominent ranges, or other information from the light lists, tide tables, tidal current tables, and sailing directions might prove helpful.

The particular preparation to be made depends upon the requirements and the personal preferences and experience of the individual navigator. The specific information selected is not important. But it *is* important that the navigator familiarize himself with his chart so that in an emergency the information needed will be available and there will be no question of its meaning.

Maintaining charts • When a chart is received, the date to which it has been corrected will be found stamped in the margin. Responsibility for maintaining it after this date lies with the user. *An uncorrected chart is a menace.* The various issues of *Notice to Mariners* and quarterly summaries of corrections subsequent to the correction date contain all the information needed for maintaining charts.

When a new edition of a chart is published, it should be obtained and the old one retired from use. The very fact that a new edition has been prepared generally indicates that there have been changes that cannot adequately be shown by hand correction.

Use and stowage of charts • Charts are among the most important aids of the navigator, and should be treated as such. When in use they should be spread out flat on a suitable chart table or desk and properly secured to prevent loss or damage. Every effort should be made to keep charts dry, for a wet chart stretches and may not return to the original dimensions after drying. The distortion thus introduced may cause inaccurate results when measurements are made on the chart. If a chart does become wet, the distortion may be minimized by ironing the chart with a warm iron until it is dry.

Permanent corrections to charts should be made in ink so that they will not be inadvertently erased. All other lines should be drawn lightly in pencil so that they can be easily erased without removing permanent information or otherwise damaging the chart. To avoid possible confusion, lines should be drawn no longer than necessary, and adequately labeled. When a voyage is completed, the charts should be carefully and thoroughly erased unless there has been an unusual incident such as a grounding or collision, when they should be preserved without change, as they will undoubtedly be requested by the investigating authority. After a chart has been erased, it should be inspected carefully for possible damage and for incompletely erased or overlooked marks that might prove confusing when the chart is next used.

When not in use charts should be stowed flat in their proper drawers or portfolios, with a minimum of folding. The stowed charts should be properly indexed so that any desired one can be found when needed. In removing or replacing a chart, care should be exercised to avoid damage to it or other charts.

A chart that is given proper care in use and stowage can have a long and useful life.

Chart lighting • In the use of charts it is important that adequate lighting be provided. However, the light on the bridge of a ship or in the cockpit of a boat underway at night should be such as to cause the least interference with the darkness-adaptation of the eyes of personnel who watch for navigational lights, running lights, dangers, etc. Experiments by the Department of the Navy have indicated that red light is least disturbing to eyes which have been adapted to maximum vision during darkness. In some instances red lights, filters, or goggles have been provided on the bridges or in chartrooms of vessels. However, the use of such light seriously affects the appearance of a chart. Red, orange, and buff disappear. Other colors may appear changed. This has led to the substitution of magenta or purple for red and orange and gray for buff on some charts. However, before a chart is used in any light except white, a preliminary test should be made and the effect noted carefully. If a glass or plastic top is provided for the chart table or desk, a dim white light *below* the chart may provide sufficient illumination to permit chart reading without objectionable disturbance of night vision.

[6]

Instruments for Piloting and Dead Reckoning

Kinds of instruments • The word *instrument* has several meanings, at least two of which apply to navigation: (1) an implement or tool, and (2) a device by which the present value of a quantity is measured. Thus, a straightedge and a mechanical log are both instruments, the first serving as a tool, and the second as a measuring device. This chapter is concerned with the navigational instruments used for plotting and those for measuring distance or speed, depth, and direction. These quantities, in conjunction with time, are the basic data in dead reckoning and piloting.

In addition to the instruments discussed, several others are important to the navigator. Binoculars are helpful in observing landmarks. A flashlight has many uses, the principal one being to illuminate the scales of instruments when they are to be read at night. Erasers should be soft, and pencils should not be so hard that they damage the surface of the chart.

Plotting Instruments

Dividers and compasses • **Dividers,** or a "pair of dividers," is an instrument originally used for dividing a line into equal segments. The instrument consists essentially of two hinged legs with pointed ends which can be separated to any distance from zero to the maximum imposed by physical limitations. The setting is retained either by friction at the hinge, as in the usual navigational dividers, or by means of a screw acting against a spring.

If one of the legs carries a pencil or ruling pen, the instrument is called **compasses.** The two legs may be attached to a bar of metal or wood instead of being hinged, thus permitting greater separation of the points. Such an instrument is called **beam compasses** or **beam dividers.**

The principal use of dividers in navigation is to measure or transfer distances on a chart, as described in Chapter 8. Compasses are used for drawing distance circles or circles of visibility (see Chapter 9), or for any plotting requiring an arc of a circle.

The friction at the hinge of most dividers and compasses can be varied, and should be adjusted so that the instrument can be manipulated easily with one hand, but will retain the separation of the points in normal handling. A drop of oil on the hinge may be required occasionally. The points should be sharp and should have equal length, permitting them to be brought close together for the measurement of very short distances.

For navigation, it is desirable to have dividers and compasses with comparatively long legs, to provide adequate range for most requirements. It is desirable to learn to manipulate dividers or compasses with one hand.

Parallel rulers • Parallel rulers are an instrument for transferring a line parallel to itself. In its most common form it consists of two parallel bars or rulers, connected in such a manner that when one is held in place on a flat surface, the other can be moved, remaining parallel to its original direction. Firm pressure is required on one ruler while the other is being moved, to prevent slippage. The principal use of parallel rulers in navigation is to transfer the direction of a charted line to a compass rose, and vice versa.

The edges of the rulers should be truly straight and, in the case of double-edged rulers, should be parallel to each other in order that either edge can be used. Parallelism can be tested by comparison of all edges with the same straight line, as a meridian or parallel of a Mercator chart. The linkage can be tested for looseness and lack of parallelism by "walking" the rulers between parallel lines on opposite sides of the chart and back again.

Some metal parallel rulers have a protractor engraved on the upper surface to permit orientation of the ruler at any convenient meridian.

In one type of instrument, parallelism during transfer is obtained by supporting a single ruler on two knurled rollers. Both rollers have the same diameter, and the motion of one is transmitted to the other by an axle having a cover which provides a convenient handle. This type of ruler is convenient and accurate, and is less likely to slip than the linked double-ruler type. However, care is necessary to prevent its rolling off the chart table when the vessel is rolling or pitching.

Directions can also be transferred by means of two triangles such as are used in drafting, or by one triangle and a straightedge. One edge of a triangle is aligned in the desired direction and the triangle is then moved along a straightedge held firmly against one of its other edges until the first edge is at the desired place on the chart. Some triangles have pro-

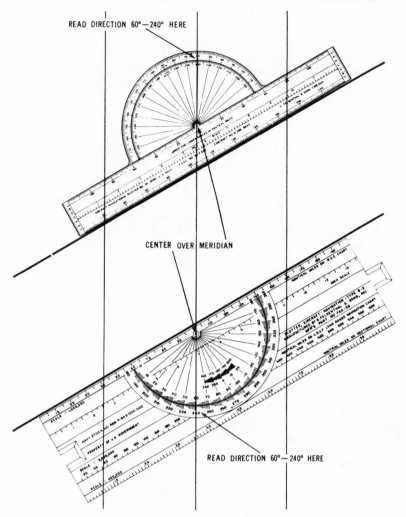

Fig. 6.1. Two plotters having no movable parts.

tractors engraved on them to assist in transferring lines. Such a triangle becomes a form of plotter.

Protractor • **A protractor** is a device for measuring angles on a chart or other surface. It consists essentially of a graduated arc, usually of 180°, on suitable material such as metal or plastic.

Plotter • The increased popularity of graphical methods in practical navigation during recent decades has resulted in the development of a wide variety of devices to facilitate plotting. In its most common form, such a device consists essentially of a protractor combined with a straightedge.

There are two general types, one having no movable parts, and the other having a pivot at the center of the arc of the protractor, to permit rotation of the straightedge around the protractor. Examples of the fixed type are illustrated in Figure 6.1. Those shown were designed for air navigation, but are applicable to many processes of marine navigation. The direction of the straightedge is controlled by placing the center of the protractor arc and the desired scale graduation on the same reference line. If the reference line is a meridian, the directions shown by the straightedge are true geographic directions. If it is desired to plot a line perpendicular to another line, the direction may be measured from a parallel of latitude or its equivalent, instead of adding or subtracting 90° from the value and measuring from a meridian. Some fixed-type plotters have auxiliary scales labeled to indicate true direction if a parallel is used as the reference.

Most plotters also provide linear distance scales, as shown in figure 6.1. In the movable-arm type of plotter, a protractor is aligned with a meridian, and the movable arm is rotated until it is in the desired direction.

Drafting machine • If a chart table of sufficient size is available, a **drafting machine** (fig. 6.2) is probably the most desirable plotting instrument. The straightedge of this instrument can be clamped so as to retain its direction during movement over the entire plotting area. Straightedges of various lengths and linear scales are interchangeable. Some models make provision for mounting two straightedges perpendicular to each other. However, for

Fig. 6.2. Drafting machine.

most purposes of navigation, the perpendicular is more conveniently obtained by the use of a triangle with a single straightedge. The movable protractor also retains its orientation and can be adjusted to conform to the compass rose of a chart secured in any position on the chart table. Directions of the straightedge can then be read or set on the protractor without reference to charted compass roses. Use of the clamped protractor requires that charted meridians be straight and parallel, as on a Mercator chart. Its use is restricted with projections such as the Lambert conformal, on which meridians converge.

When a drafting machine is used, the chart or plotting sheet is first secured to the chart table. The straightedge is aligned with a meridian (or parallel) and clamped in position. The protractor is then adjusted so that 000° and 180° (090° and 270° if a parallel is used) are at the ruler indices, and clamped. With this setting, any subsequent position of the ruler is indicated as a true direction. If the protractor is offset by the amount of the compass error (see Chapter 7), true directions can be plotted by setting the straightedge at the compass direction on the protractor, without need for applying compass error arithmetically. However, it is generally preferable to keep it set to true directions and apply compass error mentally.

Distance and Speed Measurement

Units of measurement • Mariners generally measure horizontal distances in nautical miles, but occasionally in yards or feet. Either feet or fathoms are used for measuring depth of water, and feet for measuring height above water. Nautical miles are 6,076.11549 feet (approximately) and land or statute miles are 5,280 feet.

Speed is customarily expressed in knots or, for some purposes, in kilometers per hour, or yards or feet per minute. For short distances, a nautical mile can be considered equal to 2,000 yards or 6,000 feet. This is a useful relationship because $\dfrac{6,000 \text{ feet}}{60 \text{ minutes}} = 100$ feet per minute. Thus, speed in knots is equal approximately to hundreds of feet per minute, or hundreds of yards per 3-minute interval.

Distance, speed, and time are related by the formula

$$\text{distance} = \text{speed} \times \text{time}.$$

Therefore, if any two of the three quantities are known, the third can be found. The units, of course, must be consistent. Thus, if speed is measured in knots, and time in hours, the answer is in nautical miles. Similarly, if distance is measured in yards, and time in minutes, the answer is in yards per minute.

The solution of problems involving distance, speed, and time can easily be accomplished by means of a slide rule. If the index of scale *C* is set opposite speed in knots on scale *D*, the distance in nautical miles appears on scale *D* opposite time in hours on scale *C*. If 60 of scale *C* is set opposite speed in knots on scale *D*, the distance covered in any number of *minutes* is shown on scale *D* opposite the minutes on scale *C*. Several circular slide rules particularly adapted for solution of distance, speed, and time problems have been devised.

Measurement of distance to an object • Measurement of distance to an object can be made in a variety of ways, as by radar, sonar, RAR beacon, distance finding station, sextant angle, range finder, or **stadimeter.***

Measurement of distance traveled • Measurement of distance traveled may be made directly, or the distance can be determined indirectly by means of the speed and time, as explained earlier.

One of the simplest mechanical distance-measuring devices is the **taffrail log,** consisting of (1) a rotator which turns like a screw propeller when it is towed through the water; (2) a braided *log line*, up to 100 fathoms in length, which tows the rotator and transmits its rotation to an indicator on the vessel; and (3) a dial and pointer mechanism which registers the distance traveled through the water. In some installations, the readings of the register are transferred electrically to a dial.

The taffrail log is usually streamed from the ship's quarter, although it may be carried at the end of a short boom extending outboard from the vessel. The log line should be sufficiently long, and attached in such position, that the rotator is clear of the disturbed water of the wake of the vessel; otherwise an error is introduced. Errors may also be introduced by a head or following sea; by mechanical wear or damage, such as a bent fin; or by fouling of the rotator, as by seaweed or refuse.

An accurately calibrated taffrail log in good working order provides information of sufficient reliability for most purposes of navigation. Its readings should be checked at various speeds by towing it over a known distance in an area free from currents. Usually, the average of several runs, preferably in opposite directions, is more accurate than a single one. If an error is found, it is expressed as a percentage and applied to later readings. The calibration should be checked from time to time.

Although a taffrail log is included in the equipment carried by many oceangoing vessels, the convenience and reliability of other methods of determining distance or speed have reduced the dependence formerly placed upon this instrument.

---

* Ed. note: The coastal pilot without such equipment can fix his position (see Chapter 9) and measure the distance to an object on his chart.

Measurement of speed • Speed can be determined indirectly by means of distance and time, or it can be measured directly. All instruments now in common use for measuring speed determine rate of motion *through the water*. This is done (1) electromagnetically, (2) by measuring the water pressure due solely to the forward motion of the vessel, (3) by means of a small screw propeller having a speed of rotation proportional to speed of the vessel, and (4) by determining the relationship between ship speed and speed of rotation of its screw or screws. Instruments for measuring speed, like those for measuring distance, are called **logs.**

Speed over the bottom can be determined (1) by direct measurement; (2) by measuring on the chart or plotting sheet the distance made good between fixes, and dividing this by the time; or (3) by finding the vector sum of velocity through the water and velocity of the current. A suitable instrument for measuring speed over the bottom is not generally available, although some developmental work along this line has been done. Measurement of the distance between two fixes requires a method of obtaining accurate fixes. The third method requires knowledge of velocity through the water, and current. An estimate of the current can be used to determine the approximate course and speed over the bottom. However, estimates are not always accurate, and an instrument to measure current would provide better results. Such an instrument, called the **geomagnetic electrokinetograph (GEK),** has been developed, but it has been used primarily by oceanographers in their study of ocean currents, and has not been adapted for use in ordinary navigation.

The electromagnetic type underwater log • This log consists essentially of a rodmeter, an oscillator-amplifier, and an indicator-transmitter. The rodmeter, which protrudes below the hull of the vessel, contains an electromagnetic sensing element which produces a voltage directly proportional to speed through the water. This voltage is amplified in the oscillator-amplifier and is converted to pointer and synchro indications of speed in the indicator-transmitter. The speed signals are also converted to distance, by means of a roller-and-disk mechanism in the indicator-transmitter. This system has no orifice or moving parts external to the vessel, and has high precision and accuracy from zero speed to full scale.

Speed measurement by dynamic water pressure • When an object is moving through a fluid such as water or air, its forward side is exposed to a *dynamic* pressure which is proportional to the speed at which the object is moving, in addition to the *static* pressure due to depth and density of the fluid above the object. When the fluid is water, and ship speeds are involved, dynamic pressure is equal to

$$P = \frac{S^2}{1.832g}$$

where P is dynamic pressure, S is speed through the water, and g is the acceleration due to gravity (32.2 feet per second per second, approximately). If this formula is solved for S, it becomes

$$S = 1.353 \sqrt{gP}.$$

If 32.2 is substituted for g:

$$S = 7.68 \sqrt{P}.$$

Therefore, if dynamic pressure can be measured, this principle can be used for determining speed.

One of the most widely used means of measuring dynamic pressure is by a **Pitot tube.** This device consists of a tube having an opening on its forward side or end. If the tube is stationary in the water, this opening is subject to static pressure only. But when the tube is in motion, the pressure at the opening is the sum of static and dynamic pressures. This is called **Pitot pressure** or **total pressure.** The Pitot tube is surrounded by an outer tube which has openings along its athwartship sides. Whether the tube is stationary or in motion, these openings are subject to static pressure only.

In the **Pitot-static log** the Pitot tube is in the form of a vertical "rod-meter" which extends through and is supported by a sea valve in the vessel's bottom. The tube extends 24 to 30 inches below the bottom of the vessel, into water relatively undisturbed by motion of the hull. The two pressures, Pitot and static, are led to separate bellows attached to opposite ends of a centrally pivoted lever. This lever is electrically connected to a mechanism which controls the speed of a pump. When the vessel is dead in the water, the pressures are equal, and the pump is stopped. When the ship is moving, the pump speed is regulated so that the pressures in the two bellows are equalized. Thus, the pump speed is proportional to the ship speed.

Through suitable gearing, the pump provides a mechanical output at the rate of 60 revolutions per nautical mile. This rotation is transmitted electrically to the master indicator, where the distance traveled appears on the distance counter in units of 0.01 nautical mile. In addition, the master indicator has a timing device which transforms distance and time into speed, the latter appearing on the speed dial.

Both speed and distance indications may be transmitted to various **repeaters** throughout the ship. Logs of this type have been replaced in ships of the U.S. Navy by those of the electromagnetic type to provide greater accuracy both at each calibration speed and over a given range of speeds.

Various less accurate instruments have been devised for determining speed by measuring water pressure due to forward motion of the vessel. These are relatively simple, inexpensive instruments intended primarily for use by small craft. One instrument has a finger which the water pressure forces aft against a calibrated spring. A flexible hydraulic cable transmits the motion to a speed indicator. Another instrument uses a small scoop attached to the hull of the vessel. The pressure of the water scooped up is transmitted by tubing to the speed indicator, which is essentially a pressure gage graduated in knots. A third type measures the drag of a small towed object. The accuracy of such devices depends to a large extent upon the refinements of design, manufacture, installation, maintenance, and calibration.

Impeller-type log • An impeller-type log has a small propeller-driven alternating-current generator located near the outer end of a rodmeter which extends through a sea valve on the hull plating, and projects into the water. The propeller rotates as it moves through the water. The number of its revolutions is proportional to the distance traveled through the water, and its speed of rotation is proportional to the ship's speed. The output of the generator is amplified and passed to the master indicator-transmitter, where the number of cycles, reduced by gearing, is recorded on mileage counter dials in units of 0.01 nautical mile. The frequency of the alternating current, being proportional to ship speed, is transmitted to a tachometer mechanism geared to the pointer of the speed indicator. Calibration is accomplished by adjusting the position of driving rollers along the radius of a driven disk.

The speed and distance indications of the master indicator can be transmitted to remote indicators. Speed indications of this equipment are accurate to approximately 0.15 knot at speeds between 0.25 knot and 25 knots.

Speed by engine revolution counter • The number of turns of a propeller shaft is proportional to the distance traveled. If the element of time is added, speed can be determined. If the screw were advancing through a solid substance, the distance it would advance in one revolution would be the **pitch** of the screw. Thus, if a propeller having a pitch of ten feet turns at 200 revolutions per minute, it advances 2,000 feet in one minute, equivalent to a speed of 19.75 knots. It does not do so in water because of **slip,** the difference between the distance it would advance in a solid substance and actual distance traveled, expressed as a percentage of the former. For example, if slip is 18 percent, both the ship's speed and distance covered are reduced by this percentage. Thus, instead of 19.75 knots, the speed is only $19.75 \times 0.82 = 16.2$ knots.

Slip depends upon the type and speed of rotation of the propeller, the type of ship, the condition of loading and ship's bottom, the state of the sea and the ship's course relative to it, and the apparent wind. Despite the many variables, slip can be determined with sufficient accuracy for practical navigation. This is usually accomplished by steaming a known distance and noting the time of passage. The speed corresponding to the number of revolutions being used can then be determined by means of the distance-speed-time formula in the form

$$\text{speed} = \frac{\text{distance}}{\text{time.}}$$

Thus, speed can be determined directly, without computing slip, and a table or curve of ship speed for various engine revolution speeds can be made. In determining speed in this manner, the average speed of two runs (one in each direction) should be used. The vessel should be on course and speed long enough to stabilize slip before starting each run. Any suitable distance can be used, but a distance of one nautical mile has been measured at various convenient locations. Each such **measured mile** is suitably marked on the beach, and shown on the chart, with the course to steer.

By means of an **engine revolution counter** the number of revolutions during any suitable time interval can be measured. If a **tachometer** is available, the *rate* of shaft revolution is determined, usually in revolutions per minute. For best results, allowance should be made for condition of the bottom, draft and trim of the vessel, and the state of the sea.

Depth Measurement

Importance • Accurate knowledge of the depth of water under a vessel is of such navigational importance that there is a legal requirement that American merchant vessels of 500 gross tons or more engaged in ocean and coastwise service "shall be fitted with an efficient mechanical deep-sea sounding apparatus in addition to the deep-sea hand leads."

The lead • The lead (lĕd) is a device consisting of a suitably marked line having a weight attached to one of its ends. It is used for measuring depth of water. Although the lead is probably the oldest of all navigational aids, it is still a highly useful device, particularly in periods of reduced visibility. Although its greatest service is generally in the shoal water near the shore, it sometimes can provide valuable information when the vessel is out of sight of land.

Two types of lead are in common use, the **hand lead,** weighing from about 5 to 14 pounds and having a line marked to about 25 fathoms; and the **deep-sea (dipsey) lead,** weighing from 30 to 100 pounds and having a line marked to 100 fathoms or more in length. Standard markings appear at specified intervals along the line.

Fathoms marked on the lead line are called **marks.** The intermediate whole fathoms are called **deeps.** In reporting depths it is customary to use these terms, as "by the mark five," "deep six," etc. The only fractions of a fathom usually reported are halves and quarters, the customary expressions being "and a half, eight," "less a quarter, four," etc. A practice sometimes followed is to place distinctive markings on the hand lead line at each foot near the critical depths of the vessel with which it is to be used. The markings should be placed on the lead line when it is wet, and the accuracy of the marking should be checked from time to time to detect any changes in the length of the line. The distance from the hand of the leadsman to the surface of the water under various conditions of loading should be determined so that correct allowance can be made when the marking nearest the surface cannot be observed.

The lead itself has a recess in its bottom. If this recess is filled with tallow or other suitable substance, a sample of the bottom can sometimes be obtained. This information can prove helpful in establishing the position of the vessel. If tallow is not available, some other substance can be used. Soap is suitable if it is replaced from time to time. When the recess is filled for obtaining a sample, the lead is said to be **armed** with the substance used.

Echo sounder • Most soundings are now made by means of an **echo sounder.** This instrument produces an underwater sound-wave signal, and measures the elapsed time until return of an echo from the bottom. It is a form of **sonar,** although this term is usually applied only to similar equipment which directs the sound-wave signal horizontally to measure range. An echo sounder operating within the range of audible sound (about 20 to 20,000 cycles per second) may be called a **sonic depth finder.** One using sound waves of a higher frequency may be called an **ultrasonic depth finder.** The trend has been toward higher frequency, to reduce interference from ship noise.

There are many forms of echo sounder. In a typical installation a light tube is mounted vertically behind an opaque shield which rotates at a predetermined speed. A narrow slot in the shield permits the light to be seen at one place only. This slot is under or adjacent to a circular scale graduated in depth. The sound-wave signal is transmitted when the slot is at the top or zero of the scale. At this instant, the light flashes. When an echo is received, the light again flashes. The graduation adjacent to the second flash indicates the depth. Several different scales may be available for use in various depths. The scale is controlled by adjusting the speed of rotation of the opaque shield. If the depth is greater than the maximum graduation of the scale in use, an erroneous reading may be obtained unless the operator is alert. Thus, if the maximum reading is 400 fathoms, and the depth of the water is 600 fathoms, the shield will make a complete rotation and half of another before the echo returns. The scale would indicate a reading of 200 fathoms. If allowance is made for the number of complete rotations, accurate soundings can be obtained at a relatively large scale. However, there is less possibility of error if the correct scale is used. Doubt as to the correct scale can be removed by switching to a smaller scale (greater depth), if one is available. In some models the light itself rotates. Some of the newer echo sounders are equipped with a recording device that produces a written trace of the bottom, called a **bottom profile.** This is accomplished by means of an arm which moves across a graduated tape, making one transit for each sounding. When the echo is received, a short line is produced on a moving tape graduated in time and depth units.

Echo sounders of American manufacture are calibrated for a speed of sound of 4,800 feet per second. The actual speed varies primarily with the temperature, pressure, and salinity, but in the ocean is nearly always faster than the speed of calibration. The error thus introduced is on the side of safety unless the water is fresh or very cold.

Errors are sometimes introduced by false bottoms. If soft mud covers the ocean floor, some of the sound-wave energy may penetrate to a harder layer beneath, resulting in indication of two bottoms. It is not unusual in deep water to receive a strong return at a depth of about 200 fathoms during the day, and somewhat nearer the surface at night. This is called the **phantom bottom** or **deep scattering layer.** It is believed to be due to large numbers of tiny marine animals. Schools of fish return an echo sufficiently strong to make the echo sounder a valuable aid to commercial fishermen.

In modern equipment the sound waves, whether sonic or ultrasonic, are produced electrically by means of a **transducer,** a device for converting electrical energy to sound waves, or vice versa. The transducer utilizes either the piezo-electric properties of quartz or the magnetostriction properties of nickel and its alloys.

Early models produced sound signals by striking the ship's hull with a mechanical hammer in the forward part of the vessel. The echo was received by a microphone in the after part of the vessel, depth being determined by the angle at which the signal returned.

Direction Measurement

Reference directions ● A horizontal direction is generally expressed as an angle between a line extending in some **reference direction** and a line extending in the given direction. The angle is numerically equal to the difference between the two directions, called the **angular distance** from the reference direction. Unless the reference direction is stated or otherwise understood, the intended direction is in doubt. Thus, to a navigator, direction 135° is southeast; to an astronomer or surveyor, it may be northwest.

A number of reference directions are used in navigation. If a direction is stated in three figures, without designation of reference direction, it is generally understood that the direction is related to true (geographical) north. The reference direction for magnetic directions is magnetic north, and that for compass directions is compass north. For relative bearings it is the heading of the ship. In maneuvering situations, the heading of another vessel might be used as the reference direction.

The primary function of an instrument used for measuring direction is to determine the reference direction. This having been done, other directions can be indicated by a compass rose oriented in the reference direction. North is established by some form of compass. A compass rose is attached to the north-seeking element so that other directions can be determined directly. However, if one always keeps in mind that the primary function of the instrument is to indicate a reference direction, he should be able to avoid some of the mistakes commonly made in the application of compass errors.

Desirable characteristics of a navigational compass • To serve its purpose adequately, a navigational compass needs to have certain characteristics to permit it to meet requirements of accuracy, reliability, and convenience.

The most important characteristic is accuracy. No other quality, however important or to whatever extent it may be possessed, compensates for the lack of accuracy. This does not mean that the compass need be without error, but that such errors as it may possess can be readily determined. Provision should be made for removing deviation or reducing it to a minimum (see Chapter 7). If accurate horizontal directions are to be determined, the compass needs to be provided with some type of compass rose maintained in a horizontal position. Adequate sighting equipment is needed if bearings are to be observed, and an index is needed to mark the forward direction parallel to the keel if heading is to be measured. Accurate readings cannot be expected from a compass that **hunts** (oscillates) excessively. A characteristic closely related to accuracy is precision. The amount of precision required varies somewhat with the use and depends as much upon the steadiness of the compass and its design as upon its inherent qualities.

A compass is reliable when its operation is not often interrupted; when its indications are relatively free from unknown or unsuspected disturbances; when it is little affected by extremes of temperature, moisture, vibration, or shock; and when it is not so sensitive that large errors are introduced by ordinary changes in conditions or equipment near the compass.

The value of a compass is dependent somewhat upon the convenience with which it can be used. Accuracy, too, may be involved. Thus, a compass should not be installed in such a position that one must be in an unnatural or uncomfortable position to use it. A compass intended for use in obtaining bearings is of reduced value if it is installed at a location that does not permit an unobstructed view in most directions. The compass graduations and index should be clean, adequately lighted if the instrument is to be used at night, and clearly marked.

Kinds of compasses • The compasses commonly used by the mariner are (1) *magnetic* and (2) *gyroscopic.** The magnetic compass tends to align itself with the magnetic lines of force of the earth, while the gyro compass seeks the true (geographic) meridian.

A compass may be designated to indicate its principal use, as a **standard, steering,** or **boat compass.** The compass designated as standard is usually a magnetic compass installed in an exposed position having an unobstructed view in most directions, permitting position near the helm.

Magnetic compasses • If a small magnet is pivoted at its center of gravity in such manner that it is free to turn and dip, it will tend to align itself with the magnetic field of the earth (see Chapter 7). It thus provides a directional reference and becomes a simple compass. However, such a compass would not be adequate for use aboard ship. For this purpose a compass should have a stronger directive element than that provided by a single, pivoted magnet, should have provision for measuring various directions, should have some means of damping the oscillations of the directive element, should be approximately horizontal, and should have some means of neutralizing local magnetic influences.

In a mariner's compass, several magnets are mounted parallel to each other. To them is attached a **compass card** having a compass rose to indicate various directions. Both magnets and compass card are enclosed in a bowl having a glass top through which the card can be seen. The bowl is weighted at the bottom and is suspended in gimbals so that it remains nearly horizontal as the vessel rolls and pitches. In nearly all modern compasses the bowl is filled with a liquid that supplies a buoyant force almost equal to the force of gravity acting upon the directive element and card. This reduces the friction on the pivot (a metal point in a jeweled bearing), and provides a means of damping the oscillations of the compass card. The card is mounted in such manner as to remain in an essentially horizontal position. A mark called a **lubber's line** is placed on the inner surface of the bowl, adjacent to the compass card, to indicate the forward direction parallel to the keel when the bowl is correctly installed. The gimbals used for mounting the compass bowl are attached to a stand called

* Ed. note: Only the magnetic compass is likely to be of practical interest here.

a **binnacle,** which in most installations is permanently and rigidly attached to the deck of the vessel, usually on its longitudinal center line. Most binnacles provide means for neutralization of local magnetic influences due to magnetism within the vessel. A cover or "hood" is provided to protect the compass from the elements, dust, etc.

Directional information is of such importance that selection and installation of a suitable compass should be made carefully, seeking such guidance as may be needed. Common errors are the use of a compass designed for a different type craft (as an aircraft compass in a boat), permitting chrome plating of a binnacle by someone who does not know how to do this without creating a magnetic field, authorizing electric welding of steel near the compass, improper installation of magnetic equipment or electric appliances near the compass, allowing short circuits to occur in the vicinity of the compass, etc.

After the compass has been selected and installed, proper adjustment and compensation are important (see Chapter 7), and future care of the instrument should not be neglected. It should be checked and overhauled at regular intervals, and any indication of malfunctioning or deterioration, however slight, should not be overlooked. Discoloration of the liquid or the presence of a bubble, for instance, indicates a condition that should be investigated and corrected at once. If it becomes necessary to add liquid, one should be certain that he has the correct substance and should attempt to determine the source of the leak. Except as a temporary expedient, this is best done by a professional. Some compasses should be protected from prolonged exposure to sunlight, to prevent discoloration of the card and liquid.

If a vessel is to be inactive for a long period of time—at least several months—it is good practice to remove the magnetic compass from its binnacle and store it in a place relatively free from magnetic influences, and of approximately even temperature. Unless instructions indicate otherwise, the compass should be stored upside down, to remove the weight from the pivot and prevent the card from swinging.

The compass card • The compass card is composed of light, nonmagnetic material. In nearly all modern compasses the card is graduated in 360°, increasing clockwise from north through east, south, and west. An older system still used somewhat is to graduate the card through 90° in each quadrant, increasing from both north and south. Some compass cards are graduated in "points," usually in addition to the degree graduations. There are 32 **points of the compass,** 11¼ ° apart. The four **cardinal points** are north, east, south, and west. Midway between these are four **intercardinal points** at northeast, southeast, southwest, and northwest. These eight points are the only ones appearing on the cards of compasses used by the U.S. Navy. The eight points between cardinal and intercardinal points are named for the two directions between which they lie, the cardinal name being given first, as north northeast, east northeast, east southeast, etc. The remaining 16 points are named for the nearest cardinal or intercardinal point "by" the next cardinal point in the direction of measurement, as north by east, northeast by north, etc. Smaller graduations are provided by dividing each point into four "quarter points," thus producing 128 graduations altogether. There are several systems of naming the quarter points.

The naming of the various graduations of the compass card in order is called **boxing the compass,** an important attainment by the student mariner of earlier generations. The point system of indicating relative bearings (see Chapter 9) survived long after degrees became almost universally used for compass and true directions. Except for the cardinal and intercardinal points, and occasionally the two-point graduations, all of which are used to indicate directions generally (as "northwest winds," meaning winds from a general northwesterly direction), the point system has become largely historical.

A wide variety of magnetic compasses are used in ships and yachts. The basic principles of operation of all magnetic compasses are the same, the various types differing only in details of construction. A feature which is widely used in commercial compasses is a hemispherical top which provides magnification of the graduations.

Magnetic compass limitations • Because of its essential simplicity, a magnetic compass does not easily become totally inoperative. Being independent of any power supply or other service, a magnetic compass may survive major damage to its ship without losing its utility. Small boat compasses often remain serviceable under the most rigorous conditions.

Despite its great reliability, however, a magnetic compass is subject to some limitations. Since it responds to *any* magnetic field, it is affected by any change in the local magnetic situation. Hence, the undetected presence or change of position of magnetic material near the compass may introduce an unknown error. Thus, an error might be introduced by a steel wrench or paint can left near the compass, or by a change in position of equipment in the vicinity of the compass. Even such small amounts of magnetic material as might be included in a pocketknife or steel keys are sufficient to affect the compass if brought as close as they are when on the person of an individual standing by a compass. As distance from the compass increases, the strength of the magnetic field needed to introduce an error increases. A cargo of large amounts of iron or steel may be sufficient to affect the compass. The compass may also be affected by changes of the magnetic characteristics of the vessel itself. Such changes may occur during a protracted docking period, during a long sea voyage on substantially the same course, when repairs or changes of equipment are made, if the ship sustains heavy shock as by riding out a heavy sea, if the vessel is struck by lightning, or if a short circuit occurs near the compass.

The directive force acting upon a magnetic compass is the horizontal component of the earth's magnetic field. This component is strongest at or near the magnetic equator, decreasing to zero at the magnetic poles (see Chapter 7). Near the magnetic poles, therefore, the magnetic compass is useless, and in a wider area its indications are of questionable reliability. The magnetic field of the earth has a number of local anomalies due to the presence of magnetic material within the earth. During magnetic storms it may be altered considerably. Changes in the magnetic field surrounding a vessel, due either to changes of the field itself or to change of position of the vessel within the field, affect the magnetism of the vessel and the correctors used to neutralize this effect, with a possible disturbance of the balance set up between them.

For these and other reasons, frequent determination of compass error is necessary for safe navigation.

Magnetic compass accessories • Compass heading is indicated by the lubber's line. Compass bearings may be measured by sighting across the compass, bringing the object and the vertical axis of the compass in line. Accuracy in making this alignment is increased by the use of a device to direct the line of sight across the center of the compass. Perhaps the simplest device of this kind is a **bearing bar,** consisting of two vertical **sighting vanes** mounted at opposite ends of a horizontal bar having a small pivot which fits into a hole drilled part way through the glass cover of the compass, at its center. The "near" vane (nearer the eye of the observer) has a very thin, open, vertical slot through which the line of sight is directed; the "far" vane has a thin, vertical wire or thread mounted on a suitable frame. The bar is rotated until the object is in line with the two vanes. The bearing is the reading of the compass in line with the vanes, on the far side from the observer.* If a reflecting surface is pivoted to the far vane to permit observation of the azimuth of a celestial body, the device is called an **azimuth instrument.** Bearing bars and azimuth instruments are usually used only with smaller compasses, and never with an after-reading compass.

Larger compasses are usually provided with a **bearing circle** or **azimuth circle.** These devices consist essentially of two parts: (1) a pair of sighting vanes attached to a ring which fits snugly over the compass, and (2) a mirror to reflect the compass graduation into the line of sight. The use of these devices is similar to that of the bearing bar and azimuth instrument.

None of the bearing or azimuth instruments described above can be used with a compass not designed for it, such as one having a hemispherical top, or an after-reading compass.

* Ed. note: Many coastal pilots use a hand bearing compass to take such bearings.

Some modern magnetic compasses are provided with electrical pick-offs of sufficient sensitivity that the instrument can be used to control such devices as remote indicators, automatic steering equipment, course recorders, and dead reckoning equipment without disturbing the reliability of the compass. However, these devices are more commonly controlled by a gyro compass.

Pelorus • Although it is desirable to have a compass for obtaining bearings, satisfactory results can be obtained by means of an inexpensive device known as a **pelorus** (fig. 6.3). In appearance and use this device resembles a compass, with sighting vanes or a sighting telescope attached, but it has no directive properties. That is, it remains at any *relative* direction to which it is set. It is generally used by setting 000° at the lubber's line. Relative bearings are then observed. They can be converted to bearings true, magnetic, grid, etc., by *adding* the appropriate heading. The direct use of relative bearings is sometimes of value. A pelorus is useful, for instance, in determining the moment at which an aid to navigation is broad on the beam. It is also useful in measuring pairs of relative bearings for use with Table 3 or for determining distance off and distance abeam (see Chapter 9).

If the true heading is set at the lubber's line, true bearings are observed directly. Similarly, compass bearings can be observed if the compass heading is set at the lubber's line, etc. However, the vessel must be on the heading to which the pelorus is set if accurate results are to be obtained, or else a correction must be applied to the observed results. Perhaps the

Courtesy of Wilfred O. White and Sons, Inc.

Fig. 6.3. A pelorus.

easiest way of avoiding error is to have the helmsman indicate when the vessel is on course. This is usually done by calling out "mark, mark, mark" as long as the vessel is within a specified fraction of a degree of the desired heading. The observer, who is watching a distant object across the pelorus, selects an instant when the vessel is steady and is on course. An alternative method is to have the observer call out "mark" when the relative bearing is steady, and the helmsman note the heading. If the compass is swinging at the moment of observation, the observation should be rejected. The number of degrees between the desired and actual headings is *added* if the vessel is to the *right* of the course, and *subtracted* if to the *left*. Thus, if the course is 060° and the heading is 062° at the moment of observation, a correction of 2° is added to the bearing.

Each observer should determine for himself the technique that produces the most reliable results.

[7]

Compass Error

Theory of magnetism • The fact that iron can be magnetized (given the ability to attract other iron) has been known for thousands of years, but the explanation of this phenomenon has awaited the recently acquired knowledge of atomic structure. According to present theory, the magnetic field around a current-carrying wire and the magnetism of a permanent **magnet** are the same phenomenon—fields created by moving electrical charges. This occurs whether the charge is moving along a wire, flowing with the magma of the earth's core, encircling the earth at high altitude as a stream of charged particles, or rotating around the nucleus of an atom.

It has recently been shown that microscopically small regions, called **domains,** exist in iron and other ferromagnetic substances. In each domain the fields created by electrons spinning around their atomic nuclei are parallel to each other, causing the domain to be magnetized to saturation. In a piece of unmagnetized iron, the directions of the various domains are arranged in a random manner with respect to each other. If the substance is placed in a weak magnetic field, the domains rotate somewhat toward the direction of that field. Those domains which are more nearly parallel to the field increase in size at the expense of the more nonparallel ones. If the field is made sufficiently strong, entire domains rotate suddenly by angles of as much as 90° or 180° so as to become parallel to that "crystal axis" which is most nearly parallel to the direction of the field. If the strength of the field is increased to a certain value depending upon individual conditions, all of the domains rotate into parallelism with the field, and the iron itself is said to be magnetically **saturated.** If the field is removed, the domains have a tendency to rotate more or less rapidly to a more natural direction parallel to some crystal axis, and more slowly to random directions under the influence of thermal agitation.

Magnetism which is present only when the material is under the influence of an external field is called **induced magnetism.** That which remains after the magnetizing force is removed is called **residual magnetism.** That which is retained for long periods without appreciable reduction, unless the material is subjected to a demagnetizing force, is called **permanent magnetism.**

Certain substances respond readily to a magnetic field. These **magnetic materials** are principally those composed largely of iron, although nickel and cobalt also exhibit magnetic properties. The best magnets are made of an alloy composed mostly of iron, nickel, and cobalt. Aluminum and some copper may be added. Platinum and silver, properly alloyed with other material, make excellent magnets, but for ordinary purposes the increased expense is not justified by the improvement in performance. Permanent magnets occur in nature in the form of **lodestone,** a form of magnetite (an oxide of iron) possessing magnetic properties. A piece of this material constitutes a **natural magnet.**

Hard and soft iron • In some alloys of iron, the crystals can be so arranged and internally stressed that the domains remain parallel to each other indefinitely, and the metal thus becomes a **permanent magnet.** Such alloys are used for the magnets of a compass. In other kinds of iron, the domains reorient themselves rapidly to conform to the direction of a changing external field, and soon take random directions if the field is removed. A ferromagnetic substance which retains much of its magnetism in the absence of an external field, is said to have high **remanence** or **retentivity.** The strength of a reverse field (one of opposite polarity) required to reduce the magnetism of a magnet to zero is called the **coercivity** or **coercive force** of the magnet. Hence, a compass magnet should have high remanence in order to be strong, and high coercivity so that stray fields will not materially affect it. For convenience, iron is called "hard" if it has high remanence, and "soft" if it has low remanence. **Permeability** (μ) is the ratio of the strength of the magnetic field inside the metal (B) to the strength of the external field (H), or $\mu = \dfrac{B}{H}$.

Lines of force • The direction of a magnetic field is usually represented by lines, called **lines of force.** Relative intensity in different parts of a magnetic field is indicated by the spacing of the lines of force, a strong field having the lines close together. If a piece of unmagnetized iron is placed in a magnetic field, the lines of force tend to crowd into the iron, following its long axis, and the field is stronger in the vicinity of the iron, somewhat as shown in figure 7.1. If the iron becomes permanently magnetized and is removed from this field, the lines of force around the iron follow paths about as shown in figure 7.2.

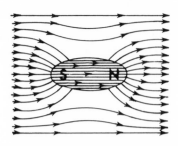 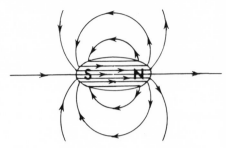

Fig. 7.1. Lines of force crowd into ferromagnetic material placed in a magnetic
field.

Fig. 7.2. Field of a permanent magnet.

Magnetic poles • The region in which the lines of force enter the iron is
called the **south pole,** and the region in which they leave the iron is called
the **north pole.** Thus, the lines of force are directed from south to north
within the magnet, and from north to south in the external field.
Every magnet has a north pole and a south pole. If a magnet is cut into
two pieces, each becomes a magnet with a north pole and south pole. A
single pole cannot exist independently.* If two magnets are brought close
together, *unlike poles attract each other and like poles repel.* Thus, a north
pole attracts a south pole but repels another north pole.

The earth itself has a magnetic field, with its magnetic poles being
some distance from the geographical poles. If a permanent bar magnet is
supported so that it can turn freely, both horizontally and vertically, it
aligns itself with the magnetic field of the earth, which at most places is
in a general north-south direction and inclined to the horizontal. Since the
north pole of the magnet points in a northerly direction, the earth's magnetic pole in the northern hemisphere has *south* magnetism. Nevertheless,
it is called the **north magnetic pole** because of its geographical location.
For a similar reason, the pole in the southern hemisphere, although it has
north magnetism, is called the **south magnetic pole.** To avoid confusion,
north magnetism is usually called "red," and south magnetism "blue."
The red (north) pole of a magnet is usually painted red, and in some
cases the south (blue) pole is painted blue. The north magnetic pole of the
earth is a blue pole, and the south magnetic pole is a red pole.

Magnetism of soft iron • The magnetism of soft iron, in which remanence
is low, depends upon the position of the iron with respect to an external
field. It is strongest if the long axis is parallel to the lines of force, and
decreases to a minimum if the material is rotated so that the long axis is
perpendicular to the lines of force. Figure 7.3 shows three positions of a
bar magnet with respect to a magnetic field. At position X the pole at the

---

* Ed. note: Scientists have recently discovered what they believe to be a single
pole magnet, but it need not be considered in this context.

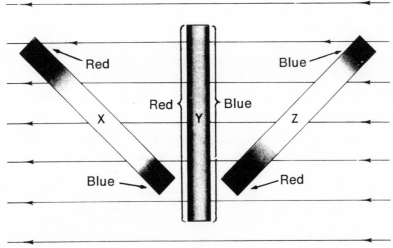

Fig. 7.3. The polarity of a soft iron bar in a magnetic field.

upper end of the bar is red and relatively strong. As the bar is rotated toward position *Y*, the upper end remains red, but its strength decreases. At position *Y*, no pole is apparent at either end, but a red pole extends along the entire left side of the bar, and a blue pole along the right side. Poles are strongest when concentrated into a small area. Hence, when spread over an entire side, as at position *Y*, they are relatively weak. At position *Z*, the upper end is blue.

The change in polarity as a bar of soft iron is rotated in a magnetic field can easily be demonstrated. If a bar of soft iron is placed vertical in northern magnetic latitudes (as in any part of the United States), the north (red) end of a compass magnet brought near it will be attracted by the upper end of the bar, and repelled by the lower end. If the bar is inverted, so that its ends are interchanged, the upper end (which as the lower end previously repelled the compass needle) will attract the north end of the needle, and the lower end will repel it. Thus, the polarity of the rod is reversed, *either* end having blue magnetism if it is at the top. This changing polarity of soft iron in the earth's field is a major factor affecting the magnetic compasses of a steel vessel.

Terrestrial magnetism • The earth itself can be considered to be a gigantic magnet. Although man has known for many centuries that the earth has a magnetic field, the origin of the magnetism is not completely understood. Nevertheless, the horizontal component of this field is a valuable reference in navigation, for it provides the directive force for the magnetic compass, which indicates the ship's heading *in relation to the horizontal component of this field*.

The world-wide pattern of the earth's magnetism is roughly like that which would result from a short, powerful, bar magnet near the earth's center, as shown in figure 7.4. The geographical poles are at the top and bottom, and the magnetic poles are offset somewhat from them. This representation, however, is greatly simplified. The actual field is more complex, and requires measurement of its strength and direction at many places before it can be defined accurately enough to be of practical use to the navigator. Not only are the magnetic poles offset from the geographical poles, but the magnetic poles themselves are not 180° apart and, in general, a magnetic compass aligned with the lines of force does not point toward either magnetic pole. The magnetic poles are not stationary. The entire magnetic field of the earth, including the magnetic poles, undergoes a small daily or **diurnal change,** and a very slow, progressive **secular change.** In addition, temporary sporadic changes occur from time to time during magnetic storms. During a severe storm, variation may change as much as 5° or more. However, such disturbances are never so rapid as to cause noticeable deflection of the compass card, and in most navigable waters the change is so little that it is not significant in practical navigation. Even when there is no temporary disturbance, the earth's field is considerably more intricate than indicated by an isomagnetic chart (see figure 7.5). Natural magnetic irregularities occurring over relatively small areas are called **magnetic anomalies** by the magneticians, but the navigator generally refers to these phenomena as **local disturbances.**

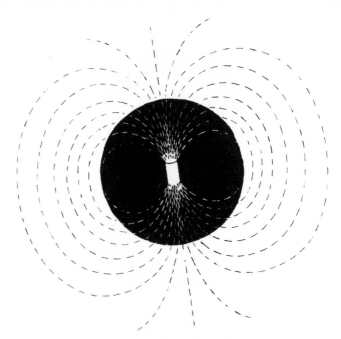

Fig. 7.4. The magnetic field of the earth.

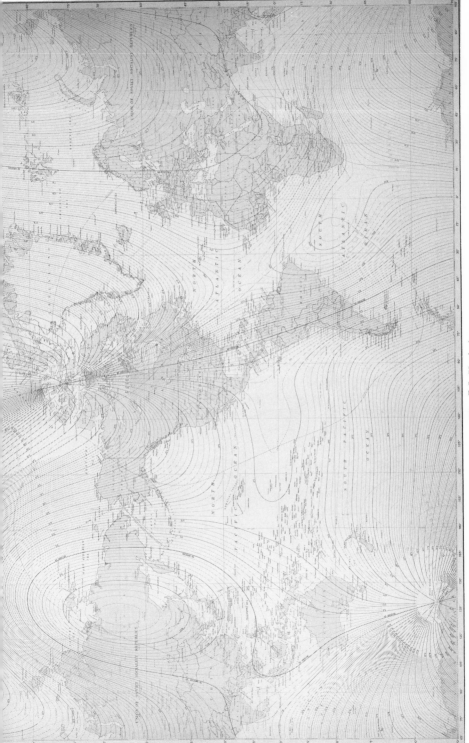

Fig. 7.5. Variation.

Notes warning of such disturbances are shown on charts. In addition, artificial disturbances may be quite severe when a vessel is in close proximity to other vessels, piers, machinery, electric currents, etc.

The elements of the earth's field are as follows:

Total intensity (F) is the strength of the field at any point, measured in a direction parallel to the field. Intensity is usually measured in **oersteds,** one oersted being equal to a force of one dyne acting on a unit pole. The range of intensity of the earth's field is about 0.25 to 0.70 oersted.

Horizontal intensity (H) is the horizontal component of the total intensity. At the **magnetic equator,** which corresponds roughly with the geographic equator, the field is parallel to the surface of the earth, and the horizontal intensity is the same as total intensity. At the magnetic poles of the earth, the field is vertical and there is no horizontal component. The direction of the horizontal component at any place defines the **magnetic meridian** at that place. This component provides the desired directive force of a magnetic compass.

North component (X) is the horizontal intensity's component along a geographic (true) meridian.

East component (Y) is the horizontal intensity's component perpendicular to the north component.

Vertical intensity (Z) is the vertical component of the total intensity. It is zero at the magnetic equator. At the magnetic poles it is the same as the total intensity. While the vertical intensity has no direct effect upon the direction indicated by a magnetic compass, it does induce magnetic fields in vertical soft iron, and these may affect the compass.

Variation (V, Var.), called **declination (D)** by magneticians, is the angle between the geographic and magnetic meridians at any place. The expression **magnetic variation** is used when it is necessary to distinguish this from other forms of variation. This element is measured in angular units and named east or west to indicate the side of true north on which the (magnetic) northerly part of the magnetic meridian lies. For computational purposes, easterly variation is sometimes designated positive $(+)$, and westerly variation negative $(-)$. **Grid variation (GV)** or **grivation** is the angle between the grid and magnetic meridians at any place, measured and named in a manner similar to variation.

Magnetic dip (I), called **inclination (I)** by magneticians, is the vertical angle, expressed in angular units, between the horizontal at any point and a line of force through that point. The **magnetic latitude** of a place is the angle having a tangent equal to half that of the magnetic dip of the place.

At a distance of several hundred miles above the earth's surface, the magnetic field surrounding the earth is believed to be uniform, as it appears in figure 7.4, and centered around two **geomagnetic poles.** These do not coincide with either the magnetic poles or the geographical poles. However, they are 180° apart, the north geomagnetic pole being at latitude

78°5 N, longitude 69° W (near Etah, Greenland) and the south geomagnetic pole being at latitude 78°5 S, longitude 111° E. The great circles through these poles are called **geomagnetic meridians.** That geomagnetic meridian passing through the south geographical pole is the origin for measurement of **geomagnetic longitude,** which is measured eastward through 360°. The complement of the arc of a geomagnetic meridian from the nearer geomagnetic pole to a place is called the **geomagnetic latitude.** When the sun is over the upper branch of the geomagnetic meridian of a place, it is **geomagnetic noon** there, and when it is over the lower branch of the geomagnetic meridian, it is **geomagnetic midnight.** The angle between the lower branch of the geomagnetic meridian of a place and the geomagnetic meridian over which the sun is located is called **geomagnetic time.** The diurnal change is related to geomagnetic time.

Measurement of the earth's magnetic field • Such measurement is made continuously throughout the world. In addition, large numbers of temporary stations are occupied for short periods to add to man's knowledge of the earth's field. In the past, measurements at sea have been made by means of nonmagnetic ships constructed especially for this purpose. However, this is a slow and expensive method, and quite inadequate to survey properly the 71 percent of the earth's surface covered with water. Since World War II, a satisfactory **airborne magnetometer** has been developed by the U.S. Navy. By means of this instrument, continuous readings can be recorded automatically during long overwater flights.

Isomagnetic charts showing lines of equality of some magnetic element are published by the Defense Mapping Agency Hydrographic Center.

The isomagnetic chart of most concern to a navigator shows variation throughout the world. A simplified version is shown in figure 7.5. The lines connecting points of equal magnetic variation are called **isogonic lines.** *These are not magnetic meridians (lines of force).* The line connecting points of zero variation is called the **agonic line.** Variation is also shown on nautical charts. Those of relatively small scale generally show isogonic lines. Those of scale larger than 1:100,000 generally give the information in the form of statements inside compass roses placed at various places on the chart, and sometimes, also, by a **magnetic compass rose** within the true compass rose and offset from it by the amount of the variation. By means of this arrangement, true directions can be plotted without arithmetically applying variation to magnetic directions, or magnetic directions can be read directly from the chart. The magnetic compass rose is generally graduated in both degrees and points. Variation is given to the nearest 15′, and the annual change to the nearest 1′. However, since the rate of change is not constant, a very old chart should not be used, even though it has been corrected for all changes shown in *Notices to Mariners.*

Another isomagnetic chart of value to the mariner shows magnetic dip (fig. 7.6). Lines connecting points of equal magnetic dip are called **isoclinal lines.** The line connecting points of zero dip is called the **magnetic equator.**

Other isomagnetic charts are listed in the DMAHC catalog.

The charts are as accurate as can be made with available information, except that the lines are smoothed somewhat, rather than depicting every small irregularity. The larger irregularities are reflected in the information shown on nautical charts, but local disturbance is indicated by warning notes at appropriate places. In areas where measurements of the magnetic field have not been made for a long period, the previous information is altered in accordance with the best information available on secular change, with some adjustment to provide continuous smooth curves. When information is thus carried forward for many years, errors may be introduced, particularly in areas where the rate of change is large and variable. Magneticians have not detected a recognizable world-wide pattern in secular change, such as would occur if it were due only to shifting of the positions of the magnetic poles. Rather, these shifts are part of the general complex, little-understood secular change.

Compass Error

Magnetic compass error • Directions relative to the northerly direction along a geographic meridian are **true.** In this case, true north is the **reference direction.** If a compass card is horizontal and oriented so that a straight line from its center to 000° points to true north, any direction measured by the card is a true direction and has no error (assuming there is no calibration or observational error). If the card remains horizontal but is rotated so that it points in any other direction, the amount of the rotation is the **compass error.** Stated differently, compass error is the angular difference between true north and **compass north** (the direction north as indicated by a magnetic compass). It is named east or west to indicate the side of true north on which compass north lies.

If a magnetic compass is influenced by no other magnetic field than that of the earth, and there is no instrumental error, its magnets are aligned with the magnetic meridian at the compass, and 000° of the compass card coincides with **magnetic north.** All directions indicated by the card are **magnetic.** As stated earlier, the angle between geographic and magnetic meridians is called **variation.** Therefore, if a compass is aligned with the magnetic meridian, compass error and variation are the same.

When a compass is mounted in a vessel, it is generally subjected to various magnetic influences other than that of the earth. These arise largely from induced magnetism in metal decks, bulkheads, masts, stacks, boat davits, etc., and from electromagnetic fields associated with direct current

Fig. 7.6. Magnetic dip.

in electrical circuits. Some metal in the vicinity of the compass may have acquired permanent magnetism. The actual magnetic field at the compass is the vector sum, or resultant, of all individual fields at that point. Since the direction of this resultant field is generally not the same as that of the earth's field alone, the compass magnets do not lie in the magnetic meridian, but in a direction that makes an angle with it. This angle is called **deviation (D, Dev.).** Thus, deviation is the angular difference between magnetic north and compass north. It is expressed in angular units and named east or west to indicate the side of magnetic north on which compass north lies. Thus, deviation is the error of the compass in pointing to magnetic north, and all directions measured with compass north as the reference direction are **compass directions.** Since variation and deviation may each be either east or west, the effect of deviation may be to either increase or decrease the error due to variation alone. The algebraic sum of variation and deviation is the total compass error.

For computational purposes, deviation and compass error, like variation, may be designated positive ($+$) if east and negative ($-$) if west.

Variation changes with location, as indicated in figure 7.5. Deviation depends upon the magnetic latitude and also upon the individual vessel, its trim and loading, whether it is pitching or rolling, the heading (orientation of the vessel with respect to the earth's magnetic field), and the location of the compass within the vessel. Therefore, deviation is not published on charts.

Deviation table • In practice aboard ship, the deviation is reduced to a minimum, as explained later in this chapter. The remaining value, called **residual deviation,** is determined on various headings and recorded in some form of **deviation table** showing the deviation for each magnetic heading. Sometimes, in the U.S. Navy, for example, a standard form is used. If the deviation is not more than about 2° on any heading, satisfactory results may be obtained by entering the values at intervals of 45° only.

If the deviation is small, no appreciable error is introduced by entering the table with either magnetic or compass heading. If the deviation on some headings is large, the desirable action is to reduce it, but if this is not practicable, a separate deviation table for compass heading entry may be useful. This may be made by applying the tabulated deviation to each entry value of magnetic heading, to find the corresponding compass heading, and then interpolating between these to find the value of deviation at each 15° compass heading. Another method is to plot the values on cross-section paper and select the desired values graphically.

Another solution is to make a deviation table with one column for magnetic heading, a second column for deviation, and a third for compass heading. Still another solution, most popular among yachtsmen, is to center a compass rose inside a larger one so that an open space is between them and a radial line would connect points of the same graduation on both roses. Each magnetic heading for which deviation has been determined is located on the outer rose, and a straight line is drawn from this point to the corresponding compass heading on the inner rose.

A variation of this method is to draw two parallel lines a short distance apart, and graduate each from 0 to 360 so that a perpendicular between the two lines connects points of the same graduation. Straight lines are drawn from magnetic directions on one line to the corresponding compass directions on the other. If the lines are horizontal and the upper one represents magnetic directions, the slope of the line indicates the direction of the deviation. That is, for westerly deviation the upper part of the connecting line is left (west) of the bottom part, and for easterly deviation it is right.

An important point to remember regarding deviation is that it varies with the *heading*. Therefore, a deviation table is *never* entered with a bearing. If the deviation table converts directly from one type heading to another, deviation is found by taking the difference between the two values. On the compass rose or straight-line type, the deviation can be written alongside the connecting line, and the intermediate values determined by estimate. If one has trouble determining whether to add or subtract deviation when bearings are involved, he has only to note which heading, magnetic or compass, is larger. The same relationship holds between the two values of bearing.

The deviation table should be protected from damage due to handling or weather, and placed in a position where it will always be available when needed. A method commonly used is to mount it on a board, cover it with shellac or varnish, and attach it to the binnacle. Another method is to post it under glass near the compass. It is good practice for the navigator to keep a second copy available at a convenient place.

Applying variation and deviation • As indicated, a single direction may have any of several numerical values depending upon the reference direction used. One should keep clearly in mind the relationship between the various expressions of a direction. Thus, true and magnetic directions differ by the variation, magnetic and compass directions differ by the deviation, and true and compass directions differ by the compass error.

If variation or deviation is easterly, the compass card is rotated in a clockwise direction. This brings smaller numbers opposite the lubber's line. Conversely, if either error is westerly, the rotation is counterclockwise and larger numbers are brought opposite the lubber's line. Thus, if the heading is 090° true (fig. 7.7, A) and variation is 6° E, the magnetic heading is 090° —6°=084° (fig. 7.7, B). If the deviation on this heading is 2° W, the compass heading is 084°+2°=086° (fig. 7.7, C). Also, compass error is 6° E—2° W=4° E, and compass heading is 090°—4°=086°. If compass error is easterly, the compass reads too low (in comparison with true directions), and if it is westerly, the reading is too high. Many rules-of-thumb have been devised as an aid to the memory, and any which assist in applying compass errors in the right direction are of value. However, one may forget the rule or its method of application, or may wish to have an independent check. If he understands the explanation given above, he can determine the correct sign without further information. Since variation and deviation are compass errors, the process of removing either from an indication of a direction (converting compass to magnetic or magnetic to true) is often called **correcting.** Conversion in the opposite direction (inserting errors) is then called **uncorrecting.**

Deviation and Its Reduction

Magnetism of a steel vessel • The materials of which a vessel is constructed are not, in general, selected for their magnetic properties. As a result, many degrees of permeability, remanence, and coercivity exist within its structure. Detailed analysis of the complex field existing at a magnetic compass is a specialized study not ordinarily required of the navigator. However, a general knowledge of the basic principles involved is of value to the navigator in helping him understand better the behavior of his magnetic compasses.

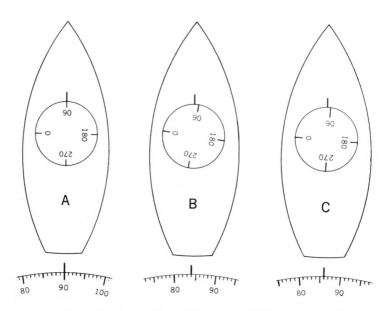

Fig. 7.7. Effect of variation and deviation on the compass card.

For most purposes, a vessel can be considered to be composed of two types of material: "hard iron" and "soft iron."

"Hard iron" is all material having some degree of permanent magnetism. This magnetism is acquired largely during construction of the vessel, when the rearrangement of the domains is facilitated by the bending, riveting, welding, and other violent mechanical processes. Since a vessel remains on a constant magnetic heading while it is on the building ways, a field of permanent magnetism becomes established, the positions of the poles being dependent largely upon the orientation of the hull with respect to the magnetic field of the earth.

The "permanent" magnetism thus acquired during construction is less permanent than that of a permanent magnet such as one of those used in a compass, and is modified somewhat after launching, particularly if the vessel remains on another heading for a considerable time during fitting out. The change is especially rapid during the first few days after launching, when the domains of the softer iron become reoriented. At this stage, deviation due to permanent magnetism may change several degrees. Further changes in the permanent magnetism may occur during long periods of being tied up or moored on a constant heading, or during a run of several days on nearly the same heading. This change is gradual and affects the strength, but usually not the polarity, of the magnetic field. The permanent field may be changed quickly, in polarity as well as in strength, if the vessel grounds, collides with another vessel, is struck by lightning, etc.

The effect that the permanent magnetism of hard iron has upon a compass depends upon the position and strength of the poles relative to the compass. When the poles are in line with the north-south axis of the compass card, the only effect is to strengthen or weaken the directive force of the compass. When the compass heading is approximately 90° away, so that the poles are east and west of the compass, the deviating effect is maximum. The direction of the deviation is the same as that of the blue pole with respect to the compass.

"Soft iron" is all that material in which induced magnetism is present. With respect to its effect upon the magnetic compass, it is classed as either vertical or horizontal. Unlike hard iron, its magnetic field changes quickly as its orientation with respect to the earth's field changes. It also changes as the strength of the earth's field changes. For some purposes induced magnetism can be treated as if it were concentrated in two bars of soft iron, one vertical and the other horizontal. The polarity depends upon the position of the vessel relative to the earth's magnetic field, and the strength depends upon the strength of the vertical and horizontal components of the earth's field. In north magnetic latitude the bottom of the vertical rod has red magnetism and the top has blue magnetism. In south magnetic latitude these are reversed. In both north and south magnetic latitudes the magnetic north end of the horizontal bar has red magnetism, and the magnetic south end has blue magnetism. Thus, whatever the position of the rod, that part in the direction of magnetic north has red magnetism, and that part in the direction of magnetic south has blue magnetism. That is, each end has magnetism opposite to that of the magnetic pole indicated by the direction in which it is pointed.

The effect upon a magnetic compass of the induced magnetism in soft iron depends upon the strength and direction of the field relative to the compass. The cumulative effect of the induced magnetism in vertical soft iron is generally on the center line of the vessel (if of conventional construction), and for a compass located forward, as on the bridge, is aft of the compass. In magnetic north latitude the effect is generally that of a blue pole at the level of the compass card. In magnetic south latitude the pole is red. On a heading of compass north or south the pole is in line with the magnets of a center line compass and serves only to strengthen or weaken the directive force. On a heading of compass east or west the pole is perpendicular to the north-south axis of the compass card, and the deviating force is greatest.

For a compass located on the center line of a vessel of conventional construction, the horizontal soft iron close enough to have appreciable effect upon the compass is arranged in a more-or-less symmetrical manner with respect to the compass. Thus, on any cardinal compass heading, the fore-and-aft and athwartship horizontal soft iron is either in line with the compass magnets or equally and similarly arranged on both sides. No error is introduced by such symmetrical horizontal soft iron because the iron north and south of the compass magnets serves only to strengthen or weaken the directive force, and that east and west of the compass sets up an equal and opposite field on each side. On intercardinal headings, the poles of the induced magnetism are offset and a maximum deviating force occurs. That part of horizontal soft iron which is not symmetrically arranged with respect to the compass—the asymmetrical soft iron—produces deviation which is maximum on the cardinal headings and zero on the intercardinal headings (by compass). This type of deviation is particularly great in a compass not mounted on the center line of the vessel. It may also produce deviation which is constant on all headings.

In nonsteel vessels such as certain yachts and small fishing vessels, one or more of these types of magnetism may be weak or entirely missing, but this does not justify the omission of any part of the correction procedure.

As far as its effect upon the compass is concerned, the magnetic field at a center line compass located forward on a vessel of conventional construction, and on an even keel, is essentially the same as that which would result from four sources: (1) the earth's magnetism; (2) a single blue pole the location and strength of which depends upon the magnetic history of the vessel; (3) a single pole which is blue in north magnetic latitude and red in south magnetic latitude, is on the center line aft of the compass, and increases in strength with higher magnetic latitude; and (4) a single blue pole on the starboard side for easterly headings and on the port side for westerly headings, being of zero strength on a heading of north or south and decreasing in strength with increased magnetic latitudes. The single pole concept assumes that the effect of one pole predominates. The locations of the poles depend partly upon the position of the compass to which they apply. The actual field surrounding any magnetic compass may be considerably more complex than indicated.

Compass adjustment • There are at least two possible solutions to the problem of compass error. The error can be permitted to remain, and the various directions interconverted by means of variation and deviation, or compass error, as explained earlier, or the error can be removed. In practice, a combination of both of these methods is used.

Variation depends upon location of the vessel, and the navigator has no control over it. Provision could be made for offsetting the lubber's line, but this would not be effective in correcting magnetic compass bearings, and this practice is not generally followed. Variation does not affect the operation of the compass itself, and so is not objectionable from this standpoint.

Deviation is undesirable because it is more troublesome to apply, and the magnetic field which causes it partly neutralizes the directive force acting upon the compass, causing it to be unsteady and sluggish. As the vessel rolls and pitches, or as it changes magnetic latitude, the magnetic field changes, producing a corresponding change in the deviation of an unadjusted compass.

Deviation is eliminated, as nearly as practicable, by introducing at the compass a magnetic field that is equal in magnitude and opposite in polarity to that of the vessel. This process is called **compass adjustment,** or sometimes **compass compensation.**

In general, the introduced field is of the same kind of magnetism as well as of the same intensity as those of the field causing deviation. That is, permanent magnets are used to neutralize permanent magnetism, and soft iron to neutralize induced magnetism, so that the adjustment remains effective with changes of heading and magnetic latitude. A relatively small mass of iron near the compass introduces a field equal to that of a much larger mass at a distance.

When a compass is properly adjusted, its remaining or **residual deviation** is small and practically constant at various magnetic latitudes, the directive force is as strong as is obtainable on all headings, and the compass returns quickly from deflections and is comparatively steady as the vessel rolls and pitches.

Effect of latitude • As indicated earlier, the magnetic field of the earth is horizontal at the magnetic equator, and vertical at the magnetic poles, the change occurring gradually as a vessel proceeds away from the magnetic equator. At any place the relative strength of the horizontal and vertical components depends upon the magnetic dip. The directive force of a magnetic compass, provided by the horizontal component of the earth's magnetic field, is maximum on or near the magnetic equator and gradually decreases to zero at the magnetic poles. Within a certain area surrounding each magnetic pole the directive force is so weak that the compass is unreliable.

Deviation changes with a change of the relative strength of either the deviating force or the directive force. Thus, with *either* an increase in deviating force or a decrease in directive force, the deviation increases. However, if both the deviating and directive forces change by the same proportion, and with the same sign, there is no change in deviation. Also, if a deviating force is neutralized by an equal and opposite force *of the same kind*, there is no change of deviation with a change of magnetic latitude.

Permanent magnetism is the same at any latitude. If the permanent magnetism of the vessel is neutralized by properly placed permanent magnets of the correct strength, a change of magnetic latitude can be made without introduction of deviation. But if residual deviation due to permanent magnetism is present, it increases with a change to higher latitude. The deviating force remains unchanged while the directive force decreases, resulting in an increase in the relative strength of the deviating force.

As magnetic latitude increases, the vertical component of the earth's magnetic field becomes stronger, increasing the amount of induced magnetism in vertical soft iron. At the same time the directive force of the compass decreases. Both effects result in increased deviation unless the deviating force is neutralized by induced magnetism in vertical soft iron.

As magnetic latitude increases, the induced magnetism in the horizontal soft iron decreases in the same proportion as the decrease in the directive force of the compass, since both are produced by the horizontal component of the earth's magnetic field. Therefore, any deviation due to this cause is the same at any latitude.

Parameters • Compass adjustment might be accomplished by locating the pole of each magnetic field, and establishing another pole of opposite polarity and equal intensity at the same place, or of less intensity and nearer to the compass; or a pole of opposite polarity and suitable intensity might be established at the correct distance on the opposite side of the compass. Thus, a blue pole east of a compass attracts the red northern ends of the compass magnets and repels the blue southern ends. Both effects cause rotation of the compass magnets and the attached compass card in a clockwise direction, producing easterly deviation. Either a red pole east of a compass, or a blue pole west of it, causes westerly deviation. If there are two fields of opposite polarity, one will tend to neutralize the other. If the intensities of the two fields are equal at the compass, one will cancel the other, and no deviation occurs.

Because of the complexities of the magnetic field of a vessel, and the fact that each individual field making up the total is present continuously, the process of isolating individual poles would be a difficult and time-consuming one. Fortunately, this is unnecessary. The vessel's field is resolved into certain specified components. Each of these components, called **parameters,** regardless of its origin or the number of individual fields contributing to it, can be neutralized separately.*

Effect of compass location • The location of a magnetic compass greatly influences the amount and type of deviation, as well as the adjustment. Thus, if a compass is on the center line, forward, the effective pole of vertical soft iron is aft of it; but if the compass is in the after part of the vessel, the effective pole is forward. If the compass is not on the center line, the magnetic field of the vessel is not symmetrical with respect to the compass. If a compass is located in a steel pilot house, the surrounding metal acts as a shield and reduces the strength of the magnetic field of the earth. This is of particular significance in high magnetic latitudes, where the directive force is weak.

A compass should not be placed off the center line if it can be placed on the center line and still serve its purpose. It should not be placed near iron or steel equipment that will frequently be moved, if this can be avoided. The immediate vicinity should be kept free from sources of deviation—particularly those of a changing nature—if this can be done. Some sources which might be overlooked are electric wires carrying direct current; magnetic instruments, searchlights, windshield wipers, electronic equipment, or motors; steel control rods, gears, or supports associated with the steering apparatus; fire extinguishers; and metal coat hangers, flashlights, keys, pocketknives, or nylon clothing. The effect of some items such as an ammeter or electric windshield wiper varies considerably at different times. If direct current is used to light the compass, the wires should be twisted.

A magnetic compass cannot be expected to give reliable service unless it is properly installed and protected from disturbing magnetic influences.

The binnacle • The compass is housed in a **binnacle.** This may vary from a simple wooden box to an elaborate device of bronze or other nonmag-

---

* Since few yachtsmen will be doing their own correcting for magnetic fields of this complexity, further details will not be given.

netic material. Most binnacles provide means for housing or supporting the various objects used for compass adjustment.

Adjustment

Preliminary steps • Efficient and accurate adjustment is preceded by certain preliminary steps best made while a vessel is tied up or at anchor.

The magnetic environment of the compass should be carefully inspected. Stray magnetic influences should be eliminated. Permanently installed equipment of magnetic material should be placed in the positions they normally occupy at sea.

The compass itself should be checked carefully for bubbles, and to be sure it is centered on the vertical axis of the binnacle. An adjustment should be made to the gimbal rings if the compass is off center. There should be no play in the position of the compass once it is centered.

The lubber's line, too, should be checked to be sure it is in line with the longitudinal axis of the vessel, as should the lubber's line of any other instrument to be used in determining deviation.

Plans for the actual adjustment should be made carefully. A suitable time and location should be selected. If landmarks are to be used, suitable ones should be selected to provide the information desired. Areas of heavy traffic should be avoided. Any necessary recording and work forms should be made up. Each person to participate in the adjustment should be instructed regarding the general plan and his specific duties.*

* Ed. note: A correctly adjusted compass is a necessity for accurate piloting. The procedure outlined in Bowditch is much too complex for the layman and is pertinent mainly for very large vessels. Compass adjustment even on a small yacht is difficult, and it is recommended that the yachtsman engage the services of a professional adjuster.

[8]

Dead Reckoning

Introduction • **Dead reckoning** (**DR**) is the determination of position by advancing a known position for courses and distances. It is reckoning relative to something stationary or "dead" in the water, and hence applies to courses and speeds *through the water*. Because of leeway due to wind, inaccurate allowance for compass error, imperfect steering, or error in measuring speed, the actual motion through the water is seldom determined with complete accuracy. In addition, if the water itself is in motion, the course and speed over the bottom differ from those through the water. It is good practice to use the true course *steered* and the best determination of *measured* speed, which is normally speed *through the water*, for dead reckoning. Hence, geographically, a **dead reckoning position** is an approximate one which is corrected from time to time as the opportunity presents itself. Although of less than the desired accuracy, dead reckoning is the only method by which a position can be determined at *any* time and therefore might be considered *basic* navigation, with all other methods only appendages to provide means for correcting the dead reckoning. The prudent navigator keeps his direction- and speed- or distance-measuring instruments in top condition and accurately calibrated, for his dead reckoning is no more accurate than his measurement of these elements.

If a navigator can accurately assess the disturbing elements introducing geographical errors into his dead reckoning, he can determine a better position than that established by dead reckoning alone. This is properly called an **estimated position** (**EP**). It may be established either by applying an estimated correction to a dead reckoning position, or by estimating the course and speed being made good over the bottom. The expression "dead reckoning" is sometimes applied loosely to such reckoning, but it is better practice to keep this "estimated reckoning" distinct from dead reckoning, if for no other reason than to provide a basis for evaluating the accuracy of one's estimates. When good information regarding current, wind, etc., is available, it should be used, but the practice of applying corrections based upon information of uncertain accuracy is, at best, questionable, and may introduce an error. Estimates should be based upon judgment and experience. Positional information which is incomplete or of uncertain accuracy may be available to assist in making the estimate. However, before adequate experience is gained, one should be cautious in applying corrections, for the estimates of the inexperienced are often quite inaccurate.

Dead reckoning not only provides means for continuously establishing an approximate position, but also is of assistance in determining times of sunrise and sunset, the predicted availability of electronic aids to navigation, the suitability and interpretation of soundings for checking position, the predicted times of making landfalls or sighting lights, and estimates of arrival times, and in evaluating the reliability and accuracy of position-determining information. Because of the importance of accurate dead reckoning, a careful log is kept of all courses and speeds, times of all changes, and compass errors. These may be recorded directly in the log or first in a **navigator's notebook** for later recording in the log, but whatever the form, a careful record is important.

Modern navigators almost invariably keep their dead reckoning by plotting directly on the chart or plotting sheet, drawing lines to represent the direction and distance of travel and indicating dead reckoning and estimated positions from time to time. This method is simple and direct. Large errors are often apparent as inconsistencies in an otherwise regular plot.

Plotting position on the chart • A position is usually expressed in units of latitude and longitude, generally to the nearest 0.1, but it may be expressed as bearing and distance from a known position, such as a landmark or aid to navigation.

To plot a position on a Mercator chart, or to determine the coordinates of a point on such a chart, proceed as follows:

To plot a position when its latitude and longitude are known: Mark the given latitude on a convenient latitude scale along a meridian, being careful to note the unit of the smallest division on the scale. Place a straightedge at this point and parallel to a parallel of latitude (perpendicular to a meridian). Holding the straightedge in place, set one point of a pair of dividers at the given longitude on the longitude scale at the top or bottom of the chart (or along any parallel) and the other at a convenient printed meridian. Without changing the spread of the dividers, place one point on the same printed meridian at the edge of the straightedge, and the second point at the edge of the straightedge in the direction of the given longitude. This second point is at the given position. *Lightly* prick the chart. Remove first the straightedge and then the dividers, watching the point to be sure of identifying it. Make a dot at the point, enclose it with a small circle or square as appropriate (a circle for a fix or a DR position; a square for an EP), and label it. If the dividers are set to the correct spread for longitude *before* the latitude is marked, one point of the dividers can be used to locate the latitude and place the straightedge, if one is careful not to disturb the setting of the dividers.

To determine the coordinates of a point on the chart: Place a straightedge at the given point and parallel to a parallel of latitude. Read the latitude where the straightedge crosses a latitude scale. Keeping the straightedge in place, set one leg of a pair of dividers at the given point and the other at the intersection of the straightedge and a convenient printed meridian. Without changing the spread of the dividers, place one end on a longitude scale, at the same printed meridian, and the other point on the scale, in the direction of the given point. Read the longitude at this second point.

Several variations of these procedures may suggest themselves. That method which seems most natural and is least likely to result in error should be used.

Measuring direction on the chart • Since the Mercator chart, commonly used by the marine navigator, is *conformal*, directions and angles are correctly represented. It is customary to orient the chart with 000° (north) at the top; other directions are in their correct relations to north and each other.

As an aid in measuring direction, **compass roses** are placed at convenient places on the chart or plotting sheet. A desired direction can be measured by placing a straightedge along the line from the center of a compass rose to the circular graduation representing the desired direction. The straightedge is then in the desired direction, which may be transferred to any other part of the chart by parallel motion, as by parallel rulers or two triangles (see Chapter 6). The direction between two points is determined by transferring that direction to a compass rose. If a drafting machine or some form of plotter or protractor is used, measurement can be made directly at the desired point, without using the compass rose.

Measurement of direction, whether or not by compass rose, can be made at any convenient place on a Mercator chart, since meridians are parallel to each other and a line making a desired angle with any one makes the same angle with all others. Such a line is a **rhumb line,** the kind commonly used for course lines, except in polar regions. For direction on a chart having nonparallel meridians, measurement can be made at the meridian involved if the chart is conformal, or by special technique if it is not. The only nonconformal chart commonly used by navigators is the gnomonic, and instructions for measuring direction on this chart are usually given on the chart itself.

Compass roses for both true and magnetic directions may be given. A drafting machine can be oriented to any reference direction—true, magnetic, compass, or grid. When a plotter or protractor is used for measuring an angle with respect to a meridian, the resulting direction is true unless other than true meridians are used. For most purposes of navigation it is good practice to plot true directions only, and to label them in true coordinates.

Measuring distance on the chart • The length of a line on a chart is usually measured in nautical miles, to the nearest 0.1 mile. For this purpose it is customary to use the latitude scale, considering one minute of latitude equal to one nautical mile. The error introduced by this assumption is not great over distances normally measured. It is maximum near the equator or geographical poles.

Since the latitude scale on a Mercator chart expands with increased latitude, measurement should be made at approximately the mid latitude. For a chart covering a relatively small area, such as a harbor chart, this precaution is not important because of the slight difference in scale over the chart. On such charts a separate mile scale may be given, and it may safely be used over the entire chart. However, habit is strong, and mistakes can probably be avoided by *always* using the mid latitude.

For long distances the line should be broken into a number of parts or *legs*, each one being measured at its mid latitude. The length of a line that should be measured in a single step varies with latitude, decreasing in higher latitudes. No realistic numerical value can be given, since there are too many considerations. With experience a navigator determines this for himself. On the larger scale charts this is not a problem because the usual dividers used for this purpose will not span an excessively long distance.

In measuring distance, the navigator spans with his dividers the length of the line to be measured and then, without altering the setting, transfers this length to the latitude scale, carefully noting the graduations so as to avoid an error in reading. This precaution is needed because of the difference from chart to chart. In measuring a desired length along a line, the navigator spans this length on the latitude scale opposite the line and then transfers his dividers to the line, without changing the setting. For a long line the navigator sets his dividers to some convenient distance and steps off the line, counting the number of steps, multiplying this by the length of the step, and adding any remainder. If the line extends over a sufficient spread of latitude to make scale difference a factor, he resets his dividers to the scale for the approximate mid latitude of each leg. The distance so measured is the length of the rhumb line.

For measuring distance on a nearly-constant-scale chart, such as the Lambert conformal, the mid-latitude precaution is usually unnecessary. Such charts generally have a mile scale independent of the latitude scale. On a gnomonic chart a special procedure is needed, and this is usually explained on the chart.

Plotting and labeling the course line and positions • **Course** is the intended horizontal direction of travel. A **course line** is a line extending in the direction of the course. From a known position of the ship the course line is drawn in the direction indicated by the course. It is good practice to label all lines and points of significance as they are drawn, for an unlabeled line or point can easily be misinterpreted later. Any simple, clear, logical, unambiguous system of labels is suitable. The following is widely used and might well be considered standard.

Label a course line with direction and speed. *Above* the course line place a capital C followed by three figures to indicate the course steered. It is customary to label and steer courses to the nearest whole degree. The course label should indicate *true* direction, starting with 000° at true north and increasing clockwise through 360°. *Below* the course line, and under the direction label, place a capital S followed by figures representing the speed in knots. Since the course is *always* given in degrees true and the speed in knots, it is not necessary to indicate the units or the reference direction (figure 8.1).

A point to be labeled is enclosed by a small circle in the case of a **fix** (an accurate position determined without reference to any former position) or dead reckoning position, and by a small square in the case of an estimated position. It is labeled with the time, usually to the nearest minute, and the nature of the position (FIX, EP, DR). Time is usually expressed in four figures without punctuation, on a 24-hour basis. Zone time is usually used, but Greenwich mean time may be employed. A course line is a succession of an infinite number of dead reckoning positions. Only selected points are labeled.

The labels of a *line* are placed *along* the line, and those of a *point* are at an *angle to the line*.

Dead reckoning by plot • As a vessel clears a harbor and proceeds out to sea, the navigator obtains one last good fix while identifiable landmarks

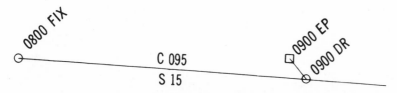

Fig. 8.1. A course line with labels.

are still available. This is called **taking departure,** and the position determined is called the **departure.** Piloting (see Chapter 9) comes to an end, and the course is set for the open sea. The course line is drawn and labeled, and some future position is indicated as a DR position. The number of points selected for labeling depends primarily upon the judgment and individual preference of the navigator. It is good practice to label each point where a change of course or speed occurs. If such changes are frequent, no additional points need be labeled. With infrequent changes, it is good practice to label points at some regular interval, as every two hours. From departure, the dead reckoning plot continues unbroken until a new well-established position is obtained, when both DR and fix are shown. The fix serves as the start of a new dead reckoning plot. Although estimated positions are shown, it is generally not good practice to begin a new DR at these points.

A typical dead reckoning plot is shown in figure 8.2, indicating procedures both when there are numerous changes of course and speed and when there is a long continuous course. It is assumed that no fix is

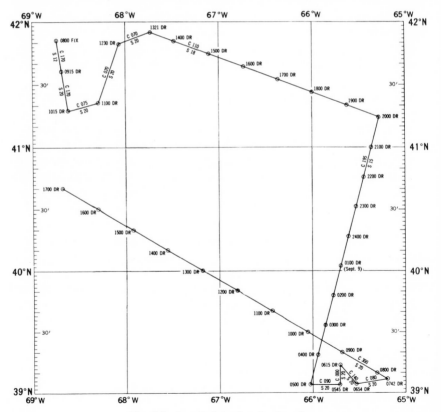

Fig. 8.2. A typical dead reckoning plot.

obtained after the initial one at 0800 on September 8. Note that course lines are not extended beyond their limits of usefulness. One should keep a neat plot and leave no doubt as to the meaning of each line and marked point. *A neat, accurate plot is the mark of a good navigator.* The plot should be kept extended to some future time. A good navigator is always ahead of his ship. In shoal water or when near the shore, aids to navigation, dangers, etc., it is customary to keep the dead reckoning plot on a chart. A chart overprinted with loran or other electronic position lines may be used at a considerable distance from shore.

Current • Water in essentially horizontal motion over the surface of the earth is called **current.** The direction in which the water is moving is called the **set,** and the speed is called the **drift.** In navigation it is customary to use the term "current" to include all factors introducing geographical error in the dead reckoning, whether their immediate effects are on the vessel or the water. When a fix is obtained, one assumes that the current has set *from* the DR position at the same time *to* the fix, and that the drift is equal to the distance in miles between these positions, divided by the number of hours since the last fix. This is true regardless of the number of changes of course or speed since the last fix.

If set and drift since the last fix are known, or can be estimated, a better position can be obtained by applying a correction to that obtained by dead reckoning. This is conveniently done by drawing a straight line in the direction of the set for a distance equal to the drift multiplied by the number of hours since the last fix, as shown in figure 8.1. The direction of a straight line from the last fix to the EP is the estimated **course made good,** and the length of this line divided by the time is the estimated **speed made good.** These estimated values are sometimes called the **course of advance (COA)** and **speed of advance (SOA),** respectively. The course and speed actually made good over the ground are then called the **course over the ground (COG)** and **speed over the ground (SOG),** respectively.

If a current is setting in the same direction as the course, or its reciprocal, the course over the ground is the same as that through the water. The effect on the speed can be found by simple arithmetic. If the course and set are in the same direction, the speeds are added; if in opposite directions, the smaller is subtracted from the larger. This situation is not unusual when a ship encounters a tidal current while entering or leaving port. If a ship is *crossing* a current, solution can be made graphically by vector diagram (see figs. 8.3–8.5) since velocity over the ground is the vector sum of velocity *through* the water and velocity *of* the water.* Although *distances* can be used, it is generally easier to use *speeds.*

---

* A vector quantity has both *magnitude* and *direction.* Therefore, if a vessel is traveling x knots on course y, the combination of x knots and course y constitutes a vector quantity.

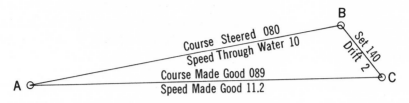

Fig. 8.3. Finding course and speed made good through a current.

Example 1. A ship on course 080°, speed ten knots, is steaming through a current having an estimated set of 140° and drift of two knots.

Required. Estimated course and speed made good.

Solution (fig. 8.3). (1) From *A*, any convenient point, draw *AB*, the course and speed of the ship, in direction 080°, for a distance of ten miles.

(2) From *B* draw *BC*, the set and drift of the current, in direction 140°, for a distance of two miles.

(3) The direction and length of *AC* are the estimated course and speed made good. Determine these by measurement.

Answers. Estimated course made good 089°, estimated speed made good 11.2 kn.

If it is required to find the course to steer at a given speed to make good a desired course, plot the current vector from the origin, *A*, instead of from *B*.

Example 2. The captain desires to make good a course of 095° through a current having a set of 170° and a drift of 2.5 knots, using a speed of 12 knots.

Required. The course to steer and the speed made good.

Solution (fig. 8.4). (1) From *A*, any convenient point, draw line *AB* extending in the direction of the course to be made good, 095°.

(2) From *A* draw *AC*, the set and drift of the current.

(3) Using *C* as a center, swing an arc of radius *CD*, the speed through the water (12 knots), intersecting line *AB* at *D*.

(4) Measure the direction of line *CD*, 083°.5. This the course to steer.

(5) Measure the length *AD*, 12.4 knots. This is the speed made good.

Answers. Course to steer 084°.5, speed made good 12.4 kn.

If it is required to find the course to steer and the speed to use to make good a desired course and speed, proceed as follows:

Example 3. The captain desires to make good a course of 265° and

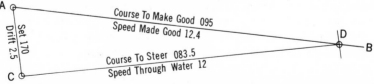

Fig. 8.4. Finding the course to steer at a given speed to make good a given course through a current.

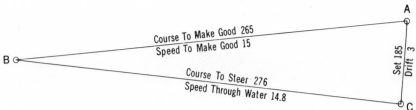

Fig. 8.5. *Finding the course to steer and the speed to use to make good a given course and speed through a current.*

a speed of 15 knots through a current having a set of 185° and a drift of three knots.

Required. The course to steer and the speed to use.

Solution (fig. 8.5). (1) From *A*, any convenient point, draw *AB* in the direction of the course to be made good, 265°, and for a length equal to the speed to be made good, 15 knots.

(2) From *A* draw *AC*, the set and drift of the current.

(3) Draw a straight line from *C* to *B*. The direction of this line, 276°, is the required course to steer; and the length, 14.8 knots, is the required speed.

Answers. Course to steer 276°, speed to use 14.8 kn.

Such vector solutions can be made to any convenient scale and at any convenient place, such as the center of a compass rose, an unused corner of the plotting sheet, a separate sheet, or directly on the plot.

Leeway • Leeway is the leeward motion of a vessel due to wind. It may be expressed as distance, speed, or angular difference between course steered and course through the water. However expressed, its amount varies with the speed and relative direction of the wind, type of vessel, amount of freeboard, trim, speed of the vessel, state of the sea, and depth of water. If information on the amount of leeway to be expected under various conditions is not available for the type vessel involved, it should be determined by observation. When sufficient data have been collected, suitable tables or graphs can be made for quick and convenient estimate. The accuracy of the information should be checked whenever convenient, and corrections made when sufficient evidence indicates the need.

Leeway is most conveniently applied by adding its effect to that of current and other elements introducing geographical error in the dead reckoning. It is customary to consider the combined effect of all such elements as current, and to make allowance for this as explained in the preceding section. In sailing ship days it was common practice to consider leeway in terms of its effect upon the course only, and to.apply it as a correction in the same manner that variation and deviation are applied. While this method has merit even with power vessels, it is generally considered inferior to that of considering leeway as part of current.

Automatic dead reckoning • Several types of devices are in use for performing automatically all or part of the dead reckoning, but few are used by coastal pilots.

Dead reckoning by computation • Dead reckoning involves the determination of position by means of course and distance from a known position. A closely related problem is that of finding the course and distance from one point to another. Although both of these problems are customarily solved by plotting directly on the chart, it occasionally becomes desirable to solve by computation, usually by logarithms or traverse table.*

* Because the coastal pilot is not likely to be out of sight of land for long periods, however, dead reckoning by plot should serve his purposes.

[9]

Piloting

Introduction • On the high seas, where there is no immediate danger of grounding, navigation is a comparatively leisurely process. Courses and speeds are maintained over relatively long periods, and fixes are obtained at convenient intervals. Under favorable conditions a vessel might continue for several days with no positions other than those obtained by dead reckoning, or by estimate, and with no anxiety on the part of the captain or navigator. Errors in position can usually be detected and corrected before danger threatens.

In the vicinity of shoal water the situation is different. Frequent or continuous positional information is usually essential to the safety of the vessel. An error which at sea may be considered small may in pilot waters be intolerably large. Frequent changes of course and speed are common. The proximity of other vessels increases the possibility of collision. Navigation under these conditions is called **piloting** or **pilotage.**

No other form of navigation requires the continuous alertness needed in piloting. At no other time is navigational experience and judgment so valuable. The ability to work rapidly and to correctly interpret all available information, always keeping "ahead of the vessel," may mean the difference between safety and disaster.

In piloting, positions are commonly obtained by reference to nearby landmarks, or the bottom. Advancements in electronics have provided additional aids which are of particular value in piloting, and have extended the range of piloting techniques far to sea.

Preparation for piloting • Because the time element is often of vital importance in piloting, adequate preparation is important. Long-range preparation includes the acquisition of a thorough knowledge of the methods and techniques of piloting, and the organization and training of those who will assist in any way. This includes the helmsman, who will be granted less tolerance in straying from the prescribed course than when farther offshore.

The more immediate preparation includes a study of the charts and publications of the area to familiarize oneself with the channels, shoals, tides, currents, aids to navigation, etc. One seldom has time to seek such information once he is proceeding in pilot waters.

Position

Lines of position • Piloting makes extensive use of **lines of position.** Such a line is one on some point of which the vessel may be presumed to be located, as a result of observation or measurement. It may be highly reliable, or of questionable accuracy. Lines of position are of great value, but one should always keep in mind that *they can be in error* because of imperfections in instruments used for obtaining them and human limitations in those who use the instruments and utilize the results. The extent to which one can have confidence in various lines of position is a matter of judgment acquired from experience.

A line of position might be a straight line (actually a part of a great circle), an arc of a circle, or part of some other curve. An appropriate label should be placed on the plot of a line of position *at the time it is drawn*, to avoid possible error or confusion. A label should include all information essential for identification, but no extraneous information. The labels shown in this volume are recommended.

Bearings • A **bearing** is the horizontal direction of one terrestrial point from another. It is usually expressed as the angular difference between a reference direction and the given direction. In navigation, north is generally used as the reference direction, and angles are measured clockwise through 360°. It is customary to express all bearings in three digits, using preliminary zeros where needed. Thus, north is 000° or 360°, a direction 7° to the right of north is 007°, east is 090°, southwest is 225°, etc.

For plotting, *true* north is used as the reference direction. A bearing measured from this reference is called a **true bearing (TB).** A **magnetic, compass,** or **grid bearing (MB, CB,** or **GB)** results from using magnetic, compass, or grid north, respectively, as the reference direction. This is similar to the designation of courses. In the case of bearings, however, one additional reference direction is often convenient. This is the heading of the ship. A bearing expressed as angular distance from the heading is called a **relative bearing (RB).** It is usually measured clockwise through

360°, but for some purposes it is more conveniently measured either clockwise or counterclockwise through 180°, and designated *right* or *left*, respectively. A relative bearing may be expressed in still another way, as indicated in figure 9.1. Except for dead ahead and points at 45° intervals from it, this method is used principally for indicating directions obtained visually, without precise measurement. An even more general indication of relative bearing may be given by such directions as "ahead," "on the starboard bow," "on the port quarter," "astern." The term *abeam* may be used as the equivalent of either the general "on the beam" or, sometimes, the more precise "broad on the beam." Degrees are sometimes used instead of points to express relative bearings by the system illustrated in figure 9.1. However, if degrees are used, a better practice is to use the 360° or 180° system. Thus, a relative bearing of "20° forward of the port beam" is better expressed as "290°," or "70° left."

True, magnetic, and compass bearings are interconverted by the use of variation and deviation, or compass error, in the same manner as courses. Interconversion of relative and other bearings is accomplished by means of the heading. If true heading is added to a relative bearing, true bearing results (RB+TH=TB). If magnetic, compass, or grid heading (MH, CH, GH) is added to relative bearing, the corresponding magnetic, compass, or grid bearing is obtained.

A **bearing line** extending in the direction of an observed bearing of a charted object is one of the most widely used lines of position. If one knows that an identified landmark has a certain bearing from his vessel, the vessel can only be on the line at which such a bearing might be observed, for at any other point the bearing would be different. This line extends outward from the landmark, along the *reciprocal* of the observed bearing. Thus, if a lighthouse is *east* of a ship, that ship is *west* of the lighthouse. If a beacon bears 156°, the observer must be on a line extending 156°+180°=336° from the beacon. Since observed bearing lines are great circles, this relationship is not strictly accurate, but the error is significant only where the great circle departs materially from the rhumb line, as in high latitudes.

Bearings are obtained by compass, pelorus, radar, etc. One type of bearing can be obtained by eye without measurement. When two objects appear directly in line, one behind the other, they are said to be "in range," and together they constitute a **range.** For accurately charted objects, a range provides the most accurate line of position obtainable, and one of the easiest to observe. Tanks, steeples, towers, cupolas, etc., sometimes form natural ranges. A navigator should be familiar with prominent ranges in his operating area, particularly those which can be used to mark turning points, indicate limits of shoals, or define an approach heading or let-go point of the anchorage of a naval vessel. So useful is the range in marking a course that artificial ranges, usually in the form of two lighted beacons,

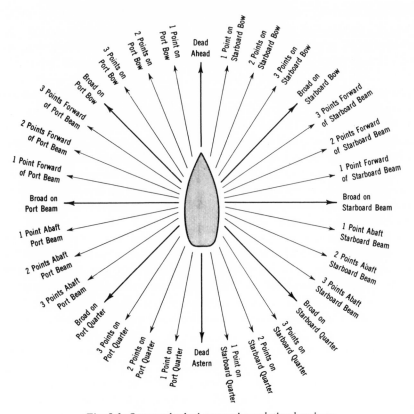

Fig. 9.1. One method of expressing relative bearings.

have been installed in line with channels in many ports. A vessel proceeding along the channel has only to keep the beacons in range to remain in the center of the channel. If the *farther* beacon (customarily the higher one) appears to "open out" (move) to the right of the forward (lower) beacon, one knows that he is to the right of his desired course line. Similarly, if it opens out to the left, the vessel is off course to the left.

It is good practice to plot only a short part of a line of position in the vicinity of the vessel, to avoid unnecessary confusion and to reduce the chart wear by erasure. Particularly, one should avoid drawing lines through the chart symbol indicating the landmark used. In the case of a range, a straightedge is placed along the two objects, and the desired portion of the line is plotted. One need not know the numerical value of the bearing represented by the line. However, if there is any doubt as to the identification of the objects observed, the measurement of the bearing should prove useful.

A bearing line is labeled with the time above the line, and the bearing below the line. A range is labeled with the time only.

Distance • If a vessel is known to be a certain distance from an identified point on the chart, it must be somewhere on a circle with that point as the center and the distance as the radius. An arc of the circle can be drawn and labeled with the time above the line and the distance below the line.

The fix • A line of position, however obtained, represents a series of possible positions, but not a single position. However, if *two simultaneous, nonparallel* lines of position are available, the only position that satisfies the requirements of being on both lines at the same time is the intersection of the two lines. This point is one form of **fix.** Examples of several types of fix are given in the illustrations. In figure 9.2 a fix is obtained from two bearing lines. The fix of figure 9.3 is obtained by two distance circles. Figure 9.4 illustrates a fix from a range and a distance. In figure 9.5 a bearing and distance of a single object are used.

Some consideration should be given to the selection of objects to provide a fix. It is essential, for instance, that the objects be identified. The angle between lines of position is important. The ideal is 90°. If the angle is small, a slight error is measuring or plotting either line results in a relatively large error in the indicated position. In the case of a bearing line, nearby objects are preferable to those at a considerable distance, because the linear (distance) error resulting from an angular error increases with distance. Thus, an error of 1° represents an error of about 100 feet if the object is one mile distant, 1,000 feet if the object is ten miles away, and one mile if the object is 60 miles from the observer.

Another consideration is the type of object. Lighthouses, spires, flagpoles, etc., are good objects because the point of observation is well defined. A large building, most nearby mountains, a point of land, etc.,

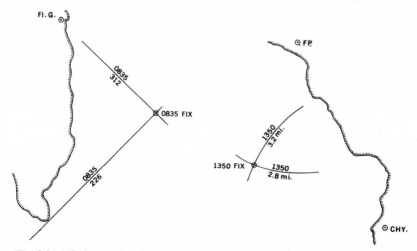

Fig. 9.2. A fix by two bearing lines.   Fig. 9.3. A fix by two distances.

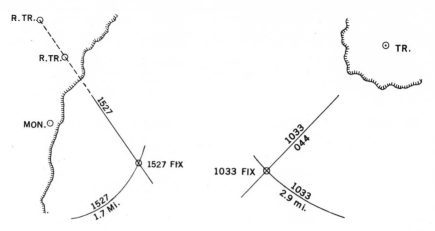

Fig. 9.4. A fix by a range and distance.   Fig. 9.5. A fix by distance and bearing of single object.

may leave some reasonable doubt as to the exact point used for observation. If a tangent is used (fig. 9.2), there is a possibility that a low spit may extend seaward from the part observed. A number of towers, chimneys, etc., close together require careful identification. A buoy or a lightship may drag anchor and be out of position. Most buoys are secured by a single anchor and so have a certain radius of swing as the tide, current, and wind change.

Although two accurate nonparallel lines of position completely define a position, if they are taken at the same time, an element of doubt always exists as to the accuracy of the lines. Additional lines of position can serve as a check on those already obtained, and, usually, reduce any existing error. If three lines of position cross at a common point, or form a small triangle, it is usually a reasonable assumption that the position is reliable, and defined by the center of the figure. However, this is not *necessarily* so, and one should be aware of the possibility of an erroneously indicated position. Sometimes an error can be identified. For instance, if several fixes obtained by bearings on three objects produce triangles of about the same size, one might reasonably suspect a constant error in the observation of the bearings, particularly if the same instrument is used for all observations, or in the plotting of the lines. If the application of a constant error to all bearings results in a point, or near-point fix, the navigator is usually justified in applying such a correction. This situation is illustrated in figure 9.6, where the solid lines indicate the original plot, and the broken lines indicate each line of position moved 3° in a clockwise direction. If different instruments are used for observation, one of them might be consistently in error. This might be detected by altering all bearings observed by that instrument by a fixed amount and producing good fixes. However, one seldom has time for much experimentation of this kind while piloting. If an error is suspected, such experiments might better be conducted while

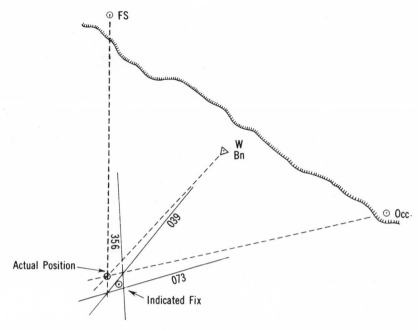

Fig. 9.6. Adjusting a fix for inaccurate bearings.

at anchor or moored alongside a pier. Underway, other instruments, such as radar, might better be used if available.

Lines of position obtained by observation of bearings or distances can be used with lines of position obtained in any other manner, as by radio direction finder, loran, etc. If an object such as a buoy is passed close aboard, a fix is obtained without plotting. Similarly, there should be no doubt as to the position of a vessel which is observed to be midway between two channel buoys a short distance apart.

Nonsimultaneous observations • For fully accurate results, observations made to fix the position of a moving vessel should be made simultaneously, or nearly so. On a slow-moving vessel, relatively little error is introduced by making several observations in quick succession. A wise precaution is to observe the objects more nearly ahead or astern first, since these are least affected by the motion of the observer. For more accurate results, all readings but the last can be repeated in reverse order, and the mean of each pair used. Thus, if three bearings (on objects *A*, *B*, and *C*) are to be used, five readings can be taken, as follows: *A, B, C, B, A*. The two *B* readings are averaged, and also the two *A* readings. The time of the *C* reading is considered the time of all readings. Approximately equal intervals should elapse between readings. An indication of the error introduced by *not* observing this precaution is the fact that at ten knots a vessel moves

1,000 feet in one minute. At 20 knots, this distance is doubled. If the angle between lines of position is small, and the earlier bearings are of objects near the beam, the position indicated by the fix might be in error by more than the motion of the vessel, particularly if the objects on which later bearings are taken are abaft those of earlier bearings.

Sometimes it is not possible or desirable to make simultaneous or nearly simultaneous observations. Such a situation may arise, for instance, when a single object is available for observation, or when all available objects are on nearly the same or reciprocal bearings, and there is no means of determining distance. Under such conditions, a period of several minutes or more may be permitted to elapse between observations to provide lines of position crossing at suitable angles. When this occurs, the lines can be adjusted to a common time to obtain a **running fix.** Refer to figure 9.7. A ship is proceeding along a coast on course 020°, speed 15 knots. At 1505 lighthouse L bears 310°. If the line of position is accurate, the ship is somewhere on it at the time of observation. Ten minutes later the ship will have traveled 2.5 miles in direction 020°. If the ship was at A at 1505, it will be at A' at 1515. However, if the position at 1505 was

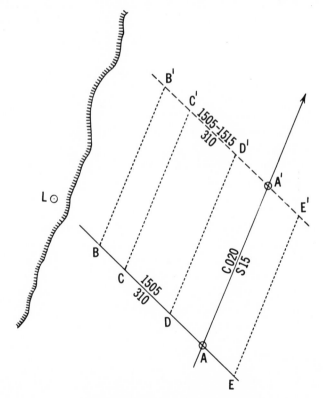

Fig. 9.7. Advancing a line of position.

B, the position at 1515 will be B'. A similar relationship exists between C and C', D and D', E and E', etc. Thus, if *any* point on the original line of position is moved a distance equal to the distance run, and in the direction of the motion, a line through this point, parallel to the original line of position, represents all possible positions of the ship at the later time. This process is called **advancing** a line of position. The moving of a line *back* to an *earlier* time is called **retiring** a line of position.

The accuracy of an adjusted line of position depends not only upon the accuracy of the original line, but also upon the reliability of the information used in moving the line. A small error in the course made good has little effect upon the accuracy of a bearing line of an object near the beam, but maximum effect upon the bearing line of an object nearly ahead or astern. Conversely, the effect of an error in speed is maximum upon the bearing line of an object abeam. The opposite is true of circles of position. The best estimate of course and speed made good should be used in advancing or retiring a line of position.

If there are any changes of course or speed, these should be considered, for the motion of the line of position should reflect as accurately as possible the motion of the observer between the time of observation and the time to which the line is adjusted. Perhaps the easiest way to do this is to measure the direction and distance between dead reckoning or estimated

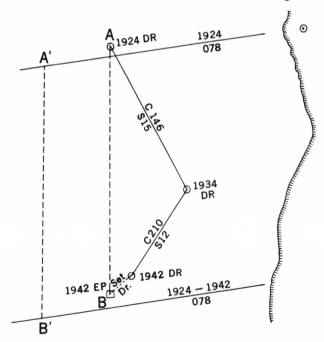

Fig. 9.8. Advancing a line of position with a change in course and speed, and allowing for current.

positions at the two times, and use these to adjust some point on the line of position. This method is shown is figure 9.8. In this illustration allowance is made for the estimated combined effect of wind and current, this effect being plotted as an additional course and distance. If courses and speeds made good over the ground are used, the separate plotting of the wind and current effect is not used. In the illustration, point *A* is the DR position at the time of observation, and point *B* is the estimated position (the DR position adjusted for wind and current) at the time to which the line of position is adjusted. Line *A'B'* is of the same length and in the same direction as line *AB*.

Other techniques may be used. The position of the object observed may be advanced or retired, and the line of position drawn in relation to the adjusted position. This is the most satisfactory method for a circle of position, as shown in figure 9.9. When the position of the landmark is adjusted, the advanced line of position can be laid down without plotting the original line, which need be shown only if it serves a useful purpose. This not only eliminates part of the work, but reduces the number of lines on the chart, and thereby decreases the possibility of error. Another method is to draw any line, such as a perpendicular, from the dead reckon-

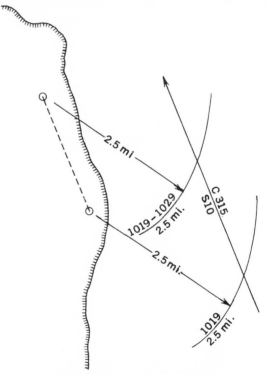

Fig. 9.9. Advancing a circle of position.

ing position at the time of observation to the line of position. A line of the same length and in the same direction, drawn from the DR position or EP at the time to which the line is adjusted, locates a point on the adjusted line, as shown in figure 9.10. If a single course and speed is involved, common practice is to measure from the intersection of the line of position and the course line. If the dividers are set to the distance run between bearings and placed on the chart so that one point is on the first bearing line and the other point is on the second bearing line, and the line connecting the points is parallel to the course line, the points will indicate the positions of the vessel at the times of the bearings.

An adjusted line of position is labeled the same as an unadjusted one, except that both the time of observation and the time to which the line is adjusted are shown, as in the figures illustrating these pages. Because of additional sources of error in adjusted lines of position, they are not used when satisfactory simultaneous lines can be obtained.

The running fix • As stated in the previous discussion, a fix obtained by means of lines of position taken at different times and adjusted to a common time is called a **running fix.** In piloting, common practice is to *advance* earlier lines to the time of the last observation. Figure 9.11 illustrates a running fix obtained from two bearings of the same object. In

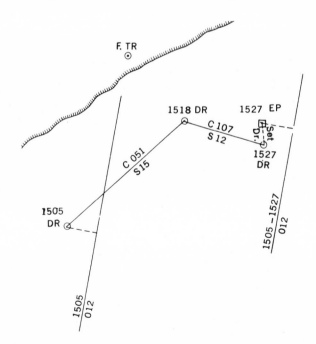

Fig. 9.10. Advancing a line of position by its relation to the dead reckoning.

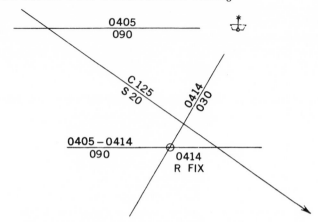

Fig. 9.11. A running fix by two bearings on the same object.

figure 9.12 the ship changes course and speed between observations of two objects. A running fix by two circles of position is shown in figure 9.13.

When simultaneous observations are not available, a running fix may provide the most reliable position obtainable. The time between observations should be no longer than necessary, for the uncertainty of course and distance made good increases with time.

The errors applicable to a running fix are those resulting from errors of the individual lines of position. However, a given error may have quite a different effect upon the fix than upon the line of position. Consider, for example, the situation of an unknown head current. In figure 9.14 a ship is proceeding along a coast, on course 250°, speed 12 knots. At 0920 lighthouse *A* bears 190°, and at 0930 it bears 143°. If the earlier bearing line is advanced a distance of two miles (ten minutes at 12 knots) in the direction of the course, the running fix is as shown by the solid lines. However, if there is a head current of two knots, the ship is making good a speed of only ten knots, and in ten minutes will travel a distance of only 1⅔ miles. If the first bearing line is advanced this distance, as shown by the broken line, the actual position of the ship is at *B*. *This is nearer the beach than the running fix*, and therefore a dangerous situation. A following current gives an indication of position too far from the object. Therefore, if a current *parallel* to the course (either head or following) is suspected, a *minimum* estimate of speed made good will result in a possible margin of safety. If the second bearing is of a different object, a *maximum* estimate of speed should be made if the second object is on the same side and farther forward, or on the opposite side and farther aft, than the first object was when observed. All of these situations assume that danger is on the same side as the object observed first. If there is either a head or following current, a series of running fixes based upon a number of bearings of the same object will plot in a straight line parallel to the course

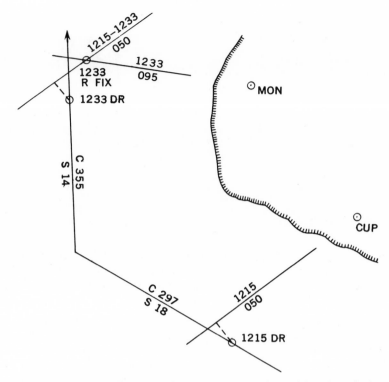

Fig. 9.12. A running fix with a change of course and speed between observations on separate landmarks.

line, as shown in figure 9.15. The plotted line will be too close to the object observed if there is a following current, and too far out if there is a head current. The existence of the current will not be apparent unless the actual speed over the ground is known. The position of the plotted line relative to the dead reckoning course line is not a reliable guide.

A current oblique to the course will result in an incorrect position, but the direction of the error is indeterminate. In general, the effect of a

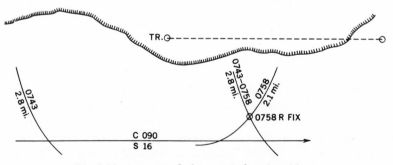

Fig. 9.13. A running fix by two circles of position.

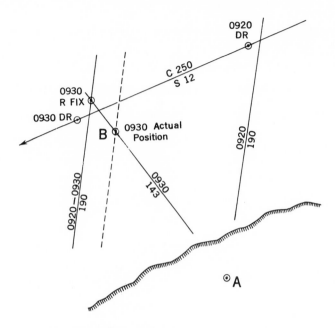

0920
DR

C 250
S 12

0930
R FIX

0930 DR

0930 Actual
Position

B

0920
190

0920—0930
190

0930
143

⊙ A

Fig. 9.14. Effect of a head current on a running fix.

current with a strong head or following component is similar to that of a head or following current, respectively. The existence of an oblique current, but not its amount, can be detected by observing and plotting several bearings of the same object. The running fix obtained by advancing one bearing line to the time of the next one will not agree with the running fix obtained by advancing an earlier line. Thus, if bearings *A*, *B*, and *C* (as in figure 9.16) are observed at five-minute intervals, the running fix obtained by advancing *B* to the time of *C* will not be the same as that obtained by advancing *A* to the time of *C*.

Whatever the current, the *direction* of the course made good (assuming constant current) can be determined. On the chart, plot the various bearing lines (fig. 9.17, left). Draw a straight line on a piece of transparent material, and along it mark off the distances run (using any assumed speed) between bearings (fig. 9.17, right). If transparent material is not available, mark off the distances along the edge of a piece of paper. By trial and error, fit the distances to the bearing lines on the chart, so that each mark falls on its bearing line (fig. 9.18). The direction of the line is the course being made good. Its distance from the track is in error by an amount proportional to the ratio of the speed being made good to the speed assumed for the solution. If a good fix (not a running fix) is obtained at some time before the first bearing for the running fix, and the current has not changed, the track can be determined by drawing a line from the

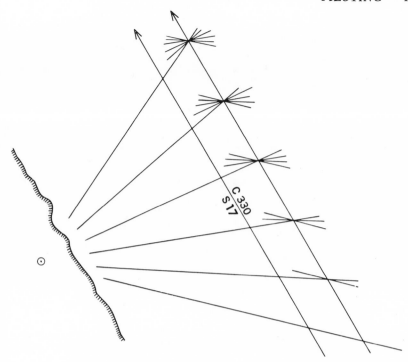

Fig. 9.15. A number of running fixes with a following current.

fix, in the direction of the course made good. The intersection of the track with any of the bearing lines is an actual position.

The current can be determined whenever a dead reckoning position and fix are available for the same time. The direction *from* the dead reckoning position *to* the fix is the set of the current. The distance between these two positions, divided by the time (expressed in hours and tenths) since the last fix, is the drift of the current in knots. For accurate results, the dead reckoning position must be run up from the previous fix without any allowance for current. Any error in either the dead reckoning position (such as poor steering, unknown compass error, inaccurate log, wind, etc.) or the fix will be reflected in the determination of current. When the dead reckoning position and fix are close together, a relatively small error in either may introduce a large error in the apparent set of the current.

Solution without a plot • A running fix can be obtained by utilizing the mathematical relationships involved. Refer to figure 9.19. A ship steams past landmark D. At any point A a bearing of D is observed and expressed as degrees right or left of the course (a relative bearing if the ship is on course). At some later time, at B, a second bearing of D is observed and expressed as before. At C the landmark is broad on the beam. The angles

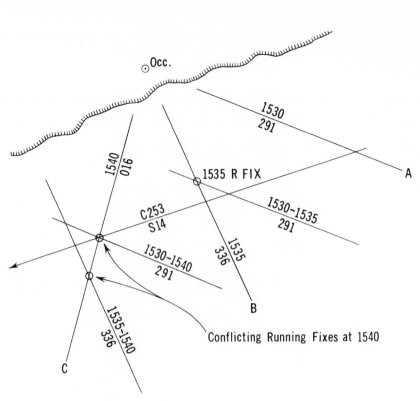

Fig. 9.16. Detecting the existence of an oblique current by a series of running fixes.

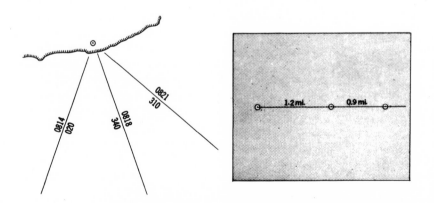

Fig. 9.17. Preparing to determine the course made good.

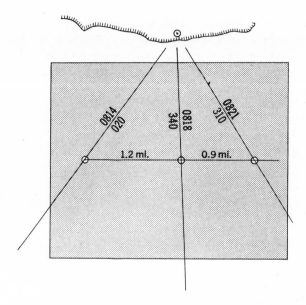

Fig. 9.18. Determining the course made good.

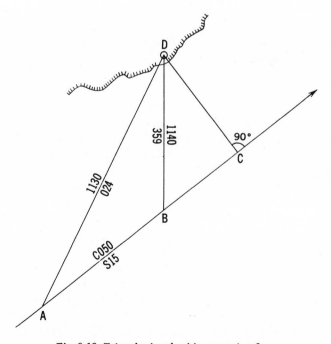

Fig. 9.19. Triangles involved in a running fix.

at *A*, *B*, and *C* are known, and also the distance run between points. The various triangles could be solved by trigonometry to find the distance from *D* at any bearing. Distance and bearing provide a fix.

Table 3 provides a quick and easy solution. The table is entered with the difference between the course and first bearing (angle *BAD* in fig. 9.19) along the top of the table, and the difference between the course and second bearing (angle *CBD*) at the left of the table. For each pair of angles listed, two numbers are given. To find the distance from the landmark at the time of the second bearing (*BD*), multiply the distance run between bearings by the first number from Table 3. To find the distance when the object is abeam (*CD*), multiply the distance run between *A* and *B* by the second number from the table. If the run between bearings is exactly one mile, the tabulated values are the distances sought.

Example. A ship is steaming on course 050°, speed 15 knots. At 1130 a lighthouse bears 024°, and at 1140 it bears 359°.

Required. (1) Distance from the light at 1140.

(2) Distance from the light when it is broad on the port beam.

Solution (fig. 9.19). (1) The difference between the course and the first bearing (050°—024°) is 26°, and the difference between the course and the second bearing (050°+360°—359°) is 51°.

(2) From Table 3 the two numbers (factors) are 1.04 and 0.81, found by interpolation.

(3) The distance run between bearings is 2.5 miles (10 minutes at 15 knots).

(4) The distance from the lighthouse at the time of the second bearing is 2.5×1.04=2.6 miles.

(5) The distance from the lighthouse when it is broad on the beam is 2.5×0.81=2.0 miles.

Answers. (1) D 2.6 mi., (2) D 2.0 mi.

Certain combinations of angles provide quick mental solution without the need for Table 3. If the second difference (angle *CBD*) is double the first difference (angle *BAD*), triangle *BAD* is isosceles, with equal angles at *A* and *D*. Therefore side *AB* (the run) is equal to side *BD* (the distance off at the time of the second bearing). This is called **doubling the angle on the bow.** If the first angle is 45° and the second 90°, the distance run equals the distance when broad on the beam. These are called **bow and beam bearings.** If the first angle is 63°5 and the second 90°, the distance off when abeam is about twice the distance run. If the angles are 71°5 and 90°, the distance off when abeam is about three times the distance run. If the first angle is 22°5 and the second 45°, the distance at which the object will be passed abeam is about 7/10 of the distance run between bearings. If the angles are 22°5 and 26°5, the distance abeam will be about 7/3 of the distance run. If the angles are 30° and 60°, the distance of the object when abeam will be about 7/8 of the distance run between

TABLE 3

Distance of an Object by Two Bearings

Difference between the course and second bearing	Difference between the course and first bearing												
	20°		22°		24°		26°		28°		30°		32°
°													
30	1.97	0.98											
32	1.64	0.87	2.16	1.14									
34	1.41	0.79	1.80	1.01	2.34	1.31							
36	1.24	0.73	1.55	0.91	1.96	1.15	2.52	1.48					
38	1.11	0.68	1.36	0.84	1.68	1.04	2.11	1.30	2.70	1.66			
40	1.00	0.64	1.21	0.78	1.48	0.95	1.81	1.16	2.26	1.45	2.88	1.85	
42	0.91	0.61	1.10	0.73	1.32	0.88	1.59	1.06	1.94	1.30	2.40	1.61	3.05 2.04
44	0.84	0.58	1.00	0.69	1.19	0.83	1.42	0.98	1.70	1.18	2.07	1.44	2.55 1.77
46	0.78	0.56	0.92	0.66	1.09	0.78	1.28	0.92	1.52	1.09	1.81	1.30	2.19 1.58
48	0.73	0.54	0.85	0.64	1.00	0.74	1.17	0.87	1.37	1.02	1.62	1.20	1.92 1.43
50	0.68	0.52	0.80	0.61	0.93	0.71	1.08	0.83	1.25	0.96	1.46	1.12	1.71 1.31
52	0.65	0.51	0.75	0.59	0.87	0.68	1.00	0.79	1.15	0.91	1.33	1.05	1.55 1.22
54	0.61	0.49	0.71	0.57	0.81	0.66	0.93	0.76	1.07	0.87	1.23	0.99	1.41 1.14
56	0.58	0.48	0.67	0.56	0.77	0.64	0.88	0.73	1.00	0.83	1.14	0.95	1.30 1.08
58	0.56	0.47	0.64	0.54	0.73	0.62	0.83	0.70	0.94	0.80	1.07	0.90	1.21 1.03
60	0.53	0.46	0.61	0.53	0.69	0.60	0.78	0.68	0.89	0.77	1.00	0.87	1.13 0.98
62	0.51	0.45	0.58	0.51	0.66	0.58	0.75	0.66	0.84	0.74	0.94	0.83	1.06 0.94
64	0.49	0.44	0.56	0.50	0.63	0.57	0.71	0.64	0.80	0.72	0.89	0.80	1.00 0.90
66	0.48	0.43	0.54	0.49	0.61	0.56	0.68	0.62	0.76	0.70	0.85	0.78	0.95 0.87
68	0.46	0.43	0.52	0.48	0.59	0.54	0.66	0.61	0.73	0.68	0.81	0.75	0.90 0.84
70	0.45	0.42	0.50	0.47	0.57	0.53	0.63	0.59	0.70	0.66	0.78	0.73	0.86 0.81
72	0.43	0.41	0.49	0.47	0.55	0.52	0.61	0.58	0.68	0.64	0.75	0.71	0.82 0.78
74	0.42	0.41	0.48	0.46	0.53	0.51	0.59	0.57	0.65	0.63	0.72	0.69	0.79 0.76
76	0.41	0.40	0.46	0.45	0.52	0.50	0.57	0.56	0.63	0.61	0.70	0.67	0.76 0.74
78	0.40	0.39	0.45	0.44	0.50	0.49	0.56	0.54	0.61	0.60	0.67	0.66	0.74 0.72
80	0.39	0.39	0.44	0.44	0.49	0.48	0.54	0.53	0.60	0.59	0.65	0.64	0.71 0.70
82	0.39	0.38	0.43	0.43	0.48	0.47	0.53	0.52	0.58	0.57	0.63	0.63	0.69 0.69
84	0.38	0.38	0.42	0.42	0.47	0.47	0.52	0.51	0.57	0.56	0.62	0.61	0.67 0.67
86	0.37	0.37	0.42	0.42	0.46	0.46	0.51	0.51	0.55	0.55	0.60	0.60	0.66 0.65
88	0.37	0.37	0.41	0.41	0.45	0.45	0.50	0.50	0.54	0.54	0.59	0.59	0.64 0.64
90	0.36	0.36	0.40	0.40	0.45	0.45	0.49	0.49	0.53	0.53	0.58	0.58	0.62 0.62
92	0.36	0.36	0.40	0.40	0.44	0.44	0.48	0.48	0.52	0.52	0.57	0.57	0.61 0.61
94	0.36	0.35	0.39	0.39	0.43	0.43	0.47	0.47	0.51	0.51	0.56	0.55	0.60 0.60
96	0.35	0.35	0.39	0.39	0.43	0.43	0.47	0.46	0.51	0.50	0.55	0.54	0.59 0.59
98	0.35	0.35	0.39	0.38	0.42	0.42	0.46	0.46	0.50	0.50	0.54	0.53	0.58 0.57
100	0.35	0.34	0.38	0.38	0.42	0.41	0.46	0.45	0.49	0.49	0.53	0.52	0.57 0.56
102	0.35	0.34	0.38	0.37	0.42	0.41	0.45	0.44	0.49	0.48	0.53	0.51	0.56 0.55
104	0.34	0.33	0.38	0.37	0.41	0.40	0.45	0.43	0.48	0.47	0.52	0.50	0.56 0.54
106	0.34	0.33	0.38	0.36	0.41	0.39	0.45	0.43	0.48	0.46	0.52	0.50	0.55 0.53
108	0.34	0.32	0.38	0.36	0.41	0.39	0.44	0.42	0.48	0.45	0.51	0.49	0.55 0.52
110	0.34	0.32	0.37	0.35	0.41	0.38	0.44	0.41	0.47	0.44	0.51	0.48	0.54 0.51
112	0.34	0.32	0.37	0.35	0.41	0.38	0.44	0.41	0.47	0.44	0.50	0.47	0.54 0.50
114	0.34	0.31	0.37	0.34	0.41	0.37	0.44	0.40	0.47	0.43	0.50	0.46	0.54 0.49
116	0.34	0.31	0.38	0.34	0.41	0.37	0.44	0.39	0.47	0.42	0.50	0.45	0.53 0.48
118	0.35	0.31	0.38	0.33	0.41	0.36	0.44	0.39	0.47	0.41	0.50	0.44	0.53 0.47
120	0.35	0.30	0.38	0.33	0.41	0.36	0.44	0.38	0.47	0.41	0.50	0.43	0.53 0.46
122	0.35	0.30	0.38	0.32	0.41	0.35	0.44	0.37	0.47	0.40	0.50	0.42	0.53 0.45
124	0.35	0.29	0.38	0.32	0.41	0.34	0.44	0.37	0.47	0.39	0.50	0.42	0.53 0.44
126	0.36	0.29	0.39	0.31	0.42	0.34	0.45	0.36	0.47	0.38	0.50	0.41	0.53 0.43
128	0.36	0.28	0.39	0.31	0.42	0.33	0.45	0.35	0.48	0.38	0.50	0.40	0.53 0.42
130	0.36	0.28	0.39	0.30	0.42	0.32	0.45	0.35	0.48	0.37	0.51	0.39	0.54 0.41
132	0.37	0.27	0.40	0.30	0.43	0.32	0.46	0.34	0.48	0.36	0.51	0.38	0.54 0.40
134	0.37	0.27	0.40	0.29	0.43	0.31	0.46	0.33	0.49	0.35	0.52	0.37	0.54 0.39
136	0.38	0.26	0.41	0.28	0.44	0.30	0.47	0.32	0.49	0.34	0.52	0.36	0.55 0.38
138	0.39	0.26	0.42	0.28	0.45	0.30	0.47	0.32	0.50	0.33	0.53	0.35	0.55 0.37
140	0.39	0.25	0.42	0.27	0.45	0.29	0.48	0.31	0.51	0.33	0.53	0.34	0.56 0.36
142	0.40	0.25	0.43	0.27	0.46	0.28	0.49	0.30	0.51	0.32	0.54	0.33	0.56 0.35
144	0.41	0.24	0.44	0.26	0.47	0.28	0.50	0.29	0.52	0.31	0.55	0.32	0.57 0.34
146	0.42	0.24	0.45	0.25	0.48	0.27	0.51	0.28	0.53	0.30	0.56	0.31	0.58 0.32
148	0.43	0.23	0.46	0.25	0.49	0.26	0.52	0.27	0.54	0.29	0.57	0.30	0.59 0.31
150	0.45	0.22	0.48	0.24	0.50	0.25	0.53	0.26	0.55	0.28	0.58	0.29	0.60 0.30
152	0.46	0.22	0.49	0.23	0.52	0.24	0.54	0.25	0.57	0.27	0.59	0.28	0.61 0.29
154	0.48	0.21	0.50	0.22	0.53	0.23	0.56	0.24	0.58	0.25	0.60	0.26	0.62 0.27
156	0.49	0.20	0.52	0.21	0.55	0.22	0.57	0.23	0.60	0.24	0.62	0.25	0.64 0.26
158	0.51	0.19	0.54	0.20	0.57	0.21	0.59	0.22	0.61	0.23	0.63	0.24	0.66 0.25
160	0.53	0.18	0.56	0.19	0.59	0.20	0.61	0.21	0.63	0.22	0.65	0.22	0.67 0.23

TABLE 3
Distance of an Object by Two Bearings

Difference between the course and second bearing °	34°		36°		38°		40°		42°		44°		46°	
44	3.22	2.24												
46	2.69	1.93	3.39	2.43										
48	2.31	1.72	2.83	2.10	3.55	2.63								
50	2.03	1.55	2.43	1.86	2.96	2.27	3.70	2.84						
52	1.81	1.43	2.13	1.68	2.54	2.01	3.09	2.44	3.85	3.04				
54	1.63	1.32	1.90	1.54	2.23	1.81	2.66	2.15	3.22	2.60	4.00	3.24		
56	1.49	1.24	1.72	1.42	1.99	1.65	2.33	1.93	2.77	2.29	3.34	2.77	4.14	3.43
58	1.37	1.17	1.57	1.33	1.80	1.53	2.08	1.76	2.43	2.06	2.87	2.44	3.46	2.93
60	1.28	1.10	1.45	1.25	1.64	1.42	1.88	1.63	2.17	1.88	2.52	2.18	2.97	2.57
62	1.19	1.05	1.34	1.18	1.51	1.34	1.72	1.52	1.96	1.73	2.25	1.98	2.61	2.30
64	1.12	1.01	1.25	1.13	1.40	1.26	1.58	1.42	1.79	1.61	2.03	1.83	2.33	2.09
66	1.06	0.96	1.18	1.07	1.31	1.20	1.47	1.34	1.65	1.51	1.85	1.69	2.10	1.92
68	1.00	0.93	1.11	1.03	1.23	1.14	1.37	1.27	1.53	1.42	1.71	1.58	1.92	1.78
70	0.95	0.89	1.05	0.99	1.16	1.09	1.29	1.21	1.43	1.34	1.58	1.49	1.77	1.66
72	0.91	0.86	1.00	0.95	1.10	1.05	1.21	1.15	1.34	1.27	1.48	1.41	1.64	1.56
74	0.87	0.84	0.95	0.92	1.05	1.01	1.15	1.10	1.26	1.21	1.39	1.34	1.53	1.47
76	0.84	0.81	0.91	0.89	1.00	0.97	1.09	1.06	1.20	1.16	1.31	1.27	1.44	1.40
78	0.80	0.79	0.88	0.86	0.96	0.94	1.04	1.02	1.14	1.11	1.24	1.22	1.36	1.33
80	0.78	0.77	0.85	0.83	0.92	0.91	1.00	0.98	1.09	1.07	1.18	1.16	1.28	1.27
82	0.75	0.75	0.82	0.81	0.89	0.88	0.96	0.95	1.04	1.03	1.13	1.12	1.22	1.21
84	0.73	0.73	0.79	0.79	0.86	0.85	0.93	0.92	1.00	0.99	1.08	1.07	1.17	1.16
86	0.71	0.71	0.77	0.77	0.83	0.83	0.89	0.89	0.96	0.96	1.04	1.04	1.12	1.12
88	0.69	0.69	0.75	0.75	0.80	0.80	0.86	0.86	0.93	0.93	1.00	1.00	1.08	1.07
90	0.67	0.67	0.73	0.73	0.78	0.78	0.84	0.84	0.90	0.90	0.97	0.97	1.04	1.04
92	0.66	0.66	0.71	0.71	0.76	0.76	0.82	0.82	0.87	0.87	0.93	0.93	1.00	1.00
94	0.65	0.64	0.69	0.69	0.74	0.74	0.79	0.79	0.85	0.85	0.91	0.90	0.97	0.97
96	0.63	0.63	0.68	0.67	0.73	0.72	0.78	0.77	0.83	0.82	0.88	0.88	0.94	0.93
98	0.62	0.62	0.67	0.66	0.71	0.70	0.76	0.75	0.81	0.80	0.86	0.85	0.91	0.90
100	0.61	0.60	0.65	0.64	0.70	0.69	0.74	0.73	0.79	0.78	0.84	0.83	0.89	0.88
102	0.60	0.59	0.64	0.63	0.68	0.67	0.73	0.71	0.77	0.76	0.82	0.80	0.87	0.85
104	0.60	0.58	0.63	0.61	0.67	0.65	0.72	0.69	0.76	0.74	0.80	0.78	0.85	0.82
106	0.59	0.57	0.63	0.60	0.66	0.64	0.70	0.68	0.74	0.72	0.79	0.76	0.83	0.80
108	0.58	0.55	0.62	0.59	0.66	0.62	0.69	0.66	0.73	0.70	0.77	0.74	0.81	0.77
110	0.58	0.54	0.61	0.57	0.65	0.61	0.68	0.64	0.72	0.68	0.76	0.71	0.80	0.75
112	0.57	0.53	0.61	0.56	0.64	0.59	0.68	0.63	0.71	0.66	0.75	0.69	0.79	0.73
114	0.57	0.52	0.60	0.55	0.63	0.58	0.67	0.61	0.70	0.64	0.74	0.68	0.78	0.71
116	0.56	0.51	0.60	0.54	0.63	0.57	0.66	0.60	0.70	0.63	0.73	0.66	0.77	0.69
118	0.56	0.50	0.59	0.52	0.63	0.55	0.66	0.58	0.69	0.61	0.72	0.64	0.76	0.67
120	0.56	0.49	0.59	0.51	0.62	0.54	0.65	0.57	0.68	0.59	0.72	0.62	0.75	0.65
122	0.56	0.47	0.59	0.50	0.62	0.53	0.65	0.55	0.68	0.58	0.71	0.60	0.74	0.63
124	0.56	0.46	0.59	0.49	0.62	0.51	0.65	0.54	0.68	0.56	0.71	0.58	0.74	0.61
126	0.56	0.45	0.59	0.48	0.62	0.50	0.64	0.52	0.67	0.54	0.70	0.57	0.73	0.59
128	0.56	0.44	0.59	0.46	0.62	0.49	0.64	0.51	0.67	0.53	0.70	0.55	0.73	0.57
130	0.56	0.43	0.59	0.45	0.62	0.47	0.64	0.49	0.67	0.51	0.70	0.53	0.72	0.55
132	0.56	0.42	0.59	0.44	0.62	0.46	0.64	0.48	0.67	0.50	0.70	0.52	0.72	0.54
134	0.57	0.41	0.59	0.43	0.62	0.45	0.64	0.46	0.67	0.48	0.69	0.50	0.72	0.52
136	0.57	0.40	0.60	0.41	0.62	0.43	0.65	0.45	0.67	0.47	0.70	0.48	0.72	0.50
138	0.58	0.39	0.60	0.40	0.63	0.42	0.65	0.43	0.67	0.45	0.70	0.47	0.72	0.48
140	0.58	0.37	0.61	0.39	0.63	0.40	0.65	0.42	0.68	0.43	0.70	0.45	0.72	0.46
142	0.59	0.36	0.61	0.38	0.63	0.39	0.66	0.41	0.68	0.42	0.70	0.43	0.72	0.45
144	0.60	0.35	0.62	0.36	0.64	0.38	0.66	0.39	0.68	0.40	0.71	0.41	0.73	0.43
146	0.60	0.34	0.63	0.35	0.65	0.36	0.67	0.37	0.69	0.39	0.71	0.40	0.73	0.41
148	0.61	0.32	0.63	0.34	0.66	0.35	0.68	0.36	0.70	0.37	0.72	0.38	0.74	0.39
150	0.62	0.31	0.64	0.32	0.66	0.33	0.68	0.34	0.70	0.35	0.72	0.36	0.74	0.37
152	0.63	0.30	0.65	0.31	0.67	0.32	0.69	0.33	0.71	0.33	0.73	0.34	0.75	0.35
154	0.65	0.28	0.67	0.29	0.68	0.30	0.70	0.31	0.72	0.32	0.74	0.32	0.76	0.33
156	0.66	0.27	0.68	0.28	0.70	0.28	0.72	0.29	0.73	0.30	0.75	0.30	0.77	0.31
158	0.67	0.25	0.69	0.26	0.71	0.27	0.73	0.27	0.74	0.28	0.76	0.28	0.78	0.29
160	0.69	0.24	0.71	0.24	0.73	0.25	0.74	0.25	0.76	0.26	0.77	0.26	0.79	0.27

TABLE 3
Distance of an Object by Two Bearings

Difference between the course and second bearing °	48°		50°		52°		54°		56°		58°		60°	
58	4.28	3.63												
60	3.57	3.10	4.41	3.82										
62	3.07	2.71	3.68	3.25	4.54	4.01								
64	2.70	2.42	3.17	2.85	3.79	3.41	4.66	4.19						
66	2.40	2.20	2.78	2.54	3.26	2.98	3.89	3.55	4.77	4.36				
68	2.17	2.01	2.48	2.30	2.86	2.65	3.34	3.10	3.99	3.71	4.88	4.53		
70	1.98	1.86	2.24	2.10	2.55	2.39	2.94	2.76	3.43	3.22	4.08	3.83	4.99	4.69
72	1.83	1.74	2.04	1.94	2.30	2.19	2.62	2.49	3.01	2.86	3.51	3.33	4.17	3.96
74	1.70	1.63	1.88	1.81	2.10	2.02	2.37	2.27	2.68	2.58	3.08	2.96	3.58	3.44
76	1.58	1.54	1.75	1.70	1.94	1.88	2.16	2.10	2.42	2.35	2.74	2.66	3.14	3.05
78	1.49	1.45	1.63	1.60	1.80	1.76	1.99	1.95	2.21	2.16	2.48	2.43	2.80	2.74
80	1.40	1.38	1.53	1.51	1.68	1.65	1.85	1.82	2.04	2.01	2.26	2.23	2.53	2.49
82	1.33	1.32	1.45	1.43	1.58	1.56	1.72	1.71	1.89	1.87	2.08	2.06	2.31	2.29
84	1.26	1.26	1.37	1.36	1.49	1.48	1.62	1.61	1.77	1.76	1.93	1.92	2.13	2.12
86	1.21	1.20	1.30	1.30	1.41	1.41	1.53	1.52	1.66	1.65	1.81	1.80	1.98	1.97
88	1.16	1.16	1.24	1.24	1.34	1.34	1.45	1.45	1.56	1.56	1.70	1.70	1.84	1.84
90	1.11	1.11	1.19	1.19	1.28	1.28	1.38	1.38	1.48	1.48	1.60	1.60	1.73	1.73
92	1.07	1.07	1.14	1.14	1.23	1.23	1.31	1.31	1.41	1.41	1.52	1.52	1.63	1.63
94	1.03	1.03	1.10	1.10	1.18	1.17	1.26	1.26	1.35	1.34	1.44	1.44	1.55	1.54
96	1.00	0.99	1.06	1.06	1.13	1.13	1.21	1.20	1.29	1.28	1.38	1.37	1.47	1.47
98	0.97	0.96	1.03	1.02	1.10	1.08	1.16	1.15	1.24	1.23	1.32	1.31	1.41	1.39
100	0.94	0.93	1.00	0.98	1.06	1.04	1.12	1.11	1.19	1.18	1.27	1.25	1.35	1.33
102	0.92	0.90	0.97	0.95	1.03	1.01	1.09	1.06	1.15	1.13	1.22	1.19	1.29	1.27
104	0.90	0.87	0.95	0.92	1.00	0.97	1.06	1.02	1.12	1.08	1.18	1.14	1.25	1.21
106	0.88	0.84	0.92	0.89	0.97	0.94	1.03	0.99	1.09	1.04	1.14	1.10	1.20	1.16
108	0.86	0.82	0.90	0.86	0.95	0.90	1.00	0.95	1.05	1.00	1.11	1.05	1.17	1.11
110	0.84	0.79	0.88	0.83	0.93	0.87	0.98	0.92	1.02	0.96	1.08	1.01	1.13	1.06
112	0.83	0.77	0.87	0.80	0.91	0.84	0.95	0.88	1.00	0.93	1.05	0.97	1.10	1.02
114	0.81	0.74	0.85	0.78	0.89	0.82	0.93	0.85	0.98	0.89	1.02	0.93	1.07	0.98
116	0.80	0.72	0.84	0.75	0.88	0.79	0.92	0.82	0.96	0.85	1.00	0.90	1.04	0.94
118	0.79	0.70	0.83	0.73	0.86	0.76	0.90	0.79	0.94	0.83	0.98	0.86	1.02	0.90
120	0.78	0.68	0.82	0.71	0.85	0.74	0.89	0.77	0.91	0.80	0.96	0.83	1.00	0.87
122	0.77	0.66	0.81	0.68	0.84	0.71	0.87	0.74	0.90	0.77	0.95	0.80	0.98	0.83
124	0.77	0.63	0.80	0.66	0.83	0.69	0.86	0.71	0.90	0.74	0.93	0.77	0.96	0.80
126	0.76	0.61	0.79	0.64	0.82	0.66	0.85	0.69	0.88	0.71	0.91	0.74	0.95	0.77
128	0.75	0.59	0.78	0.62	0.81	0.64	0.84	0.66	0.87	0.69	0.90	0.71	0.93	0.74
130	0.75	0.57	0.78	0.60	0.81	0.62	0.83	0.64	0.86	0.66	0.89	0.68	0.92	0.71
132	0.75	0.56	0.77	0.57	0.80	0.59	0.83	0.61	0.85	0.64	0.88	0.66	0.91	0.68
134	0.74	0.54	0.77	0.55	0.80	0.57	0.82	0.59	0.85	0.61	0.87	0.63	0.90	0.65
136	0.74	0.52	0.77	0.53	0.80	0.55	0.82	0.57	0.84	0.58	0.87	0.60	0.89	0.62
138	0.74	0.50	0.77	0.51	0.79	0.53	0.81	0.54	0.84	0.56	0.86	0.58	0.89	0.59
140	0.74	0.48	0.77	0.49	0.79	0.51	0.81	0.52	0.83	0.54	0.86	0.55	0.88	0.57
142	0.74	0.46	0.77	0.47	0.79	0.49	0.81	0.50	0.83	0.51	0.85	0.52	0.87	0.54
144	0.75	0.44	0.77	0.45	0.79	0.46	0.81	0.48	0.83	0.49	0.85	0.50	0.87	0.51
146	0.75	0.42	0.77	0.43	0.79	0.44	0.81	0.45	0.83	0.46	0.85	0.47	0.87	0.49
148	0.76	0.40	0.77	0.41	0.79	0.42	0.81	0.43	0.83	0.44	0.85	0.45	0.87	0.46
150	0.76	0.38	0.78	0.39	0.80	0.40	0.81	0.41	0.83	0.42	0.85	0.42	0.87	0.43
152	0.77	0.36	0.78	0.37	0.80	0.38	0.82	0.38	0.83	0.39	0.85	0.40	0.87	0.41
154	0.77	0.34	0.79	0.35	0.81	0.35	0.82	0.36	0.84	0.37	0.85	0.37	0.87	0.38
156	0.78	0.32	0.80	0.32	0.81	0.33	0.83	0.34	0.84	0.34	0.86	0.35	0.87	0.35
158	0.79	0.30	0.81	0.30	0.82	0.31	0.83	0.31	0.85	0.32	0.86	0.32	0.87	0.33
160	0.80	0.27	0.82	0.28	0.83	0.28	0.84	0.29	0.85	0.29	0.86	0.30	0.88	0.30

Difference between the course and first bearing

TABLE 3
Distance of an Object by Two Bearings

Difference between the course and second bearing °	62°		64°		66°		68°		70°		72°		74°		76°	
72	5. 08	4. 84														
74	4. 25	4. 08	5. 18	4. 98												
76	3. 65	3. 54	4. 32	4. 19	5. 26	5. 10										
78	3. 20	3. 13	3. 72	3. 63	4. 39	4. 30	5. 34	5. 22								
80	2. 86	2. 81	3. 26	3. 21	3. 78	3. 72	4. 46	4. 39	5. 41	5. 33						
82	2. 58	2. 56	2. 91	2. 88	3. 31	3. 28	3. 83	3. 80	4. 52	4. 48	5. 48	5. 42				
84	2. 36	2. 34	2. 63	2. 61	2. 96	2. 94	3. 36	3. 35	3. 88	3. 86	4. 57	4. 55	5. 54	5. 51		
86	2. 17	2. 17	2. 40	2. 39	2. 67	2. 66	3. 00	2. 99	3. 41	3. 40	3. 93	3. 92	4. 62	4. 61	5. 59	5. 57
88	2. 01	2. 01	2. 21	2. 21	2. 44	2. 44	2. 71	2. 71	3. 04	3. 04	3. 45	3. 45	3. 97	3. 97	4. 67	4. 66
90	1. 88	1. 88	2. 05	2. 05	2. 25	2. 25	2. 48	2. 48	2. 75	2. 75	3. 08	3. 08	3. 49	3. 49	4. 01	4. 01
92	1. 77	1. 76	1. 91	1. 91	2. 08	2. 08	2. 28	2. 28	2. 51	2. 51	2. 78	2. 78	3. 11	3. 11	3. 52	3. 52
94	1. 67	1. 66	1. 80	1. 79	1. 95	1. 94	2. 12	2. 11	2. 31	2. 30	2. 54	2. 53	2. 81	2. 80	3. 14	3. 13
96	1. 58	1. 57	1. 70	1. 69	1. 83	1. 82	1. 97	1. 96	2. 14	2. 13	2. 34	2. 33	2. 57	2. 55	2. 84	2. 82
98	1. 50	1. 49	1. 61	1. 59	1. 72	1. 71	1. 85	1. 84	2. 00	1. 98	2. 17	2. 15	2. 36	2. 34	2. 59	2. 56
100	1. 43	1. 41	1. 53	1. 51	1. 63	1. 61	1. 75	1. 72	1. 88	1. 85	2. 03	2. 00	2. 19	2. 16	2. 39	2. 35
102	1. 37	1. 34	1. 46	1. 43	1. 55	1. 52	1. 66	1. 62	1. 77	1. 73	1. 90	1. 86	2. 05	2. 00	2. 21	2. 16
104	1. 32	1. 28	1. 40	1. 36	1. 48	1. 44	1. 58	1. 53	1. 68	1. 63	1. 79	1. 74	1. 92	1. 87	2. 07	2. 01
106	1. 27	1. 22	1. 34	1. 29	1. 42	1. 37	1. 51	1. 45	1. 60	1. 54	1. 70	1. 63	1. 81	1. 74	1. 94	1. 87
108	1. 23	1. 17	1. 29	1. 23	1. 37	1. 30	1. 44	1. 37	1. 53	1. 45	1. 62	1. 54	1. 72	1. 63	1. 83	1. 74
110	1. 19	1. 12	1. 25	1. 17	1. 32	1. 24	1. 39	1. 30	1. 46	1. 37	1. 54	1. 45	1. 64	1. 54	1. 74	1. 63
112	1. 15	1. 07	1. 21	1. 12	1. 27	1. 18	1. 33	1. 24	1. 40	1. 30	1. 48	1. 37	1. 56	1. 45	1. 65	1. 53
114	1. 12	1. 02	1. 17	1. 07	1. 23	1. 12	1. 29	1. 18	1. 35	1. 24	1. 42	1. 30	1. 50	1. 37	1. 58	1. 44
116	1. 09	0. 98	1. 14	1. 03	1. 19	1. 07	1. 25	1. 12	1. 31	1. 17	1. 37	1. 23	1. 44	1. 29	1. 51	1. 36
118	1. 07	0. 94	1. 11	0. 98	1. 16	1. 02	1. 21	1. 07	1. 26	1. 12	1. 32	1. 17	1. 38	1. 22	1. 45	1. 28
120	1. 04	0. 90	1. 08	0. 94	1. 13	0. 98	1. 18	1. 02	1. 23	1. 06	1. 28	1. 11	1. 34	1. 16	1. 40	1. 21
122	1. 02	0. 86	1. 06	0. 90	1. 10	0. 93	1. 15	0. 97	1. 19	1. 01	1. 24	1. 05	1. 29	1. 10	1. 35	1. 14
124	1. 00	0. 83	1. 04	0. 86	1. 08	0. 89	1. 12	0. 93	1. 16	0. 96	1. 21	1. 00	1. 25	1. 04	1. 31	1. 08
126	0. 98	0. 79	1. 02	0. 82	1. 05	0. 85	1. 09	0. 88	1. 13	0. 92	1. 18	0. 95	1. 22	0. 99	1. 27	1. 02
128	0. 97	0. 76	1. 00	0. 79	1. 03	0. 82	1. 07	0. 84	1. 11	0. 87	1. 15	0. 90	1. 19	0. 94	1. 23	0. 97
130	0. 95	0. 73	0. 98	0. 75	1. 02	0. 78	1. 05	0. 80	1. 09	0. 83	1. 12	0. 86	1. 16	0. 89	1. 20	0. 92
132	0. 94	0. 70	0. 97	0. 72	1. 00	0. 74	1. 03	0. 77	1. 06	0. 79	1. 10	0. 82	1. 13	0. 84	1. 17	0. 87
134	0. 93	0. 67	0. 96	0. 69	0. 99	0. 71	1. 01	0. 73	1. 04	0. 75	1. 08	0. 77	1. 11	0. 80	1. 14	0. 82
136	0. 92	0. 64	0. 95	0. 66	0. 97	0. 68	1. 00	0. 69	1. 03	0. 71	1. 06	0. 74	1. 09	0. 76	1. 12	0. 78
138	0. 91	0. 61	0. 94	0. 63	0. 96	0. 64	0. 99	0. 66	1. 01	0. 68	1. 04	0. 70	1. 07	0. 72	1. 10	0. 74
140	0. 90	0. 58	0. 93	0. 60	0. 95	0. 61	0. 97	0. 63	1. 00	0. 64	1. 03	0. 66	1. 05	0. 68	1. 08	0. 70
142	0. 90	0. 55	0. 92	0. 57	0. 94	0. 58	0. 96	0. 59	0. 99	0. 61	1. 01	0. 62	1. 04	0. 64	1. 06	0. 65
144	0. 89	0. 52	0. 91	0. 54	0. 93	0. 55	0. 96	0. 56	0. 98	0. 57	1. 00	0. 59	1. 02	0. 60	1. 05	0. 62
146	0. 89	0. 50	0. 91	0. 51	0. 93	0. 52	0. 95	0. 53	0. 97	0. 54	0. 99	0. 55	1. 01	0. 57	1. 03	0. 58
148	0. 89	0. 47	0. 90	0. 48	0. 92	0. 49	0. 94	0. 50	0. 96	0. 51	0. 98	0. 52	1. 00	0. 53	1. 02	0. 54
150	0. 88	0. 44	0. 90	0. 45	0. 92	0. 46	0. 94	0. 47	0. 95	0. 48	0. 97	0. 49	0. 99	0. 50	1. 01	0. 50
152	0. 88	0. 41	0. 90	0. 42	0. 92	0. 43	0. 93	0. 44	0. 95	0. 45	0. 97	0. 45	0. 98	0. 46	1. 00	0. 47
154	0. 88	0. 39	0. 90	0. 39	0. 91	0. 40	0. 93	0. 41	0. 94	0. 41	0. 96	0. 42	0. 98	0. 43	0. 99	0. 43
156	0. 89	0. 36	0. 90	0. 37	0. 91	0. 37	0. 93	0. 38	0. 94	0. 38	0. 96	0. 39	0. 97	0. 39	0. 99	0. 40
158	0. 89	0. 33	0. 90	0. 34	0. 91	0. 34	0. 93	0. 35	0. 94	0. 35	0. 95	0. 36	0. 97	0. 36	0. 98	0. 37
160	0. 89	0. 30	0. 90	0. 31	0. 91	0. 31	0. 93	0. 32	0. 94	0. 32	0. 95	0. 33	0. 96	0. 33	0. 98	0. 33

TABLE 3
Distance of an Object by Two Bearings

Difference between the course and second bearing	78°	80°	82°	84°	86°	88°	90°	92°
	Difference between the course and first bearing							
88	5. 63 5. 63							
90	4. 70 4. 70	5. 67 5. 67						
92	4. 04 4. 04	4. 74 4. 73	5. 70 5. 70					
94	3. 55 3. 54	4. 07 4. 06	4. 76 4. 75	5. 73 5. 71				
96	3. 17 3. 15	3. 57 3. 55	4. 09 4. 07	4. 78 4. 76	5. 74 5. 71			
98	2. 86 2. 83	3. 19 3. 16	3. 59 3. 56	4. 11 4. 07	4. 80 4. 75	5. 76 5. 70		
100	2. 61 2. 57	2. 88 2. 84	3. 20 3. 16	3. 61 3. 55	4. 12 4. 06	4. 81 4. 73	5. 76 5. 67	
102	2. 40 2. 35	2. 63 2. 57	2. 90 2. 83	3. 22 3. 15	3. 62 3. 54	4. 13 4. 04	4. 81 4. 70	5. 76 5. 63
104	2. 23 2. 16	2. 42 2. 35	2. 64 2. 56	2. 91 2. 82	3. 23 3. 13	3. 63 3. 52	4. 13 4. 01	4. 81 4. 66
106	2. 08 2. 00	2. 25 2. 16	2. 43 2. 34	2. 65 2. 55	2. 92 2. 80	3. 23 3. 11	3. 63 3. 49	4. 13 3. 97
108	1. 96 1. 86	2. 10 2. 00	2. 26 2. 15	2. 45 2. 33	2. 66 2. 53	2. 92 2. 78	3. 24 3. 08	3. 63 3. 45
110	1. 85 1. 73	1. 97 1. 85	2. 11 1. 98	2. 27 2. 13	2. 45 2. 31	2. 67 2. 51	2. 92 2. 75	3. 23 3. 04
112	1. 75 1. 62	1. 86 1. 72	1. 98 1. 83	2. 12 1. 96	2. 28 2. 11	2. 46 2. 28	2. 67 2. 48	2. 92 2. 71
114	1. 66 1. 52	1. 76 1. 61	1. 87 1. 71	1. 99 1. 82	2. 12 1. 94	2. 28 2. 08	2. 46 2. 25	2. 67 2. 44
116	1. 59 1. 43	1. 68 1. 51	1. 77 1. 59	1. 88 1. 69	2. 00 1. 79	2. 13 1. 91	2. 28 2. 05	2. 46 2. 21
118	1. 52 1. 34	1. 60 1. 41	1. 68 1. 49	1. 78 1. 57	1. 88 1. 66	2. 00 1. 76	2. 13 1. 88	2. 28 2. 01
120	1. 46 1. 27	1. 53 1. 33	1. 61 1. 39	1. 69 1. 47	1. 78 1. 54	1. 89 1. 63	2. 00 1. 73	2. 13 1. 84
122	1. 41 1. 19	1. 47 1. 25	1. 54 1. 31	1. 62 1. 37	1. 70 1. 44	1. 79 1. 52	1. 89 1. 60	2. 00 1. 70
124	1. 36 1. 13	1. 42 1. 18	1. 48 1. 23	1. 55 1. 28	1. 62 1. 34	1. 70 1. 41	1. 79 1. 48	1. 89 1. 56
126	1. 32 1. 06	1. 37 1. 11	1. 43 1. 15	1. 48 1. 20	1. 55 1. 26	1. 62 1. 31	1. 70 1. 38	1. 79 1. 45
128	1. 28 1. 01	1. 33 1. 04	1. 38 1. 08	1. 43 1. 13	1. 49 1. 17	1. 55 1. 23	1. 62 1. 28	1. 70 1. 34
130	1. 24 0. 95	1. 29 0. 98	1. 33 1. 02	1. 38 1. 06	1. 44 1. 10	1. 49 1. 14	1. 56 1. 19	1. 62 1. 24
132	1. 21 0. 90	1. 25 0. 93	1. 29 0. 96	1. 34 0. 99	1. 39 1. 03	1. 44 1. 07	1. 49 1. 11	1. 55 1. 16
134	1. 18 0. 85	1. 22 0. 88	1. 26 0. 90	1. 30 0. 93	1. 34 0. 97	1. 39 1. 00	1. 44 1. 04	1. 49 1. 07
136	1. 15 0. 80	1. 19 0. 83	1. 22 0. 85	1. 26 0. 88	1. 30 0. 90	1. 34 0. 93	1. 39 0. 97	1. 44 1. 00
138	1. 13 0. 76	1. 16 0. 78	1. 19 0. 80	1. 23 0. 82	1. 27 0. 85	1. 30 0. 87	1. 35 0. 90	1. 39 0. 93
140	1. 11 0. 71	1. 14 0. 73	1. 17 0. 75	1. 20 0. 77	1. 23 0. 79	1. 27 0. 82	1. 31 0. 84	1. 34 0. 86
142	1. 09 0. 67	1. 12 0. 69	1. 14 0. 70	1. 17 0. 72	1. 20 0. 74	1. 24 0. 76	1. 27 0. 78	1. 30 0. 80
144	1. 07 0. 63	1. 10 0. 64	1. 12 0. 66	1. 15 0. 67	1. 18 0. 69	1. 21 0. 71	1. 24 0. 73	1. 27 0. 75
146	1. 05 0. 59	1. 08 0. 60	1. 10 0. 62	1. 13 0. 63	1. 15 0. 64	1. 18 0. 66	1. 21 0. 67	1. 24 0. 69
148	1. 04 0. 55	1. 06 0. 56	1. 08 0. 57	1. 11 0. 59	1. 13 0. 60	1. 16 0. 61	1. 18 0. 62	1. 21 0. 64
150	1. 03 0. 51	1. 05 0. 52	1. 07 0. 53	1. 09 0. 54	1. 11 0. 55	1. 13 0. 57	1. 15 0. 58	1. 18 0. 59
152	1. 02 0. 48	1. 04 0. 49	1. 05 0. 49	1. 07 0. 50	1. 09 0. 51	1. 11 0. 52	1. 13 0. 53	1. 15 0. 54
154	1. 01 0. 44	1. 02 0. 45	1. 04 0. 46	1. 06 0. 46	1. 08 0. 47	1. 09 0. 48	1. 11 0. 49	1. 13 0. 50
156	1. 00 0. 41	1. 01 0. 41	1. 03 0. 42	1. 05 0. 43	1. 06 0. 43	1. 08 0. 44	1. 09 0. 45	1. 11 0. 45
158	0. 99 0. 37	1. 01 0. 38	1. 02 0. 38	1. 03 0. 39	1. 05 0. 39	1. 06 0. 40	1. 08 0. 40	1. 09 0. 41
160	0. 99 0. 34	1. 00 0. 34	1. 01 0. 35	1. 02 0. 35	1. 04 0. 35	1. 05 0. 36	1. 06 0. 36	1. 08 0. 37

°	94°	96°	98°	100°	102°	104°	106°	108°
104	5. 74 5. 57							
106	4. 80 4. 61	5. 73 5. 51						
108	4. 12 3. 92	4. 78 4. 55	5. 70 5. 42					
110	3. 62 3. 40	4. 11 3. 86	4. 76 4. 48	5. 67 5. 33				
112	3. 23 2. 99	3. 61 3. 35	4. 09 3. 80	4. 74 4. 40	5. 63 5. 22			
114	2. 92 2. 66	3. 22 2. 94	3. 59 3. 28	4. 07 3. 72	4. 70 4. 30	5. 59 5. 10		
116	2. 66 2. 39	2. 91 2. 61	3. 20 2. 88	3. 57 3. 21	4. 04 3. 63	4. 67 4. 19	5. 54 4. 98	
118	2. 45 2. 17	2. 65 2. 34	2. 90 2. 56	3. 19 2. 83	3. 55 3. 13	4. 01 3. 54	4. 62 4. 08	5. 48 4. 84
120	2. 28 1. 97	2. 45 2. 12	2. 64 2. 29	2. 88 2. 49	3. 17 2. 74	3. 52 3. 05	3. 97 3. 44	4. 57 3. 96
122	2. 12 1. 80	2. 27 1. 92	2. 43 2. 06	2. 63 2. 23	2. 86 2. 43	3. 14 2. 66	3. 49 2. 96	3. 93 3. 33
124	2. 00 1. 65	2. 12 1. 76	2. 26 1. 87	2. 42 2. 01	2. 61 2. 16	2. 84 2. 35	3. 11 2. 58	3. 45 2. 86
126	1. 88 1. 52	1. 99 1. 61	2. 11 1. 71	2. 25 1. 82	2. 40 1. 95	2. 59 2. 10	2. 81 2. 27	3. 08 2. 49
128	1. 78 1. 41	1. 88 1. 48	1. 98 1. 56	2. 10 1. 65	2. 23 1. 76	2. 39 1. 88	2. 57 2. 02	2. 78 2. 19
130	1. 70 1. 30	1. 78 1. 36	1. 87 1. 43	1. 97 1. 51	2. 08 1. 60	2. 21 1. 70	2. 36 1. 81	2. 54 1. 94
132	1. 62 1. 20	1. 69 1. 26	1. 77 1. 32	1. 86 1. 38	1. 96 1. 45	2. 07 1. 54	2. 19 1. 63	2. 34 1. 74
134	1. 55 1. 12	1. 62 1. 16	1. 68 1. 21	1. 76 1. 27	1. 85 1. 33	1. 94 1. 40	2. 05 1. 47	2. 17 1. 56
136	1. 49 1. 04	1. 55 1. 07	1. 61 1. 12	1. 68 1. 16	1. 75 1. 22	1. 83 1. 27	1. 92 1. 34	2. 03 1. 41
138	1. 44 0. 96	1. 49 0. 99	1. 54 1. 03	1. 60 1. 07	1. 66 1. 11	1. 74 1. 16	1. 81 1. 21	1. 90 1. 27
140	1. 39 0. 89	1. 43 0. 92	1. 48 0. 95	1. 53 0. 98	1. 59 1. 02	1. 65 1. 06	1. 72 1. 10	1. 79 1. 15
142	1. 34 0. 83	1. 38 0. 85	1. 43 0. 88	1. 47 0. 91	1. 52 0. 94	1. 58 0. 97	1. 64 1. 01	1. 70 1. 05
144	1. 30 0. 77	1. 34 0. 79	1. 38 0. 81	1. 42 0. 83	1. 46 0. 86	1. 51 0. 89	1. 56 0. 92	1. 62 0. 95
146	1. 27 0. 71	1. 30 0. 73	1. 33 0. 75	1. 37 0. 77	1. 41 0. 79	1. 45 0. 81	1. 50 0. 84	1. 54 0. 86
148	1. 23 0. 65	1. 26 0. 67	1. 29 0. 69	1. 33 0. 70	1. 36 0. 72	1. 40 0. 74	1. 44 0. 76	1. 48 0. 78
150	1. 20 0. 60	1. 23 0. 61	1. 26 0. 63	1. 29 0. 64	1. 32 0. 66	1. 35 0. 67	1. 38 0. 69	1. 42 0. 71
152	1. 18 0. 55	1. 20 0. 56	1. 22 0. 57	1. 25 0. 59	1. 28 0. 60	1. 31 0. 61	1. 34 0. 63	1. 37 0. 64
154	1. 15 0. 50	1. 17 0. 51	1. 19 0. 52	1. 22 0. 53	1. 24 0. 54	1. 27 0. 56	1. 29 0. 57	1. 32 0. 58
156	1. 13 0. 46	1. 15 0. 47	1. 17 0. 47	1. 19 0. 48	1. 21 0. 49	1. 23 0. 50	1. 25 0. 51	1. 28 0. 52
158	1. 11 0. 42	1. 13 0. 42	1. 14 0. 43	1. 16 0. 44	1. 18 0. 44	1. 20 0. 45	1. 22 0. 46	1. 24 0. 47
160	1. 09 0. 37	1. 11 0. 38	1. 12 0. 38	1. 14 0. 39	1. 15 0. 39	1. 17 0. 40	1. 19 0. 41	1. 21 0. 41

TABLE 3
Distance of an Object by Two Bearings

Difference between the course and second bearing.

Difference between the course and first bearing.

Difference between the course and second bearing.	110°		112°		114°		116°		118°		120°		122°	
120	5.41	4.69												
122	4.52	3.83	5.34	4.53										
124	3.88	3.22	4.46	3.70	5.26	4.36								
126	3.41	2.76	3.83	3.10	4.39	3.55	5.18	4.19						
128	3.04	2.40	3.36	2.65	3.78	2.98	4.32	3.41	5.08	4.01				
130	2.75	2.10	3.00	2.30	3.31	2.54	3.72	2.85	4.25	3.25	4.99	3.82		
132	2.51	1.86	2.71	2.01	2.96	2.20	3.26	2.42	3.65	2.71	4.17	3.10	4.88	3.63
134	2.31	1.66	2.48	1.78	2.67	1.92	2.91	2.09	3.20	2.30	3.58	2.57	4.08	2.93
136	2.14	1.49	2.28	1.58	2.44	1.69	2.63	1.83	2.86	1.98	3.14	2.18	3.51	2.44
138	2.00	1.34	2.12	1.42	2.25	1.50	2.40	1.61	2.58	1.73	2.80	1.88	3.08	2.06
140	1.88	1.21	1.97	1.27	2.08	1.34	2.21	1.42	2.36	1.52	2.53	1.63	2.74	1.76
142	1.77	1.09	1.85	1.14	1.95	1.20	2.05	1.26	2.17	1.34	2.31	1.42	2.48	1.53
144	1.68	0.99	1.75	1.03	1.83	1.07	1.91	1.13	2.01	1.18	2.13	1.25	2.26	1.33
146	1.60	0.89	1.66	0.93	1.72	0.96	1.80	1.01	1.88	1.05	1.98	1.10	2.08	1.17
148	1.53	0.81	1.58	0.84	1.63	0.87	1.70	0.90	1.77	0.94	1.84	0.98	1.93	1.03
150	1.46	0.73	1.51	0.75	1.55	0.78	1.61	0.80	1.67	0.83	1.73	0.87	1.81	0.90
152	1.40	0.66	1.44	0.68	1.48	0.70	1.53	0.72	1.58	0.74	1.63	0.77	1.70	0.80
154	1.35	0.59	1.39	0.61	1.42	0.62	1.46	0.64	1.50	0.66	1.55	0.68	1.60	0.70
156	1.31	0.53	1.33	0.54	1.37	0.56	1.40	0.57	1.43	0.58	1.47	0.60	1.52	0.62
158	1.26	0.47	1.28	0.48	1.32	0.49	1.34	0.50	1.37	0.51	1.41	0.53	1.44	0.54
160	1.23	0.42	1.25	0.43	1.27	0.43	1.29	0.44	1.32	0.45	1.35	0.46	1.38	0.47

	124°		126°		128°		130°		132°		134°		136°	
134	4.77	3.43												
136	3.99	2.77	4.66	3.23										
138	3.43	2.29	3.89	2.60	4.54	3.04								
140	3.01	1.93	3.34	2.15	3.79	2.44	4.41	2.84						
142	2.68	1.65	2.94	1.81	3.26	2.01	3.68	2.27	4.28	2.63				
144	2.42	1.42	2.62	1.54	2.86	1.68	3.17	1.86	3.57	2.10	4.14	2.43		
146	2.21	1.24	2.37	1.32	2.55	1.43	2.78	1.55	3.07	1.72	3.46	1.93	4.00	2.24
148	2.04	1.08	2.16	1.14	2.30	1.22	2.48	1.31	2.70	1.43	2.97	1.58	3.34	1.77
150	1.89	0.95	1.99	0.99	2.10	1.05	2.24	1.12	2.40	1.20	2.61	1.30	2.87	1.44
152	1.77	0.83	1.85	0.87	1.94	0.91	2.04	0.96	2.17	1.02	2.33	1.09	2.52	1.18
154	1.66	0.73	1.72	0.76	1.80	0.79	1.88	0.83	1.98	0.87	2.10	0.92	2.25	0.99
156	1.56	0.64	1.62	0.66	1.68	0.68	1.75	0.71	1.83	0.74	1.92	0.78	2.03	0.83
158	1.48	0.56	1.53	0.57	1.58	0.59	1.63	0.61	1.70	0.64	1.77	0.66	1.85	0.69
160	1.41	0.48	1.45	0.49	1.49	0.51	1.53	0.52	1.58	0.54	1.64	0.56	1.71	0.58

	138°		140°		142°		144°		146°		148°		150°	
148	3.85	2.04												
150	3.22	1.61	3.70	1.85										
152	2.77	1.30	3.09	1.45	3.55	1.66								
154	2.43	1.06	2.66	1.16	2.96	1.30	3.38	1.48						
156	2.17	0.88	2.33	0.95	2.54	1.04	2.83	1.15	3.22	1.31				
158	1.96	0.73	2.08	0.78	2.23	0.84	2.43	0.91	2.69	1.01	3.05	1.14		
160	1.79	0.61	1.88	0.64	1.99	0.68	2.13	0.73	2.31	0.79	2.55	0.87	2.88	0.98

bearings.* If the two angles are such that their natural cotangents differ by unity, the distance abeam will be equal approximately to the distance run between bearings. Some combinations having approximately this relationship are 22°–34°, 25°–41°, 27°–46°, 32°–59°, and 40°–79°.

If either the course or speed is in error, the result will be inaccurate.

Safe piloting without a fix • A fix or running fix is not always necessary to insure safety of the vessel. If a ship is proceeding up a dredged channel, for instance, the only knowledge needed to prevent grounding is that the ship is within the limits of the dredged area. This information might be provided by a range in line with the channel. A fix is not needed except to mark the point at which the range can no longer be followed with safety. Such a point is usually marked by a buoy.

Under favorable conditions a **danger bearing** might be used to insure safe passage past a shoal or other danger. Refer to figure 9.20. A vessel is proceeding along a coast, on course line *AB*. A shoal is to be avoided. A line *HX* is drawn from lighthouse *H*, tangent to the outer edge of the danger. As long as the bearing of light *H* is *less* than *XH*, the danger bearing, the vessel is in safe water. An example is *YH*, no part of the bearing line passing through the danger area. Any bearing *greater* than *XH*, such as *ZH*, indicates a *possible* dangerous situation. If the object is passed on the port side, the safe bearing is *less* than the danger bearing, as shown in figure 9.20. If the object is passed on the starboard side, the danger bearing represents the minimum bearing, safe ones being *greater*. To be effective, a danger bearing should not differ greatly from the course, and the object of which bearings are to be taken should be easily identifiable and visible over the entire area of usefulness of the danger bearing. A margin of safety might be provided by drawing line *HX* through a point a short distance off the danger. If a natural or artificial range is available as a danger bearing, it should be used.

A vessel proceeding along a coast may be in safe water as long as it remains a minimum distance off the beach. This information may be provided by any means available. One method useful in avoiding particular dangers is the use of a **danger angle.** Refer to figure 9.21. A ship is proceeding along a coast on course line *AB*, and the captain wishes to remain outside a danger *D*. Prominent landmarks are located at *M* and *N*. A circle is drawn through *M* and *N* and tangent to the outer edge of the danger. If *X* is a point on this circle, angle *MXN* is the same as at any other point on the circle (except that part between *M* and *N*). Anywhere within the circle the angle is *larger* and anywhere outside the circle it is *smaller*. Therefore, any angle smaller than *MXN* indicates a safe position

---

* Refer also to the Glossary under "seven-eighths rule," "seven-tenths rule," and "seven-thirds rule."

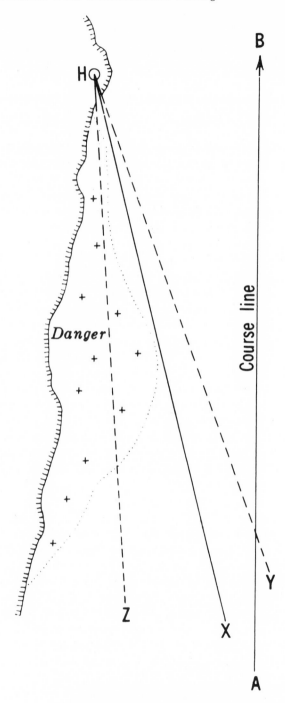

Fig. 9.20. A danger bearing.

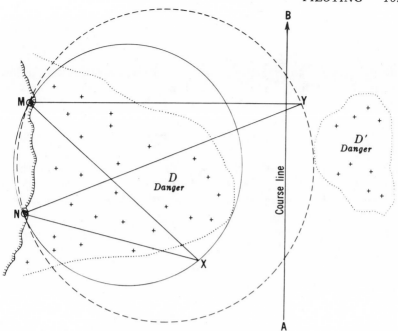

Fig. 9.21. Horizontal danger angles.

and any angle larger than *MXN* indicates possible danger. Angle *MXN* is therefore a maximum **horizontal danger angle.** A minimum horizontal danger angle is used when a vessel is to pass *inside* an offlying danger, as at *D'*. In this case the circle is drawn through *M* and *N* and tangent to the *inner* edge of the danger area. The angle is kept larger than *MYN*. If a vessel is to pass *between* two danger areas, as in figure 9.21, the horizontal angle should be kept smaller than *MXN* but larger than *MYN*. The minimum danger angle is effective only while the vessel is inside the larger circle through *M* and *N*. Bearings on either landmark might be used to indicate the entering and leaving of the larger circle. A margin of safety can be provided by drawing the circles through points a short distance off the dangers. Any method of measuring the angles, or difference of bearing of *M* and *N*, can be used.

A vessel may sometimes be kept in safe water by means of a **danger sounding.** The value selected depends upon the draft of the vessel and the slope of the bottom. It should be sufficiently deep to provide adequate maneuvering room for the vessel to reach deeper water before grounding, once the minimum depth is obtained. In an area where the shoaling is gradual, a smaller margin of depth can be considered safe than in an area of rapid shoaling. Where the shoaling is very abrupt, no danger sounding is practical. It is good practice to prominently mark the danger sounding line on the chart. A colored pencil is useful for this purpose.

If it is desired to round a point marked by a prominent landmark, without approaching closer than a given minimum distance, this can be done by steaming until the minimum distance is reached and then immediately changing course so as to bring the landmark broad on the beam. Frequent small changes of course are then used to keep the landmark near, *but not forward of*, the beam. This method is not reliable if the vessel is being moved laterally by wind or current.

An approximation of the distance off can be found by noting the rate at which the bearing changes. If the landmark is kept abeam, the change is indicated by a change of heading. During a change of 57°5, the distance off is about the same as the distance run. For a change of 28°5, the distance is about twice the run; for 19° it is about three times the run; for 14°5 it is about four times the run; and for 11°5 it is about five times the run. Another variation is to measure the number of seconds required for a change of 16°. The distance off is equal to this interval multiplied by the speed in knots and divided by 1,000. That is, $D = \frac{St}{1,000}$, where D is the distance in nautical miles, S is the speed in knots, and t is the time interval in seconds. This method can also be used for straight courses (with bearings 8° forward and abaft the beam), but with somewhat reduced accuracy.

Soundings • The most important use of soundings is to determine whether the depth is sufficient to provide a reasonable margin of safety for the vessel. For this reason, soundings should be taken continuously in pilot waters. A study of the chart and the establishment of a danger sounding should indicate the degree of safety of the vessel at any time.

Under favorable conditions, soundings can be a valuable aid in establishing the position of the vessel. Their value in this regard depends upon the configuration of the bottom, the amount and accuracy of information given on the chart, the type and accuracy of the sounding equipment available aboard ship, and the knowledge and skill of the navigator. In an area having a flat bottom devoid of distinctive features, or in an area where detailed information is not given on the chart, little positional information can be gained from soundings. However, in an area where depth curves run roughly parallel to the shore, a sounding might indicate distance from the beach. In any area where a given depth curve is sharply defined and relatively straight, it serves as a line of position which can be used with other lines, such as those obtained by bearings of landmarks, to obtain a fix. The crossing of a sharply defined trench, ridge, shoal, or flat-topped seamount (a **guyot**) might provide valuable positional information.

In any such use, identification of the feature observed is important. In an area of rugged underwater terrain, identification might be difficult unless an almost continuous determination of position is maintained, for it is not unusual for a number of features within a normal radius of uncertainty to be similar. If the echo sounder produces a continuous recording of the depth, called a **bottom profile**, this can be matched to the chart in the vicinity of the course line. If no profile is available, a rough approximation of one can be constructed as follows: Record a series of soundings at short intervals, the length being dictated by the scale of the chart and the existing situation. For most purposes the interval might be each minute, or perhaps each half-mile or mile. Draw a straight line on transparent material and, at the scale of the chart, place marks along the line at the distance intervals at which soundings were made. For this purpose the line might be superimposed over the latitude scale or a distance scale of the chart. At each mark record the corresponding sounding. Then place the transparency over the chart and, by trial and error, match the recorded soundings to those indicated on the chart. Keep the line on the transparency parallel or nearly parallel to the course line plotted on the chart. A current may cause some difference between the plotted course line and the course made good. Also, speed over the bottom might be somewhat different from that used for the plot. This should be reflected in the match. This method should be used with caution, because it may be possible to fit the **line of soundings** to several places on the chart.

Exact agreement with the charted bottom should not be expected at all times. Inaccuracies in the soundings, tide, or incomplete data on the chart may affect the match, but general agreement should be sought. Any marked discrepancy should be investigated, particularly if it indicates less depth than anticipated. If such a discrepancy cannot be reconciled, the wisest decision might well be to haul off into deeper water or anchor and wait for more favorable conditions or additional information.

Most probable position (**MPP**) • Since information sufficient to establish an *exact* position is seldom available, the navigator is frequently faced with the problem of establishing the most probable position of the vessel. If three reliable bearing lines cross at a point, there is usually little doubt as to the position, and little or no judgment is needed. But when conflicting information or information of questionable reliability is received, a decision is required to establish the MPP. At such a time the experience of the navigator can be of great value. Judgment can be improved if the navigator will continually try to account for all apparent discrepancies, even under favorable conditions. If a navigator habitually analyzes the situation whenever positional information is received, he will develop judgment as to the reliability of various types of information, and will learn something of the conditions under which certain types should be treated with caution.

When complete positional information is lacking, or when the available information is considered of questionable reliability, the most probable position might well be considered an **estimated position (EP).** Such a position might be determined from a single line of position, from a line of soundings, from lines of position which are somewhat inconsistent, from a dead reckoning position with a correction for current or wind, etc.

Whether the most probable position is a fix, running fix, estimated position, or dead reckoning position, it should be kept continually in mind, together with some estimate of its reliability. The practice of continuing a dead reckoning plot from one good fix to another is advisable, whether or not information is available to indicate a most probable position differing from the dead reckoning position, for the DR plot provides an indication of current and leeway. A series of estimated positions may not be consistent because of the continual revision of the estimate as additional information is received. However, it is good practice to plot all MPP's, and sometimes to maintain a separate EP plot based upon the best estimate of course and speed being made good over the ground, for this should furnish valuable information to indicate whether the present course is a safe one.

Aids to Navigation

Kinds of aids • When piloting, a navigator is concerned primarily with the position of his vessel relative to nearby land, shoals, and other dangers. It is natural, therefore, that he make extensive use of **landmarks,** which are conspicuous objects, structures, or lights serving as indicators for guidance or warning of a craft. Such an object visible from a distance to seaward is called a **seamark.** Either type of mark may be called a **daymark** if useful only during daylight, or a **nightmark** if useful primarily during darkness. A natural or artificial mark used to assist a vessel in avoiding a particular hazard may be called a **clearing mark.** If an uncharted landmark is discovered, its position might be established from available information and plotted on the chart for future use. A permanent feature might well be reported to the appropriate government charting agency.

A mark established by man, to serve as a landmark, is called an **aid to navigation.** This should not be confused with the expression **navigational aid,** which includes, in addition to aids to navigation, such items as instruments, charts, tables, etc. The principal aids to navigation are:

Lighthouse. A lighthouse is a structure exhibiting a major light designed to serve as an aid to navigation. Lighthouses vary in appearance because of location, relative importance, the type of soil upon which they are constructed, prevalence of violent storms, backgrounds against which they are seen, distances the lights are to be seen, etc. Some are located on land, and some in the water. The type of structure and its coloring assist in daylight identification.

Beacon. In a general sense, a beacon is anything serving as a signal or indication, either for guidance or warning. However, as a distinctive type of aid to navigation, a beacon is either a *fixed* aid (not a floating one) or an unlighted aid (sometimes called a **daybeacon**). As thus defined, a lighthouse is a beacon. However, the term "beacon" is generally applied particularly to secondary fixed structures, whether lighted or not.

Lightship. This is a distinctively marked vessel anchored or moored at a charted point to serve as an aid to navigation. By night it displays a characteristic masthead light and a less brilliant light on the forestay. The forestay indicates the direction in which the vessel is headed, and hence the direction of the current (or wind), since lightships head into the wind or current. By day a lightship displays the International Code signal of the station when requested, or if an approaching vessel does not seem to recognize it. The name of the station is painted in large letters on the side of the vessel. A lightship may be equipped with certain auxiliary devices such as a fog signal, submarine sound signal, and radiobeacon. When under way or off station a lightship displays the lights and sounds the signals prescribed by the rules of the road, and flies the International Code signal flags "PC," signifying that it is not then serving as an aid to navigation. It does not then show or sound any of the signals of a lightship. A lightship is the floating equivalent of a lighthouse. Most U.S. lightships eventually will be replaced by structures.

Buoy. A buoy is a floating object, other than a lightship, moored to the bottom as an aid to navigation. There are many different types of buoys to serve different purposes. Buoys are the most numerous aid to navigation.

Any lighted aid to navigation may be called a **light.**

Along the coasts of the United States and in the Great Lakes (United States side) most aids to navigation are installed and maintained by the U.S. Coast Guard. Along certain rivers they are under the control of other government agencies, notably the United States Army Corps of Engineers. A number of privately maintained aids are in use. An example of such aids are lights at the ends of privately owned piers.

Lights • A light extends the use of various aids to navigation to periods of darkness. If such a light is to serve its purpose, the user must be able to distinguish it from the general background of shore lights, and to determine *which* navigational light it is. That is, one must be able to *identify* the light. For this purpose each light is given a distinctive sequence of light and dark periods, and in some cases a distinctive color, or color sequence. These features are called the **characteristics** of the light (fig. 9.22). No two lights are given the same characteristics if they are so located that one might be mistaken for the other.

The U.S. Coast Guard publishes a *Light List* in five volumes: one for the Atlantic coast, one for the Atlantic and Gulf coast, and one each for the Pacific coast and islands, Great Lakes, and Mississippi River system. The Defense Mapping Agency Hydrographic Center publishes seven *Lists of Lights* giving characteristics of lights of foreign waters and the principal lights along the coasts of the United States. Characteristics are also indicated on charts. The letter *W* indicates a white light, *R* a red light, and *G* a green light. Other colors are not used by the Coast Guard. If no color indication is given, a light is white. Colors are produced by glass shades or screens. The **period** of a light is the time required for one complete sequence of characteristics.

Some lights provide bearing indication by a system of **light sectors,** different colors being exhibited in the various sectors. As an observer crosses the boundary between sectors, he can note the change of color. The boundaries are indicated in the light lists and by broken lines on charts. The bearings given in these indications are those *of* the light as observed at a distance, not the direction outward *from* the light. In general, red sectors are used to indicate obstruction areas. In using light sectors to determine bearing, one should remember that the line of demarcation is not always sharply defined, and that when haze or smoke is present, a white light might have a reddish hue.

Visibility of lights • Usually a navigator wants to know not only the identity of a light, but also the area in which he might reasonably expect to observe it. His track is planned to take him within range of lights which can prove useful during periods of darkness. If lights are not sighted within a reasonable time after prediction, a dangerous situation may exist, requiring resolution or action to insure safety of the vessel.

The area in which a light can be observed is normally a circle with the light as the center, and the range of visibility as the radius. However, on some bearings the range may be reduced by obstructions. In this case the obstructed arc might differ with height of eye and distance. Also, lights of different colors may be seen at different distances. This fact should be considered not only in predicting the distance at which a light can be seen, but also in identifying it. The condition of the atmosphere has a considerable effect upon the distance at which lights can be seen. Sometimes lights are obscured by fog, haze, dust, smoke, or precipitation which may be present at the light, or between it and the observer, but may be unknown to the observer. There is always the possibility of a light being extinguished. In the case of unwatched lights, this condition might not be detected and corrected at once.

On a dark, clear night the range of visibility is limited primarily in two ways: (1) luminosity and (2) curvature of the earth. A weak light cannot normally be expected to be seen beyond a certain range, regardless of the height of eye. This distance is called **luminous range.** Light travels

Illustration	Symbols and meaning		Phase description
	Lights which do not change color	Lights which show color variations	
	F. = Fixed	Alt. = Alternating.	A continuous steady light.
	F. Fl. = Fixed and flashing.	Alt. F. Fl. = Alternating fixed and flashing.	A fixed light varied at regular intervals by a flash of greater brilliance.
	F. Gp. Fl. = Fixed and group flashing.	Alt. F. Gp. Fl. = Alternating fixed and group flashing	A fixed light varied at regular intervals by groups of 2 or more flashes of greater brilliance.
	Fl. = Flashing....	Alt. Fl. Alternating flashing.	Shows a single flash at regular intervals, the duration of light always being less than the duration of darkness. Shows not more than 30 flashes per minute.
	Gp. Fl. = Group flashing.	Alt. Gp. Fl. = Alternating group flashing.	Shows at regular intervals groups of 2 or more flashes.
	Qk. Fl. = Quick flashing.	----------------	Shows not less than 60 flashes per minute.
	I. Qk. Fl. = Interrupted quick flashing.	----------------	Shows quick flashes for about 4 seconds, followed by a dark period of about 4 seconds.
	S-L. Fl. = Short-long flashing.	----------------	Shows a short flash of about 0.4 second, followed by a long flash of 4 times that duration.
	Occ. = Occulting.	Alt. Occ. = Alternating occulting.	A light totally eclipsed at regular intervals, the duration of light always equal to or greater than the duration of darkness.
	Gp. Occ. = Group occulting.	----------------	A light with a group of 2 or more eclipses at regular intervals.

Light colors used and abbreviations: W = white, R = red, G = green.

Fig. 9.22. Light characteristics.

in almost straight lines, so that an observer below the visible horizon of the light should not expect to see the light, although the loom extending upward from the light can sometimes be seen at greater distances. Table 4 gives the distance to the horizon at various heights. The tabulated distances assume normal refraction. Abnormal conditions might extend this range somewhat (or in some cases reduce it). Hence, the **geographic range,** like the luminous range, is not subject to exact prediction at any given time.

The geographic range depends upon the height of both the light and the observer, as shown in figure 9.23. This illustration shows a light 150 feet above the water. At this height, the distance to the horizon, by Table 4, is 14.0 miles. Within this range the light, if powerful enough and if atmospheric conditions permit, is visible regardless of the height of eye of the observer (if there is no obstruction). Beyond this range, the visibility depends upon the height of eye. Thus, by Table 4 an observer with height of eye of five feet can see the light on his horizon if he is 2.6 miles beyond the horizon of the light, or a total of 16.6 miles. For a height of 30 feet the distance is $14.0+6.3 = 20.3$ miles. If the height of eye is 70 feet, the geographic range is $14.0+9.6 = 23.6$ miles.

The range of important lights is given in the light lists, and also on the charts. *The tabulated or charted range is for mean high water and a height of eye of 15 feet,* and because of various uncertainties is given only to the nearest whole mile. Where the luminous range is less than the charted range, the shorter distance is given. This fact is not indicated. Therefore, in predicting the range at which a light can be seen, one should first determine the geographic range and compare this with the charted range. This is done by *adding* 4.4 miles (the distance to the horizon at a height of 15 feet) to the value from Table 4 for the height of the light. If this value approximates the charted range, one is generally safe in assuming that the charted range is the geographic range. The predicted range is then found by adding the distance to the horizon for both the light and the observer, as indicated above, or, approximately, by taking the *difference* between 4.4 and the distance for the height of eye of the observer (a constant for any given height) and *adding* this value to the charted range (subtracting if the height of eye is less than 15 feet). In making a prediction, one should keep in mind the possibility of the luminous range *between* the charted range and the predicted range. The *power* of the light should be of some assistance in identifying this condition.

If one is approaching a light, and wishes to predict the *time* at which it should be sighted, he first predicts the range. It is then good practice to draw a circle indicating the limit of visibility. The point at which the course line crosses the circle of visibility is the predicted position of the vessel at the time of sighting the light. The predicted time of arrival at this point is the predicted time of sighting the light. The direction of the light from this point is the predicted bearing at which the light should be sighted. Conversion of the true bearing to a relative bearing is usually helpful in sighting the light. The accuracy of the predictions depends upon the accuracy of the predicted range, and the accuracy of the predicted time and place of crossing the circle of visibility. If the course line crosses the circle of visibility at a small angle, a small lateral error in track may result in a large error of prediction, both of bearing and time. This is particularly apparent if the vessel is *farther* from the light than predicted, in which case the light might be passed without being sighted. Thus, if a light is not sighted at the predicted time, the error *may* be on the side of safety. However, such an interpretation should not be given unless confirmed by other information, for there is always the possibility of reduced range of visibility, or of the light being extinguished.

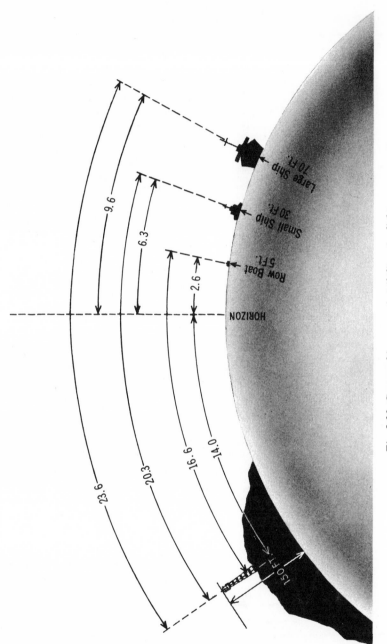

Fig. 9.23. Geographic range of visibility of a light.

TABLE 4

Distance of the Horizon

Height feet	Nautical miles	Statute miles	Height feet	Nautical miles	Statute miles	Height feet	Nautical miles	Statute miles
1	1. 1	1. 3	120	12. 5	14. 4	940	35. 1	40. 4
2	1. 6	1. 9	125	12. 8	14. 7	960	35. 4	40. 8
3	2. 0	2. 3	130	13. 0	15. 0	980	35. 8	41. 2
4	2. 3	2. 6	135	13. 3	15. 3	1, 000	36. 2	41. 6
5	2. 6	2. 9	140	13. 5	15. 6	1, 100	37. 9	43. 7
6	2. 8	3. 2	145	13. 8	15. 9	1, 200	39. 6	45. 6
7	3. 0	3. 5	150	14. 0	16. 1	1, 300	41. 2	47. 5
8	3. 2	3. 7	160	14. 5	16. 7	1, 400	42. 8	49. 3
9	3. 4	4. 0	170	14. 9	17. 2	1, 500	44. 3	51. 0
10	3. 6	4. 2	180	15. 3	17. 7	1, 600	45. 8	52. 7
11	3. 8	4. 4	190	15. 8	18. 2	1, 700	47. 2	54. 3
12	4. 0	4. 6	200	16. 2	18. 6	1, 800	48. 5	55. 9
13	4. 1	4. 7	210	16. 6	19. 1	1, 900	49. 9	57. 4
14	4. 3	4. 9	220	17. 0	19. 5	2, 000	51. 2	58. 9
15	4. 4	5. 1	230	17. 3	20. 0	2, 100	52. 4	60. 4
16	4. 6	5. 3	240	17. 7	20. 4	2, 200	53. 7	61. 8
17	4. 7	5. 4	250	18. 1	20. 8	2, 300	54. 9	63. 2
18	4. 9	5. 6	260	18. 4	21. 2	2, 400	56. 0	64. 5
19	5. 0	5. 7	270	18. 8	21. 6	2, 500	57. 2	65. 8
20	5. 1	5. 9	280	19. 1	22. 0	2, 600	58. 3	67. 2
21	5. 2	6. 0	290	19. 5	22. 4	2, 700	59. 4	68. 4
22	5. 4	6. 2	300	19. 8	22. 8	2, 800	60. 5	69. 7
23	5. 5	6. 3	310	20. 1	23. 2	2, 900	61. 6	70. 9
24	5. 6	6. 5	320	20. 5	23. 6	3, 000	62. 7	72. 1
25	5. 7	6. 6	330	20. 8	23. 9	3, 100	63. 7	73. 3
26	5. 8	6. 7	340	21. 1	24. 3	3, 200	64. 7	74. 5
27	5. 9	6. 8	350	21. 4	24. 6	3, 300	65. 7	75. 7
28	6. 1	7. 0	360	21. 7	25. 0	3, 400	66. 7	76. 8
29	6. 2	7. 1	370	22. 0	25. 3	3, 500	67. 7	77. 9
30	6. 3	7. 2	380	22. 3	25. 7	3, 600	68. 6	79. 0
31	6. 4	7. 3	390	22. 6	26. 0	3, 700	69. 6	80. 1
32	6. 5	7. 5	400	22. 9	26. 3	3, 800	70. 5	81. 2
33	6. 6	7. 6	410	23. 2	26. 7	3, 900	71. 4	82. 2
34	6. 7	7. 7	420	23. 4	27. 0	4, 000	72. 4	83. 3
35	6. 8	7. 8	430	23. 7	27. 3	4, 100	73. 3	84. 3
36	6. 9	7. 9	440	24. 0	27. 6	4, 200	74. 1	85. 4
37	7. 0	8. 0	450	24. 3	27. 9	4, 300	75. 0	86. 4
38	7. 1	8. 1	460	24. 5	28. 2	4, 400	75. 9	87. 4
39	7. 1	8. 2	470	24. 8	28. 6	4, 500	76. 7	88. 3
40	7. 2	8. 3	480	25. 1	28. 9	4, 600	77. 6	89. 3
41	7. 3	8. 4	490	25. 3	29. 2	4, 700	78. 4	90. 3
42	7. 4	8. 5	500	25. 6	29. 4	4, 800	79. 3	91. 2
43	7. 5	8. 6	520	26. 1	30. 0	4, 900	80. 1	92. 2
44	7. 6	8. 7	540	26. 6	30. 6	5, 000	80. 9	93. 1
45	7. 7	8. 8	560	27. 1	31. 2	6, 000	88. 6	102. 0
46	7. 8	8. 9	580	27. 6	31. 7	7, 000	95. 7	110. 2
47	7. 8	9. 0	600	28. 0	32. 3	8, 000	102. 3	117. 8
48	7. 9	9. 1	620	28. 5	32. 8	9, 000	108. 5	124. 9
49	8. 0	9. 2	640	28. 9	33. 3	10, 000	114. 4	131. 7
50	8. 1	9. 3	660	29. 4	33. 8	15, 000	140. 1	161. 3
55	8. 5	9. 8	680	29. 8	34. 3	20, 000	161. 8	186. 3
60	8. 9	10. 2	700	30. 3	34. 8	25, 000	180. 9	208. 2
65	9. 2	10. 6	720	30. 7	35. 3	30, 000	198. 1	228. 1
70	9. 6	11. 0	740	31. 1	35. 8	35, 000	214. 0	246. 4
75	9. 9	11. 4	760	31. 5	36. 3	40, 000	228. 8	263. 4
80	10. 2	11. 8	780	31. 9	36. 8	45, 000	242. 7	279. 4
85	10. 5	12. 1	800	32. 4	37. 3	50, 000	255. 8	294. 5
90	10. 9	12. 5	820	32. 8	37. 7	60, 000	280. 2	322. 6
95	11. 2	12. 8	840	33. 2	38. 2	70, 000	302. 7	348. 4
100	11. 4	13. 2	860	33. 5	38. 6	80, 000	323. 6	372. 5
105	11. 7	13. 5	880	33. 9	39. 1	90, 000	343. 2	395. 1
110	12. 0	13. 8	900	34. 3	39. 5	100, 000	361. 8	416. 5
115	12. 3	14. 1	920	34. 7	39. 9	200, 000	511. 6	589. 0

TABLE 5

Distance by Vertical Angle

Angle	Difference in feet between height of object and height of eye of observer												Angle
	50	60	70	80	90	100	110	120	130	140	160	180	
° ′	Miles	Miles	Miles	Miles	Miles	Miles	Miles	Miles	Miles	Miles	Miles	Miles	° ′
0 10	2. 55	3. 01	3. 45	3. 89	4. 31	4. 72	5. 11	5. 51	5. 89	6. 26	6. 99	7. 68	0 10
0 11	2. 36	2. 79	3. 20	3. 61	4. 01	4. 40	4. 78	5. 15	5. 51	5. 87	6. 57	7. 24	0 11
0 12	2. 19	2. 59	2. 99	3. 37	3. 75	4. 12	4. 48	4. 83	5. 18	5. 53	6. 19	6. 84	0 12
0 13	2. 04	2. 42	2. 80	3. 16	3. 52	3. 87	4. 21	4. 55	4. 89	5. 21	5. 85	6. 48	0 13
0 14	1. 91	2. 27	2. 62	2. 97	3. 31	3. 64	3. 97	4. 30	4. 61	4. 93	5. 54	6. 14	0 14
0 15	1. 79	2. 13	2. 46	2. 79	3. 12	3. 43	3. 75	4. 06	4. 36	4. 66	5. 25	5. 83	0 15
0 20	1. 37	1. 64	1. 90	2. 16	2. 42	2. 68	2. 93	3. 18	3. 43	3. 68	4. 16	4. 64	0 20
0 25	1. 11	1. 33	1. 54	1. 76	1. 97	2. 18	2. 39	2. 60	2. 81	3. 02	3. 42	3. 83	0 25
0 30	0. 93	1. 11	1. 29	1. 47	1. 65	1. 83	2. 01	2. 19	2. 37	2. 54	2. 89	3. 24	0 30
0 35	0. 80	0. 96	1. 11	1. 27	1. 43	1. 58	1. 74	1. 89	2. 05	2. 20	2. 51	2. 81	0 35
0 40	0. 70	0. 84	0. 98	1. 12	1. 26	1. 39	1. 53	1. 67	1. 81	1. 94	2. 21	2. 48	0 40
0 45	0. 62	0. 74	0. 87	0. 99	1. 12	1. 24	1. 36	1. 48	1. 61	1. 73	1. 97	2. 21	0 45
0 50	0. 56	0. 67	0. 78	0. 89	1. 01	1. 12	1. 23	1. 34	1. 45	1. 56	1. 78	2. 00	0 50
0 55	0. 51	0. 61	0. 72	0. 82	0. 92	1. 02	1. 12	1. 22	1. 32	1. 43	1. 63	1. 83	0 55
1 00	0. 47	0. 56	0. 65	0. 75	0. 84	0. 93	1. 02	1. 12	1. 21	1. 30	1. 49	1. 67	1 00
1 10	0. 40	0. 48	0. 56	0. 64	0. 72	0. 80	0. 88	0. 96	1. 04	1. 12	1. 28	1. 44	1 10
1 20	0. 35	0. 42	0. 49	0. 56	0. 63	0. 70	0. 77	0. 84	0. 91	0. 98	1. 12	1. 26	1 20
1 30	0. 31	0. 38	0. 44	0. 50	0. 56	0. 63	0. 69	0. 75	0. 81	0. 87	1. 00	1. 12	1 30
1 40	0. 28	0. 34	0. 39	0. 45	0. 51	0. 57	0. 62	0. 67	0. 73	0. 79	0. 90	1. 02	1 40
1 50	0. 26	0. 31	0. 36	0. 42	0. 47	0. 52	0. 56	0. 61	0. 66	0. 72	0. 82	0. 92	1 50
2 00	0. 24	0. 28	0. 33	0. 38	0. 43	0. 47	0. 53	0. 57	0. 62	0. 65	0. 77	0. 85	2 00
2 15	0. 21	0. 26	0. 30	0. 34	0. 38	0. 42	0. 46	0. 50	0. 54	0. 57	0. 65	0. 73	2 15
2 30	0. 19	0. 23	0. 26	0. 30	0. 34	0. 38	0. 41	0. 45	0. 49	0. 53	0. 60	0. 68	2 30
2 45	0. 17	0. 21	0. 24	0. 27	0. 31	0. 34	0. 37	0. 41	0. 44	0. 48	0. 55	0. 62	2 45
3 00	0. 16	0. 19	0. 22	0. 25	0. 28	0. 31	0. 35	0. 38	0. 41	0. 44	0. 50	0. 56	3 00
3 20	0. 14	0. 17	0. 20	0. 22	0. 25	0. 28	0. 31	0. 34	0. 37	0. 39	0. 45	0. 51	3 20
3 40	0. 13	0. 15	0. 18	0. 21	0. 23	0. 26	0. 28	0. 31	0. 33	0. 36	0. 41	0. 46	3 40
4 00	0. 12	0. 14	0. 16	0. 19	0. 21	0. 24	0. 26	0. 28	0. 31	0. 33	0. 38	0. 42	4 00
4 20	0. 11	0. 13	0. 15	0. 17	0. 19	0. 22	0. 24	0. 26	0. 28	0. 30	0. 35	0. 39	4 20
4 40	0. 10	0. 12	0. 14	0. 16	0. 18	0. 20	0. 22	0. 24	0. 26	0. 28	0. 32	0. 36	4 40
5 00		0. 11	0. 13	0. 15	0. 17	0. 19	0. 21	0. 22	0. 25	0. 26	0. 30	0. 34	5 00
5 20		0. 11	0. 12	0. 14	0. 16	0. 17	0. 19	0. 21	0. 23	0. 25	0. 28	0. 32	5 20
5 40		0. 10	0. 12	0. 13	0. 15	0. 17	0. 18	0. 20	0. 21	0. 23	0. 27	0. 30	5 40
6 00			0. 11	0. 12	0. 14	0. 15	0. 17	0. 19	0. 20	0. 22	0. 25	0. 28	6 00
6 20			0. 10	0. 12	0. 13	0. 15	0. 16	0. 18	0. 19	0. 21	0. 23	0. 27	6 20
6 40				0. 11	0. 12	0. 14	0. 15	0. 17	0. 18	0. 19	0. 22	0. 25	6 40
7 00				0. 10	0. 12	0. 13	0. 14	0. 16	0. 17	0. 18	0. 21	0. 24	7 00
7 20				0. 10	0. 12	0. 13	0. 14	0. 15	0. 17	0. 18	0. 20	0. 23	7 20
7 40				0. 10	0. 11	0. 12	0. 13	0. 15	0. 16	0. 17	0. 19	0. 22	7 40
8 00					0. 10	0. 11	0. 13	0. 14	0. 15	0. 16	0. 19	0. 21	8 00
8 20					0. 10	0. 11	0. 13	0. 13	0. 14	0. 15	0. 18	0. 20	8 20
8 40						0. 11	0. 12	0. 13	0. 14	0. 15	0. 17	0. 19	8 40
9 00						0. 10	0. 12	0. 12	0. 14	0. 14	0. 17	0. 19	9 00
9 30						0. 10	0. 11	0. 12	0. 13	0. 14	0. 16	0. 18	9 30
10 00							0. 10	0. 11	0. 12	0. 13	0. 15	0. 17	10 00
10 30							0. 10	0. 11	0. 11	0. 12	0. 14	0. 16	10 30
11 00								0. 10	0. 11	0. 12	0. 13	0. 15	11 00
11 30								0. 10	0. 11	0. 12	0. 13	0. 14	11 30
12 00									0. 10	0. 11	0. 12	0. 14	12 00
12 30									0. 10	0. 11	0. 12	0. 14	12 30
13 00										0. 10	0. 11	0. 12	13 00
13 30										0. 10	0. 11	0. 12	13 30
14 00											0. 10	0. 12	14 00
14 30											0. 10	0. 12	14 30
15 00												0. 11	15 00
16 00												0. 10	16 00
17 00													17 00
18 00													18 00
19 00													19 00
20 00													20 00

When a light is first sighted, one might determine whether it is on the horizon by immediately reducing the height of eye by several feet, as by squatting or changing position to a lower height. If the light disappears, and reappears when the original height is resumed, it is on the horizon. This process is called **bobbing a light.** If a vessel has considerable vertical motion due to the condition of the sea, a light sighted on the horizon may alternately appear and disappear. This may lead the unwary to assign faulty characteristics and hence to err in its identification. The true characteristics should be observed after the distance has decreased, or by increasing the height of eye of the observer.

Buoys • The primary functions of buoys are to delineate channels, indicate shoals, mark obstructions, and warn the mariner of danger.

The principal types of buoys used by the United States, illustrated in figure 9.24, are as follows:

Can, a buoy built up of steel plates in the shape of an ordinary cylindrical "tin" can.

Nun, a buoy built up of steel plates, the above-water portion being in the shape of a truncated cone.

Spar, a large log, trimmed, shaped, and appropriately painted. Some spar buoys of the same shape are constructed of steel.

Bell, a steel float surmounted by a short skeleton tower in which the bell is located. Older bell buoys are sounded by the motion of the buoys in the sea. In newer types the bells are struck by compressed gas or electrically operated hammers. A **gong buoy** is similar to a bell buoy, but instead of a bell it has a set of gongs, each of which has a distinctive tone.

Whistle, a steel float surmounted by a small tower in which a whistle is located.

Lighted, a steel float surmounted by a skeleton tower with the light at the top.

Combination, a buoy having more than one means of conveying intelligence, as a **lighted bell buoy** or **lighted whistle buoy.**

Some unlighted buoys are fitted with reflectors to assist in their location and identification by searchlight at night. The colors of the reflectors have the same significance as those of lights. Radar reflectors are fitted to some buoys to increase the strength of the returned signal. A buoy may be equipped with a marker radiobeacon.

Most maritime countries use either the **lateral system** of buoyage or the **cardinal system,** or both. In the lateral system, used on all navigable waters of the United States, the coloring, shape, numbering, and lighting of buoys indicate the direction to a danger relative to the course which should be followed. In the cardinal system the coloring, shape, and lighting of buoys indicate the direction to a danger relative to the buoy itself. The color, shape, lights, and numbers of buoys in the lateral system as used

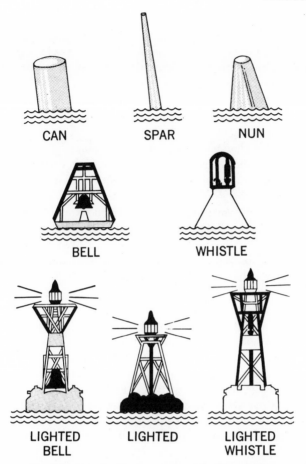

Fig. 9.24. Principal buoy types used by United States.

by the United States are determined relative to a direction *from* seaward. Along the *coasts* of the United States, the *clockwise* direction around the country is arbitrarily considered to be the direction "from seaward." Some countries using the lateral system have methods of coloring their buoys and lights opposite to that of the United States.

In United States waters the following distinctive system of identification is used:

Red nun buoys mark the *right* side of channels for an inbound vessel, and obstructions which should be kept to starboard. They have *even* numbers which increase from seaward.

Black can buoys mark the *left* side of channels for an inbound vessel, and obstructions which should be kept to port. They have *odd* numbers which increase from seaward.

Red and black horizontally banded buoys mark junctions or bifurcations of channels, or an obstruction that can be passed on either side. The color (red or black) of the top band and the shape (nun or can) indicate the side on which the buoy should be passed by a vessel proceeding along the principal channel (black top, preferred channel to starboard; red top, preferred channel to port).

Black and white vertically striped buoys mark the center of a channel and should be passed close aboard. These "mid-channel buoys" may be either nuns or cans.

In fairways and channels solid red or solid black buoys have numbers. Others may have letter designations. Along channels certain numbers may be omitted to maintain the approximate sequence on both sides of the channels.

Lights. Red lights are used only on red buoys and buoys with a red band at the top, green lights are used only on black buoys and buoys with a black band at the top. White lights are used without any color significance. Lights on red and black buoys, if not fixed, are always regularly flashing or regularly occulting. Quick flashing lights are used when a light of distinct cautionary significance is desired, as at a sharp turn or constriction in the channel. Interrupted quick flashing lights are used on red and black horizontally banded buoys. White short-long flashing lights are used on black and white vertically striped buoys.

Special purpose buoys. White buoys mark anchorages. Yellow buoys mark quarantine anchorages. White buoys with green tops are used in dredging and survey operations. Black and white horizontally banded buoys mark fish net areas. White and orange banded, either horizontally or vertically, are used for special purposes.

Wreck buoys are generally placed on the seaward or channel side, as near the wreck as conditions permit. The possibility of the wreck having shifted position due to sea action since the buoy was placed should not be overlooked.

Station buoys are placed close to some lightships and important buoys to mark the position if the regular aid is not at the assigned position. Such buoys are colored and numbered the same as the regular aid, lightship station buoys having the letters "LS" above the initials of the station.

Buoys are secured by anchor, and swing in a circle of small radius as the current changes. In this respect, they are inferior to fixed aids for position fixing. They may be shifted, carried away, capsized, or sunk. Lighted buoys may be extinguished and sound buoys may not function.

Dates shown in light lists for seasonal buoys are approximations which vary with local conditions.

Fog signals • Any sound-producing device may serve as a fog signal to warn the mariner of danger or to assist him in establishing the position of his vessel. If a fog signal is to be fully effective for the second of these functions, the mariner must be able to recognize it as a fog signal and to know from what point it is sounded. Bells, whistles, etc., which are sounded by action of the sea are erratic in operation, and positive identification is not always possible. At most lighthouses and lightships fog signals are operated by mechanical means, providing a definite sequence of sounds and silent periods resembling the characteristics of lights. The sequence, stated in the light list, is an aid to identification. The distinctive sound of each type of signal apparatus is helpful in this respect. Charts indicate whether fog signals are bells, horns, whistles, or gongs.

Rariobeacons, radar, and other electronic aids to navigation can be of considerable assistance to a vessel equipped to use them.

Tides and Currents

Tidal effects • The daily rise and fall of the **tide,** with its attendant flood and ebb of **tidal current,** is familiar to every mariner. He is aware, also, that at **high water** and **low water** the depth of water is momentarily constant, a condition called **stand.** Similarly, there is a moment of **slack water** as a tidal current reverses direction. As a general rule, the *change* in height or the current *speed* is at first very slow, increasing to a maximum about midway between the two extremes, and then decreasing again. If plotted against time, the height of tide or speed of a tidal current takes the general form of a sine curve. Sample curves, and more complete information about causes, types, and features of tides and tidal currents, are given in Chapter 10. The present chapter is concerned primarily with the application of tides and currents to piloting, and predicting the tidal conditions that might be encountered at any given time.

Although tides and tidal currents are caused by the same phenomena, the time relationship between them varies considerably from place to place. For instance, if an estuary has a wide entrance and does not extend far inland, the time of maximum speed of current occurs at about the mid time between high water and low water. However, if an extensive tidal basin is connected to the sea by a small opening, the maximum current may occur at about the time of high water or low water outside the basin, when the difference in height is maximum.

The *height of tide* should not be confused with *depth of water.* For reckoning tides a reference level is selected. Soundings shown on the largest scale charts are the vertical distances from this level to the bottom. At any time the actual depth is this charted depth *plus* the height of tide. In most places the reference level is some form of low water. But all low waters at a place are not the same height, and the selected reference level is seldom the *lowest* tide that occurs at the place. When lower tides occur, these are indicated by a negative sign. Thus, at a spot where the charted depth is 15 feet, the actual depth is 15 feet plus height of tide. When the tide is three feet, the depth is $15+3=18$ feet. When it is $(-)1$ foot, the depth is $15-1=14$ feet. It is well to remember that *the actual depth can be less than the charted depth.* In an area where there is a considerable **range of tide** (the difference between high water and low water), the height of tide might be an important consideration in using soundings to assist in determining position, or whether the vessel is in safe water.

One should remember that heights given in the tide tables are *predictions*, and that when conditions vary considerably from those used in making the predictions, the heights shown may be considerably in error. Heights lower than predicted are particularly to be anticipated when the atmospheric pressure is higher than normal, or when there is a persistent strong offshore wind. Along coasts where there is a large inequality between the two high or two low tides during a tidal day the height predictions are less reliable than elsewhere.

The current encountered in pilot waters is due primarily to tidal action, but other causes are sometimes present. The tidal current tables give the best prediction of total current, regardless of cause. The predictions for a river may be considerably in error following heavy rains or a drought. The effect of current is to alter the course and speed made good over the bottom. Due to the configuration of land (or shoal areas) and water, the set and drift may vary considerably over different parts of a harbor. Since this is generally an area in which small errors in position of a vessel are of considerable importance to its safety, a knowledge of predicted currents can be critical, particularly if the visibility is reduced by fog, rain, etc. If the vessel is proceeding at reduced speed, the effect of current with respect to distance traveled is greater than normal. Strong currents are particularly to be anticipated in narrow passages connecting larger bodies of water. Currents of more than five knots are encountered from time to time in the Golden Gate at San Francisco. Currents of more than 13 knots sometimes occur at Seymour Narrows, British Columbia.

In straight portions of rivers and channels the strongest currents usually occur in the middle, but in curved portions the swiftest currents (and deepest water) usually occur near the outer edge of the curve. Counter-currents and eddies may occur on either side of the main current of a river or narrow passage, especially near obstructions and in bights.

In general, the range of tide and the speed of tidal current are at a minimum upon the open ocean or along straight coasts. The greatest tidal effects are usually encountered in rivers, bays, harbors, inlets, bights, etc. A vessel proceeding along a coast can be expected to encounter stronger sets toward or away from the shore while passing an indentation than when the coast is straight.

Predictions of tides and currents to be expected at various places are published annually by the National Ocean Survey. These are supplemented by sets of **Tidal Current Charts,** each set consisting of 12 charts, one for each hour of the tidal cycle. On these charts the set of the current at various places in the area is shown by arrows, and the drift by numbers. Since these are *average* conditions, they indicate in a general way the tidal conditions on any day and during any year. They are designed to be used with the tidal current tables (except those for New York Harbor and Narragansett Bay, which are used with the tide tables). Current arrows are sometimes shown on nautical charts. These represent average conditions and should not be considered reliable predictions of the conditions to be encountered at any given time. When a strong current sets over an irregular bottom, or meets an opposing current, ripples may occur on the surface. These are called **tide rips.** Areas where they occur frequently are shown on charts.

Usually, the mariner obtains tidal information from tide and tidal current tables. However, if these are not available, or if they do not include information at a desired place, the mariner may be able to obtain locally the **mean high water lunitidal interval** or the **high water full and change.** The approximate *time* of high water can be found by adding either interval to the time of transit (either upper or lower) of the moon. Low water occurs approximately ¼ tidal day (about 6^h12^m) before and after the time of high water. The actual interval varies somewhat from day to day, but approximate results can be obtained in this manner. Similar information for tidal currents (**lunicurrent interval**) is seldom available.

Tide tables • Tide tables for various parts of the world are published in four volumes by the National Ocean Survey. Each volume is arranged as follows:

Table 1 contains a complete list of the predicted times and heights of the tide for each day of the year at a number of places designated as **reference stations.**

Table 2 gives differences and ratios which can be used to modify the tidal information for the reference stations to make it applicable to a relatively large number of **subordinate stations.**

Table 3 provides information for use in finding the approximate height of the tide at any time between high water and low water.

Table 4 is a sunrise-sunset table at five-day intervals for various latitudes.

Table 5 provides an adjustment to convert the local mean time of table 4 to zone or standard time.

Table 6 gives the zone time of moonrise and moonset for each day of the year at certain selected places.

The volume also gives certain astronomical data.

Tide predictions for reference stations • Table 6 reproduces the table 1 daily predictions for New York (The Battery) for the first quarter of 1975. As indicated at the bottom of the page, times are for Eastern Standard Time (+5 zone, time meridian 75° W). Daylight saving time is not used. Times are given on the 24-hour basis. The tidal reference level for this station is mean low water.

For each day, the date and day of week are given, and the time and height of each high and low water are given in chronological order. Although high and low waters are not labeled as such, they can be distinguished by the relative heights given immediately to the right of the times. Since *two* high tides and *two* low tides occur each tidal day, the type of tide at this place is *semidiurnal* (see Chapter 10). The *tidal* day being longer than the *civil* day (because of the revolution of the moon eastward around the earth), any given tide occurs *later* from day to day. Thus, on Friday, March 14, the first tide that occurs is the lower low water (−0.4 foot at 0313). The following high water (lower high water) is 4.3 feet above the reference level (a 4.7 foot rise from the preceding low water), and occurs at 0912. This is followed by the higher low water (−0.3 feet) at 1525, and then the higher high water of 4.5 feet at 2126. The cycle is repeated on the following day with variations in height, and later times.

Because of later times of corresponding tides from day to day, certain days have only one high water or only one low water. Thus, on January 1 high tides occur at 1043 and 2321. The next following high tides are at 1138 on January 2 and 0017 on January 3. Thus, only one high tide occurs on January 2, the previous one being shortly before midnight on the first, and the next one occurring early in the morning of the third, as shown.

Tide predictions for subordinate stations • Table 7 reproduces a page of table 2 of the tide tables. For each subordinate station listed, the following information is given:

Number. The stations are listed in geographical order and given consecutive numbers. At the end of each volume an alphabetical listing is given, and for each entry the consecutive number is shown, to assist in finding the entry in table 2.

Place. The list of places includes both subordinate and reference stations, the latter being given in bold type.

Position. The approximate latitude and longitude are given to assist in locating the station. The latitude is north or south, and the longitude east or west, depending upon the letters (N, S, E, W) next *above* the entry. These may not be the same as those at the *top* of the column.

Differences. The differences are to be applied to the predictions for the reference station shown in bold capitals next *above* the entry on the page. Time and height differences are given separately for high and low

TABLE 6   From 1975 TIDE TABLES (Table 1)

TIMES AND HEIGHTS OF HIGH AND LOW WATERS

JANUARY

DAY	TIME H.M.	HT. FT.	DAY	TIME H.M.	HT. FT.
1 W	0422	-0.8	16 TH	0431	0.0
	1043	5.1		1045	4.1
	1659	-1.1		1656	-0.2
	2321	4.6		2319	3.8
2 TH	0516	-0.6	17 F	0501	0.2
	1138	4.9		1120	3.9
	1749	-0.9		1722	0.0
				2357	3.7
3 F	0017	4.6	18 SA	0533	0.4
	0615	-0.4		1154	3.7
	1234	4.6		1746	0.2
	1847	-0.6			
4 SA	0111	4.6	19 SU	0029	3.7
	0724	-0.1		0613	0.6
	1329	4.3		1228	3.5
	1951	-0.4		1818	0.3
5 SU	0207	4.6	20 M	0108	3.8
	0835	0.0		0727	0.7
	1428	4.0		1311	3.4
	2053	-0.3		1917	0.4
6 M	0307	4.5	21 TU	0156	3.9
	0939	-0.1		0856	0.7
	1530	3.7		1404	3.3
	2153	-0.3		2050	0.4
7 TU	0407	4.5	22 W	0255	4.0
	1038	-0.2		1001	0.4
	1635	3.6		1515	3.2
	2247	-0.3		2157	0.2
8 W	0508	4.6	23 TH	0404	4.2
	1131	-0.3		1057	0.1
	1735	3.7		1637	3.4
	2339	-0.3		2256	0.0
9 TH	0603	4.7	24 F	0510	4.5
	1222	-0.4		1150	-0.2
	1828	3.8		1742	3.7
				2352	-0.3
10 F	0028	-0.4	25 SA	0609	4.9
	0649	4.8		1242	-0.6
	1310	-0.5		1838	4.0
	1915	3.9			
11 SA	0117	-0.4	26 SU	0048	-0.6
	0733	4.8		0701	5.2
	1354	-0.6		1330	-1.0
	1959	3.9		1929	4.4
12 SU	0202	-0.4	27 M	0140	-0.9
	0814	4.8		0749	5.4
	1436	-0.6		1419	-1.3
	2040	3.9		2019	4.7
13 M	0242	-0.4	28 TU	0231	-1.1
	0854	4.7		0840	5.5
	1516	-0.6		1505	-1.4
	2122	3.9		2110	4.9
14 TU	0321	-0.3	29 W	0321	-1.2
	0931	4.5		0931	5.4
	1552	-0.5		1550	-1.5
	2202	3.9		2203	5.0
15 W	0358	-0.1	30 TH	0410	-1.2
	1011	4.3		1024	5.2
	1625	-0.4		1635	-1.3
	2242	3.8		2258	5.0
			31 F	0459	-0.9
				1120	4.9
				1725	-1.0
				2354	4.9

FEBRUARY

DAY	TIME H.M.	HT. FT.	DAY	TIME H.M.	HT. FT.
1 SA	0554	-0.6	16 SU	0503	0.2
	1213	4.5		1111	3.8
	1818	-0.7		1704	0.1
				2338	4.0
2 SU	0047	4.8	17 M	0535	0.3
	0659	-0.2		1149	3.6
	1309	4.1		1733	0.2
	1919	-0.3			
3 M	0142	4.6	18 TU	0020	4.0
	0808	0.0		0621	0.5
	1405	3.8		1231	3.5
	2024	-0.1		1818	0.4
4 TU	0240	4.4	19 W	0108	4.1
	0915	0.1		0759	0.6
	1508	3.6		1329	3.4
	2129	0.0		1932	0.5
5 W	0341	4.3	20 TH	0211	4.1
	1015	0.0		0926	0.5
	1612	3.5		1439	3.3
	2225	0.0		2125	0.4
6 TH	0444	4.3	21 F	0327	4.2
	1110	-0.1		1026	0.2
	1715	3.5		1607	3.5
	2320	0.0		2233	0.1
7 F	0542	4.4	22 SA	0444	4.5
	1200	-0.2		1123	-0.2
	1811	3.7		1718	3.9
				2334	-0.3
8 SA	0009	-0.1	23 SU	0545	4.8
	0629	4.5		1214	-0.6
	1246	-0.3		1816	4.4
	1856	3.9			
9 SU	0057	-0.2	24 M	0030	-0.7
	0713	4.6		0640	5.2
	1329	-0.5		1306	-1.0
	1937	4.0		1909	4.8
10 M	0141	-0.3	25 TU	0123	-1.0
	0752	4.6		0731	5.4
	1410	-0.5		1354	-1.2
	2015	4.1		1959	5.2
11 TU	0222	-0.4	26 W	0215	-1.3
	0829	4.6		0820	5.4
	1449	-0.6		1441	-1.4
	2053	4.2		2048	5.4
12 W	0300	-0.4	27 TH	0305	-1.4
	0906	4.5		0912	5.3
	1523	-0.5		1526	-1.4
	2129	4.2		2139	5.4
13 TH	0335	-0.3	28 F	0352	-1.4
	0941	4.3		1003	5.1
	1555	-0.4		1612	-1.2
	2203	4.1		2232	5.3
14 F	0407	-0.2			
	1011	4.1			
	1622	-0.2			
	2235	4.1			
15 SA	0435	0.0			
	1043	3.9			
	1643	-0.1			
	2307	4.0			

MARCH

DAY	TIME H.M.	HT. FT.	DAY	TIME H.M.	HT. FT.
1 SA	0442	-1.0	16 SU	0416	-0.1
	1058	4.8		1013	4.0
	1658	-0.9		1613	0.0
	2325	5.1		2223	4.4
2 SU	0533	-0.6	17 M	0443	0.0
	1152	4.4		1043	3.8
	1749	-0.5		1637	0.2
				2259	4.4
3 M	0021	4.9	18 TU	0517	0.2
	0631	-0.2		1124	3.7
	1247	4.1		1708	0.3
	1847	0.0		2346	4.3
4 TU	0115	4.6	19 W	0602	0.4
	0739	0.1		1218	3.6
	1344	3.8		1752	0.5
	1956	0.3			
5 W	0212	4.3	20 TH	0042	4.3
	0848	0.3		0724	0.5
	1443	3.6		1318	3.6
	2103	0.4		1906	0.6
6 TH	0312	4.1	21 F	0146	4.3
	0949	0.3		0853	0.4
	1545	3.5		1429	3.6
	2204	0.4		2106	0.5
7 F	0415	4.1	22 SA	0300	4.3
	1041	0.2		0959	0.2
	1649	3.6		1548	3.9
	2258	0.3		2217	0.2
8 SA	0513	4.2	23 SU	0417	4.5
	1131	0.0		1056	-0.2
	1744	3.8		1658	4.3
	2347	0.1		2315	-0.2
9 SU	0603	4.3	24 M	0524	4.8
	1216	-0.1		1147	-0.5
	1830	4.1		1755	4.8
10 M	0033	0.0	25 TU	0011	-0.6
	0645	4.4		0620	5.0
	1259	-0.3		1238	-0.8
	1909	4.3		1848	5.2
11 TU	0117	-0.2	26 W	0107	-1.0
	0726	4.5		0712	5.2
	1341	-0.4		1328	-1.1
	1946	4.4		1938	5.6
12 W	0158	-0.3	27 TH	0157	-1.2
	0803	4.5		0802	5.3
	1418	-0.4		1416	-1.2
	2022	4.5		2025	5.7
13 TH	0237	-0.4	28 F	0247	-1.3
	0837	4.5		0852	5.2
	1453	-0.4		1502	-1.1
	2054	4.5		2114	5.7
14 F	0313	-0.4	29 SA	0334	-1.2
	0912	4.3		0942	4.9
	1525	-0.3		1547	-0.9
	2126	4.5		2206	5.5
15 SA	0346	-0.3	30 SU	0422	-0.9
	0941	4.2		1037	4.7
	1551	-0.1		1632	-0.6
	2152	4.5		2259	5.3
			31 M	0512	-0.6
				1132	4.3
				1721	-0.2
				2352	4.9

TIME MERIDIAN 75° W. 0000 IS MIDNIGHT. 1200 IS NOON.
HEIGHTS ARE RECKONED FROM THE DATUM OF SOUNDINGS ON CHARTS OF THE LOCALITY WHICH IS MEAN LOW WATER.

TABLE 7—From TIDE TABLES 1975

No.	PLACE	POSITION		DIFFERENCES				RANGES		Mean Tide Level
		Lat.	Long.	Time		Height		Mean	Spring	
				High water	Low water	High water	Low water			
		° ′	° ′	h. m.	h. m.	feet	feet	feet	feet	feet
	NEW YORK and NEW JERSEY — Continued									
	Hudson River‡	N.	W.	on NEW YORK, p.56						
	Time meridian, 75°W.									
1513	Jersey City, Pa. RR. Ferry, N. J────	40 43	74 02	+0 07	+0 07	−0.1	0.0	4.4	5.3	2.2
1515	New York, Desbrosses Street─────────	40 43	74 01	+0 10	+0 10	−0.1	0.0	4.4	5.3	2.2
1517	New York, Chelsea Docks─────────────	40 45	74 01	+0 17	+0 16	−0.2	0.0	4.3	5.2	2.1
1519	Hoboken, Castle Point, N. J─────────	40 45	74 01	+0 17	+0 16	−0.2	0.0	4.3	5.2	2.1
1521	Weehawken, Days Point, N. J─────────	40 46	74 01	+0 24	+0 23	−0.3	0.0	4.2	5.0	2.1
1523	New York, Union Stock Yards─────────	40 47	74 00	+0 27	+0 26	−0.3	0.0	4.2	5.0	2.1
1525	New York, 130th Street──────────────	40 49	73 58	+0 37	+0 35	−0.5	0.0	4.0	4.8	2.0
1527	George Washington Bridge────────────	40 51	73 57	+0 46	+0 43	−0.6	0.0	3.9	4.6	1.9
1529	Spuyten Duyvil, West of RR. bridge──	40 53	73 56	+0 58	+0 53	−0.7	0.0	3.8	4.5	1.9
1531	Yonkers─────────────────────────────	40 56	73 54	+1 09	+1 10	−0.8	0.0	3.7	4.4	1.8
1533	Dobbs Ferry─────────────────────────	41 01	73 53	+1 29	+1 40	−1.1	0.0	3.4	4.0	1.7
1535	Tarrytown───────────────────────────	41 05	73 52	+1 45	+1 54	−1.3	0.0	3.2	3.7	1.6
1537	Ossining────────────────────────────	41 10	73 52	+1 53	+2 14	−1.4	0.0	3.1	3.6	1.5
1539	Haverstraw──────────────────────────	41 12	73 58	+1 59	+2 25	−1.6	0.0	2.9	3.4	1.4
1541	Peekskill───────────────────────────	41 17	73 56	+2 24	+3 00	−1.3	+0.3	2.9	3.4	1.7
1543	West Point──────────────────────────	41 24	73 57	+3 16	+3 37	−1.5	+0.3	2.7	3.1	1.6
1545	Newburgh────────────────────────────	41 30	74 00	+3 42	+4 00	−1.5	+0.2	2.8	3.2	1.6
1547	New Hamburg─────────────────────────	41 35	73 57	+4 00	+4 25	−1.5	+0.1	2.9	3.3	1.5
1549	Poughkeepsie────────────────────────	41 42	73 57	+4 30	+4 43	−1.3	+0.1	3.1	3.5	1.6
1551	Hyde Park───────────────────────────	41 47	73 57	+4 56	+5 09	−1.3	0.0	3.2	3.6	1.6
1553	Kingston Point──────────────────────	41 56	73 58	+5 16	+5 31	−0.9	−0.1	3.7	4.2	1.7
1555	Tivoli──────────────────────────────	42 04	73 56	+5 46	+6 01	−0.8	−0.2	3.9	4.4	1.7
1557	Catskill────────────────────────────	42 13	73 51	+6 37	+6 55	−0.7	−0.3	4.1	4.6	1.7
1559	Hudson──────────────────────────────	42 15	73 48	+6 54	+7 09	−0.9	−0.4	4.0	4.4	1.6
				on ALBANY, p.60						
1561	Coxsackie───────────────────────────	42 21	73 48	−1 01	−1 38	−0.5	+0.2	3.9	4.3	2.1
1563	New Baltimore───────────────────────	42 27	73 47	−0 34	−0 56	−0.1	+0.4	4.1	4.5	2.4
1565	Castleton-on-Hudson─────────────────	42 32	73 46	−0 17	−0 29	−0.2	+0.1	4.3	4.7	2.2
1567	ALBANY──────────────────────────────	42 39	73 45	Daily predictions				4.6	5.0	2.5
1569	Troy────────────────────────────────	42 44	73 42	+0 08	+0 10	+0.1	0.0	4.7	5.1	2.3
	The Kills and Newark Bay			on NEW YORK, p.56						
	Kill Van Kull									
1571	Constable Hook──────────────────	40 39	74 05	−0 34	−0 21	0.0	0.0	4.5	5.4	2.2
1573	New Brighton────────────────────	40 39	74 05	−0 12	−0 18	0.0	0.0	4.5	5.4	2.2
1575	Port Richmond───────────────────	40 38	74 08	−0 03	+0 05	0.0	0.0	4.5	5.4	2.2
1577	Bergen Point────────────────────	40 39	74 08	+0 03	+0 03	+0.1	0.0	4.6	5.5	2.3
1579	Shooters Island─────────────────────	40 39	74 10	+0 06	+0 18	+0.1	0.0	4.6	5.5	2.3
1581	Port Newark Terminal────────────────	40 41	74 08	−0 01	+0 18	+0.6	0.0	5.1	6.1	2.5
1583	Newark, Passaic River───────────────	40 44	74 10	+0 22	+0 52	+0.6	0.0	5.1	6.1	2.5
1585	Passaic, Gregory Ave. bridge────────	40 51	74 07	+0 49	+1 57	+0.6	0.0	5.1	6.1	2.5
	Hackensack River									
1586	Kearny Point────────────────────	40 44	74 06	+0 09	+0 33	+0.5	0.0	5.0	6.0	2.5
1587	Secaucus────────────────────────	40 48	74 04	+1 13	+1 09	+0.6	0.0	5.1	6.1	2.6
1588	Little Ferry────────────────────	40 51	74 02	+1 22	+1 14	+0.8	0.0	5.3	6.4	2.7
1589	Hackensack──────────────────────	40 53	74 02	+1 33	+1 58	+0.8	0.0	5.3	6.4	2.6
				on SANDY HOOK, p.64						
	Arthur Kill									
1591	Elizabethport───────────────────	40 39	74 11	+0 25	+0 39	+0.3	0.0	4.9	5.9	2.4
1593	Chelsea─────────────────────────	40 36	74 12	+0 24	+0 35	+0.4	0.0	5.0	6.0	2.5
1595	Carteret────────────────────────	40 35	74 13	+0 23	+0 31	+0.5	0.0	5.1	6.2	2.6
1597	Rossville───────────────────────	40 33	74 13	+0 17	+0 25	+0.7	0.0	5.3	6.4	2.6
1599	Tottenville─────────────────────	40 31	74 15	+0 03	+0 13	+0.7	0.0	5.3	6.4	2.6
1601	Perth Amboy─────────────────────	40 30	74 16	+0 13	+0 19	+0.6	0.0	5.2	6.3	2.6

‡Values for the Hudson River above the George Washington Bridge are based upon averages for the six months May to October, when the fresh-water discharge is a minimum.

waters. Where differences are omitted, they are either unreliable or unknown.

The time difference is the number of hours and minutes to be applied to the time at the reference station to find the time of the corresponding tide at the subordinate station. This interval is added if preceded by a plus sign (+), and subtracted if preceded by a minus sign (−). Special conditions occurring at a few stations are indicated by footnotes on the applicable pages. In some instances, the corresponding tide falls on a different date at reference and subordinate stations.

Height differences are shown in a variety of ways. For most entries separate height differences in feet are given for high water and low water. These are applied to the height given for the reference station. In many cases a *ratio* is given for either high water or low water, or both. The height at the reference station is multiplied by this ratio to find the height at the subordinate station. For a few stations, *both* a ratio and difference are given. In this case the height at the reference station is first multiplied by the ratio, and the difference is then applied. An example is given in each volume of tide tables. Special conditions are indicated in the table or by footnote (see Table 7).

Ranges. Various ranges are given, as indicated in the tables. In each case this is the difference in height between high water and low water for the tides indicated.

Example. List chronologically the times and heights of all tides at Yonkers (No. 1531) on January 10, 1975.

Solution.

Date	January 10, 1975
Subordinate station	Yonkers
Reference station	New York
High water time difference	(+) 1ʰ09ᵐ
Low water time difference	(+) 1ʰ10ᵐ
High water height difference	(−) 0.8 ft.
Low water height difference	0.0 ft.

	New York			Yonkers	
LW	0028	(−) 0.4 ft.	0138	(−) 0.4 ft.
HW	0649	4.8 ft.	0758	4.0 ft.
LW	1310	(−) 0.5 ft.	1420	(−) 0.5 ft.
HW	1915	3.9 ft.	2024	3.1 ft.

Finding height of tide at any time • Table 3 of the tide tables provides means for determining the approximate height of tide at any time. It is based upon the assumption that a plot of height versus time is a sine curve. Instructions for use of the table are given in a footnote below the table.

Tidal current tables • Tidal current tables are somewhat similar to tide tables, but the coverage is less extensive, being given in two volumes. Each volume is arranged as follows:

Table 1 contains a complete list of predicted times of maximum currents and slack, with the velocity (speed) of the maximum currents, for a number of reference stations.

Table 2 gives differences, ratios, and other information related to a relatively large number of subordinate stations.

Table 3 provides information for use in finding the speed of the current at any time between tabulated entries in tables 1 and 2.

Table 4 gives the number of minutes the current does not exceed stated amounts, for various maximum speeds.

Table 5 (Atlantic Coast of North America only) gives information on rotary tidal currents.

Each volume contains additional useful information related to currents.

Tidal current predictions for reference stations • Table 8 reproduces tidal current tables for The Narrows, New York Harbor. Times are given on the 24-hour basis, for meridian 75° W.

For each day, the date and day of week are given, with complete current information. Since the cycle is repeated twice each tidal day, currents at this place are semidiurnal. On most days there are four slack waters and four maximum currents, two of them floods (F) and two of them ebbs (E). However, since the tidal day is longer than the civil day, the corresponding condition occurs later from day to day, and on certain days there are only three slack waters or three maximum currents. At some places, the current on some days runs maximum flood twice, but ebb only once, a minimum flood occurring in place of the second ebb. The tables show this information.

As indicated, the sequence of currents at The Narrows on Sunday, January 19, 1975, is as follows:

0000 Flood current, 51^m after maximum velocity (speed).
0218 Slack, ebb begins.
0530 Maximum ebb of 1.6 knots, setting 160°.
0920 Slack, flood begins.
1130 Maximum flood of 1.3 knots, setting 340°.
1424 Slack, ebb begins.
1745 Maximum ebb of 1.7 knots, setting 160°.
2132 Slack, flood begins.
2358 Maximum flood of 1.5 knots, setting 340°.
2400 Flood current, 2^m after maximum velocity (speed).

Tidal current predictions for subordinate stations • For each subordinate station listed in table 2 of the tidal current tables, the following information is given:

TABLE 8—From TIDAL CURRENT Tables

F-FLOOD, DIR. 340° TRUE   E-EBB, DIR. 160° TRUE

JANUARY

Days 1–15

DAY	SLACK WATER TIME H.M.	MAXIMUM CURRENT TIME H.M.	VEL. KNOTS
1 W	0617	0254	2.4E
	1211	0857	2.2F
	1901	1526	2.5E
		2132	2.0F
2 TH	0037	0345	2.3E
	0716	0952	2.1F
	1301	1614	2.4E
	1954	2227	2.0F
3 F	0132	0440	2.2E
	0819	1049	1.9F
	1352	1708	2.3E
	2050	2321	2.0F
4 SA	0230	0542	2.1E
	0924	1147	1.7F
	1445	1807	2.1E
	2146		
5 SU	0331	0018	1.9F
	1027	0648	2.0E
	1543	1244	1.5F
	2242	1909	2.0E
6 M	0434	0119	1.9F
	1129	0751	2.0E
	1643	1352	1.4F
	2337	2007	2.0E
7 TU	0537	0232	1.9F
	1230	0850	2.0E
	1744	1515	1.3F
		2102	2.0E
8 W	0033	0343	1.9F
	0635	0946	2.0E
	1328	1623	1.4F
	1841	2154	1.9E
9 TH	0127	0442	2.0F
	0727	1037	2.1E
	1423	1714	1.4F
	1932	2242	1.9E
10 F	0219	0527	2.0F
	0814	1126	2.1E
	1511	1757	1.5F
	2020	2336	1.9E
11 SA	0307	0609	2.0F
	0857	1215	2.1E
	1556	1836	1.5F
	2106		
12 SU	0351	0023	1.9E
	0938	0638	2.0F
	1637	1300	2.1E
	2150	1906	1.5F
13 M	0434	0108	1.9E
	1018	0709	1.9F
	1717	1340	2.2E
	2235	1937	1.5F
14 TU	0515	0151	1.9E
	1058	0743	1.8F
	1756	1418	2.1E
	2318	2010	1.5F
15 W	0557	0231	1.9E
	1137	0822	1.7F
	1836	1455	2.1E
		2051	1.5F

Days 16–31

DAY	SLACK WATER TIME H.M.	MAXIMUM CURRENT TIME H.M.	VEL. KNOTS
16 TH	0002	0310	1.8E
	0641	0907	1.6F
	1217	1532	2.0E
	1917	2139	1.5F
17 F	0046	0351	1.7E
	0730	0954	1.5F
	1257	1611	1.9E
	2000	2224	1.5F
18 SA	0131	0437	1.6E
	0823	1043	1.4F
	1339	1654	1.8E
	2045	2309	1.5F
19 SU	0218	0530	1.6E
	0920	1130	1.3F
	1424	1745	1.7E
	2132	2358	1.5F
20 M	0310	0631	1.5E
	1017	1220	1.2F
	1514	1842	1.6E
	2220		
21 TU	0407	0047	1.6F
	1114	0728	1.6E
	1610	1313	1.1F
	2310	1940	1.6E
22 W	0505	0140	1.6F
	1211	0823	1.7E
	1710	1410	1.1F
		2033	1.7E
23 TH	0001	0237	1.7F
	0602	0917	1.9E
	1305	1509	1.2F
	1808	2124	1.8E
24 F	0055	0337	1.9F
	0655	1007	2.0E
	1357	1612	1.4F
	1903	2215	2.0E
25 SA	0148	0434	2.1F
	0745	1059	2.2E
	1445	1703	1.6F
	1955	2309	2.1E
26 SU	0240	0523	2.3F
	0834	1150	2.4E
	1531	1751	1.8F
	2046		
27 M	0330	0003	2.3E
	0922	0611	2.4F
	1615	1241	2.5E
	2138	1838	2.0F
28 TU	0420	0057	2.4E
	1011	0658	2.5F
	1659	1329	2.6E
	2231	1925	2.2F
29 W	0510	0148	2.5E
	1100	0745	2.4F
	1745	1416	2.7E
	2324	2015	2.2F
30 TH	0602	0237	2.6E
	1149	0838	2.3F
	1833	1503	2.6E
		2106	2.2F
31 F	0017	0327	2.5E
	0659	0932	2.1F
	1238	1551	2.5E
	1925	2201	2.1F

FEBRUARY

Days 1–15

DAY	SLACK WATER TIME H.M.	MAXIMUM CURRENT TIME H.M.	VEL. KNOTS
1 SA	0111	0420	2.3E
	0759	1027	1.9F
	1328	1643	2.3E
	2021	2258	2.1F
2 SU	0207	0517	2.1E
	0902	1124	1.7F
	1420	1738	2.1E
	2118	2355	2.0F
3 M	0305	0621	2.0E
	1005	1222	1.5F
	1516	1839	1.9E
	2216		
4 TU	0408	0056	1.8F
	1107	0727	1.9E
	1617	1331	1.3F
	2314	1943	1.8E
5 W	0511	0207	1.7F
	1208	0830	1.9E
	1720	1455	1.2F
		2039	1.8E
6 TH	0011	0322	1.7F
	0611	0925	1.9E
	1306	1602	1.3F
	1820	2133	1.8E
7 F	0107	0422	1.8F
	0704	1016	1.9E
	1359	1655	1.4F
	1913	2226	1.8E
8 SA	0200	0511	1.8F
	0751	1104	2.0E
	1447	1741	1.5F
	2001	2313	1.8E
9 SU	0248	0552	1.9F
	0833	1149	2.0E
	1530	1818	1.5F
	2045		
10 M	0333	0000	1.9E
	0912	0625	1.9F
	1609	1232	2.1E
	2128	1845	1.6F
11 TU	0414	0044	1.9E
	0951	0650	1.8F
	1647	1312	2.1E
	2209	1911	1.6F
12 W	0455	0127	2.0E
	1029	0718	1.8F
	1723	1350	2.1E
	2251	1942	1.7F
13 TH	0534	0207	2.0E
	1108	0757	1.7F
	1800	1426	2.1E
	2332	2019	1.7F
14 F	0616	0245	1.9E
	1147	0838	1.6F
	1836	1501	2.0E
		2102	1.7F
15 SA	0015	0323	1.9E
	0700	0923	1.5F
	1226	1536	1.9E
	1915	2149	1.6F

Days 16–28

DAY	SLACK WATER TIME H.M.	MAXIMUM CURRENT TIME H.M.	VEL. KNOTS
16 SU	0058	0404	1.8E
	0751	1011	1.4F
	1307	1615	1.8E
	1958	2236	1.6F
17 M	0144	0451	1.7E
	0846	1100	1.3F
	1350	1656	1.7E
	2046	2325	1.6F
18 TU	0233	0547	1.6E
	0944	1151	1.2F
	1439	1800	1.6E
	2138		
19 W	0329	0015	1.6F
	1041	0650	1.6E
	1535	1242	1.1F
	2234	1903	1.6E
20 TH	0429	0108	1.6F
	1138	0752	1.7E
	1638	1337	1.1F
	2331	2004	1.7E
21 F	0529	0205	1.7F
	1233	0848	1.9E
	1741	1439	1.2F
		2100	1.9E
22 SA	0030	0308	1.8F
	0627	0941	2.1E
	1325	1544	1.5F
	1840	2154	2.1E
23 SU	0127	0408	2.0F
	0720	1032	2.2E
	1415	1639	1.7F
	1935	2248	2.2E
24 M	0222	0504	2.2F
	0810	1123	2.4E
	1502	1730	2.0F
	2027	2343	2.4E
25 TU	0315	0552	2.4F
	0859	1214	2.5E
	1547	1818	2.2F
	2119		
26 W	0405	0037	2.6E
	0947	0641	2.4F
	1632	1304	2.6E
	2211	1903	2.4F
27 TH	0455	0129	2.7E
	1036	0726	2.4F
	1718	1353	2.7E
	2303	1952	2.4F
28 F	0547	0218	2.7E
	1125	0816	2.2F
	1805	1439	2.6E
	2356	2041	2.3F

TIME MERIDIAN 75° W.   0000 IS MIDNIGHT.   1200 IS NOON.

Number. Table stations are listed in geographical order and given consecutive numbers, as in the tide tables. At the end of each volume an alphabetical listing is given, and for each entry the consecutive number is shown, to assist in finding the entry in table 2.

Place. The list of places includes both subordinate and reference stations, the latter being given in **bold type.**

Position. The approximate latitude and longitude are given to assist in locating the station. The latitude is north or south and the longitude east or west as indicated by the letters (N, S, E, W) next *above* the entry. The current given is for the center of the channel unless another location is indicated by the station name.

Time difference. Two time differences are tabulated. One is the number of hours and minutes to be applied to the tabulated times of slack water at the reference station to find the times of slack waters at the subordinate station. The other time difference is applied to the times of maximum current at the reference station to find the times of the corresponding maximum current at the subordinate station. The intervals, which are added or subtracted in accordance with their signs, include any difference in time between the two stations, so that the answer is correct for the standard time of the subordinate station. Limited application and special conditions are indicated by footnotes.

Velocity (speed) ratios. Speed of the current at the subordinate station is found by multiplying the speed at the reference station by the tabulated ratio. Separate ratios may be given for flood and ebb currents. Special conditions are indicated by footnotes.

As indicated in Table 9, the currents at Chelsea Docks (No. 2385) can be found by *adding* 1ʰ30ᵐ for slack water and 1ʰ40ᵐ for maximum current to the times for The Narrows, and multiplying flood currents by 1.0 and ebb currents by 1.0. Applying these to the values for Sunday, January 19, 1975, the sequence is as follows:

0000 Flood current, 49ᵐ before maximum velocity (speed).
0049 Maximum flood of 1.5 knots, setting 020°.
0348 Slack, ebb begins.
0710 Maximum ebb of 1.6 knots, setting 185°.
1050 Slack, flood begins.
1310 Maximum flood of 1.3 knots, setting 020°.
1554 Slack, ebb begins.
1925 Maximum ebb of 1.7 knots, setting 185°.
2302 Slack, flood begins.
2400 Flood current, 58ᵐ after slack.

Finding speed of tidal current at any time • Table 3 of the tidal current tables provides means for determining the approximate velocity (speed) at any time. Instructions for its use are given below the table.

TABLE 9—From TIDAL CURRENT Tables

No.	PLACE	POSITION Lat.	POSITION Long.	TIME DIFFERENCES Slack water	TIME DIFFERENCES Maximum current	VELOCITY RATIOS Maximum flood	VELOCITY RATIOS Maximum ebb	MAXIMUM CURRENTS Flood Direction (true)	Flood Average velocity	MAXIMUM CURRENTS Ebb Direction (true)	Ebb Average velocity
		° ′	° ′	h. m.	h. m.			deg.	knots	deg.	knots
	LONG ISLAND, South Coast—Continued	N.	W.	on THE NARROWS, p.46							
	Time meridian, 75°W.										
2245	Ponquogue bridge, Shinnecock Bay------	40 51	72 30	+0 40	+0 35	0.5	0.3	250	0.8	090	0.6
2250	Shinnecock Inlet----------------------	40 51	72 29	-0 20	-0 40	1.5	1.2	350	2.5	170	2.3
2255	Fire I. Inlet, 0.5 mi. S. of Oak Beach	40 38	73 18	+0 15	0 00	1.4	1.2	080	2.4	245	2.4
2260	Jones Inlet---------------------------	40 35	73 34	-1 00	-0 55	1.8	1.3	035	3.1	215	2.6
2265	Long Beach, inside, between bridges---	40 36	73 40	-0 10	+0 10	0.3	0.3	075	0.5	275	0.6
2270	East Rockaway Inlet-------------------	40 35	73 45	-1 25	-1 35	1.3	1.2	040	2.2	225	2.3
2275	Ambrose Light-------------------------	40 27	73 49	See table 5.							
228 ٠	Sandy Hook App. Lighted Horn Buoy 2A--	40 27	73 55	See table 5.							
	JAMAICA BAY										
2285	Rockaway Inlet------------------------	40 34	73 56	-1 45	-2 15	1.1	1.3	085	1.8	245	2.7
2290	Barren Island, east of---------------	40 35	73 53	-2 00	-2 25	0.7	0.9	005	1.2	190	1.7
2295	Canarsie (midchannel, off pier)-------	40 38	73 53	-1 35	-1 50	0.3	0.3	045	0.5	220	0.7
2300	Beach Channel (bridge)----------------	40 35	73 49	-1 20	-1 20	1.1	1.0	060	1.9	225	2.0
2305	Grass Hassock Channel-----------------	40 37	73 47	-1 10	-1 00	0.6	0.5	050	1.0	230	1.0
	NEW YORK HARBOR ENTRANCE										
2310	Ambrose Channel entrance-------------	40 30	73 58	-1 10	-1 05	1.0	1.2	310	1.7	110	2.3
2315	Ambrose Channel, SE. of West Bank Lt--	40 32	74 01	(¹)	-0 25	0.8	0.9	310	1.3	170	1.8
2320	Coney Island Lt., 1.6 miles SSW. of---	40 33	74 01	-0 10	(²)	0.5	0.8	330	0.8	145	1.5
2325	Ambrose Channel, north end------------	40 34	74 02	+0 05	+0 15	0.8	0.9	330	1.3	175	1.9
2330	Coney Island, 0.2 mile west of---·----	40 35	74 01	-0 55	-0 55	0.9	1.0	330	1.5	170	2.0
2335	Ft. Lafayette, channel east of--------	40 36	74 02	(³)	(³)	0.6	0.5	345	1.1	195	0.9
2340	THE NARROWS, midchannel--------------	40 37	74 03	Daily predictions				340	1.7	160	2.0
	NEW YORK HARBOR, Upper Bay										
2345	Tompkinsville-------------------------	40 38	74 04	-0 10	+0 20	0.9	1.0	005	1.6	170	2.0
2350	Bay Ridge Channel---------------------	40 39	74 02	-0 35	-0 45	0.6	0.6	040	1.0	220	1.1
2355	Red Hook Channel---------------------	40 40	74 01	-0 35	-0 35	0.6	0.4	355	1.0	170	0.7
2360	Robbins Reef Light, east of----------	40 39	74 03	+0 10	+0 20	0.8	0.8	015	1.3	205	1.6
2365	Red Hook, 1 mile west of-------------	40 41	74 02	+0 45	+1 00	0.8	1.2	025	1.3	205	2.3
2370	Statue of Liberty, east of-----------	40 42	74 02	+0 55	+1 00	0.8	1.0	030	1.4	205	1.9
	HUDSON RIVER, Midchannel⁴										
2375	The Battery, northwest of------------	40 43	74 02	+1 30	+1 35	0.9	1.2	015	1.5	195	2.3
2380	Desbrosses Street---------------------	40 43	74 01	+1 35	+1 40	0.9	1.2	010	1.5	----	2.3
2385	Chelsea Docks-------------------------	40 45	74 01	+1 30	+1 40	1.0	1.0	020	1.7	185	2.0
2390	Forty-second Street-------------------	40 46	74 00	+1 35	+1 45	1.0	1.2	030	1.7	----	2.3
2395	Ninety-sixth Street-------------------	40 48	73 59	+1 40	+1 50	1.0	1.2	030	1.7	----	2.3
2400	Grants Tomb, 123d Street-------------	40 49	73 58	+1 45	+1 55	0.9	1.2	025	1.6	----	2.3
2405	George Washington Bridge-------------	40 51	73 57	+1 45	+2 00	0.9	1.1	020	1.6	200	2.2
2410	Spuyten Duyvil-----------------------	40 53	73 56	+2 00	+2 10	0.9	1.1	020	1.6	----	2.1
2415	Riverdale----------------------------	40 54	73 55	+2 05	+2 20	0.8	1.0	015	1.4	200	2.0
2420	Dobbs Ferry--------------------------	41 01	73 53	+2 25	+2 40	0.8	0.9	010	1.3	----	1.7
2425	Tarrytown----------------------------	41 05	73 53	+2 40	+2 55	0.6	0.8	000	1.1	----	1.5
2430	Ossining-----------------------------	41 10	73 54	+2 55	+3 10	0.5	0.7	320	0.9	----	1.3
2435	Haverstraw---------------------------	41 12	73 57	+3 05	+3 15	0.5	0.7	335	0.8	----	1.3
2440	Peekskill----------------------------	41 17	73 57	+3 20	+3 35	0.5	0.6	000	0.8	----	1.2
2445	Bear Mountain Bridge-----------------	41 19	73 59	+3 25	+3 40	0.5	0.6	000	0.8	----	1.1
2450	Highland Falls-----------------------	41 22	73 58	+3 35	+3 50	0.6	0.6	005	1.0	185	1.2
2455	West Point, off Duck Island----------	41 24	73 57	+3 40	+3 55	0.5	0.6	010	1.0	----	1.1

¹Current is rotary, turning clockwise. Minimum current of 0.9 knot sets SW. about time of "Slack, flood begins" at The Narrows. Minimum current of 0.5 knot sets NE. about 1 hour before "Slack, ebb begins" at The Narrows.
²Maximum flood, -0ʰ 50ᵐ; maximum ebb, +0ʰ 55ᵐ.
³Flood begins, -2ʰ 15ᵐ; maximum flood, -0ʰ 05ᵐ; ebb begins, +0ʰ 05ᵐ; maximum ebb, -1ʰ 50ᵐ.
⁴The values for the Hudson River are for the summer months, when the fresh-water discharge is a minimum.

Current diagrams • A current diagram is a graph showing the speed of the current along a channel at different stages of the tidal current cycle. Such diagrams are included in the tidal current tables and can be used when the pilot needs such exact information.

Miscellaneous

Allowing for turning characteristics of vessel • When precise piloting is necessary (as in an area where maneuvering space is limited or when a specified anchorage is approached), the turning characteristics of the vessel should be considered. That is, a ship does not complete a turn instantaneously, but follows a curve the characteristics of which depend upon the vessel's length, beam, underwater contour, draft, etc. From the moment the rudder is put over until the new course is reached, the vessel moves a certain distance in the direction of the original course. This distance is called **advance.** The distance the vessel moves perpendicular to the original course line during the turn is called **transfer.** The amount of advance and transfer for a given vessel depends primarily upon the amount of rudder used and the angle through which the ship is to be turned. The speed of the vessel has little effect. Allowance for advance and transfer is illustrated in the following example.

Example (fig. 9.25). A ship proceeding on course 100° is to turn 60° to the left to come on a range which will guide it up a channel. For a 60° turn and the amount of rudder used, the advance is 920 yards and the transfer is 350 yards.

Required. The bearing of flagpole "FP." when the rudder is put over.

Solution. (1) Extend the original course line, *AB.*

(2) At a perpendicular distance of 350 yards, the transfer, draw a line *A'B'* parallel to the original course line *AB.* The point of intersection, *C,* of *A'B'* with the new course line (located by the range) is the place at which the turn is to be completed.

(3) From *C* draw a perpendicular, *CD,* to the original course line, intersecting it at *D.*

(4) From *D* measure the advance, 920 yards, *back* along the original course line. This locates *E,* the point at which the turn should be started.

(5) The direction of "FP." from *E,* 058°, is the bearing when the turn should be started.

Answer. B 058°.

Anchoring • If a large vessel is to anchor at a predetermined point, as in an assigned berth, an established procedure should be followed to insure accuracy of placing the anchor. In the case of naval vessels, it is desired that the error not exceed ten yards. This requires a high order of naviga-

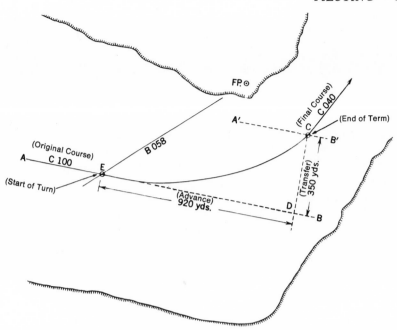

Fig. 9.25. Allowing for advance and transfer.

tional accuracy. Several procedures have been devised. The following is representative (fig. 9.26).

The position selected for anchoring is located on the chart. The direction of approach is then determined, considering limitations of land, shoals, other vessels, etc. Where conditions permit, the approach should be made heading into the current or, if the wind has a greater affect upon the vessel, into the wind. It is desirable to approach from such direction that a prominent object, or preferably a range, is available dead ahead to serve as a steering guide. It is also desirable to have a range or prominent object near the beam at the point of letting go the anchor. If practicable a straight approach long enough to permit the vessel to steady on the required course should be provided. The track is then drawn in, allowing for advance and transfer during any turns.

Next, a circle is drawn with the selected position of the anchor as the center, and with a radius equal to the distance between the hawsepipe and pelorus or other instrument used for measuring bearings. The intersection of this circle and the approach track, point *A*, is the position of the vessel (bearing-measuring instrument) at the moment of letting go. A number of arcs of circles are then drawn and labeled as shown in figure 9.26. The desired position of the anchor is the common center of these arcs. The selected radii may be chosen at will. Those shown in figure 9.26 have been found to be generally suitable for a large ship. In each case the

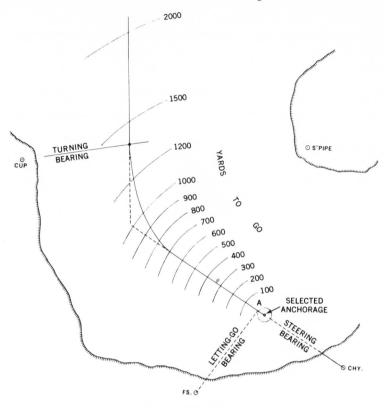

Fig. 9.26. Anchoring.

distance indicated is from the small circle. Turning bearings may also be indicated.

During the approach to the anchorage, fixes are plotted at frequent intervals, the measurement and plotting of bearings going on continuously, usually to the nearest half or quarter degree. The navigator advises the captain of any tendency of the vessel to drift from the desired track, so that adjustments can be made. The navigator also keeps the captain informed of the distance to go, to permit adjustment of the speed so that the vessel will be nearly dead in the water when the anchor is let go.

At the moment of letting go, the position of the vessel should be determined as accurately as possible, preferably by simultaneous or nearly simultaneous bearings of a number of prominent landmarks.

A number of variations may suggest themselves. One occasionally mentioned is as follows: An inverted compass rose (0° at south) is placed around each landmark used. A thumb tack with an attached thread is inserted at the symbol of two landmarks. One observer continually notes the bearing of each object. Alternately they call out the bearings. The navigator takes one thread in each hand and maintains a slight strain. As each bearing is called out, he adjusts the appropriate thread by means of the reverse compass rose. The point of intersection of the two threads is the position of the vessel. By this means the ship can be "walked in" to the anchorage. This method is particularly to be recommended when one landmark is on each bow.

The exact procedure to use depends upon local conditions, number and training of available personnel, equipment, and personal preference of individuals concerned.

Piloting and electronics • Many of the familiar electronic aids to navigation are used primarily in piloting. The radio direction finder provides bearings through fog and at greater distance from the aids. Distance finding stations provide distances which might not otherwise be available. The sonic depth finder provides frequent or continuous soundings. Radar provides bearings, distances, and information on the location and identity of various targets. Some of the longer range systems such as loran extend piloting techniques far to sea, where nearness of shoals and similar dangers are not a problem.

Practical piloting • In pilot waters, navigation is primarily an art. It is essential that the principles explained in this chapter be mastered and applied intelligently. From every experience the wise navigator acquires additional knowledge and improves his judgment. The mechanical following of a set procedure should not be expected always to produce satisfactory results.

While piloting, the successful navigator is somewhat of an opportunist, fitting his technique to the situation at hand. If a vessel is steaming in a large area having relatively weak currents and moderate traffic, like Chesapeake Bay, fixes may be obtained at relatively long intervals, with a dead reckoning plot between. In a narrow channel with swift currents and heavy traffic, like the East River between Manhattan and Long Island, New York City, an almost continuous fix is needed. In such an area the navigator may draw the desired track on the chart and obtain fixes every few minutes, or even seconds, directing the vessel back on the track as it begins to drift to one side.

If the navigator is to traverse unfamiliar waters, he studies the chart, sailing directions or coast pilot, tide and tidal current tables, and light lists to familiarize himself with local conditions. The experienced navigator learns to interpret the signs around him. The ripple of water around buoys and other obstructions, the direction and angle of tilt of buoys, the direction at which vessels ride at anchor, provide meaningful information regarding currents. The wise navigator learns to interpret such signs when the position of his vessel is not in doubt. When visibility is poor, or available information is inconsistent, the ability developed at favorable times can be of great value.

With experience, a navigator learns when a danger angle or danger bearing is useful, and what ranges are reliable and how they should be used. However familiar one is with an area, he should not permit himself to become careless in the matter of timing lights for identification, plotting his progress on a chart, or keeping a good recent position. Fog sometimes creeps in unnoticed, obscuring landmarks before one realizes its presence. A series of frequent fixes obtained while various aids are visible provides valuable information on position and current.

Practical piloting requires a thorough familiarity with principles involved and local conditions, constant alertness, and judgment. A study of avoidable groundings reveals that in most cases the problem is not lack of knowledge, but failure to use or interpret available information. Among the more common errors are:

1. Failure to obtain or evaluate soundings.
2. Failure to identify aids to navigation.
3. Failure to use all available navigational aids.
4. Failure to correct charts.
5. Failure to adjust a magnetic compass or maintain an accurate table of corrections.
6. Failure to apply deviation, or error in its application.
7. Failure to apply variation, or to allow for change in variation.
8. Failure to check compass readings at frequent and regular intervals.
9. Failure to keep a dead reckoning plot.
10. Failure to plot information received.
11. Failure to properly evaluate information received.
12. Poor judgment.
13. Failure to do own navigating (following another vessel).
14. Failure to obtain and use information available on charts and in various publications.
15. Poor ship organization.
16. Failure to "keep ahead of the vessel."

[10]

Tides and Tidal Currents

The tidal phenomenon is the periodic motion of the waters of the sea due to differences in the attractive forces of various celestial bodies, principally the moon and sun, upon different parts of the rotating earth. It can be either a help or hindrance to the mariner—the water's rise and fall may at certain times provide enough depth to clear a bar and at others may prevent him from entering or leaving a harbor. The flow of the current may help his progress or hinder it, may set him toward dangers or away from them. By understanding this phenomenon and by making intelligent use of predictions published in tide and tidal current tables and of descriptions in sailing directions, the mariner can set his course and schedule his passage to make the tide serve him, or at least to avoid its dangers.

Tide and current • In its rise and fall, the tide is accompanied by a periodic horizontal movement of the water called **tidal current.** The two movements, tide and tidal current, are intimately related, forming parts of the same phenomenon brought about by the tide-producing forces of the sun and moon, principally.

It is necessary, however, to distinguish clearly between tide and tidal current, for the relation between them is not a simple one nor it is everywhere the same. For the sake of clearness and to avoid misunderstanding, it is desirable that the mariner adopt the technical usage: **tide** for the vertical rise and fall of the water, and **current** for the horizontal flow. The tide rises and falls, the tidal current floods and ebbs.

Cause • Tides result from differences in the gravitational attraction of various celestial bodies, principally the moon and sun, upon different parts of the rotating earth. The gravity of the earth acts approximately toward the earth's center, and tends to hold the earth in the shape of a sphere. But the moon and sun provide disturbing, or tide-producing, forces. Consider the earth and moon. The moon appears to revolve about the earth, but actually the moon and earth revolve about their common center of mass. They are held together by gravitational attraction and kept apart by an equal and opposite centrifugal force. In this earth-moon system, the tide-producing force on the earth's hemisphere nearer the moon is in the direction of the moon's attraction, or toward the moon. On the hemisphere opposite the moon the tide-producing force is in the direction of the centrifugal force, or away from the moon.

At the sublunar point, and its antipode, the moon's attractive force is vertical, in the opposite direction to gravity. Along the great circle midway between these points, the force is horizontal, parallel to the earth's surface. At any other point, the moon's tide-producing force can be resolved into horizontal and vertical components. Both are very small compared to the earth's gravity. Since the horizontal component is not operating against gravity and can draw particles of water over the surface of the earth, it is the more effective in generating tides.

The tide-producing forces, then, tend to create high tides on the sides of the earth nearest to and farthest from the moon, with a low tide belt between them. As the earth rotates, a point on earth passes through two high and two low areas each day if the moon is over the equator (fig. 10.1, A). When the moon is north or south of the equator, the force pattern is as shown in figure 10.1, B, and a point on the equator passes through two equal highs, but a point in higher latitudes passes through two unequal highs or only one high. Thus, due to changes in the moon's declination, there is introduced a diurnal inequality in the pattern of the tidal forces at a particular place. There are similar forces due to the sun,

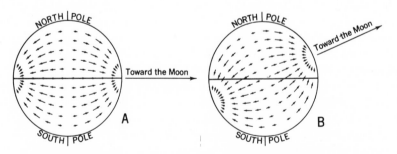

Fig. 10.1. Tide-producing forces. The arrows represent the magnitude and direction of the horizontal component of the tide-producing force on the earth's surface. A. When the moon is in the plane of the equator, the forces are equal in magnitude at the two points on the same parallel of latitude and 180° apart in longitude. B. When the moon is at north (or south) declination, the forces are unequal at such points and tend to cause an inequality in the two high waters and the two low waters of a day.

and the total tide producing force is the resultant of the two. Minute tidal effects are caused by other celestial bodies.

The mathematician develops his formulas by considering the difference in attraction between a point on the earth's surface and a point at the earth's center. In accordance with Newton's law, gravitational attraction of an astronomical body varies directly as its mass and inversely as the *square* of its distance. But the tide-producing (differential) force varies directly as the mass and inversely as the *cube* of the distance. As a consequence, only the moon and sun produce any appreciable tidal effect upon the earth. Further, although the moon's mass is but a fraction of the sun's, dividing such masses by the cube of their respective distances—$(238,862)^3$ statute miles and $(92,900,000)^3$ statute miles, respectively—reduces the sun's tide-producing force to only 0.46 that of the moon. It is because of this that the timing of the tides is identified so closely with the motions of the moon.

Though the tide-producing forces are distributed over the earth in a regular manner, the sizes and shapes of the ocean basins and the interference of the land masses prevent the tides of the oceans from assuming a simple, regular pattern. The way in which the waters in different parts of the oceans, as well as in the smaller waterways, respond to these known regular forces is dependent in large part upon the size, depth, and configuration of the basin or waterway.

Tide

General features • **Tide** is the periodic rise and fall of the water accompanying the tidal phenomenon. At most places it occurs twice daily. The tide rises until it reaches a maximum height, called **high tide** or **high water,** and then falls to a minimum level called **low tide** or **low water.**

The rate of rise and fall is not uniform. From low water, the tide begins to rise slowly at first but at an increasing rate until it is about halfway to high water. The rate of rise then decreases until high water is reached and the rise ceases. The falling tide behaves in a similar manner. The period at high or low water during which there is no sensible change of level is called **stand.** The difference in height between consecutive high and low waters is the **range.**

Figure 10.2 is a graphical representation of the rise and fall of the tide at New York during a 24-hour period.

Types of tide • A body of water has a natural period of oscillation that is dependent upon its dimensions. None of the oceans appears to be a single oscillating body, but rather each one is made up of a number of oscillating basins. As such basins are acted upon by the tide-producing forces, some

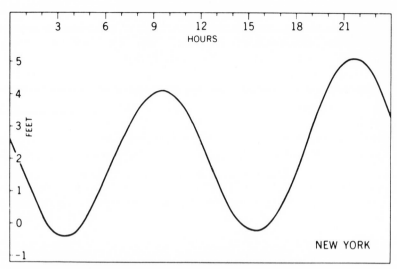

Fig. 10.2. The rise and fall of the tide at New York, shown graphically.

respond more readily to daily or diurnal forces, others to semidiurnal forces, and others almost equally to both. Hence, tides at a place are classified as one of three types—**semidiurnal, diurnal,** or **mixed**—according to the characteristics of the tidal pattern occurring at the place.

In the **semidiurnal** type of tide, there are two high and two low waters each tidal day, with relatively small inequality in the high and low water heights. Tides on the Atlantic coast of the United States are representative of the semidiurnal type, which is illustrated in figure 10.3 by the tide curve for Boston Harbor.

In the **diurnal** type of tide, only a single high and single low water occur each tidal day. Tides of the diurnal type occur along the northern shore of the Gulf of Mexico, in the Java Sea, the Gulf of Tonkin, and in a few other localities. The tide curve for Pakhoi, China, illustrated in figure 10.4, is an example of the diurnal type.

In the **mixed** type of tide, the diurnal and semidiurnal oscillations are both important factors and the tide is characterized by a large inequality

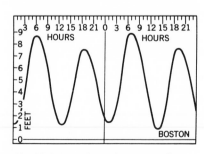

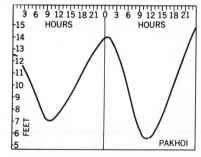

Fig. 10.3. Semidiurnal type of tide.   *Fig. 10.4. Diurnal type of tide.*

in the high water heights, low water heights, or in both. There are usually two high and two low waters each day, but occasionally the tide may become diurnal. Such tides are prevalent along the Pacific coast of the United States and in many other parts of the world. Examples of mixed types of tide are shown in figure 10.5. At Los Angeles, it is typical that the inequalities in the high and low waters are about the same. At Seattle the greater inequalities are typically in the low waters, while at Honolulu it is the high waters that have the greater inequalities.

Solar tide • The natural period of oscillation of a body of water may accentuate either the solar or the lunar tidal oscillations. Though it is a general rule that the tides follow the moon, the relative importance of the solar effect varies in different areas. There are a few places, primarily in the South Pacific and the Indonesian areas, where the solar oscillation is the more important, and at those places the high and low waters occur at about the same time each day. At Port Adelaide, Australia (fig. 10.6), the solar and lunar semidiurnal oscillations are equal and nullify one another at neaps, which will be discussed later.

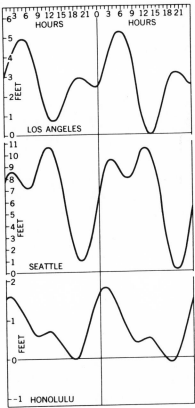

Fig. 10.5. Mixed types of tide.

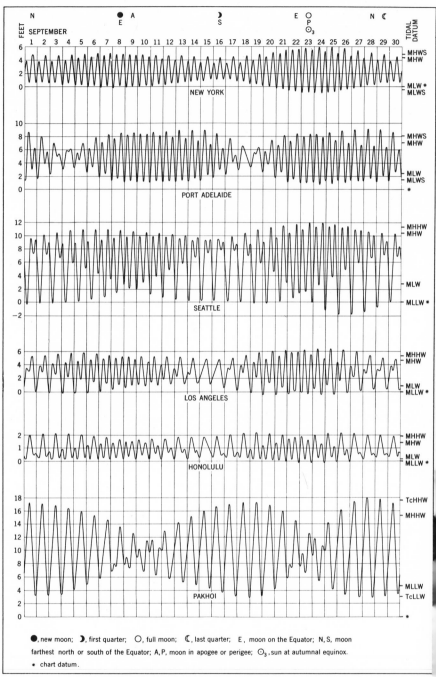

Fig. 10.6. Tidal variations at various places during a month.

Special effects • As a progressive wave enters shallow water, its speed is decreased. Since the trough is shallower than the crest, its retardation is greater, resulting in a steepening of the wave front. Therefore, in many rivers, the duration of rise is considerably less than the duration of fall. In a few estuaries, the advance of the low water trough is so much retarded that the crest of the rising tide overtakes the low, and advances upstream as a churning, foaming wall of water called a **bore.** Bores that are large and dangerous at times of large tidal ranges may be mere ripples at those times of the month when the range is small. The tide tables indicate where bores occur.

Other special features are the **double low water** (as at Hoek Van Holland) and the **double high water** (as at Southampton, England). At such places there is often a slight fall or rise in the middle of the high or low water period. The practical effect is to create a longer period of stand at high or low tide. The tide tables direct attention to these and other peculiarities where they occur.

Variations in range • Though the tide at a particular place can be classified as to type, it exhibits many variations during the month (fig. 10.6). The range of the tide varies in accordance with the intensity of the tide-producing force, though there may be a lag of a day or two (**age of tide**) between a particular astronomic cause and the tidal effect.

Thus, when the moon is at the point in its orbit nearest the earth (at *perigee*), the lunar semidiurnal range is increased and **perigean** tides occur; when the moon is farthest from the earth (at *apogee*), the smaller **apogean** tides occur. When the moon and sun are in line and pulling together, as at new and full moon, **spring** tides occur (the term *spring* has nothing to do with the season of year); when the moon and sun oppose each other, as at the quadratures, the smaller **neap** tides occur.

When certain of these phenomena coincide, the great **perigean spring** tides, the small **apogean neap** tides, etc., occur.

These are variations in the semidiurnal portion of the tide. Variations in the diurnal portion occur as the moon and sun change declination. When the moon is at its maximum semi-monthly declination (either north or south), **tropic** tides occur in which the diurnal effect is at a maximum; when it crosses the equator, the diurnal effect is a minimum and **equatorial** tides occur.

It should be noted that when the range of tide is increased, as at spring tides, there is more water available only at *high* tide; at *low* tide there is less, for the high waters rise higher and the low waters fall lower at these times. There is more water at neap low water than at spring low water. With tropic tides, there is usually more depth at one low water during the day than at the other. While it is desirable to know the meanings of these terms, the best way of determining the height of the tide at any place and time is to examine the tide predictions for the place as given in the tide tables. Figure 10.7 illustrates variations in the ranges and heights of tides in a locality where the water level always exceeds the charted depth.

Tidal cycles • Tidal oscillations go through a number of cycles. The shortest cycle, completed in about 12 hours and 25 minutes for a semi-diurnal tide, extends from any phase of the tide to the next recurrence of the same phase. During a **lunar day** (averaging 24 hours and 50 minutes) there are two highs and two lows (two of the shorter cycles) for a semi-diurnal tide. The effect of the phase variation is completed in about two weeks as the moon varies from new to full or full to new. The effect of the moon's declination is also repeated about each two weeks. The cycle involving the moon's distance requires approximately a **lunar month** (a synodical month of about 29½ days). The sun's declination and distance cycles are respectively a half year and a year in length. An important lunar cycle, called the **nodal period,** is 18.6 years (usually expressed in round

TIDES AND TIDAL CURRENTS

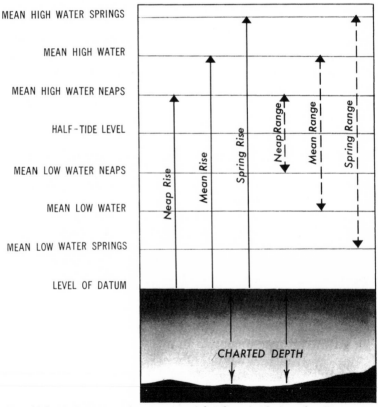

Fig. 10.7. Variations in the ranges and heights of tide in a locality where the water level always exceeds the charted depth.

figures as 19 years). For a tidal value, particularly a range, to be considered a true mean, it must be either based upon observations extended over this period of time or adjusted to take account of variations known to occur during the cycle.

Time of tide • Since the lunar tide-producing force has the greater effect in producing tides at most places, the tides "follow the moon." Because of the rotation of the earth, high water lags behind meridian passage (upper and lower) of the moon. The **tidal day,** which is also the **lunar day,** is the time between consecutive transits of the moon, or 24 hours and 50 minutes on the average. Where the tide is largely semidiurnal in type, the **lunitidal interval**—the interval between the moon's meridian transit and a particular phase of tide—is fairly constant throughout the month, varying somewhat with the tidal cycles. There are many places, however, where solar or diurnal oscillations are effective in upsetting this relationship, and the newer editions of charts of many countries now omit intervals because of the tendency to use them for prediction even though accurate predictions are available in tide tables. However, the lunitidal interval may be encountered. The interval generally given is the average elapsed time from the meridian transit (upper or lower) of the moon until the next high tide. This may be called **mean high water lunitidal interval** or **establishment of the port.** The **high water full and change (HWF&C)** or **vulgar establishment,** sometimes given, is the average interval on days of full or new moon, and approximates the mean high water lunitidal interval.

In the ocean, the tide may be of the nature of a progressive wave with the crest moving forward, a stationary or standing wave which oscillates in a seesaw fashion, or a combination of the two. Consequently, caution should be used in inferring the time of tide at a place from tidal data for nearby places. In a river or estuary, the tide enters from the sea and is usually sent upstream as a progressive wave, so that the tide occurs progressively later at various places upstream.

Tidal datums • A **tidal datum** is a level from which heights and depths are measured. There are a number of such levels of reference that are important to the mariner. The relation of the tide each day during a month to these datums is shown, for certain places, in figure 10.6.

The most important level of reference to the mariner is the datum of soundings on charts. Since the tide rises and falls continually while soundings are being taken during a hydrographic survey, the tide should be observed during the survey so that soundings taken at all stages of the tide can be reduced to a common datum. Soundings on charts show depths below a selected low water datum (occasionally mean sea level), and tide predictions in tide tables show heights above the same level. The depth of water available at any time is obtained by adding the height of the tide at the time in question to the charted depth, or by subtracting the predicted height if it is negative.

By international agreement, the level used as chart datum should be just low enough so that low waters do not go far below it. At most places, however, the level used is one determined from a mean of a number of low waters (usually over a 19-year period); therefore some low waters can be expected to fall below it. The following are some of the datums in general use.

The highest low water datum in considerable use is **mean low water (MLW),** which is the average height of all low waters at a place. About half of the low waters fall below it. **Mean low water springs (MLWS),** usually shortened to **low water springs,** is the average level of the low waters that occur at the times of spring tides. **Mean lower low water (MLLW)** is the average height of the lower low waters at a place. **Tropic lower low water (TcLLW)** is the average height of the lower low waters (or of the single daily low waters if the tide becomes diurnal) that occur when the moon is near maximum declination and the diurnal effect is most pronounced. This datum is not in common use as a tidal reference. **Indian spring low water (ISLW),** sometimes called **Indian tide plane** or **harmonic tide plane,** is a low datum that includes the spring effect of the semidiurnal portion of the tide and the tropic effect of the diurnal portion. It is about the level of lower low water of mixed tides at the time that the moon's maximum declination coincides with the time of new or full moon. **Mean lower low water springs** is the average level of the lower of the two low waters on the days of spring tides. Some still lower datums used on charts are determined from tide observations and some are determined arbitrarily and later referred to the tide. Most of them fall close to one or the other of the following two datums. **Lowest normal low water** is a datum that approximates the average height of monthly lowest low waters, discarding any tides disturbed by storms. **Lowest low water** is an extremely low datum. It conforms generally to the lowest tide observed, or even somewhat lower. Once a tidal datum is established, it is generally retained for an indefinite period, even though it might differ slightly from a better determination from later observations. When this occurs, the established datum may be called **low water datum, lower low water datum,** etc.

In some areas where there is little or no tide, such as the Baltic Sea, **mean sea level (MSL)** is used as chart datum. This is the average height of the surface of the sea for all stages of the tide over a 19-year period. This may differ slightly from **half-tide level,** which is the level midway between mean high water and mean low water.

Inconsistencies of terminology are found among charts of different countries and between charts issued at different times. For example, the spring effect as defined here is a feature of only the semidiurnal tide, yet it is sometimes used synonymously with tropic effect to refer to times of increased range of a diurnal tide. Such inconsistencies are being reduced through increased international cooperation.

Large-scale charts usually specify the datum of soundings and may contain a tide note giving mean heights of the tide at one or more places on the chart. These heights are intended merely as a rough guide to the change in depth to be expected under the specified conditions. They should not be used for the prediction of heights on any particular day. Such predictions should be obtained from *tide tables* (see Chapter 9).

High water datums • Heights of land features are usually referred on nautical charts to a high water datum. The one used on charts of the United States, its territories and possessions, and widely used elsewhere, is **mean high water (MHW),** which is the average height of all high waters over a 19-year period. Any other high water datum in use on charts is likely to be higher than this. Other high water datums are **mean high water springs (MHWS),** which is the average level of the high waters that occur at the time of spring tides; **mean higher high water (MHHW),** which is the average height of the higher high waters of each day; and **tropic higher high water (TcHHW),** which is the average height of the higher high waters (or the single daily high waters if the tide becomes diurnal) that occur when the moon is near maximum declination and the diurnal effect is most pronounced. A reference merely to "high water" leaves some doubt as to the specific level referred to, for the height of high water varies from day to day. Where the range is large, the variation during a two-week period may be considerable.

Meteorological effects • The foregoing discussion of tide behavior assumes normal weather conditions. The level of the sea is affected by wind and atmospheric pressure. In general, onshore winds raise the level and offshore winds lower it, but the amount of change varies at different places. During periods of low atmospheric pressure, the water level tends to be higher than normal. For a stationary low, the increase in elevation can be found by the formula

$$R_0 = 0.0325\,(1010 - P),$$

in which R_0 is the increase in elevation in feet, and P is the atmospheric pressure in millibars. This is equal approximately to one centimeter per millibar depression, or one foot (13.6 inches) per inch depression. For a moving low, the increase in elevation is given by the formula

$$R = \frac{R_0}{1 - \dfrac{C^2}{gh}},$$

in which R is the increase in elevation in feet, R_0 is the increase in feet for a stationary low, C is the rate of motion of the low in feet per second, g is the acceleration due to gravity (32.2 feet per second), and h is the depth of water in feet.

Where the range of tide is very small, the meteorological effect may sometimes be greater than the normal tide.

Tidal Current

Tidal and nontidal currents • Horizontal movement of the water is **current.** It may be classified as "tidal" and "nontidal." **Tidal current** is the periodic horizontal flow of water accompanying the rise and fall of the tide, and results from the same cause. **Nontidal current** is any current not due to the tidal movement. Nontidal currents include the permanent currents in the general circulatory system of the oceans as well as temporary currents arising from meteorological conditions. The current experienced at any time is usually a combination of tidal and nontidal currents.

In navigation, the effect of the tidal current is often of more importance than the changing depth due to the tide, and many mariners speak of "the tide," when they have in mind the flow of the tidal current.

General features • Offshore, where the direction of flow is not restricted by any barriers, the tidal current is **rotary;** that is, it flows continuously, with the direction changing through all points of the compass during the tidal period. The tendency for the rotation in direction has its origin in the deflecting force of the earth's rotation, and unless modified by local conditions, the change is clockwise in the northern hemisphere and counterclockwise in the southern hemisphere. The speed usually varies throughout the tidal cycle, passing through two maximums in approximately opposite directions, and two minimums about halfway between the maximums in time and direction. Rotary currents can be depicted as in figure 10.8, by a series of arrows representing the direction and speed of the current at each hour. This is sometimes called a **current rose.** Because of the elliptical pattern formed by the ends of the arrows, it is also referred to as a **current ellipse.**

In rivers or straits, or where the direction of flow is more or less restricted to certain channels, the tidal current is **reversing;** that is, it flows alternately in approximately opposite directions with an instant or short period of little or no current, called **slack water,** at each reversal of the current. During the flow in each direction, the speed varies from zero at the time of slack water to a maximum, called **strength of flood** or **ebb,** about midway between the slacks. Reversing currents can be indicated graphically, as in figure 10.9, by arrows that represent the speed of the current at each hour. The flood is usually depicted above the slack water

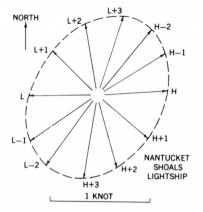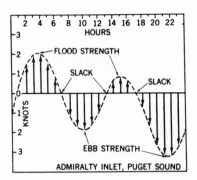

Fig. 10.8. Rotary tidal current. Times are hours before and after high and low tide at Nantucket Shoals Lightship. The bearing and length of each arrow represents the hourly direction and speed of the current. See fig. 10.13.
Fig. 10.9. Reversing tidal current. See figure 10.14.

line and the ebb below it. The tidal current curve formed by the ends of the arrows has the same characteristic sine form as the tide curve. (In illustrations for certain purposes, as in figures 10.11 and 10.14, it is convenient to omit the arrows and show only the curve.)

A slight departure from the sine form is exhibited by the reversing current in a strait, such as East River, New York, that connects two tidal bodies of water. The tides at the two ends of a strait are seldom in phase or equal in range, and the current, called **hydraulic current,** is generated largely by the continuously changing difference in height of water at the two ends. The speed of a hydraulic current varies nearly as the square root of the difference in height. The speed reaches a maximum more quickly and remains at strength for a longer period than shown in figure 10.9, and the period of weak current near the time of slack is considerably shortened.

The current *direction* or **set** is the direction *toward* which the current flows. The *speed* is sometimes called the **drift.** The term "velocity" is often used as the equivalent of "speed" when referring to current, although strictly "velocity" implies direction as well as speed. The term "strength" is also used to refer to speed, but more often to greatest speed between consecutive slack waters. The movement toward shore or upstream is the **flood,** the movement away from shore or downstream is the **ebb.** In a purely semidiurnal type of current unaffected by nontidal flow, the flood and ebb each last about six hours and 13 minutes. But if there is either diurnal inequality or nontidal flow, the durations of flood and ebb may be quite unequal.

Types of tidal current • Tidal currents may be of the **semidiurnal, diurnal,** or **mixed** type; corresponding to a considerable degree to the type of tide at the place, but often with a stronger semidiurnal tendency.

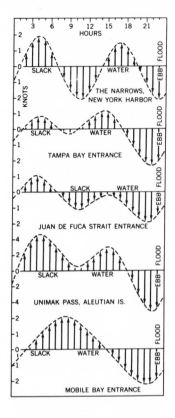

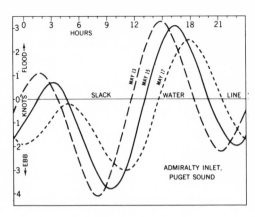

Fig. 10.10. *Several types of reversing current. The pattern changes gradually from day to day, particularly for mixed types, passing through cycles somewhat similar to that shown for tides in figure 10.6.*

Fig. 10.11. *Changes in a current of the mixed type. Note that each day as the inequality increases, the morning slacks draw together in time until on the 17th the morning flood disappears. On that day the current ebbs throughout the morning.*

The tidal currents in tidal estuaries along the Atlantic coast of the United States are examples of the semidiurnal type of reversing current. At Mobile Bay entrance they are almost purely diurnal. At most places, however, the type is mixed to a greater or lesser degree. At Tampa and Galveston entrances there are only one flood and one ebb each day when the moon is near its maximum declination, and two floods and two ebbs each day when the moon is near the equator. Along the Pacific coast of the United States there are generally two floods and two ebbs every day, but one of the floods or ebbs has a greater speed and longer duration than the other, the inequality varying with the declination of the moon. The inequalities in the current often differ considerably from place to place even within limited areas, such as adjacent passages in Puget Sound and various passages between the Aleutian Islands. Figure 10.10 shows several types of reversing current. Figure 10.11 shows how the flood disappears as the diurnal inequality increases at one station.

Offshore rotary currents that are purely semidiurnal repeat the elliptical pattern (fig. 10.8) each tidal cycle of 12 hours and 25 minutes. If there is considerable diurnal inequality, the plotted hourly current arrows de-

scribe a set of two ellipses of different sizes during a period of 24 hours
and 50 minutes, as shown in figure 10.12, and the greater the diurnal inequality, the greater the difference between the sizes of the two ellipses.
In a completely diurnal rotary current, the smaller ellipse disappears and
only one ellipse is produced in 24 hours and 50 minutes.

Variations and cycles • Tidal currents have periods and cycles similar to
those of the tides and are subject to similar variations, but flood and ebb
of the current do not necessarily occur at the same times as the rise and
fall of the tide. The relationship is explained further later.

The speed at strength increases and decreases during the two-week
period, month, and year with the variations in the range of tide. Thus,
the stronger **spring** and **perigean currents** occur near the times of new and
full moon and near the times of the moon's perigee, or at times of spring
and perigean tides; the weaker **neap** and **apogean currents** occur at the
times of neap and apogean tides; **tropic currents** with increased diurnal
speeds or with larger diurnal inequalities in speed occur at times of tropic
tides; and **equatorial currents** with a minimum diurnal effect occur at
times of equatorial tides; etc.

As with the tide, a *mean value* represents an average obtained from
a 19-year series. Since a series of current observations is usually limited
to a day or two, and seldom covers more than a month or two, it is
necessary to adjust the observed values, usually by comparison with tides
at a nearby place, to obtain such a mean.

Effect of nontidal flow • The current existing at any time is seldom purely
tidal, but usually includes also a nontidal current that is due to drainage,
oceanic circulation, wind, or other cause. The method in which tidal and

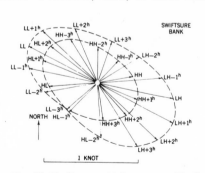 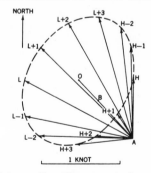

Fig. 10.12. *Rotary tidal current with diurnal inequality. Times are in hours
referred to tides (higher high, lower low, lower high, and higher low) at
Swiftsure Bank.*

Fig. 10.13. *Effect of nontidal current on the rotary tidal current of figure
10.8. If the nontidal current is northwest at 0.3 knot, it may be represented
by* BO, *and all hourly directions and speeds will then be measured from* B.
If it is 1.0 knot, it will be represented by AO *and the actual resultant hourly
directions and speeds will be measured from* A, *as shown by the arrows.*

nontidal currents combine is best explained graphically, as in figures 10.13 and 10.14. The pattern of the tidal current remains unchanged, but the curve is shifted from the point or line from which the currents are measured in the direction of the nontidal current and by an amount equal to it. It is sometimes more convenient graphically merely to move the line or point of origin in the opposite direction.

Thus, the speed of the current flowing in the direction of the nontidal current is increased by an amount equal to the magnitude of the nontidal current, and the speed of the current flowing in the opposite direction is decreased by an equal amount. In figure 10.13 a nontidal current is represented both in direction and speed by the vector AO. Since this is greater than the speed of the tidal current in the opposite direction, the point A is outside the ellipse. The direction and speed of the combined tidal and nontidal currents at any time is represented by a vector from A to that point on the curve representing the given time, and can be scaled from the graph. The strongest and weakest currents may no longer be in the directions of the maximum and minimum of the tidal current. In a reversing current (fig. 10.14), the effect is to advance the time of one slack and to retard the following one. If the speed of the nontidal current exceeds that of the reversing tidal current, the resultant current flows continuously in one direction without coming to a slack. In this case, the speed varies from a maximum to a minimum and back to a maximum in each tidal

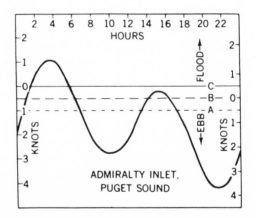

Fig. 10.14. Effect of nontidal current on the reversing tidal current of figure 10.9. If the nontidal current is 0.5 knot in the ebb direction, the ebb is increased by moving the slack water line from position A up 0.5 knot to position B. Speeds will then be measured from this broken line as shown by the scale on the right, and times of slack are changed. If the nontidal current is 1.0 knot in the ebb direction, as shown by line C, the speeds are as shown on the left, and the current will not reverse to a flood in the afternoon; it will merely slacken at about 1500.

cycle. In figure 10.14 the horizontal line *A* represents slack water if only tidal currents are present. Line *B* represents the effect of a 0.5-knot non-tidal ebb, and line *C* the effect of a 1.0-knot nontidal ebb. With the condition shown at *C* there is only one flood each tidal day. If the nontidal ebb were to increase to approximately two knots, there would be no flood, two maximum ebbs and two minimum ebbs occurring during a tidal day.

Relation between time of tidal current and time of tide • At many places where current and tide are both semidiurnal, there is a definite relation between times of current and times of high and low water in the locality. Current atlases and notes on nautical charts often make use of this relationship by presenting for particular locations the direction and speed of the current at each succeeding hour after high and low water at a place for which tide predictions are available.

In localities where there is considerable diurnal inequality in tide or current, or where the type of current differs from the type of tide, the relationship is not constant, and it may be hazardous to try to predict the times of current from times of tide. Note the current curve for Unimak Pass in the Aleutions in figure 10.10. It shows the current as predicted in the tidal current tables. Predictions of high and low waters in the tide tables might have led one to expect the current to change from flood to ebb in the late morning, whereas actually the current continued to run flood with some strength at that time.

Since the relationship between times of tidal current and tide is not everywhere the same, and may be variable at the same place, one should exercise extreme caution in using general rules. The belief that slacks occur at local high and low tides and that the maximum flood and ebb occur when the tide is rising or falling most rapidly may be approximately true at the seaward entrance to, and in the upper reaches of, an inland tidal waterway. But generally this is not true in other parts of inland waterways. When an inland waterway is extensive or its entrance constricted, the slacks in some parts of the waterway often occur midway between the times of high and low tide. Usually in such waterways the relationship changes from place to place as one progresses upstream, slack water getting progressively later with respect to the local tide until at the head of tidewater (the inland limit of water affected by a tide) the slacks occur at the times of high and low tide.

Relation between speed of current and range of tide • The variation in the speed of the tidal current from place to place is not necessarily consistent with the range of tide. It may be the reverse. For example, currents are weak in the Gulf of Maine, where the tides are large, and strong near Nantucket Island and in Nantucket Sound, where the tides are small.

At any one place, however, the speed of the current at strength of flood and ebb varies during the month in about the same proportion as the range of tide, and one can use this relationship to determine the relative strength of currents on any day.

Variation across an estuary • In inland tidal waterways the *time* of tidal current varies across the channel from shore to shore. On the average, the current turns earlier near shore than in midstream, where the speed is greater. Differences of half an hour to an hour are not uncommon, but the difference varies and the relationship may be nullified by the effect of nontidal flow.

The *speed* of the current also varies across the channel, usually being greater in midstream or midchannel than near shore, but in a winding river or channel the strongest currents occur near the concave shore. Near the opposite (convex) shore the currents are weak or may eddy.

Variation with depth • In tidal rivers the subsurface current acting on the lower portion of the hull may differ considerably from the surface current. An appreciable subsurface current may be present when the surface movement appears to be practically slack, and the subsurface current may even be flowing with appreciable speed in the opposite direction to the surface current.

In a tidal estuary, particularly in the lower reaches where there is considerable difference in density from top to bottom, flood usually begins earlier near the bottom than at the surface. The differences may be an hour or two or as little as a few minutes, depending upon the estuary, the location in the estuary, and freshet conditions. Even when the fresh water runoff becomes so great as to prevent the surface current from flooding, it may still flood below the surface. The difference in time of ebb from surface to bottom is normally small but subject to variation with time and location.

The ebb speed at strength usually decreases gradually from top to bottom, but the speed of flood at strength often is stronger at subsurface depths than at the surface.

Tidal current tables and other sources of information • The navigator should not attempt to predict currents without specific information for the locality in which he is interested. Such information is contained in various forms in many navigational publications.

Tidal current tables, issued annually, list daily predictions of the times and strengths of flood and ebb currents, and of the times of intervening slacks. Due to lack of observational data, coverage is considerably more limited than for the tides. The tidal current tables do include supplemental data by which tidal current predictions can be determined for many places in addition to those for which daily predictions are given. The use of tidal current tables is explained in Chapter 9.

Sailing directions and **coast pilots** issued by maritime nations include general descriptions of current behavior in various localities throughout the world.

Tidal current charts. A number of important harbors and waterways are covered by sets of tidal current charts showing graphically the hourly current movement.

[11]

Weather Observations

Introduction • Weather forecasts are generally based upon information acquired by observations made at a large number of stations. Ashore, these stations are located so as to provide adequate coverage of the area of interest. Most observations at sea are made by mariners, wherever they happen to be. Since the number of observations at sea is small compared to the number ashore, marine observations are of importance in areas where little or no information is available from other sources.

The analysis of the weather map can be no better than the weather reports used for making the map. A knowledge of weather elements and the instruments used to measure them is therefore of importance to the mariner who hopes to benefit from weather forecasts.

Instruments of various types have been developed to aid in making weather observations. Some have been in use for many years, while others have been developed only recently. Electronic devices have aided materially, but the full impact of electronics upon meteorology has not yet been felt. Several new types of electronic weather instruments are in various stages of development.

Atmospheric pressure measurement • The sea of air surrounding the earth exerts a pressure of about 14.7 pounds per square inch on the surface of the earth. This **atmospheric pressure,** sometimes called **barometric pressure,** varies from place to place, and at the same place it varies with time.

Atmospheric pressure is one of the basic elements of a meteorological observation. When the pressure at each station is plotted on a synoptic chart, lines of equal atmospheric pressure, called **isobars,** are drawn to indicate the areas of high and low pressure and their centers. These are useful in making weather predictions, because certain types of weather are characteristic of each type area, and often the wind patterns over large areas are deduced from the isobars.

Atmospheric pressure is measured by means of a **barometer**. A **mercurial barometer** does this by balancing the weight of a column of air against that of a column of mercury. The **aneroid barometer** has a partly evacuated, thin-metal cell which is compressed by atmospheric pressure, the amount of the compression being related to the pressure.

Early mercurial barometers were calibrated to indicate the height, usually in inches or millimeters, of the column of mercury needed to balance the column of air above the point of measurement. While the units **inches of mercury** and **millimeters of mercury** are still widely used, many modern barometers are calibrated to indicate the centimeter-gram-second unit of pressure, the **millibar,** which is equal to 1,000 dynes per square centimeter. A **dyne** is the force required to accelerate a mass of one gram at the rate of one centimeter per second per second.

The mercurial barometer in its simplest form consists of a glass tube a little more than 30 inches in length and of uniform internal diameter; one end being closed, the tube is filled with mercury, and inverted into a cup of mercury. The mercury in the tube falls until the column is just supported by the pressure of the atmosphere on the open cup, leaving a vacuum at the upper end of the tube. The height of the column indicates atmospheric pressure, greater pressures supporting higher columns of mercury. The mercurial barometer has been largely replaced at sea by the aneroid barometer.

The aneroid barometer (**fig. 11.1**) measures atmospheric pressure by means of the force exerted by the pressure on a partly evacuated, thin-metal element called a **sylphon cell.** A small spring is used, either internally or externally, to partly counteract the tendency of the atmospheric pressure to crush the cell. Atmospheric pressure is indicated directly by a scale and a pointer connected to the cell by a combination of levers. The linkage provides considerable magnification of the slight motion of the cell, to permit readings to higher precision than could be obtained without it.

An aneroid barometer should be mounted permanently. Prior to installation, the barometer should be carefully set to station pressure (see later section). An adjustment screw is provided for this purpose. The error in the reading of the instrument is determined by comparison with a mercurial barometer or a standard precision aneroid barometer. If a qualified meteorologist is not available to make this adjustment, it is good practice to remove only one-half the apparent error. The case should then be tapped gently to assist the linkage to adjust itself, and the process repeated. If the remaining error is not more than half a millibar (0.015 inch), no attempt should be made to remove it by further adjustment. Instead, a correction should be applied to the readings. The accuracy of this correction should be checked from time to time.

Fig. 11.1. An aneroid barometer.

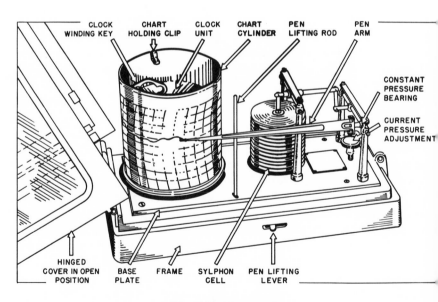

Fig. 11.2. A barograph.

A **precision aneroid barometer** used at weather stations ashore, and for comparison of shipboard instruments, is constructed and tested to more exacting tolerances than the ordinary barometer, and provides readings to greater accuracy.

The barograph (fig. 11.2) is a recording barometer. Basically, it is the same as a nonrecording aneroid barometer except that the pointer carries a pen at its outer end, and the scale is replaced by a slowly rotating cylinder around which a prepared chart is wrapped. A clock mechanism inside the cylinder rotates the cylinder so that a continuous line is traced on the chart to indicate the pressure at any time.

A **microbarograph** is a precise barograph with greater magnification of deformations due to pressure changes, and a correspondingly expanded chart. Two sylphon cells are used, one being mounted over the other in tandem. Minor fluctuations due to shocks or vibrations are eliminated by damping. Since oil-filled dashpots are used for this purpose, the instrument should not be inverted.

The barograph is usually mounted on a shelf or desk in a room open to the atmosphere, and in a location which minimizes the effect of the ship's vibration. Shock-absorbing material such as sponge rubber is placed under the instrument to minimize the transmission of shocks.

The pen should be checked and the inkwell filled each time the chart is changed, every week in the case of the barograph, and each four days in the case of the microbarograph. The dashpots of the microbarograph should be kept filled with dashpot oil to within three-eighths inch of the top.

Both instruments require checking from time to time to insure correct indication of pressure. The position of the pen is adjusted by a small knob provided for this purpose. The adjustment should be made in stages, eliminating half the apparent error, tapping the case to insure linkage adjustment to the new setting, and then repeating the process.

Adjustment of barometer readings • Atmospheric pressure as indicated by a barometer or barograph may be subject to several errors, as follows:

Instrument error. Any inaccuracy due to imperfection or incorrect adjustment of the instrument can be determined by comparison with a standard instrument. The National Weather Service provides a comparison service. In certain ports a representative brings a standard barometer on board ships for comparison, or a barometer can be taken to a local National Weather Service office, and comparison can be made there. The correct sea-level pressure can be obtained by telephone. The shipboard barometer should be corrected for height, as explained below, before comparison with this telephoned value. If there is reason to believe that the barometer is in error, it should be compared with a standard, and if an error is found, the barometer should be adjusted to the correct reading, or a correction applied to all readings.

Height error. Since atmospheric pressure is caused by the weight of air above the place, the pressure decreases as height increases. The correct value at the barometer is called **station pressure.** Isobars adequately reflect wind conditions and geographic distribution of pressure only when they are drawn for pressure at constant height (or the varying height at which a constant pressure exists). On synoptic charts it is customary to show the equivalent pressure at sea level, called **sea level pressure.** This is found by applying a correction to station pressure. The correction, given in Table 10, depends upon the height of the barometer and the average temperature of the air between this height and the surface. The outside air temperature taken aboard ship is sufficiently accurate for this purpose. *This is an important correction which should be applied to all readings of any type barometer.*

Gravity error. Mercurial barometers are calibrated for standard sea-level gravity at latitude 45°32′40″. If the gravity differs from this amount, an error is introduced and must be corrected. *This correction does not apply to readings of an aneroid barometer.* Gravity also changes with height above sea level, but the effect is negligible for the first few hundred feet, and so is not needed for readings taken aboard ship.

TABLE 10

Correction of Barometer Reading for Height Above Sea Level

All barometers.   All values positive.

Height in feet	Outside temperature in degrees Fahrenheit													Height in feet
	−20°	−10°	0°	10°	20°	30°	40°	50°	60°	70°	80°	90°	100°	
	Inches	*Inches*	*Inches*	*Inches*	*Inches*	*Inches*	*Inches*	*Inches*	*Inches*	*Inches*	*Inches*	*Inches*	*Inches*	
5	0. 01	0. 01	0. 01	0. 01	0. 01	0. 01	0. 01	0. 01	0. 01	0. 01	0. 01	0. 01	0. 01	5
10	0. 01	0. 01	0. 01	0. 01	0. 01	0. 01	0. 01	0. 01	0. 01	0. 01	0. 01	0. 01	0. 01	10
15	0. 02	0. 02	0. 02	0. 02	0. 02	0. 02	0. 02	0. 02	0. 02	0. 02	0. 02	0. 02	0. 02	15
20	0. 03	0. 02	0. 02	0. 02	0. 02	0. 02	0. 02	0. 02	0. 02	0. 02	0. 02	0. 02	0. 02	20
25	0. 03	0. 03	0. 03	0. 03	0. 03	0. 03	0. 03	0. 03	0. 03	0. 03	0. 03	0. 03	0. 03	25
30	0. 04	0. 04	0. 04	0. 04	0. 04	0. 03	0. 03	0. 03	0. 03	0. 03	0. 03	0. 03	0. 03	30
35	0. 04	0. 04	0. 04	0. 04	0. 04	0. 04	0. 04	0. 04	0. 04	0. 04	0. 04	0. 04	0. 04	35
40	0. 05	0. 05	0. 05	0. 05	0. 05	0. 05	0. 04	0. 04	0. 04	0. 04	0. 04	0. 04	0. 04	40
45	0. 06	0. 06	0. 05	0. 05	0. 05	0. 05	0. 05	0. 05	0. 05	0. 05	0. 05	0. 05	0. 05	45
50	0. 06	0. 06	0. 06	0. 06	0. 06	0. 06	0. 06	0. 06	0. 05	0. 05	0. 05	0. 05	0. 05	50
55	0. 07	0. 07	0. 07	0. 07	0. 07	0. 06	0. 06	0. 06	0. 06	0. 06	0. 06	0. 06	0. 06	55
60	0. 08	0. 07	0. 07	0. 07	0. 07	0. 07	0. 07	0. 07	0. 06	0. 06	0. 06	0. 06	0. 06	60
65	0. 08	0. 08	0. 08	0. 08	0. 08	0. 07	0. 07	0. 07	0. 07	0. 07	0. 07	0. 07	0. 07	65
70	0. 09	0. 09	0. 09	0. 08	0. 08	0. 08	0. 08	0. 08	0. 08	0. 08	0. 07	0. 07	0. 07	70
75	0. 10	0. 09	0. 09	0. 09	0. 09	0. 09	0. 09	0. 08	0. 08	0. 08	0. 08	0. 08	0. 08	75
80	0. 10	0. 10	0. 10	0. 10	0. 09	0. 09	0. 09	0. 09	0. 09	0. 08	0. 08	0. 08	0. 08	80
85	0. 11	0. 11	0. 10	0. 10	0. 10	0. 10	0. 10	0. 09	0. 09	0. 09	0. 09	0. 09	0. 09	85
90	0. 11	0. 11	0. 11	0. 11	0. 11	0. 10	0. 10	0. 10	0. 10	0. 10	0. 09	0. 09	0. 09	90
95	0. 12	0. 12	0. 12	0. 11	0. 11	0. 11	0. 11	0. 11	0. 10	0. 10	0. 10	0. 10	0. 10	95
100	0. 13	0. 12	0. 12	0. 12	0. 12	0. 11	0. 11	0. 11	0. 11	0. 11	0. 11	0. 10	0. 10	100
105	0. 13	0. 13	0. 13	0. 13	0. 12	0. 12	0. 12	0. 12	0. 11	0. 11	0. 11	0. 11	0. 11	105
110	0. 14	0. 14	0. 13	0. 13	0. 13	0. 13	0. 12	0. 12	0. 12	0. 12	0. 11	0. 11	0. 11	110
115	0. 15	0. 14	0. 14	0. 14	0. 13	0. 13	0. 13	0. 13	0. 12	0. 12	0. 12	0. 12	0. 12	115
120	0. 15	0. 15	0. 15	0. 14	0. 14	0. 14	0. 13	0. 13	0. 13	0. 13	0. 12	0. 12	0. 12	120
125	0. 16	0. 16	0. 15	0. 15	0. 15	0. 14	0. 14	0. 14	0. 13	0. 13	0. 13	0. 13	0. 12	125

Temperature error. Barometers are calibrated at a standard temperature of 32° F. The liquid of a mercurial barometer expands as the temperature of the mercury rises, and contracts as it decreases, and another correction must be applied to readings of mercurial barometers. Modern aneroid barometers are compensated for temperature changes by the use of different metals having unequal coefficients of linear expansion.

Wind measurement • Wind measurement consists of determination of the direction *from* which the wind is blowing, and the speed of the wind. Wind direction is measured by a **wind vane,** and wind speed by an **anemometer.**

A wind vane consists of a device pivoted on a vertical shaft, with more surface area on one side of the pivot than on the other, so that the wind exerts more force on one side, causing the smaller end to point into the wind. An indicator may be connected to the shaft to provide continuous measurement of wind direction.

In its simplest form, an anemometer consists of a number of cups mounted on short horizontal arms attached to a longer vertical shaft which rotates as the wind blows against the cups. The speed at which the shaft rotates is directly proportional to the wind speed. The number of rotations may be indicated by a counter or by marks on a revolving drum, or the speed may be indicated directly by a device similar to an automobile speedometer. Still another method is to connect a buzzer or flashing light so calibrated that the number of signals per unit time is the speed in knots or miles per hour.

The standard anemometer used aboard ship has three cups, although some anemometers have four. An anemometer which uses a propeller as the rotor to measure wind speed, and has a streamlined, tail-type vane to indicate direction, is being installed on some ships. Similar equipment is used ashore, customarily mounted on a guyed mast 13 feet high. Wind direction is transmitted to an indicator or recorder by a synchronous motor, while wind speed is transmitted as a voltage generated by a direct-current magneto driven by the propeller. A synchro system is connected to some wind-measuring equipment to provide remote indication of the velocity (both direction and speed). Lightweight, portable, hand-held instruments for measuring and indicating wind speed in knots are used on some ships.

Several types of wind speed and direction **recorders** are available. Each instrument is normally supplied with a description and complete operating instructions.

If no anemometer is available, wind speed can be estimated by its effect upon the sea and objects in its path, as explained later.

True and apparent wind • An observer aboard a vessel proceeding through still air experiences an **apparent wind** which is from dead ahead and has an apparent speed equal to the speed of the vessel. Thus, if the actual or **true wind** is zero and the speed of the vessel is ten knots, the apparent wind is from dead ahead at ten knots. If the true wind is from dead ahead at 15 knots, and the speed of the vessel is ten knots, the apparent wind is $15+10=25$ knots from dead ahead. If the vessel makes a 180° turn, the apparent wind is $15-10=5$ knots from dead astern.

In any case, the apparent wind is the vector sum of the true wind and the *reciprocal* of the vessel's course and speed vector. Since wind vanes and anemometers measure *apparent* wind, the usual problem aboard a vessel equipped with an anemometer is to convert this to true wind. There are several ways of doing this. Perhaps the simplest is by the graphical solution illustrated in the following example:

Example 1. A ship is proceeding on course 150° at a speed of 17 knots. The apparent wind is from 40° off the starboard bow, speed 15 knots.

Required. The relative direction, true direction, and speed of the true wind.

Solution (fig. 11.3). Starting at the center of a maneuvering board or other suitable form (see fig. 11.3), draw a line in the relative direction *from* which the apparent wind is blowing. Locate point 1 on this line, at a distance from the center equal to the speed of the apparent wind (2:1 scale is used in figure 11.3). From point 1, draw a line vertically *downward*. Locate point 2 on this line at a distance from point 1 equal to the speed of the vessel in knots, to the same scale as the first line. The relative direction of the true wind is *from* point 2 (120°) toward the center, and the speed of the true wind is the distance of point 2 from the center, to the same scale used previously (11 kn.). The true direction of the wind is the relative direction plus the true heading, or $120°+150°=270°$.

Answers. True wind from 120° relative, 270° true, at 11 knots.

A quick solution can be made without an actual plot, in the following manner: On a maneuvering board, label the circles 5, 10, 15, 20, etc., from the center, and draw vertical lines tangent to these circles. Cut out the 5:1 scale and discard that part having graduations greater than the maximum speed of the vessel. Keep this equipment for all solutions. (For durability, the two parts can be mounted on cardboard or other suitable material.) To find true wind, spot in point 1 by eye. Place the zero of the 5:1 scale on this point and align the scale (inverted) by means of the vertical lines. Locate point 2 at the speed of the vessel as indicated on the 5:1 scale. It is always vertically *below* point 1. Read the relative direction and the speed of the true wind using eye interpolation if needed.

Such problems can be solved by the use of true directions and a regular vector solution, but the use of relative directions simplifies the plot because

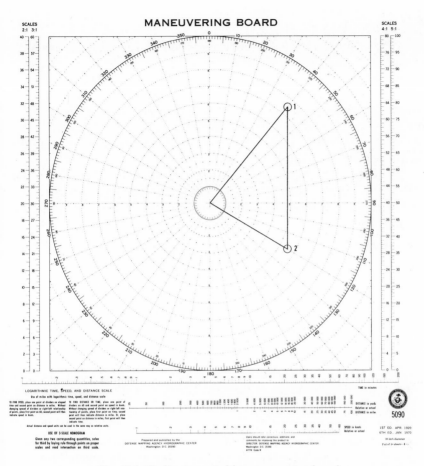

Fig. 11.3. Finding true wind by maneuvering board.

that component of the apparent wind due to the vessel's motion is always parallel (but reversed) to the vessel's motion, and the apparent wind is always *forward* of the true wind.

A tabular solution based upon the same principle can be made by means of Table 11. The entering values for this table are the apparent wind speed *in units of ship's speed*, and the difference between the heading and the apparent wind direction. The values taken from the table are the relative direction (right or left) of the true wind, and the speed of the true wind *in units of ship's speed*. If a vessel is proceeding at 12 knots, six knots constitutes one-half (0.5) unit, 12 knots one unit, 18 knots 1.5 units, 24 knots two units, etc.

Example 2. A ship is proceeding on course 270° at a speed of ten knots. The apparent wind is from 10° off the port bow, speed 30 knots.

Required. The relative direction, true direction, and speed of the true wind by Table 10.

Solution. The apparent wind speed is $\frac{30}{10}=3.0$ ship's speed units. Enter Table 10 with 3.0 and 10° and find the relative direction of the true wind to be 15° off the port bow (345° relative), and the speed to be 2.02 times the ship's speed, or $2.02\times10=20$ knots, approximately. The true direction is $345°+270°=255°$.

Answers. True wind from 345° relative, 255° true, at 20 knots.

Wind speed determined by appearance of the sea is the speed of the true wind. The sea also provides an indication of the direction of the true wind, because waves move in the same direction as the generating wind. If a wind vane is used, the direction of the apparent wind thus determined can be used with the speed of the true wind to determine the direction of the true wind by vector diagram. If a maneuvering board is used, draw a circle about the center equal to the speed of the true wind. From the center, plot the ship's vector (true course and speed). From the end of this vector draw a line in the direction in which the apparent wind is blowing (reciprocal of the direction from which it is blowing) until it intersects the speed circle. This line is the apparent wind vector, its length denotes the speed. A line from the center of the board to the end of the apparent wind vector is the true wind vector. The reciprocal of this vector is the direction from which the true wind is blowing. If the true wind speed is less than the speed of the vessel, two solutions are possible. If solution is by Table 11, the true speed, in units of ship's speed, is found in the column for the direction of the apparent wind. The number to the left is the relative direction of the true wind. The number on the same line in the side columns is the speed of the apparent wind in units of ship's speed. Again, two solutions are possible if true wind speed is less than ship's speed.

TABLE 11
Direction and Speed of True Wind in Units of Ship's Speed

Apparent wind speed	Difference between the heading and apparent wind direction										Apparent wind speed
	0°		10°		20°		30°		40°		
0. 0	180	1. 00	180	1. 00	180	1. 00	180	1. 00	180	1. 00	0. 0
0. 1	180	0. 90	179	0. 90	178	0. 91	177	0. 91	176	0. 93	0. 1
0. 2	180	0. 80	178	0. 80	175	0. 81	173	0. 83	171	0. 86	0. 2
0. 3	180	0. 70	176	0. 71	172	0. 73	169	0. 76	166	0. 79	0. 3
0. 4	180	0. 60	173	0. 61	168	0. 64	163	0. 68	160	0. 74	0. 4
0. 5	180	0. 50	170	0. 51	162	0. 56	156	0. 62	152	0. 70	0. 5
0. 6	180	0. 40	166	0. 42	155	0. 48	148	0. 57	144	0. 66	0. 6
0. 7	180	0. 30	159	0. 33	145	0. 42	138	0. 53	136	0. 65	0. 7
0. 8	180	0. 20	147	0. 25	132	0. 37	127	0. 50	136	0. 64	0. 8
0. 9	180	0. 10	126	0. 19	117	0. 34	116	0. 50	118	0. 66	0. 9
1. 0	calm	0. 00	95	0. 17	100	0. 35	105	0. 52	110	0. 68	1. 0
1. 1	0	0. 10	66	0. 21	85	0. 38	95	0. 55	103	0. 72	1. 1
1. 2	0	0. 20	49	0. 28	73	0. 43	86	0. 60	96	0. 78	1. 2
1. 3	0	0. 30	39	0. 36	64	0. 50	79	0. 66	90	0. 84	1. 3
1. 4	0	0. 40	33	0. 45	57	0. 57	73	0. 73	85	0. 90	1. 4
1. 5	0	0. 50	29	0. 54	51	0. 66	68	0. 81	81	0. 98	1. 5
1. 6	0	0. 60	26	0. 64	47	0. 74	64	0. 89	78	1. 05	1. 6
1. 7	0	0. 70	24	0. 74	44	0. 83	61	0. 97	75	1. 13	1. 7
1. 8	0	0. 80	22	0. 83	42	0. 93	58	1. 06	72	1. 22	1. 8
1. 9	0	0. 90	21	0. 93	40	1. 02	56	1. 15	70	1. 30	1. 9
2. 0	0	1. 00	20	1. 03	38	1. 11	54	1. 24	68	1. 39	2. 0
2. 5	0	1. 50	17	1. 52	32	1. 60	47	1. 71	60	1. 85	2. 5
3. 0	0	2. 00	15	2. 02	29	2. 09	43	2. 19	56	2. 32	3. 0
3. 5	0	2. 50	14	2. 52	28	2. 58	41	2. 68	53	2. 81	3. 5
4. 0	0	3. 00	13	3. 02	26	3. 08	39	3. 17	51	3. 30	4. 0
4. 5	0	3. 50	13	3. 52	25	3. 58	38	3. 67	50	3. 79	4. 5
5. 0	0	4. 00	12	4. 02	25	4. 08	37	4. 16	49	4. 28	5. 0
6. 0	0	5. 00	12	5. 02	24	5. 07	36	5. 16	47	5. 27	6. 0
7. 0	0	6. 00	12	6. 02	23	6. 07	35	6. 15	46	6. 27	7. 0
8. 0	0	7. 00	11	7. 02	23	7. 07	34	7. 15	45	7. 26	8. 0
9. 0	0	8. 00	11	8. 02	22	8. 07	34	8. 15	44	8. 26	9. 0
10. 0	0	9. 00	11	9. 02	22	9. 06	33	9. 15	44	9. 26	10. 0
	50°		60°		70°		80°		90°		
0. 0	180	1. 00	180	1. 00	180	1. 00	180	1. 00	180	1. 00	0. 0
0. 1	175	0. 94	175	0. 95	174	0. 97	174	0. 99	174	1. 00	0. 1
0. 2	170	0. 88	169	0. 92	169	0. 95	168	0. 99	169	1. 02	0. 2
0. 3	164	0. 84	163	0. 89	163	0. 94	163	0. 99	163	1. 04	0. 3
0. 4	158	0. 80	157	0. 87	156	0. 94	157	1. 01	158	1. 08	0. 4
0. 5	151	0. 78	150	0. 87	150	0. 95	152	1. 04	153	1. 12	0. 5
0. 6	143	0. 77	143	0. 87	145	0. 97	147	1. 07	149	1. 17	0. 6
0. 7	136	0. 77	137	0. 89	139	1. 01	142	1. 12	145	1. 22	0. 7
0. 8	128	0. 78	131	0. 92	134	1. 05	138	1. 17	141	1. 28	0. 8
0. 9	121	0. 81	125	0. 95	129	1. 09	134	1. 22	138	1. 35	0. 9
1. 0	115	0. 85	120	1. 00	125	1. 15	130	1. 29	135	1. 41	1. 0
1. 1	109	0. 89	115	1. 05	121	1. 21	127	1. 35	132	1. 49	1. 1
1. 2	104	0. 95	111	1. 11	118	1. 27	124	1. 42	130	1. 56	1. 2
1. 3	99	1. 01	107	1. 18	114	1. 34	121	1. 50	128	1. 64	1. 3
1. 4	95	1. 08	104	1. 25	112	1. 42	119	1. 57	126	1. 72	1. 4
1. 5	92	1. 15	101	1. 32	109	1. 49	117	1. 65	124	1. 80	1. 5
1. 6	89	1. 23	98	1. 40	107	1. 57	115	1. 73	122	1. 89	1. 6
1. 7	86	1. 31	96	1. 48	105	1. 65	113	1. 82	120	1. 97	1. 7
1. 8	84	1. 39	94	1. 56	103	1. 73	111	1. 90	119	2. 06	1. 8
1. 9	81	1. 47	92	1. 65	101	1. 82	110	1. 99	118	2. 15	1. 9
2. 0	79	1. 56	90	1. 73	100	1. 91	108	2. 07	117	2. 24	2. 0
2. 5	72	2. 01	83	2. 18	94	2. 35	103	2. 53	112	2. 69	2. 5
3. 0	68	2. 48	79	2. 65	89	2. 82	99	2. 99	108	3. 16	3. 0
3. 5	65	2. 96	76	3. 12	87	3. 29	96	3. 47	106	3. 64	3. 5
4. 0	63	3. 44	74	3. 61	84	3. 78	94	3. 95	104	4. 12	4. 0
4. 5	61	3. 93	72	4. 09	83	4. 26	93	4. 44	103	4. 61	4. 5
5. 0	60	4. 42	71	4. 58	81	4. 75	92	4. 93	101	5. 10	5. 0
6. 0	58	5. 41	69	5. 57	79	5. 74	90	5. 91	99	6. 08	6. 0
7. 0	57	6. 40	68	6. 56	78	6. 72	88	6. 90	98	7. 07	7. 0
8. 0	56	7. 40	67	7. 55	77	7. 72	87	7. 89	97	8. 06	8. 0
9. 0	55	8. 39	66	8. 54	76	8. 71	86	8. 88	96	9. 06	9. 0
10. 0	55	9. 39	65	9. 54	76	9. 70	86	9. 88	96	10. 01	10. 0

TABLE 11
Direction and Speed of True Wind in Units of Ship's Speed

Apparent wind speed	90°		100°		110°		120°		130°		Apparent wind speed
0.0	180	1.00	180	1.00	180	1.00	180	1.00	180	1.00	0.0
0.1	174	1.00	174	1.02	175	1.04	175	1.05	176	1.07	0.1
0.2	169	1.02	169	1.05	170	1.08	171	1.11	172	1.14	0.2
0.3	163	1.04	164	1.09	166	1.14	167	1.18	169	1.21	0.3
0.4	158	1.08	160	1.14	162	1.20	164	1.25	166	1.29	0.4
0.5	153	1.12	156	1.19	158	1.26	161	1.32	164	1.38	0.5
0.6	149	1.17	152	1.25	155	1.33	158	1.40	162	1.46	0.6
0.7	145	1.22	148	1.32	152	1.40	156	1.48	160	1.55	0.7
0.8	141	1.28	145	1.38	149	1.48	154	1.56	158	1.63	0.8
0.9	138	1.35	143	1.46	147	1.56	152	1.65	156	1.72	0.9
1.0	135	1.41	140	1.53	145	1.64	150	1.73	155	1.81	1.0
1.1	132	1.49	138	1.61	143	1.72	148	1.82	154	1.90	1.1
1.2	130	1.56	136	1.69	141	1.81	147	1.91	153	2.00	1.2
1.3	128	1.64	134	1.77	140	1.89	146	2.00	152	2.09	1.3
1.4	126	1.72	132	1.86	138	1.98	145	2.09	151	2.18	1.4
1.5	124	1.80	130	1.94	137	2.07	143	2.18	150	2.28	1.5
1.6	122	1.89	129	2.03	136	2.16	142	2.27	149	2.37	1.6
1.7	120	1.97	128	2.12	135	2.25	141	2.36	148	2.46	1.7
1.8	119	2.06	127	2.21	134	2.34	141	2.46	147	2.56	1.8
1.9	118	2.15	125	2.30	133	2.43	140	2.55	147	2.66	1.9
2.0	117	2.24	124	2.39	132	2.52	139	2.65	146	2.75	2.0
2.5	112	2.69	120	2.85	128	2.99	136	3.12	144	3.23	2.5
3.0	108	3.16	117	3.32	126	3.47	134	3.61	142	3.72	3.0
3.5	106	3.64	115	3.80	124	3.96	132	4.09	140	4.21	3.5
4.0	104	4.12	113	4.29	122	4.44	131	4.58	139	4.71	4.0
4.5	103	4.61	112	4.78	121	4.93	130	5.07	138	5.20	4.5
5.0	101	5.10	111	5.27	120	5.42	129	5.57	138	5.69	5.0
6.0	99	6.08	109	6.25	118	6.41	128	6.56	137	6.69	6.0
7.0	98	7.07	108	7.24	117	7.40	127	7.55	136	7.68	7.0
8.0	97	8.06	107	8.23	116	8.39	126	8.54	135	8.68	8.0
9.0	96	9.06	106	9.23	116	9.39	125	9.54	135	9.67	9.0
10.0	96	10.01	106	10.22	115	10.39	125	10.54	134	10.67	10.0

Apparent wind speed	140°		150°		160°		170°		180°		Apparent wind speed
0.0	180	1.00	180	1.00	180	1.00	180	1.00	180	1.00	0.0
0.1	177	1.08	177	1.09	178	1.09	179	1.10	180	1.10	0.1
0.2	174	1.16	175	1.18	177	1.19	178	1.20	180	1.20	0.2
0.3	171	1.24	173	1.27	175	1.29	178	1.30	180	1.30	0.3
0.4	169	1.33	172	1.36	174	1.38	177	1.40	180	1.40	0.4
0.5	167	1.42	170	1.45	173	1.48	177	1.50	180	1.50	0.5
0.6	165	1.51	169	1.55	173	1.58	176	1.60	180	1.60	0.6
0.7	164	1.60	168	1.64	172	1.68	176	1.69	180	1.70	0.7
0.8	162	1.69	167	1.74	171	1.77	176	1.79	180	1.80	0.8
0.9	161	1.79	166	1.84	171	1.87	175	1.89	180	1.90	0.9
1.0	160	1.88	165	1.93	170	1.97	175	1.99	180	2.00	1.0
1.1	159	1.97	164	2.03	170	2.07	175	2.09	180	2.10	1.1
1.2	158	2.07	164	2.13	169	2.17	175	2.19	180	2.20	1.2
1.3	157	2.16	163	2.22	169	2.27	174	2.29	180	2.30	1.3
1.4	157	2.26	162	2.32	168	2.36	174	2.39	180	2.40	1.4
1.5	156	2.36	162	2.42	168	2.46	174	2.49	180	2.50	1.5
1.6	155	2.45	161	2.52	168	2.56	174	2.59	180	2.60	1.6
1.7	155	2.55	161	2.61	167	2.66	174	2.69	180	2.70	1.7
1.8	154	2.65	161	2.71	167	2.76	174	2.79	180	2.80	1.8
1.9	154	2.74	160	2.81	167	2.86	173	2.89	180	2.90	1.9
2.0	153	2.84	160	2.91	167	2.96	173	2.99	180	3.00	2.0
2.5	151	3.33	158	3.40	166	3.46	173	3.49	180	3.50	2.5
3.0	150	3.82	157	3.90	165	3.95	172	3.99	180	4.00	3.0
3.5	149	4.31	157	4.39	164	4.45	172	4.49	180	4.50	3.5
4.0	148	4.81	156	4.89	164	4.95	172	4.99	180	5.00	4.0
4.5	147	5.31	155	5.39	164	5.45	172	5.49	180	5.50	4.5
5.0	146	5.80	155	5.89	163	5.95	172	5.99	180	6.00	5.0
6.0	145	6.80	154	6.88	163	6.95	171	6.99	180	7.00	6.0
7.0	145	7.79	154	7.88	162	7.95	171	7.99	180	8.00	7.0
8.0	144	8.79	153	8.88	162	8.95	171	8.99	180	9.00	8.0
9.0	144	9.79	153	9.88	162	9.95	171	9.99	180	10.00	9.0
10.0	143	10.78	153	10.88	162	10.95	171	10.98	180	11.00	10.0

Wind and the sea • There is a relationship between the speed of the wind and the state of the sea in the immediate vicinity of the wind. This is useful in predicting the sea conditions to be anticipated when future wind speed forecasts are available. It can also be used to estimate the speed of the wind, which may be desirable when an anemometer is not available.

Wind speeds are usually grouped in accordance with the **Beaufort scale,** named after Admiral Sir Francis Beaufort, who devised it in 1806. As adopted in 1838, Beaufort numbers ranged from 0, calm, to 12, hurricane. They have now been extended to 17. The wind speed and the appearance of the sea at Beaufort scale numbers from 0 through 12 are shown in figures 11.4 through 11.16.

Temperature • Temperature is the intensity or degree of heat. It is measured in degrees. Several different temperature scales are in use.

On the **Fahrenheit (F)** scale commonly used in the United States and other English-speaking countries, pure water freezes at 32° and boils at 212°.

On the **Celsius (C)** scale commonly used with the metric system, the freezing point of pure water is 0° and the boiling point is 100°. This scale has been known by various names in different countries. In the United States it was formerly called the **centigrade** scale.

Réaumur temperature is based upon a scale in which water freezes at 0° and boils at 80°.

Absolute zero is considered to be the lowest possible temperature, at which there is no molecular motion and a body has no heat. For some purposes, it is convenient to express temperature by a scale at which 0° is absolute zero. This is called **absolute** temperature. If Fahrenheit degrees are used, it may be called **Rankine (R)** temperature; and if Celsius, **Kelvin (K)** temperature. The Kelvin scale is more widely used than the Rankine. Absolute zero is at $(-)459°67$ F or $(-)273°15$ C.

Temperature by one scale can be converted to that at another by means of the relationship that exists between the scales. Thus,

$$C=\frac{5}{9}(F-32)$$

and

$$F=\frac{9}{5}C+32.$$

Temperature measurement is made by means of a **thermometer.** Most thermometers are based upon the principle that materials expand with increase of temperature, and contract as temperature decreases. In its most usual form a thermometer consists of a bulb filled with mercury and connected to a tube of very small cross-sectional area. The mercury only

Fig. 11.4. Beaufort scale 0: under 1 knot.

Fig. 11.5. Beaufort scale 1: 1-3 knots.

Fig. 11.6. Beaufort scale 2: 4-6 knots.

Fig. 11.7. Beaufort scale 3: 7-10 knots.

Fig. 11.6. Beaufort scale 2: 4-6 knots.

Fig. 11.7. Beaufort scale 3: 7-10 knots.

Fig. 11.8. Beaufort scale 4: 11-16 knots.

Fig. 11.9. Beaufort scale 5: 17-21 knots.

Fig. 11.10. Beaufort scale 6: 22-27 knots.

Fig. 11.11. Beaufort scale 7: 28-33 knots.   *Fig. 11.12. Beaufort scale 8: 34-40 knots.*

Fig. 11.13. Beaufort scale 9: 41-47 knots.   *Fig. 11.14. Beaufort scale 10: 48-55 knots.*

Fig. 11.15. Beaufort scale 11: 56-63 knots.   *Fig. 11.16. Beaufort scale 12: 64-71 knots.*

partly fills the tube. In the remainder is a vacuum created during construction of the instrument. The air is driven out by boiling the mercury, and the top of the tube is then sealed by a flame. As the mercury expands or contracts with changing temperature, the length of the mercury column in the tube changes. Temperature is indicated by the position of the top of the column of mercury with respect to a scale etched on the glass tube or placed on the thermometer support.

A **maximum thermometer** has a constriction in the tube, near the bulb. As temperature increases, the expanding mercury is forced past the constriction, but will not return as temperature decreases. Thus, it indicates the highest temperature which has occurred since the last setting. This principle is utilized in clinical thermometers, used for measuring body temperature. The mercury can be forced back into the bulb by centrifugal force applied by swinging the arm rapidly. Meteorologists have a device called a "Townsend support" for accomplishing this with less effort and less possibility of breakage.

A **minimum thermometer** uses alcohol instead of mercury. The upper part of the tube contains air under slight pressure, to prevent evaporation of the alcohol with resultant "breaks" in the column as the alcohol later condenses. The thermometer contains an index which is so constructed as to allow alcohol to flow past it up the tube with rising temperatures, but which moves downward in the tube if the temperature falls below it, being drawn down by the effect of surface tension exerted by the bottom of the meniscus (curved upper surface) of the column of alcohol as it reaches the index. Due to this effect, the index remains at the lowest temperature which has occurred since the last setting. Setting is accomplished by tilting the thermometer until the bulb is uppermost, when the index returns to the current temperature. The thermometer is normally maintained at an angle of about 5° to the horizontal, with the bulb at the lower end. A Townsend support is used for this purpose.

Temperature can be measured by means of a **thermograph,** which is a recording thermometer. In its outward appearance this instrument is similar to a barograph (fig. 11.2). The pen arm is connected, through a linkage, to the thermometric element, which usually consists of a metal tube shaped in the form of an arc and containing alcohol. As the alcohol expands with temperature increase, it tends to straighten the tube; and as the temperature decreases, the contracting alcohol permits the tube to resume its curved shape. The linkage magnifies these variations and transmits them to the pen, which records the temperature on a chart placed around a clock-driven, revolving cylinder.

Temperature measuring equipment should be placed in a shelter which protects it from mechanical damage and direct rays of the sun. The shelter should have louvered sides to permit free access of air. Aboard ship, the shelter should be placed in an exposed position as far as practicable from metal bulkheads. On vessels where shelters are not available, the temperature measurement should be made in shade at an exposed position on the windward side.

Sea water temperature is normally measured at the condenser intake. Although this is not a true measure of surface water temperature, the error is generally small. Measurement should be made near the entrance of the intake.

If the temperature of the water at the surface is desired, a sample should be obtained by bucket, preferably a canvas bucket, from a forward position well clear of any discharge lines. The sample should be taken immediately to a place where it is sheltered from wind and sun. The water should then be stirred with the thermometer, keeping the bulb submerged, until an essentially constant reading is obtained.

Humidity • Humidity is the condition of the atmosphere with reference to its water vapor content. **Absolute humidity** is a measure of the mass of vapor per unit volume of air. **Relative humidity** is the ratio (stated as a percentage) of the existing vapor pressure to the vapor pressure corresponding to saturation at the prevailing temperature and atmospheric pressure. This is very nearly the ratio of the amount of water vapor present to the amount that the air could hold at the same temperature and pressure if it were saturated.

As air cools, its capacity for holding water vapor decreases. Therefore, as air temperature decreases, the relative humidity increases. At some point, saturation takes place, and any further cooling results in condensation of some of the moisture. The temperature at which this occurs is called the **dew point,** and the moisture deposited upon natural objects is called **dew** if it forms in the liquid state, or **frost** if it forms in the frozen state.

The same process causes moisture to form on the outside of a container of cold liquid, the liquid cooling the air in the immediate vicinity of the container until it reaches the dew point. When moisture is deposited on man-made objects, it is usually called **sweat.** It occurs whenever the temperature of a surface is lower than the dew point of the air in contact with it. It is of particular concern to the mariner because of its effect upon his instruments, and possible damage to his ship or its cargo. Lenses of optical instruments may sweat, usually with such small droplets that the surface has a "frosted" appearance. When this occurs, the instrument is said to "fog" or "fog up," and is useless until the moisture is removed.

Clouds and fog form by "sweating" of minute particles of dust, salt, etc., in the air. Each particle forms a nucleus around which a droplet of water forms. If air is completely free from solid particles on which water vapor may condense, the extra moisture remains in the vapor state, and the air is said to be **supersaturated.**

Relative humidity and dew point are measured by means of a **hygrom-**

eter. One type, called a **psychrometer,** consists of two thermometers mounted together on a single strip of material. One of the thermometers is mounted a little lower than the other, and has its bulb covered with muslin. When the muslin covering is thoroughly moistened and the thermometer well ventilated, evaporation cools the bulb of the thermometer, causing it to indicate a lower reading than the other. A **sling psychrometer** is ventilated by whirling the thermometers. Some psychrometers use a fan. **Dry-bulb temperature** is indicated by the uncovered **dry-bulb thermometer,** and **wet-bulb temperature** is indicated by the muslin-covered **wet-bulb thermometer.** The difference between these two temperatures, and the dry-bulb temperature, are used to enter **psychrometric tables** to find the relative humidity and dew point. If the wet-bulb temperature is above freezing, reasonably accurate results can be obtained by a psychrometer consisting of wet- and dry-bulb thermometers mounted so that air can circulate freely around them without special ventilation. This type of installation is common aboard ship.

A recording hygrometer, called a **hygrograph,** provides a continuous record of relative humidity. In outward appearance this instrument is similar to a barograph (fig. 11.2) and a thermograph, using the same clock movement and chart cylinder. The measuring element, however, generally consists of a number of strands of human hair separated into groups kept apart by a spreader device. The hairs are kept taut by a counterbalance. As the relative humidity rises, the hairs increase in length, and as the relative humidity falls, they decrease in length. A linkage magnifies these changes and transmits them to a pen which records the relative humidity on a chart placed around the clock-driven, revolving cylinder. The hygrograph is a convenient device, but lacks accuracy, lags considerably behind changes in relative humidity, and is not reliable at low temperatures. It requires frequent calibration.

A **hygrothermograph** combines the features of both the hygrograph and the thermograph, providing a continuous record of both relative humidity and air temperature for seven days on a single chart. It has the same limitations as the hygrograph and the thermograph and its indications should be checked daily by psychrometer and thermometer.

Clouds • Clouds are visible assemblages of numerous tiny droplets of water, or ice crystals, formed by condensation of water vapor in the air, with the bases of the assemblages above the surface of the earth. **Fog** is a similar assemblage in contact with the surface of the earth.

The shape, size, height, thickness, and nature of a cloud depend upon the conditions under which it is formed. Therefore, clouds are indicators of various processes occurring in the atmosphere. The ability to recognize different types and a knowledge of the conditions associated with them are useful in predicting future weather.

Although the variety of clouds is virtually endless, they may be classified according to general type. Clouds are grouped generally into four "families" according to some common characteristic. **High clouds** are those having a mean lower level above 20,000 feet. They are composed principally of ice crystals. **Middle clouds** have a mean level between 6,500 and 20,000 feet. They are composed largely of water droplets, although the higher ones have a tendency toward ice particles. **Low clouds** have a mean upper level of less than 6,500 feet. These clouds are composed entirely of water droplets. **Clouds with vertical development** are a distinctive group formed by rising air which is cooled as it reaches greater heights. When it reaches the height of the dew point, some of its water vapor condenses. Therefore, the bottoms of such clouds are usually flat. Clouds with vertical development may begin at almost any level, but generally within the low cloud range. They may extend to great heights, well above the lower limit of high clouds. They form as water droplets, but toward the top they may freeze.

Within these four families are ten principal cloud types. The names of these are composed of various combinations and forms of the following basic words, all from Latin:

Cirrus, meaning "curl."

Cumulus, meaning "heap."

Stratus, meaning "layer."

Alto, meaning "high."

Nimbus, meaning "rain."

The first three are the basic cloud types. Individual cloud types recognize certain characteristics, variations, or combinations of these. The ten principal cloud types are:

High clouds. **Cirrus (Ci)** are detached high clouds of delicate and fibrous appearance, without shading, generally white in color, and often of a silky appearance (figs. 11.17 and 11.20). Their fibrous and feathery appearance is due to the fact that they are composed entirely of ice crystals. Cirrus appear in varied forms such as isolated tufts; long, thin lines across the sky; branching, feather-like plumes; curved wisps which may end in tufts, etc. These clouds may be arranged in parallel bands which cross the sky in great circles and appear to converge toward a point on the horizon. This may indicate, in a general way, the direction of a low pressure area. Cirrus may be brilliantly colored at sunrise and sunset. Because of their height, they become illuminated before other clouds in the morning, and remain lighted after others at sunset. Cirrus are generally associated with fair weather, but if they are followed by lower and thicker clouds, they are often the forerunner of rain or snow.

Cirrocumulus (Cc) are high clouds composed of small white flakes or scales, or of very small globular masses, usually without shadows and arranged in groups or lines, or more often in ripples resembling those of sand on the seashore (fig. 11.18). One form of cirrocumulus is popularly known as "mackerel sky" because the pattern resembles the scales on the back of a mackerel. Like cirrus, cirrocumulus are composed of ice crystals and are generally associated with fair weather, but may precede a storm if they thicken and lower. They may turn gray and appear hard before thickening.

Cirrostratus (Cs) are thin, whitish, high clouds (fig. 11.19) sometimes covering the sky completely and giving it a milky appearance and at other times presenting, more or less distinctly, a formation like a tangled web. The thin veil is not sufficiently dense to blur the outline of sun or moon. However, the ice crystals of which the cloud is composed refract the light passing through in such a way that halos (see Chapter 12) may form with the sun or moon at the center. Figure 11.20 shows cirrus thickening and changing into cirrostratus. In this form it is popularly known as "mares' tails." It if continues to thicken and lower, the ice crystals melting to form water droplets, the cloud formation is known as altostratus. When this occurs, rain may normally be expected within 24 hours. The more brushlike the cirrus when the sky appears as in figure 11.20, the stronger the wind at the level of the cloud.

Middle clouds. Altocumulus (Ac) are middle clouds consisting of a layer of large, ball-like masses that tend to merge together. The balls or patches may vary in thickness and color from dazzling white to dark gray, but they are more or less regularly arranged. They may appear as distinct patches (fig. 11.21) similar to cirrocumulus but can be distinguished by the fact that individual patches are generally larger, and show distinct shadows in some places. They are often mistaken for stratocumulus (fig. 11.25). If this form thickens and lowers, it may produce thundery weather and showers, but it does not bring prolonged bad weather. Sometimes the patches merge to form a series of big rolls that resemble ocean waves, but with streaks of blue sky (fig. 11.22). Because of perspective, the rolls appear to run together near the horizon. These regular parallel bands differ from cirrocumulus in that they occur in larger masses with shadows. These clouds move in the direction of the short dimension of the rolls, as do ocean waves. Sometimes altocumulus appear briefly in the form shown in figure 11.23, usually before a thunderstorm. They are generally arranged in a line with a flat horizontal base, giving the impression of turrets on a castle. The turreted tops may look like miniature cumulus and possess considerable depth and great length. These clouds usually indicate a change to chaotic, thundery skies.

Altostratus (As) are middle clouds having the appearance of a grayish or bluish, fibrous veil or sheet (fig. 11.24). The sun or moon, when seen through these clouds, appears as if it were shining through ground glass, with a corona (see Chapter 12) around it. Halos are not formed. If these clouds thicken and lower, or if low, ragged "scud" or rain clouds (nimbo-

Fig. 11.17. Cirrus.

Fig. 11.18. Cirrocumulus.

Fig. 11.19. Cirrostratus.

Fig. 11.20. Cirrus and cirrostratus.

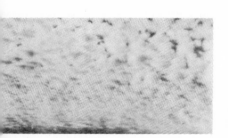

Fig. 11.21. Altocumulus in patches.

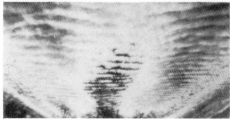

Fig. 11.22. Altocumulus in bands.

Fig. 11.23. Turreted altocumulus.

Fig. 11.24. Altostratus.

Fig. 11.25. Stratocumulus.

Fig. 11.26. Stratus.

Fig. 11.27. Cumulus.

Fig. 11.28. Cumulonimbus.

stratus) form below them, continuous rain or snow may be expected within a few hours.

Low clouds. **Stratocumulus (Sc)** are low clouds composed of soft, gray, roll-shaped masses (fig. 11.25). They may be shaped in long, parallel rolls similar to altocumulus (fig. 11.22), moving forward with the wind. The motion is in the direction of their short dimension, like ocean waves. These clouds, which vary greatly in altitude, are the final product of the characteristic daily change that takes place in cumulus clouds. They are usually followed by clear skies during the night.

Stratus (St) is a low cloud in a uniform layer (fig. 11.26) resembling fog. Often the base is not more than 1,000 feet high. A veil of thin stratus gives the sky a hazy appearance. Stratus is often quite thick, permitting so little sunlight to penetrate that it appears dark to an observer below it. From above, it looks white. Light mist may descend from stratus. Strong wind sometimes breaks stratus into shreds called "fractostratus."

Nimbostratus (Ns) is a low, dark, shapeless cloud layer, usually nearly uniform, but sometimes with ragged, wet-looking bases. Nimbostratus is the typical rain cloud. The precipitation which falls from this cloud is steady or intermittent, but not showery.

Clouds with vertical development. **Cumulus (Cu)** are dense clouds with vertical development. They have a horizontal base and dome-shaped upper surface, with protuberances extending above the dome. Cumulus appear in small patches, and never cover the entire sky. When the vertical development is not great, the clouds appear in patches resembling tufts of cotton or wool, being popularly called "woolpack" clouds (fig. 11.27). The horizontal bases of such clouds may not be noticeable. These are called "fair weather" cumulus because they always accompany good weather. However, they may merge with altocumulus, or may grow to cumulonimbus before a thunderstorm. Since cumulus are formed by updrafts, they are accompanied by turbulence, causing "bumpiness" in the air. The extent of turbulence is proportional to the vertical extent of the clouds. Cumulus are marked by strong contrasts of light and dark.

Cumulonimbus (Cb) is a massive cloud with great vertical development, rising in mountainous towers to great heights (fig. 11.28). The upper part consists of ice crystals, and often spreads out in the shape of an anvil which may be seen at such distances that the base may be below the horizon. Cumulonimbus often produces showers of rain, snow, or hail, frequently accompanied by thunder. Because of this, the cloud is often popularly called a "thundercloud" or "thunderhead." The base is horizontal, but as showers occur it lowers and becomes ragged.

Cloud height measurement • At sea, cloud heights are often determined by estimate. This is a difficult task, particularly at night. A searchlight may be of some assistance. Radar operating at the higher frequencies, particularly three-centimeter radar, indicates returns from some clouds. Certain models permit measurement of height.

Ceiling balloons are used by the Navy and Air Force to determine height of low clouds, and they do so with reasonable accuracy. Any type balloon having a known rate of ascent is suitable. Cloud height is determined by measurement of the elapsed time from release of the balloon until it disappears in the clouds. Horizontal motion due to wind generally has negligible effect upon the rate of ascent.

Ashore, measurement of cloud heights is made easier by equipment that is not suitable for use at sea. Observing stations can therefore have a continuous record of cloud height overhead.

Visibility measurement • Visibility is the extreme horizontal distance at which prominent objects can be seen and identified by the unaided eye. It is usually measured directly by the human eye. Ashore, the distances of various buildings, trees, lights, and other objects are measured and used as a guide in estimating the visibility. At sea, however, such an estimate is difficult to make with accuracy. Other ships and the horizon may be of some assistance.

Visibility is sometimes measured by a **transmissometer,** a device which measures the transparency of the atmosphere by passing a beam of light over a known short distance, and comparing it with a reference light.

Upper air observations • Upper air information provides the third dimension to the weather map. Unfortunately, the equipment necessary to obtain such information is quite expensive, and the observations are time consuming. Consequently, the network of observing stations is quite sparse compared to that for surface observations, particularly over the oceans and in isolated land areas. Where facilities exist, upper air observations are made by means of unmanned balloons in conjunction with various instruments. Observations are sometimes made by aircraft.

Storm detection radar • During World War II, it was found that certain radar equipment gave an indication of weather fronts and precipitation areas. It was of particular value near hurricanes and typhoons. Since the close of that war a great amount of work has been done in perfecting radar equipment for use in weather observation. It has proved of immense value in detecting, tracking, and interpreting weather activity out to a distance of as much as 400 miles from the observing station.

Precipitation measurement • Any type of condensed water vapor that falls to the earth's surface is called **precipitation.** It may be liquid, freezing, or frozen when it arrives at the surface. Measurement of precipitation normally includes only the determination of the amount of rain or snow that has fallen in a given period of time. For purposes of comparison, snow measurement is obtained by melting the snow to its water equivalent. Depth of snow is also measured to determine the amount of snowfall.

The usual type of **nonrecording precipitation gage** consists of a collector ring, funnel, and measuring cylinder set within a receiver. All precipitation falling on the area encompassed by the collector ring descends through the funnel into the measuring cylinder, where it is measured directly by means of a rod graduated in tenths of an inch. Since the cross-sectional area of the measuring cylinder is exactly one-tenth that of the collector ring, each 0.1 inch collected is a measure of 0.01 inch of precipitation. When precipitation is in the form of snow, the measuring tube is removed, permitting the snow to collect in the larger receiver. The receiver is placed in a container of warm water until the snow melts. The resulting liquid is then poured into the measuring tube and measured.

The most representative measurement of precipitation from snow is obtained by removing the collector ring and funnel, and using a slat screen to reduce the effect of wind.

One type of **recording rain gage** is known as the "tipping-bucket rain gage." The rainfall from a funnel-shaped collector is directed into one of two small buckets so arranged that when 0.01 inch of rain is collected, the bucket is forced downward, causing the other bucket to move into the collecting position. When a bucket is in the "down" position, its water runs into the base of the collector, where it can be measured later. As each bucket lowers in its turn, it causes a small cam to rotate into contact position and close a battery-powered electric circuit. This causes a magnetic relay at the recorder to operate a pen arm, which marks the additional 0.01 inch of rainfall on a chart secured to a clock-driven drum.

Another type of recording rain gage, used principally at locations which are not continuously attended, employs a weighing device which actuates a pen arm, causing it to trace measurements on a chart secured to a clock-driven drum.

The precipitation gage, whatever its form, should be placed in an exposed position as far as practicable from obstructions. Precipitation measurement is not ordinarily made aboard ship because the motions of the vessel, and the possibility of collecting salt spray, introduce errors into the measurement.

Automatic weather stations • Automatic weather stations provide regularly scheduled transmissions of meteorological measurements by radio. They are used at isolated and relatively inaccessible locations from which weather data are of great importance to the weather forecaster. The measurements usually obtained are of wind speed and direction, atmospheric pressure, temperature, and relative humidity.

[12]

Weather and Weather Forecasts

Introduction • **Weather** is the state of the earth's atmosphere with respect to temperature, humidity, precipitation, visibility, cloudiness, etc. In contrast, the term **climate** refers to the prevalent or characteristic meteorological conditions of a place or region.

All weather may be traced ultimately to the effect of the sun on the earth, including the lower portions of the atmosphere. Most changes in weather involve large-scale, approximately horizontal, motion of air. Air in such motion is called **wind.** This motion is produced by differences of atmospheric pressure, which are largely attributable to differences of temperature.

The weather is of considerable interest to the mariner. The wind and state of the sea affect dead reckoning. Reduced horizontal visibility limits piloting. The state of the atmosphere affects electronic navigation and radio communication. Wind is of vital importance to sailors, and even power vessels are affected considerably by wind and sea. Less fuel consumption and a more comfortable passage are to be expected if wind and sea are moderate and favorable. Pilot charts are useful in selecting suitable routes. Since longer range forecasts have become possible, some experimental work has been done in routing ocean vessels to take advantage of anticipated conditions during passage.

The atmosphere • The atmosphere is a relatively thin shell of air, water vapor, dust, smoke, etc., surrounding the earth. The air is a mixture of transparent gases and, like any gas, is elastic and highly compressible. Although extremely light, it has a definite weight which can be measured. A cubic foot of air at standard sea-level temperature and pressure weighs 1.22 ounces, or about 1/817th part of the weight of an equal volume of water. Because of this weight, the atmosphere exerts a pressure upon the surface of the earth, amounting to about 15 pounds per square inch.

As altitude increases, less atmosphere extends upward, and pressure decreases. With less pressure, the density decreases. More than three-fourths of the air is concentrated within a layer averaging about seven statute miles thick, called the **troposphere.** This is the region of most "weather," as the term is commonly understood.

The top of the troposphere is marked by a thin transition zone called the **tropopause.** Beyond this lie several other layers. The average height of the tropopause ranges from about five miles or less over the poles to about 11 miles over the equator.

The **standard atmosphere** is a conventional vertical structure of the atmosphere characterized by standard sea level pressure of 29.92 inches of mercury (1013.25 millibars), sea level temperature of 59° F (15° C), and a uniform decrease of temperature and moisture content of the air with height, the rate of temperature decrease being $3°6$ F ($2°$ C) per thousand feet to 11 kilometers (36,089 feet) and thereafter a constant temperature of ($-$)$69°7$ F ($-56°5$ C). The rate of temperature decreases with height in the standard atmosphere is called the **standard temperature lapse rate.**

Meteorologists are continually learning more of the characteristics of atmospheric processes above the lowest portions of the atmosphere. In recent years, greatly increased attention has been directed to such features as the **jet stream,** a meandering stream of air which circles the globe at speeds of 100 to more than 250 knots at heights of about 20,000 to 40,000 feet. Some similarity has been noted between major wind streams such as the jet stream and ocean currents such as the Gulf Stream.

Wind • When air is not confined, changes in temperature produce changes in volume, heated air expanding and cooled air contracting. If a large volume of air near the surface of the earth is cooled, it contracts, causing a downdraft. Air from neighboring regions aloft moves horizontally to fill the void. This results in a greater mass of air over the region, and the pressure is correspondingly increased. By a similar process in reverse, heating of air near the surface causes expansion and an updraft, resulting in decreased pressure over the heated area. Near the surface of the earth, the air tends to move from an area of high pressure to one of low pressure. Thus, a circulation is set up, air moving across the surface of the earth from an area of high pressure and low temperature to one of low pressure and high temperature, then vertically upward, then horizontally at high altitudes from the area of low pressure to that of high pressure, where it moves vertically downward to complete the circuit. The actual circulation is much more complex than this, due to such factors as rotation of the earth and continual changes in temperature and pressure.

If there were no heating and cooling, the temperature at any given altitude remaining everywhere the same, there would be no tendency for the air to move from one place to another. Air would lie sluggish and at rest on the earth's surface. There would be no wind and no variation in weather.

As a result of the position and motion of the earth in relation to the sun, and the physical processes involving radiation and absorption of energy, certain regions of the earth are always warmer than others. For similar reasons, the air over some parts of the earth is seasonally warmer than that over other parts. This general pattern is modified to a varying degree by the local heating and cooling which is continually taking place. Consequently, winds in some areas are relatively steady in both direction and speed, others are seasonal, and this general circulation is continually being modified by local conditions.

General circulation of the atmosphere • The heat required for warming the air is supplied originally by the sun. As radiant energy from the sun arrives at the earth, about 43 percent is reflected back into space by the atmosphere, about 17 percent is absorbed in the lower portions of the atmosphere, and the remaining 40 percent (approximately) reaches the surface of the earth and much of it is reradiated into space. This earth radiation is in comparatively long waves relative to the short-wave radiation from the sun, since it emanates from a cooler body. Long-wave radiation, being readily absorbed by the water vapor in the air, is primarily responsible for the warmth of the atmosphere near the earth's surface. Thus, the atmosphere acts much like the glass on the roof of a greenhouse. It allows part of the incoming solar radiation to reach the surface of the earth, but is heated by the terrestrial radiation passing outward. Over the entire earth and for long periods of time, the total outgoing energy must be equivalent to the incoming energy (minus any converted to another form and retained), or the temperature of the earth, including its atmosphere, would steadily increase or decrease. In local areas, or over relatively short periods of time, such a balance is not required, and in fact does not exist, resulting in changes such as those occurring in the different seasons, and in different parts of the day.

The more nearly perpendicular the rays of the sun as they strike the surface of the earth, the more heat energy per unit area is received at that place. Physical measurements show that in the tropics more heat per unit area is received than is radiated away, and that in polar regions the opposite is true. Unless there were some process to transfer heat from the tropics to polar regions, the tropics would be much warmer than they are, and the polar regions would be much colder. The process which brings about the required transfer of heat is the general circulation of the atmosphere.

If the earth had a uniform surface, did not rotate on its axis (but

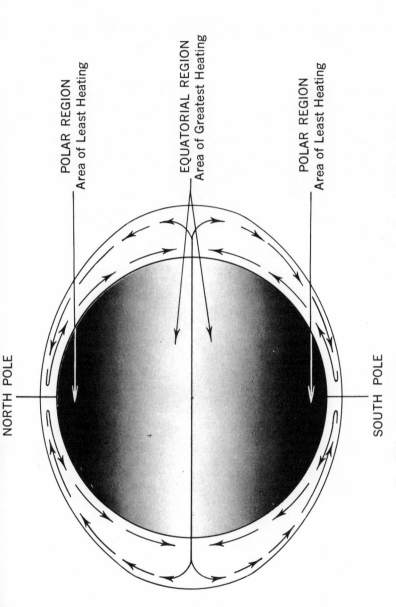

NORTH POLE

POLAR REGION
Area of Least Heating

EQUATORIAL REGION
Area of Greatest Heating

POLAR REGION
Area of Least Heating

SOUTH POLE

Fig. 12.1. Ideal atmospheric circulation for a uniform, nonrotating, non-revolving earth.

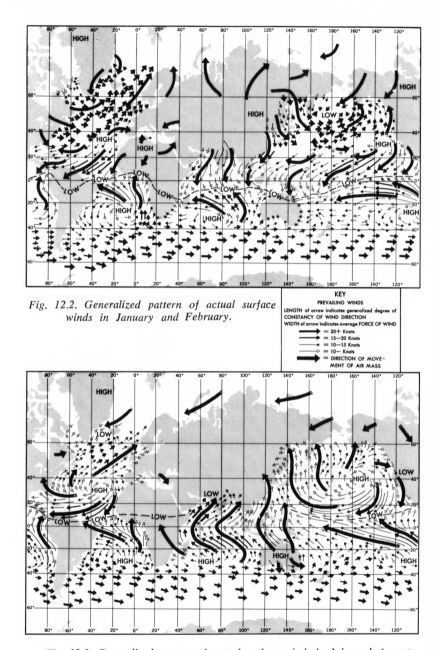

Fig. 12.2. Generalized pattern of actual surface winds in January and February.

KEY

PREVAILING WINDS

LENGTH of arrow indicates generalized degree of CONSTANCY OF WIND DIRECTION
WIDTH of arrow indicates average FORCE OF WIND

⟹ = 20+ Knots
→ = 15—20 Knots
⟶ = 10—15 Knots
⟝ = 10— Knots
⟹ = DIRECTION OF MOVEMENT OF AIR MASS

Fig. 12.3. Generalized pattern of actual surface winds in July and August.

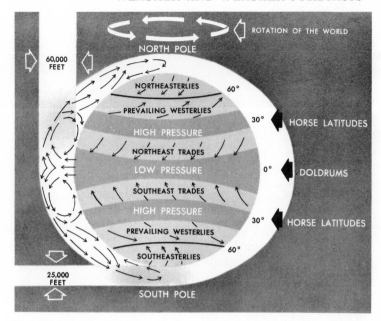

Fig. 12.4. Simplified diagram of the general circulation of the atmosphere.

received sunlight equally all around the equator), and did not revolve around the sun (with its axis tilted), a simple circulation would result, as shown in figure 12.1. However, the surface of the earth is far from uniform, being covered with an irregular distribution of land of various heights, and water; the earth rotates about its axis once in approximately 24 hours, so that the portion heated by the sun continually changes; and the axis of rotation is tilted so that as the earth moves along its orbit about the sun, seasonal changes occur in the exposure of specific areas to the sun's rays, resulting in variations in the heat balance of these areas. These factors, coupled with others, result in constantly changing large-scale movements of air. Based upon averages over long periods, however, a general circulation is discernible. Figures 12.2 and 12.3 give a generalized picture of the world's pressure distribution and wind systems as actually observed. A simplified diagram of the general pattern is shown in figure 12.4.

The rotation of the earth diverts the air from a direct path between high and low pressure areas, the diversion being toward the *right* in the northern hemisphere and toward the *left* in the southern hemisphere. At some distance above the surface of the earth, the wind tends to blow along the isobars, being called the **geostrophic wind** if the isobars are straight (great circles), and **gradient wind** if they are curved. Near the surface of the earth, friction tends to divert the wind from the isobars toward the center of low pressure. At sea, where friction is less than on land, the wind follows the isobars more closely.

The decrease of pressure with distance is called the **pressure gradient.** It is maximum along a normal (perpendicular) to the isobars, decreasing to zero along the isobars. Speed of the wind is directly proportional to the maximum pressure gradient.

The doldrums • The belt of low pressure near the equator occupies a position approximately midway between high pressure belts at about latitude 30° to 35° on each side. Except for slight diurnal changes, the atmospheric pressure along the equatorial low is almost uniform. With almost no pressure gradient, wind is practically nonexistent. The light breezes that do blow are variable in direction. Hot, sultry days are common. The sky is often overcast, and showers and thundershowers are relatively frequent.

The area involved is a thin belt near the equator, the eastern part in both the Atlantic and Pacific being wider than the western part. However, both the position and extent of the belt vary somewhat with the season. During February and March it lies immediately to the north of the equator and is so narrow that it may be considered virtually nonexistent. In July and August the belt is centered on about latitude 7° N, and is several degrees in width, even at the narrowest point.

The trade winds • The trades blow from the belts of high pressure, toward the equatorial belt of low pressure. Because of the rotation of the earth, the moving air is deflected toward the west. Therefore, the trade winds in the northern hemisphere are from the northeast and are called the **northeast trades,** while those in the southern hemisphere are from the southeast and are called the **southeast trades.** Over the eastern part of both the Atlantic and Pacific these winds extend considerably farther from the equator, and their original direction is more nearly along the meridians than in the western part of each ocean.

The trade winds are generally considered among the most constant of winds. Although they sometimes blow for days or even weeks with little change of direction or speed, their constancy is sometimes exaggerated. At times they weaken or shift direction, and there are regions where the general pattern is disrupted. A notable example is the island groups of the South Pacific, where they are practically nonexistent during January and February. Their highest development is attained in the South Atlantic and in the South Indian Ocean. Everywhere they are fresher during the winter than during the summer.

In July and August, when the belt of equatorial low pressure moves to a position some distance north of the equator, the southeast trades blow across the equator, into the northern hemisphere, where the earth's rotation diverts them toward the right, causing them to be southerly and southwesterly winds. The "southwest monsoons" of the African and Central American coasts have their origin partly in such diverted southeast trades.

Cyclonic storms generally do not enter the regions of the trade winds, although hurricanes and typhoons may originate within these areas.

The horse latitudes • Along the poleward side of each trade-wind belt, and corresponding approximately with the belt of high pressure in each hemisphere, is another region with weak pressure gradients and correspondingly light, variable winds. These are called the **horse latitudes.** The weather is generally clear and fresh, unlike that in the doldrums, and periods of stagnation are less persistent, being of a more intermittent nature. The difference is due primarily to the fact that rising currents of warm air in the equatorial low carry large amounts of moisture which condenses as the air cools at higher levels, while in the horse latitudes the air is apparently descending and becoming less humid as it is warmed at lower heights.

The prevailing westerlies • On the poleward side of the high pressure belt in each hemisphere the atmospheric pressure again diminishes. The currents of air set in motion along these gradients toward the poles are diverted by the earth's rotation toward the east, becoming southwesterly winds in the northern hemisphere and northwesterly in the southern hemisphere. These two wind systems are known as the **prevailing westerlies** of the temperate zones.

In the northern hemisphere this relatively simple pattern is distorted considerably by secondary wind circulations, due primarily to the presence of large land masses. In the North Atlantic, between latitudes 40° and 50°, winds blow from some direction between south and northwest during 74 percent of the time, being somewhat more persistent in winter than in summer. They are stronger in winter, too, averaging about 25 knots (Beaufort 6) as compared with 14 knots (Beaufort 4) in the summer.

In the southern hemisphere the westerlies blow throughout the year with a steadiness approaching that of the trade winds. The speed, though variable, is generally between 17 and 27 knots (Beaufort 5 and 6). Latitudes 40° S to 50° S (or 55° S), where these boisterous winds occur, are called the **roaring forties.** These winds are strongest at about latitude 50° S.

The greater speed and persistence of the westerlies in the southern hemisphere are due to the difference in the atmospheric pressure pattern, and its variations, from that of the northern hemisphere. In the comparatively landless southern hemisphere, the average yearly atmospheric pressure diminishes much more rapidly on the poleward side of the high pressure belt, and has fewer irregularities due to continental interference, than in the northern hemisphere.

Winds of polar regions • Because of the low temperatures near the geographical poles of the earth, the pressure tends to remain higher than in surrounding regions. Consequently, the winds blow outward from the poles, and are deflected westward by the rotation of the earth, to become **northeasterlies** in the arctic, and **southeasterlies** in the antarctic. Where these meet the prevailing westerlies, the winds are variable.

In the arctic, the general circulation is greatly modified by surrounding land masses. Winds over the Arctic Ocean are somewhat variable, and strong surface winds are rarely encountered.

In the antarctic, on the other hand, a high central land mass is surrounded by water, a condition which augments, rather than diminishes, the general circulation. The high pressure, although weaker than in some areas, is stronger than in the arctic, and of great persistence near the south pole. The upper air descends over the high continent, where it becomes intensely cold. As it moves outward and downward toward the sea, it is deflected toward the west by the earth's rotation. The winds remain strong throughout the year, frequently attaining hurricane force, and sometimes reaching speeds of 100 to 200 knots at the surface. These are the strongest surface winds encountered anywhere in the world, with the possible exception of those in well-developed tropical cyclones.

Modifications of the general circulation • The general circulation of the atmosphere as just described is greatly modified by various conditions.

The high pressure in the horse latitudes is not uniformly distributed around the belts, but tends to be accentuated at several points, as shown in figures 12.2 and 12.3. These **semipermanent highs** remain at about the same places with great persistence.

Semipermanent lows also occur in various places, the most prominent ones being west of Iceland, and over the Aleutians (winter only) in the northern hemisphere, and at the Ross Sea and Weddell Sea in the antarctic. The areas occupied by these semipermanent lows are sometimes called the graveyards of the lows, since many lows move directly into these areas and lose their identity as they merge with and reinforce the semipermanent lows. The low pressure in these areas is maintained largely by the migratory lows which stall there, but partly by the sharp temperature difference between polar regions and warmer ocean areas.

Another modifying influence is land, which undergoes greater temperature changes than does the sea. During the summer, a continent is warmer than its adjacent oceans. Therefore, low pressures tend to prevail over the land. If a belt of high pressure encounters such a continent, its pattern is distorted or interrupted. A belt of low pressure is intensified. The winds associated with belts of high and low pressure are distorted accordingly. In winter, the opposite effect takes place, belts of high pressure being intensified over land and those of low pressure being interrupted.

The general circulation is further modified by winds of cyclonic origin and various local winds.

Air masses • Because of large differences in physical characteristics of the earth's surface, particularly the oceanic and continental contrasts, the air overlying these surfaces acquires differing values of temperature, moisture, etc. The processes of radiation and convection in the lower portions of the troposphere act in differing, characteristic manners for a number of well-defined regions of the earth. The air overlying these regions acquires characteristics common to the particular area, but contrasting to those of other areas. Each distinctive part of the atmosphere, within which common characteristics prevail over a reasonably large area, is called an **air mass.**

Air masses are named according to their source regions. Four such regions are generally recognized: (1) *equatorial (E)*, the doldrum area between the north and south trades; (2) *tropical (T)*, the trade wind and lower temperate regions; (3) *polar (P)*, the higher temperate latitudes; and (4) *arctic (A)*, the north polar region of ice and snow (or, by extension, the antarctic). This classification is a general indication of relative temperature, as well as latitude of origin.

Tropical and polar air masses are further classified as *maritime (m)* or *continental (c)*, depending upon whether they form over water or land. This classification is an indication of the relative moisture content of the air mass. Since the moisture content of equatorial and arctic air is essentially independent of the surface over which they form, these sub-classifications are not applied to them. Tropical air, then, might be designated *maritime tropical (mT)* or *continental tropical (cT)*. Similarly, polar air may be either *maritime polar (mP)* or *continental polar (cP)*.

A third classification sometimes applied to tropical and polar air masses indicates whether the air mass is *warm (w)* or *cold (k)* relative to the underlying surface. Thus, the symbol *mTw* indicates maritime tropical air which is warmer than the underlying surface, and *cPk* indicates continental polar air which is colder than the underlying surface. The *w* and *k* classifications are primarily indications of stability. If the air is cold relative to the surface, the lower portion of the air mass is being heated, resulting in instability as the warmer air tends to rise by convection. Conversely, if the air is warm relative to the surface, the lower portion of the air mass is cooled, tending to remain close to the surface. This is a stable condition.

Two other types of air masses are sometimes recognized. These are *monsoon (M)*, a transitional form between *cP* and *E*; and *superior (S)*, a special type formed in the free atmosphere by the sinking and consequent warming of air aloft.

Fronts • As air masses move within the general circulation, they travel from their source regions and invade other areas dominated by air having different characteristics. There is little tendency for adjacent air masses to mix. Instead, they are separated by a thin zone in which air mass characteristics exhibit such sharp gradients as to appear as discontinuities. This is called a **frontal surface.** The intersection of a frontal surface and a horizontal plane is called a **front,** although the term "front" is commonly used as a short expression for "frontal surface" when this will not introduce an ambiguity.

Because of differences in the motion of adjacent air masses, "waves" form along the frontal surface between them.

Before the formation of frontal waves, the isobars (lines of equal atmospheric pressure) tend to run parallel to the fronts. As a wave is formed, the pattern is distorted somewhat, as shown in figure 12.5. In this illustration, colder air is north of warmer air. Isobars are shown at intervals of three millibars. The wave tends to travel in the direction of the general circulation, which in the temperate latitudes is usually in a general easterly and slightly poleward direction.

Along the leading edge of the wave, warmer air is replacing colder air. This is called the **warm front.** The trailing edge is the **cold front,** where colder air is replacing warmer air.

The warm air, being less dense, tends to ride up over the colder air it is replacing, causing the warm front to be tilted in the direction of motion. The slope is gentle, varying between 1:100 and 1:300. Because of the replacement of cold, dense air with warm, light air, the pressure decreases. Since the slope is gentle, the upper part of a warm frontal surface may be many hundreds of miles ahead of the surface portion. The decreasing pressure, indicated by a "falling barometer," is often an indication of the approach of such a wave. In a slow-moving, well-developed wave, the barometer may begin to fall several *days* before the wave arrives. Thus, the amount and nature of the change of atmospheric pressure between observations, called **pressure tendency,** is of assistance in predicting the approach of such a system.

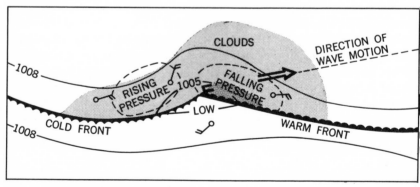

Fig. 12.5. *First stage in the development of a frontal wave (top view).*

The advancing cold air, being more dense, tends to cut under the warmer air at the cold front, lifting it to greater heights. The slope here is in the opposite direction, at a rate of about 1:25 to 1:100, being steeper than the warm front. Therefore, after a cold front has passed, the pressure increases—a "rising barometer."

In the first stages, these effects are not marked, but as the wave continues to grow, they become more pronounced, as shown in figure 12.6. As the amplitude of the wave increases, pressure near the center usually decreases, and the "low" is said to "deepen." As it deepens, its forward speed generally decreases.

The approach of a well-developed warm front is usually heralded not only by falling pressure, but also by a more-or-less regular sequence of clouds. First, cirrus appear. These give way successively to cirrostratus, altostratus, altocumulus, and nimbostratus. Brief showers may precede the steady rain accompanying the nimbostratus.

As the warm front passes, the temperature rises, the wind shifts to the right (in the northern hemisphere), and the steady rain stops. Drizzle may fall from low-lying stratus clouds, or there may be fog for some time after the wind shift. During passage of the **warm sector** between the warm front and the cold front, there is little change in temperature or pressure. However, if the wave is still growing and the low deepening, the pressure might slowly decrease. In the warm sector the skies are generally clear or partly cloudy, with cumulus or stratocumulus clouds most frequent. The warm air is usually moist, and haze or fog may often be present.

As the faster moving, steeper cold front passes, the wind shifts abruptly to the right (in the northern hemisphere), the temperature falls rapidly, and there are often brief and sometimes violent showers, frequently accompanied by thunder and lightning. Clouds are usually of the convective type. A cold front usually coincides with a well-defined **wind-shift line** (a line along which the wind shifts abruptly from southerly or southwesterly to northerly or northwesterly in the northern hemisphere and from northerly or northwesterly to southerly or southwesterly in the southern hemisphere). At sea a series of brief showers accompanied by strong, shifting winds may occur along or some distance (up to 200 miles) ahead of a cold front. These are called **squalls,** and the line along which they occur is called a **squall line.** Because of its greater speed and steeper slope, which may approach or even exceed the vertical near the earth's surface (due to friction), a cold front and its associated weather pass more quickly than a warm front. After a cold front passes, the pressure rises, often quite rapidly, the visibility usually improves, and the clouds tend to diminish.

As the wave progresses and the cold front approaches the slower moving warm front, the low becomes deeper and the warm sector becomes smaller. This is shown in figure 12.7.

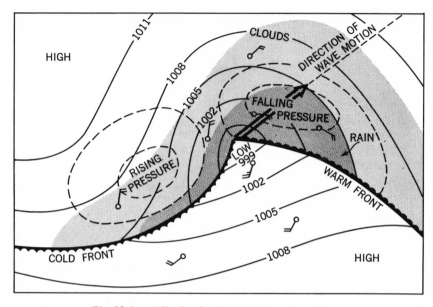

Fig. 12.6. *A fully developed frontal wave (top view).*

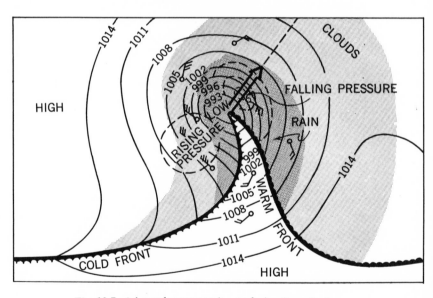

Fig. 12.7. *A frontal wave nearing occlusion (top view).*

Finally, the faster moving cold front overtakes the warm front (fig. 12.8), resulting in an **occluded front** at the surface, and an **upper front** aloft (fig. 12.9). When the two parts of the cold air mass meet, the warmer portion tends to rise above the colder part. The warm air continues to rise until the entire system dissipates. As the warmer air is replaced by colder air, the pressure gradually rises, a process called "filling." This usually occurs within a few days after an occluded front forms, but the process is sometimes delayed by a slowing of the forward motion of the wave. In general, however, a filling low increases in speed.

The sequence of weather associated with a low depends greatly upon location with respect to the path of the center. That described above assumes that the observer is so located that he encounters each part of the system. If he is poleward of the path of the center of the low, the abrupt weather changes associated with the passage of fronts are not experienced. Instead, the change from the weather characteristically found ahead of a warm front to that behind a cold front takes place gradually, the exact sequence being dictated somewhat by distance from the center, as well as severity and age of the low.

Although each low follows generally the pattern given above, no two are ever exactly alike. Other centers of low pressure and high pressure and the air masses associated with them, even though they may be 1,000 miles or more away, influence the formation and motion of individual low centers and their accompanying weather. Particularly, a high stalls or

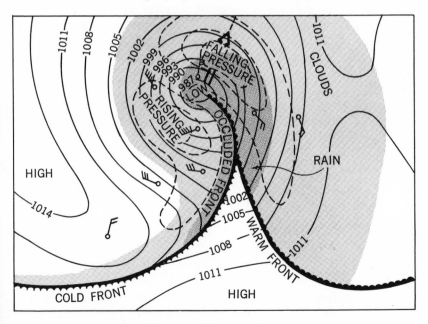

Fig. 12.8. An occluded front (top view).

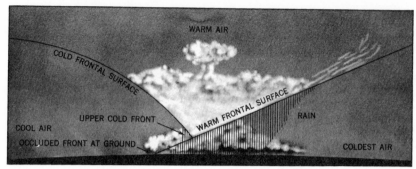

Fig. 12.9. An occluded front (cross section).

diverts a low. This is true of temporary highs as well as semipermanent highs.

Cyclones and anticyclones • An approximately circular portion of the atmosphere in the vicinity of a low pressure area is called a **cyclone.** A similar portion in the vicinity of an atmospheric high is called an **anticyclone.** These terms are used particularly in connection with the winds associated with such centers. Wind tends to blow from an area of high pressure to one of low pressure, but due to rotation of the earth, they are deflected toward the right in the northern hemisphere and toward the left in the southern hemisphere.

Because of the rotation of the earth, therefore, the circulation tends to be counterclockwise around areas of low pressure in the northern hemisphere and clockwise around areas of high pressure, the speed being proportional to the spacing of isobars. In the southern hemisphere, the direction of circulation is reversed. Based upon this condition, a general rule (**Buys Ballot's Law**) can be stated thus:

If an observer in the northern hemisphere faces the wind, the center of low pressure is toward his right, somewhat behind him; and the center of high pressure is toward his left and somewhat in front of him.

If an observer in the southern hemisphere faces the wind, the center of low pressure is toward his left and somewhat behind him; and the center of high pressure is toward his right and somewhat in front of him.

In a general way, these relationships apply in the case of the general distribution of pressure, as well as to temporary local pressure systems.

The reason for the wind shift along a front is that the isobars have an abrupt change of direction along these lines, as shown in figures 12.5–12.8. Since the direction of the wind is directly related to the direction of isobars, any change in the latter results in a shift in the wind direction.

In the northern hemisphere, the wind shifts toward the *right* when either a warm or cold front passes. In the southern hemisphere, the shift is toward the *left*. When the wind shifts in this direction (clockwise in the northern hemisphere and counterclockwise in the southern hemisphere), it is said to **veer.** If it shifts in the opposite direction, as when an observer is on the poleward side of the path of a frontal wave, it is said to **back.**

In an anticyclone, successive isobars are relatively far apart, resulting in light winds. In a cyclone, the isobars are more closely spaced. With a steeper pressure gradient, the winds are stronger.

Since an anticyclonic area is a region of outflowing winds, air is drawn into it from aloft. Descending air is warmed, and as air becomes warmer, its capacity for holding uncondensed moisture increases. Therefore, clouds tend to dissipate. Clear skies are characteristic of an anticyclone, although scattered clouds and showers are sometimes encountered.

In contrast, a cyclonic area is one of converging winds. The resulting upward movement of air results in cooling, a condition favorable to the formation of clouds and precipitation. More or less continuous rain and generally stormy weather are usually associated with a cyclone.

Between the two belts of high pressure associated with the horse latitudes, cyclones form only occasionally, generally in certain seasons, and always in certain areas at sea. These **tropical cyclones** are usually quite violent, being known under various names according to their location.

In the areas of the prevailing westerlies, cyclones are a common occurrence, the cyclonic and anticyclonic circulation being a prominent feature of temperate latitudes. These are sometimes called **extratropical cyclones** to distinguish them from the more violent tropical cyclones. Although most of them are formed at sea, their formation over land is not unusual. As a general rule, they decrease in intensity when they encounter land, and increase when they move from the land to a water area. In their early stages, cyclones are elongated, as shown in figure 12.5, but as their life cycle proceeds, they become more nearly circular (figs. 12.6–12.8).

Local winds • In addition to the winds of the general circulation and those associated with cyclones and anticyclones, there are numerous local winds which influence the weather in various places.

The most common of these are the **land** and **sea breezes,** caused by alternate heating and cooling of land adjacent to water. By day the land is warmer than the water, and by night it is cooler. This effect occurs along many coasts during the summer. Between about 0900 and 1100 the temperature of the land becomes greater than that of the adjacent water. The lower levels of air over the land are warmed, and the air rises, drawing in cooler air from the sea. This is the **sea breeze.** Late in the afternoon, when the sun is low in the sky, the temperature of the two surfaces equalizes and the breeze stops. After sunset, as the land cools below the sea temperature, the air above it is also cooled. The contracting cool air becomes more dense, increasing the pressure. This results in an outflow of winds to the sea. This is the **land breeze,** which blows during the night and dies away near sunrise. Since the atmospheric pressure changes associated with this cycle are not great, the accompanying winds do not exceed gentle breezes. The circulation is generally of limited extent, reaching a distance of perhaps 20 miles inland, and not more than five or six miles offshore, and to a height of a few hundred feet. In the tropics, this process is repeated with great regularity throughout most of the year. As the latitude increases, it becomes less prominent, being masked by winds of cyclonic origin. However, the effect may often be present to reinforce, retard, or deflect stronger prevailing winds.

Varying conditions of topography produce a large variety of local winds throughout the world. In light airs, winds tend to follow valleys, and to be deflected from high banks and shores. Many local winds have been given distinctive names. An **anabatic wind** is one which blows up an incline, as one which blows up a hillside due to surface heating. A **katabatic wind** is one which blows down an incline due to cooling of the air. The cooler air becomes heavier than surrounding air and flows downward along the incline under the force of gravity.

A dry wind with a downward component, warm for the season, is called a **foehn.** The foehn occurs when horizontally moving air encounters a mountain barrier. As it blows upward to clear the barrier, it is cooled below the dew point, resulting in loss of moisture by cloud formation and perhaps rain. As the air continues to rise, its rate of cooling is reduced because the condensing water vapor gives off heat to the surrounding atmosphere. After crossing the mountain barrier, the air flows downward along the leeward slope, being warmed by compression as it descends to lower levels. Thus, since it loses less heat on the ascent than it gains during descent, and since it loses moisture during ascent, it arrives at the bottom of the mountains as very warm, dry air. This accounts for the warm, arid regions along the eastern side of the Rocky Mountains and in similar areas. In the Rocky Mountain region this wind is known by the name **chinook.** It may occur at any season of the year, at any hour of the day or night, and have any speed from a gentle breeze to a gale. It may last for several days, or for a very short period. Its effect is most marked in winter, when it may cause the temperature to rise as much as 20° F to 30° F within 15 minutes, and cause snow and ice to melt within a few hours. On the west coast of the United States, the name "chinook" is given to a moist southwesterly wind from the Pacific Ocean, warm in winter and cool in summer. Cloudy weather and rain may accompany or follow this wind, which is thus quite different from the other chinook mentioned above. A foehn given the name **Santa Ana** blows through a pass and down a valley by that name in Southern California. This wind usually starts suddenly, without warning, and blows with such force that it may capsize small craft off the coast.

A cold wind blowing down an incline is called a **fall wind.** Although it is warmed somewhat during descent, as is the foehn, it is cold relative to the surrounding air. It occurs when cold air is dammed up in great quantity on the windward side of a mountain and then spills over suddenly, usually as an overwhelming surge down the other side. It is usually quite violent, sometimes reaching hurricane force. A different name for this type wind is given at each place where it is common. The **williwaw** of the Aleutian coast, the **tehuantepecer** of the Mexican and Central American coast, the **pampero** of the Argentine coast, the **mistral** of the western Mediterranean, and the **bora** of the eastern Mediterranean are examples of this type wind.

Many other local winds also have distinctive names.

A **blizzard** is a violent, intensely cold wind laden with snow mostly or entirely picked up from the ground, although the term is often used popularly to refer to any heavy snowfall accompanied by strong wind. A **dust whirl** is a rotating column of air about 100 to 300 feet in height, carrying dust, leaves, and other light material. This wind, which is similar to a waterspout at sea, is given various local names such as **dust devil** in southwestern United States and **desert devil** in South Africa. A **gust** is a sudden, brief increase in wind speed followed by a slackening, or the violent wind or squall that accompanies a thunderstorm. A puff of wind or a light breeze affecting a small area, such as would cause patches of ripples on the surface of water, is called a **cat's paw.**

Fog • Fog, like a cloud, is a visible assemblage of numerous tiny droplets of water, or ice crystals, formed by condensation of water vapor in the air. However, the base of a cloud is above the surface of the earth, while fog is in contact with the surface.

Radiation fog forms over low-lying land on clear, calm nights. As the land radiates heat and becomes cooler, it cools the air immediately above the surface. This causes a **temperature inversion** to form, the temperature for some distance upward *increasing* with height. If the air is cooled to its dew point, fog forms. Often, cooler and more dense air drains down surrounding slopes to heighten the effect. Radiation fog is often quite shallow, and is usually thickest at the surface. After sunrise the fog may "lift" and gradually dissipate, usually being entirely gone by noon. At sea the temperature of the water undergoes little change between day and night, and so radiation fog is seldom encountered more than ten times from shore.

Advection fog forms when warm, moist air blows over a colder surface and is cooled below its dew point. This type, most commonly encountered at sea, may be quite thick and often persists over relatively long periods. The maximum density might be at nearly any height. Advection fog is common over cold ocean currents. If the wind is strong enough to thoroughly mix the air, condensation may take place at some distance above the surface of the earth, forming low stratus clouds (see Chapter 11) rather than fog.

Off the coast of California, winds create an offshore current which displaces the warm surface water, causing an upwelling of colder water. Moist air being transported along the coast in the same wind system is cooled, and advection fog results. In the coastal valleys, fog is sometimes formed when moist air blown inland during the afternoon is cooled by radiation during the night. Both of these are called **California fog** because they are peculiar to California and its coastal valleys.

When very cold air moves over warmer water, wisps of visible water vapor may rise from the surface as the water "steams." In extreme cases this **frost smoke,** or **arctic sea smoke,** may rise to a height of several hundred feet, the portion near the surface constituting a dense fog which obscures the horizon and surface objects, but usually leaves the sky relatively clear.

Fog consisting of ice crystals is called **ice fog,** or **pogonip** by Western American Indians. Thin fog of relatively large particles, or very fine rain lighter than drizzle, is called **mist.** A mixture of smoke and fog is called **smog.**

Haze consists of fine dust or salt particles in the air, too small to be individually apparent, but in sufficient number to reduce horizontal visibility and cast a bluish or yellowish veil over the landscape, subduing its colors and making objects appear indistinct. This is sometimes called **dry haze** to distinguish it from **damp haze,** which consists of small water droplets or moist particles in the air, smaller and more scattered than light fog. In international meteorological practice, the term "haze" is used to refer to a condition of atmospheric obscurity caused by dust and smoke.

Mirage • Light is refracted (changes direction) as it passes through the atmosphere. When refraction is normal, objects appear slightly elevated, and the visible horizon is farther from the observer than it otherwise would be. Since the effects are uniformly progressive, they are not apparent to the observer. When refraction is not normal, some form of **mirage** may occur. A mirage is an optical phenomenon in which objects appear distorted, displaced (raised or lowered), magnified, multiplied, or inverted due to varying atmospheric refraction which occurs when a layer of air near the earth's surface differs greatly in density from surrounding air. This may occur when there is a rapid and sometimes irregular change of temperature or humidity with height.

If there is a temperature inversion (increase of temperature with height), particularly if accompanied by a rapid decrease in humidity, the refraction is greater than normal. Objects appear elevated, and the visible horizon is farther away. Objects which are normally below the horizon become visible. This is called **looming.** If the upper portion of an object is raised much more than the bottom part, the object appears taller than usual, an effect called **towering.** If the lower part of an object is raised more than the upper part, the object appears shorter, an effect called **stooping.** When the refraction is greater than normal, a **superior mirage** may occur. An inverted image is seen above the object, and sometimes an erect image appears over the inverted one, with the bases of the two images touching. Greater than normal refraction usually occurs when the water is much colder than the air above it.

If the temperature decrease with height is much greater than normal, refraction is less than normal, or may even cause bending in the opposite direction. Objects appear lower than normal, and the visible horizon is closer to the observer. This is called **sinking.** Towering or stooping may occur if conditions are suitable. When the refraction is reversed, an **inferior mirage** may occur. A ship or an island appears to be floating in the air above a shimmering horizon, possibly with an inverted image beneath it. Conditions suitable to the formation of an inferior mirage occur when the surface is much warmer than the air above it. This usually requires a heated land mass, and therefore is more common near the coast than at sea.

When refraction is not uniformly progressive, objects may appear distorted, taking an almost endless variety of shapes. The sun when near the horizon is one of the objects most noticeably affected. A **fata morgana** is a complex mirage characterized by marked distortion, generally in the vertical. It may cause objects to appear towering, magnified, and at times even multiplied.

Sky coloring • White light is composed of light of all colors. Color is related to wave length, the visible spectrum varying from about 0.000038 to 0.000076 centimeters. The characteristics of each color are related to its wave length (or frequency). Thus, the shorter the wave length, the greater the amount of bending when light is refracted. It is this principle that permits the separation of light from celestial bodies into a **spectrum** ranging from red, through orange, yellow, green, and blue, to violet, with long-wave infrared (black light) being slightly outside the visible range at one end and short-wave ultraviolet being slightly outside the visible range at the other end. Light of shorter wave length is scattered and diffracted more than that of longer wave length.

Light from the sun and moon is white, containing all colors. As it enters the earth's atmosphere, a certain amount of it is scattered. The blue and violet, being of shorter wave length than other colors, are scattered most. Most of the violet light is absorbed in the atmosphere. Thus, the scattered blue light is most apparent, and the sky appears blue. At great heights, above most of the atmosphere, it appears black.

When the sun is near the horizon, its light passes through more of the atmosphere than when higher in the sky, resulting in greater scattering and absorption of blue and green light, so that a larger percentage of the red and orange light penetrates to the observer. For this reason the sun and moon appear redder at this time, and when this light falls upon clouds, they appear colored. This accounts for the colors at sunset and sunrise. As the setting sun approaches the horizon, the sunset colors first appear as faint tints of yellow and orange. As the sun continues to set, the colors deepen. Contrasts occur, due principally to difference in height of clouds. As the sun sets, the clouds become a deeper red, first the lower clouds and then the higher ones, and finally they fade to a gray.

When there is a large quantity of smoke, dust, or other material in the sky, unusual effects may be observed. If the material in the atmosphere is of suitable substance and quantity to absorb the longer wave red, orange, and yellow radiations, the sky may have a greenish tint, and even the sun or moon may appear green. If the green light, too, is absorbed, the sun or moon may appear blue. A **green moon** or **blue moon** is most likely to occur when the sun is slightly below the horizon and the longer wave length light from the sun is absorbed, resulting in green or blue light being cast upon the atmosphere in front of the moon. The effect is most apparent if the moon is on the same side of the sky as the sun.

Rainbows • The familiar arc of concentric colored bands seen when the sun shines on rain, mist, spray, etc., is caused by refraction, internal reflection, and diffraction of sunlight by the drops of water. The center of the arc is a point 180° from the sun, in the direction of a line from the sun, through the observer. The radius of the brightest rainbow is 42°. The colors are visible because of the difference in the amount of refraction of the different colors making up white light, the light being spread out to form a spectrum. Red is on the outer side and blue and violet on the inner side, with orange, yellow, and green between, in that order from red.

Sometimes a secondary rainbow is seen outside the primary one, at a radius of about 50°. The order of colors of this rainbow is reversed. On rare occasions a faint rainbow is seen on the same side as the sun. The radius of this rainbow and the order of colors are the same as those of the primary rainbow.

A similar arc formed by light from the moon (a lunar rainbow) is called a **moonbow.** The colors are usually very faint. A faint, white arc of about 39° radius is occasionally seen in fog opposite the sun. This is called a **fogbow,** although its origin is controversial, some considering it a halo.

Halos • Refraction, or a combination of refraction and reflection, of light by ice crystals in the atmosphere (cirrostratus clouds, Chapter 11) may cause a **halo** to appear. The most common form is a ring of light of radius 22° or 46° with the sun or moon at the center. Occasionally a faint, white circle with a radius of 90° appears around the sun. This is called a **Hevelian halo.** It is probably caused by refraction and internal reflection of the sun's light by bipyramidal ice crystals. A halo formed by refraction is usually faintly colored like a rainbow, with red nearest the celestial body, and blue farthest from it.

A brilliant rainbow-colored arc of about a quarter of a circle with its center at the zenith, and the bottom of the arc about 46° above the sun, is called a **circumzenithal arc.** Red is on the outside of the arc, nearest the sun. It is produced by the refraction and dispersion of the sun's light striking the top of prismatic ice crystals in the atmosphere. It usually lasts for only about five minutes, but may be so brilliant as to be mistaken for an unusually bright rainbow. A similar arc formed 46° *below* the sun, with red on the upper side, is called a **circumhorizontal arc.** Any arc tangent to a heliocentric halo (one surrounding the sun) is called a **tangent arc.** As the sun increases in elevation, such arcs tangent to the halo of 22° gradually bend their ends toward each other. If they meet, the elongated curve enclosing the circular halo is called a **circumscribed halo.** The inner edge is red.

A halo consisting of a faint, white circle through the sun and parallel to the horizon is called a **parhelic circle.** A similar one through the moon is called a **paraselenic circle.** They are produced by reflection of sunlight or moonlight from vertical faces of ice crystals.

A **parhelion** (plural *parhelia*) is a form of halo consisting of an image of the sun at the same altitude and some distance from it, usually 22°, but occasionally 46°. A similar phenomenon occurring at an angular distance of 120° (sometimes 90° or 140°) from the sun is called a **paranthelion.** One at an angular distance of 180°, a rare occurrence, is called an **anthelion,** although this term is also used to refer to a luminous, colored ring or **glory** sometimes seen around the shadow of one's head on a cloud or fog bank. A parhelion is popularly called a **mock sun** or **sun dog.** Similar phenomena in relation to the moon are called **paraselene** (popularly a **mock moon** or **moon dog),** **parantiselene,** and **antiselene.** The term *parhelion* should not be confused with *perihelion,* that orbital point nearest the sun when the sun is the center of attraction.

A **sun pillar** is a glittering shaft of white or reddish light occasionally seen extending above and below the sun, usually when the sun is near the horizon. A phenomenon similar to a sun pillar, but observed in connection with the moon, is called a **moon pillar.** A rare form of halo in which horizontal and vertical shafts of light intersect at the sun is called a **sun cross.** It is probably due to the simultaneous occurrence of a sun pillar and a parhelic circle.

Corona • When the sun or moon is seen through altostratus clouds (Chapter 11), its outline is indistinct, and it appears surrounded by a glow of light called a **corona.** This is somewhat similar in appearance to the corona seen around the sun during a solar eclipse. When the effect is due to clouds, however, the glow may be accompanied by one or more rainbow-colored rings of small radii, with the celestial body at the center. These can be distinguished from a halo by their much smaller radii and also by the fact that the order of the colors is reversed, red being on the inside, nearest the body, in the case of the halo, and on the outside, away from the body, in the case of the corona.

A corona is caused by diffraction of light by tiny droplets of water. The radius of a corona is inversely proportional to the size of the water droplets. A large corona indicates small droplets. If a corona decreases in size, the water droplets are becoming larger and the air more humid. This may be an indication of an approaching rainstorm.

The glow portion of a corona is called an **aureole.**

The green flash • As light from the sun passes through the atmosphere, it is refracted. Since the amount of bending is slightly different for each color, separate images of the sun are formed in each color of the spectrum. The effect is similar to that of imperfect color printing in which the various colors are slightly out of register. However, the difference is so slight that the effect is not usually noticeable. At the horizon, where refraction is maximum, the greatest difference, which occurs between violet at one end of the spectrum and red at the other, is about ten seconds of arc. At latitudes of the United States, about 0.7 second of time is needed for the sun to change altitude by this amount when it is near the horizon. The red image, being bent least by refraction, is first to set and last to rise. The shorter wave blue and violet colors are scattered most by the atmosphere, giving it its characteristic blue color. Thus, as the sun sets, the green image may be the last of the colored images to drop out of sight. If the red, orange, and yellow images are below the horizon, and the blue and violet light is scattered and absorbed, the upper rim of the green image is the only part seen, and the sun appears green. This is the **green flash.** The shade of green varies, and occasionally the blue image is seen, either separately or following the green flash (at sunset). On rare occasions the violet image is also seen. These colors may also be seen at sunrise, but in reverse order. They are occasionally seen when the sun disappears behind a cloud or other obstruction.

The phenomenon is not observed at each sunrise or sunset, but under suitable conditions is far more common than generally supposed. Conditions favorable to observation of the green flash are a sharp horizon, clear atmosphere, a temperature inversion, and an attentive observer. Since these conditions are more frequently met when the horizon is formed by the sea than by land, the phenomenon is more common at sea. With a sharp sea horizon and clear atmosphere, an attentive observer may see the green flash at as many as 50 percent of sunsets and sunrises, although a telescope may be needed for some of the observations.

Duration of the green flash (including the time of blue and violet flashes) of as long as ten seconds has been reported, but such length is rare. Usually it lasts for a period of about half a second to two and one-half seconds with about one and a quarter seconds being average. This variability is probably due primarily to changes in the index of refraction of the air near the horizon.

Under favorable conditions, a momentary green flash has been observed at the setting of Venus and Jupiter. A telescope improves the chances of seeing such a flash from a planet, but is not a necessity.

Crepuscular rays • Crepuscular rays are beams of light from the sun passing through openings in the clouds, and made visible by illumination of dust in the atmosphere along their paths. Actually, the rays are virtually parallel, but because of perspective appear to diverge. Those appearing to extend downward are popularly called **backstays of the sun,** or **sun drawing water.** Those extending upward and across the sky, appearing to converge toward a point 180° from the sun, are called **anticrepuscular rays.**

Atmospheric electricity • Various conditions induce the formation of electrical charges in the atmosphere. When this occurs, there is often a difference of electron charge between various parts of the atmosphere, and between the atmosphere and earth or terrestrial objects. When this difference exceeds a certain minimum value depending upon the conditions, the static electricity is discharged, resulting in phenomena such as lightning and St. Elmo's fire.

Lightning is the discharge of electricity from one part of a thundercloud to another, from one such cloud to another, or between such a cloud and the earth or a terrestrial object.

Enormous electrical stresses build up within thunderclouds and between such clouds and the earth. At some point the resistance of the intervening air is overcome. At first the process is a progressive one, probably starting as a brush discharge (St. Elmo's fire) and growing by ionization. The breakdown follows an irregular path along the line of least resistance. A hundred or more individual discharges may be necessary to complete the path between points of opposite polarity. When this "leader stroke" reaches its destination, a heavy "main stroke" immediately follows in the opposite direction. This main stroke is the visible lightning, which may be tinted any color, depending upon the nature of the gases through which it passes. The illumination is due to the high degree of ionization of the air, which causes many of the atoms to be in excited states and emit radiation.

Thunder, the noise that often accompanies lightning, is caused by the heating and ionizing of the air by lightning, which results in rapid expansion of the air along its path and the sending out of a compression wave. Thunder may be heard at a distance of as much as 15 miles, but generally does not carry that far. The elapsed time between the flash of lightning and reception of the accompanying sound of thunder is an indication of the distance, because of the difference in travel time of light and sound. Since the former is comparatively instantaneous, and the speed of sound is about 1,117 feet per second, the approximate distance in nautical miles is equal to the elapsed time in seconds, divided by 5.5. If there is no accompanying thunder, the flash is called **heat lightning.**

St. Elmo's fire is a luminous discharge of electricity from pointed objects such as the masts and yardarms of ships, lightning rods, steeples, mountain tops, blades of grass, human hair, arms, etc., when there is a considerable difference in the electrical charge between the object and the air. It appears most frequently during a storm. An object from which St. Elmo's fire emanates is in danger of being struck by lightning, since this type discharge may be the initial phase of the leader stroke. Throughout history those who have not understood St. Elmo's fire have regarded it with superstitious awe, considering it a supernatural manifestation. This view is reflected in the name **corposant** (from "corpo santo," meaning "body of a saint"), sometimes given this phenomenon.

The **aurora** is a luminous glow appearing in varied forms in the thin atmosphere high above the earth, due to radiation from the sun.

Waterspouts • A waterspout is a small, whirling storm over the ocean or inland waters. Its chief characteristic is a funnel-shaped cloud extending, in a fully developed spout, from the surface of the water to the base of a cumulus type cloud (fig. 12.10). The water in a spout is mostly confined to its lower portion, and may be either salt spray drawn up by the sea surface or fresh water resulting from condensation due to the lowered pressure in the center of the vortex creating the spout. Waterspouts usually rotate in the same direction as cyclones (counterclockwise in the northern hemisphere and clockwise in the southern hemisphere), but the opposite rotation is occasionally observed. They are found most frequently in tropical regions, but are not uncommon in higher latitudes.

Waterspouts may be divided into two classes, according to their different origins and appearances. In the true waterspout, the vortex is formed in clouds by the interaction of air currents flowing in opposite directions. This type occurs mainly in the vicinity of a squall line. A similar disturbance over land is called a **tornado.** The second type, which may be considered a pseudo waterspout, originates just above the water surface, in unstable air, and builds upward, frequently under clear skies. This type is identical to the whirling pillars of sand and dust often seen on deserts and usually occurs only over very warm water surfaces.

Waterspouts vary in diameter from a few feet to several hundred feet,

Fig. 12.10. Waterspouts.

and in height from a few hundred feet to several thousand feet. Sometimes they assume fantastic shapes and may even seem to coil about themselves. Since a waterspout is often inclined to the vertical, its actual length may be much greater than indicated by its height.

Forecasting weather • The prediction of weather at some future time is based upon an understanding of weather processes, and observations of present conditions. Thus, one learns that when there is a certain sequence of cloud types (Chapter 11), rain can usually be expected to follow within a certain period. If the sky is cloudless, more heat will be received from the sun by day, and more heat will be radiated outward from the warm earth by night, than if the sky is overcast. If the wind is in such a direction that warm, moist air will be transported to a colder surface, fog can be expected. A falling barometer indicates the approach of a "low," probably accompanied by stormy weather. Thus, before the science of meteorology was developed, many individuals learned to interpret certain phenomena in terms of future weather, and to make reasonably accurate forecasts for short periods into the future.

With the establishment of weather observation stations, additional information became available. As such observations expanded, and communication facilities improved, knowledge of simultaneous conditions over wider areas became available. This made possible the collection of these "synoptic" reports from various sources.

The individual observations are made at government-operated stations on shore and aboard vessels at sea. Observations aboard merchant ships at sea are made and transmitted on a voluntary and cooperative basis. Symbols and numbers are used to indicate on a **synoptic chart,** popularly called a **weather map,** the conditions at each observation station. Isobars are drawn through lines of equal atmospheric pressure, fronts are located and marked by symbol, areas of precipitation and fog are indicated, etc.

By studying the latest synoptic weather chart and comparing it with previous charts, a trained meteorologist having a knowledge of local weather peculiarities can draw certain inferences regarding future weather and issue a forecast. Weather forecasts are essentially a form of extrapolation. Past changes and present trends are used to predict future events. In areas where certain sequences follow with great certainty, the probability of an accurate forecast is very high. In transitional areas, or areas where an inadequate number of synoptic reports is available, the forecasts are less reliable. Forecasts, then, are based upon the principles of probability, and where nature provides low probability, high reliability should not be expected. In any area, the probability of a given event occurring decreases with the lead time. Thus, a forecast for six hours after a synoptic chart is drawn should be more reliable than one for 24 hours ahead. Long-term forecasts for two weeks or a month in advance are limited to general statements. For example, a prediction is made as to which areas will have temperatures above or below normal, and how precipitation will compare with normal, but no attempt is made to state that rainfall will occur at a certain time and place.

Forecasts are issued for various areas. The national meteorological services of most maritime nations, including the United States, issue forecasts for ocean areas and warnings of the approach of storms.

Dissemination of weather information • Dissemination is carried out in a number of ways. Forecasts are widely broadcast by commercial and government radio stations, and printed in newspapers. Shipping authorities on land are kept informed by telegraph and telephone. Visual storm warnings are displayed in various ports, and storm warnings are broadcast by radio.

Through the use of codes, a simplified version of synoptic weather charts is transmitted to various stations ashore and afloat. Rapid transmission of completed maps has been made possible by the development of facsimile transmitters and receivers. This system is based upon detailed scanning, by a photoelectric detector, of properly illuminated black and white copy. The varying degrees of light intensity are converted to electric energy which is transmitted to the receiver and converted back to a black and white presentation.

Complete information on dissemination of weather information by radio is given in *Worldwide Marine Weather Broadcasts*, published by National Weather Service. Information on day and night visual storm warnings is given in the various volumes of sailing directions and coast pilots.

Interpreting the weather • The factors which determine weather are numerous and varied. Ever-increasing knowledge regarding them makes possible a continually improving weather service. However, the ability to forecast is acquired through study and long practice, and therefore the services of a trained meteorologist should be utilized whenever available.

The value of a forecast is increased if one has access to the information upon which it is based, and understands the principles and processes involved. It is sometimes as important to know the various types of weather that *might* be experienced as it is to know which of several possibilities is *most likely* to occur.

At sea, reporting stations are unevenly distributed, sometimes leaving relatively large areas with incomplete reports, or none at all. Under these conditions, the locations of highs, lows, fronts, etc., are imperfectly known, and their very existence may even be in doubt. At such times the mariner who can interpret the observations made from his own vessel may be able to predict weather during the next 24 hours more reliably than a trained meteorologist some distance away with incomplete information.

Knowledge of the various relationships given in this and the last chapter is of value, but only the more elementary principles are presented. Further information can be obtained from meteorological publications. The information obtained from these references will provide a background for proper interpretation of individual experience. If one uses every opportunity to observe and interpret weather sequences, he can develop knowledge and skill that will serve as a valuable supplement to information given in weather broadcasts, or to supply information for areas not covered by such broadcasts.

Influencing the weather • Meteorological activities are devoted primarily to understand weather processes, and predicting future weather. However, as knowledge regarding cause-and-effect relationships increases, the possibility of being able to induce certain results by artificially producing the necessary conditions becomes greater. The most promising results to date have been in the encouraging of precipitation by "seeding" supercooled clouds with powdered dry ice or silver iodide smoke. The effectiveness of this procedure is controversial. Various methods of decreasing the intensity of tropical cyclones, or of diverting their courses, have been suggested, but a satisfactory method has not been devised.

If a way is found to influence weather on a major scale, legal and possibly moral problems will be created due to conflicting interests.

Appendix A: Abbreviations

A more complete listing of abbreviations and symbols is given in H.O. Pub. No. 220, *Navigation Dictionary*, of which this is an abridgement.

AP, assumed position.
B, bearing, bearing angle.
Bn, bearing (as distinguished from bearing angle).
C, Celsius (centigrade); compass (direction); course, course angle.
CB, compass bearing.
CC, compass course.
CH, compass heading.
Cn, course (as distinguished from course angle).
D, deviation; distance.
Dev., deviation.
dist., distance.
DLo, difference of longitude (arc units).
DR, dead reckoning, dead reckoning position.
E, east.
EP, estimated position.
ETA, estimated time of arrival.
F, Fahrenheit.
Hdg., heading.
HHW, higher high water.
HLW, higher low water.
ISLW, Indian spring low water.
K, Kelvin (temperature).
L, latitude.

l, difference of latitude.
lat., latitude.
Lm, middle latitude.
long., longitude.
LW, low water.
M, magnetic (direction); meridional parts; nautical mile, miles.
m, meridional difference ($M_1 \sim M_2$); statute mile, miles.
MHHW, mean higher high water.
MHW, mean high water.
MHWN, mean high water neaps.
MHWS, mean high water springs.
mi., mile, miles.
MLLW, mean lower low water.
MLW, mean low water.
MLWN, mean low water neaps.
MLWS, mean low water springs.
N, north.
p, departure.
RB, relative bearing.
RDF, radio direction finder.
R Fix, running fix.
S, south.
SH, ship's head (heading).
T, true (direction).
TB, true bearing.

TC, true course.
TcHHW, tropic higher high water.
TcHLW, tropic higher low water.
TcLHW, tropic lower high water.
TcLLW, tropic lower low water.

TH, true heading.
TR, track.
V, variation.
Var., variation.
W, west.

Appendix B: Glossary

This appendix is an abridgment of the definitions of Pub. No. 220, *Navigation Dictionary*, to which reference should be made for complete definitions.

abeam. Bearing approximately 090° relative (*abeam to starboard*) or 270° relative (*abeam to port*).

absolute humidity. The mass of water vapor per unit of volume of air.

absolute zero. The lowest possible temperature, about $(-)459°\!.67$ F or $(-)273°\!.15$ C.

acute angle. An angle less than 90°.

advance. The distance a vessel moves in its original direction in making a turn.

advanced line of position. A line of position which has been moved forward to allow for the run since the line was established.

advection. Horizontal movement of part of the atmosphere.

agonic line. A line connecting points of no magnetic variation.

aground. Touching, resting, or lodged on the bottom.

ahead. Bearing approximately 000° relative.

aid to navigation. A device external to a craft, designed to assist in determination of position of the craft, or of a safe course, or to warn of dangers.

air mass. An extensive body of air within which the conditions of temperature and moisture in a horizontal plane are essentially uniform.

alidade. A telescope or other device mounted over a compass, compass repeater, or compass rose, for measuring direction.

alternating fixed and flashing light. A fixed light varied at regular intervals by one or more flashes of greater brilliance, with color variations in either the fixed light or flashes, or both.

alternating fixed and group flashing light. A fixed light varied at regular intervals by a group of two of more flashes of greater brilliance, with color variations in either the fixed light or flashes, or both.

alternating flashing light. A light showing one or more flashes with color variations at regular intervals, the duration of light being less than that of darkness.

alternating group flashing light. A light showing groups of flashes with color variations at regular intervals, the duration of light being less than that of darkness.

alternating group occulting light. A light having groups of total eclipses at regular intervals and having color variations, the duration of light being equal to or greater than that of darkness.

alternating light. A light having periodic color variations, particularly one with constant luminous intensity.

alternating occulting light. A light having one or more total eclipses at regular intervals and having color variations, the duration of light being equal to or greater than that of darkness.

altocumulus. A cloud layer (or patches) within the middle level (mean height 6,500–20,000 ft.) composed of rather flattened globular masses, the smallest elements of the regularly arranged layers being fairly thin, with or without shading. These elements are arranged in groups, in lines or in waves, following one or two directions, and are sometimes so close together that their edges join.

altostratus. A sheet of gray or bluish cloud within the middle level (mean height 6,500–20,000 ft.). Sometimes the sheet is composed of a compact mass of dark, thick, gray clouds of fibrous structure; at other times the sheet is thin and through it the sun or moon can be seen dimly as though gleaming through ground glass.

anchorage. An area where a vessel anchors or may anchor, either because of suitability or designation.

anchorage buoy. One of a series of buoys marking the limits of an anchorage.

anemometer. An instrument for measuring the speed of the wind. Some instruments also indicate the direction from which it is blowing.

aneroid barometer. An instrument which determines atmospheric pressure by the effect of such pressure on a thin-metal cylinder from which the air has been partly exhausted.

angle. The inclination to each other of two intersecting lines, measured by the arc of a circle intercepted between the two lines forming the angle, the center of the circle being the point of intersection.

angular distance. The angular difference between two directions, or the arc of the great circle joining two points.

antenna. A conductor or system of conductors for radiating or receiving radio waves.

antenna array. A group of antennas arranged so as to obtain directional characteristics.

anticyclone. An approximately circular portion of the atmosphere, having relatively high atmospheric pressure and winds which blow clockwise around the center in the northern hemisphere and counterclockwise in the southern hemisphere.

apogean tides. Tides of decreased range occurring when the moon is near apogee.

apogee. That orbital point farthest from the earth when the earth is the center of attraction (as in the case of the moon).

apparent wind. Wind relative to a moving point, such as a vessel.

arc. Part of a curved line, as a circle.

arc of visibility. The arc of a light sector, designated by its limited bearings as observed at points other than the light.

arming. Tallow or other substance placed in the recess at the lower end of a sounding lead, for obtaining a sample of the bottom.

astern. Bearing approximately 180° relative.

atmosphere. The envelope of air surrounding the earth or other celestial body.

atmospheric pressure. The pressure exerted by the weight of the earth's atmosphere. Its standard value at sea level is about 14.7 pounds per square inch.

atmospheric refraction. Refraction of a ray of radiant energy passing obliquely through the atmosphere.

aurora. A luminous phenomena due to electrical discharge in the upper atmosphere, most commonly seen in high latitudes.

awash. Situated so that the top is intermittently washed by waves or tidal action.

azimuth. The horizontal direction of a celestial point from a terrestrial point. It is usually measured from 000° at the reference direction clockwise through 360°.

azimuthal equidistant projection. An azimuthal map projection in which distances from the point of tangency are accurately represented according to a uniform scale.

azimuthal projection. A map projection in which the surface of a sphere or spheroid, such as the earth, is conceived as developed on a tangent plane, with the result that azimuths or bearings of any point from the center are correctly represented.

azimuth circle. A ring designed to fit snugly over a compass or compass repeater, and provided with means for observing compass bearings and azimuths.

azimuth instrument. An instrument for measuring azimuths, particularly a device which fits snugly over a central pivot in the glass cover of a magnetic compass.

back. Of the wind, to change direction counterclockwise in the northern hemisphere and clockwise in the southern hemisphere.

barograph. A recording barometer.

barometer. An instrument for measuring atmospheric pressure.

barometric pressure. Atmospheric pressure as indicated by a barometer.

bathymetric chart. A topographic chart of the bed of a body of water.

beacon. 1. A fixed aid to navigation. 2. An unlighted aid to navigation. 3. Anything serving as a signal or conspicuous indication, either for guidance or warning.

bearing. The horizontal direction of one terrestrial point from another. It is usually measured from 000° at the reference direction clockwise through 360°.

bearing angle. Bearing measured from 0° at the north or south reference direction clockwise or counterclockwise through 90° or 180°.

bearing bar. A slender bar with a vane at each end, designed to fit over a central pivot in the glass cover of a magnetic compass, for measurement of compass bearings.

bearing circle. A ring designed to fit snugly over a compass or compass repeater, and provided with vanes for observing compass bearings.

bearing line. A line extending in the direction of a bearing.

Beaufort scale. A numerical scale for indicating wind speed, named after Admiral Sir Francis Beaufort, who devised it in 1806.

binnacle. The stand in which a compass is mounted.

blue magnetism. The magnetism of the south-seeking end of a freely suspended magnet.

boat compass. A small compass mounted in a box for convenient use in small craft.

bobbing a light. Quickly lowering the height of eye several feet and then raising it again when a light is first sighted, to determine whether the observer is at the geographical range of the light.

bottom sample. A portion of the material forming the bottom, brought up for inspection.

bow and beam bearings. Successive relative bearings (right or left) of 45° and 90° of a fixed object.

boxing the compass. Stating in order the names of the points (and sometimes fractional points) of the compass.

broad on the beam. Bearing 090° relative ("broad on the starboard beam") or 270° relative ("broad on the port beam").

broad on the bow. Bearing 045° relative ("broad on the starboard bow") or 315° relative ("broad on the port bow").

broad on the quarter. Bearing 135° relative ("broad on the starboard quarter") or 225° relative ("broad on the port quarter").

buoy. A floating object, other than a lightship, moored or anchored to the bottom as an aid to navigation.

buoyage. A system of buoys.

can buoy. A buoy the above-water part of which is in the shape of a cylinder.

cardinal point. North, east, south, or west.

celestial navigation. Navigation with the aid of celestial bodies.

Celsius temperature. Temperature based upon a scale in which, under standard atmospheric pressure, water freezes at 0° and boils at 100°. Called "centigrade temperature" before 1948.

centigrade temperature. Celsius temperature.

change of tide. A reversal of the direction of motion (rising or falling) of a tide.

characteristics of a light. The sequence and length of light and dark periods and the color or colors by which a navigational light is identified.

character of the bottom. The type of material of which the bottom is composed.

chart. A map intended primarily for navigational use.

chart datum. The tidal datum to which soundings on a chart are referred.

charted depth. The vertical distance from the chart datum to the bottom.

charted visibility. The extreme distance, shown in numbers on a chart, at which a navigational light can be seen under standard conditions.

chart projection. A map projection used for a chart.

chart reading. Interpretation of the symbols, lines, abbreviations, and terms appearing on charts.

chronometer. A timepiece with a nearly constant rate.

circle of position. A circular line of position.

circle of uncertainty. A circle within which a craft is considered to be located.

circle of visibility. That circle surrounding an aid to navigation in which the aid is visible.

cirrocumulus. High clouds (mean lower level above 20,000 ft.) composed of small white flakes or of very small globular masses, usually without shadows, which are arranged in groups or lines, or more often in ripples resembling those of sand on the seashore.

cirrostratus. Thin, whitish, high clouds (mean lower level above 20,000 ft.) sometimes covering the sky completely and giving it a milky appearance and at other times presenting, more or less distinctly, a formation like a tangled web.

cirrus. Detached high clouds (mean lower level above 20,000 ft.) of delicate and fibrous appearance, without shading, generally white in color, and often of a silky appearance.

cloud. A visible assemblage of numerous tiny droplets of water or ice crystals formed by condensation of water vapor in the air, with the base above the surface of the earth.

coastal current. An ocean current flowing roughly parallel to a coast, outside the surf zone.

coast chart. A nautical chart intended for use near a shore, as in entering and leaving harbors.

coasting. Proceeding approximately parallel to a coast line and near enough to be in pilot waters most of the time.

coast pilot. A descriptive book for the use of mariners, containing detailed information of coastal waters, harbor facilities, etc., of an area, particularly along the coasts of the United States.

coast piloting. The directing of the movements of a vessel near a coast, by means of terrestrial reference points.

coastwise navigation. Navigation in the vicinity of a coast.

cold air mass. An air mass that is colder than surrounding air, and usually colder than the surface over which it is moving.

cold front. That line of discontinuity, at the earth's surface or at a horizontal plane aloft, along which an advancing cold air mass is undermining and displacing a warmer air mass.

combination buoy. A buoy having more than one means of conveying intelligence, as by light and sound.

compass. An instrument for determining a horizontal reference direction relative to the earth.

compass adjustment. The process of neutralizing the magnetic effect a vessel exerts on a magnetic compass.

compass bearing. Bearing relative to compass north.

compass bowl. That part of a compass in which the compass card is mounted.

compass card. That part of a compass on which the direction graduations are placed.

compass course. Course relative to compass north.

compass error. The angular difference between a compass direction and the corresponding true direction.

compasses. An instrument for drawing circles.

compass heading. Heading relative to compass north.

compass north. The direction north as indicated by a magnetic compass.

compass points. The 32 divisions of a compass, at intervals of 11¼°.

compass rose. A circle graduated in degrees, clockwise from 0° at the reference direction to 360°, or in compass points, or in both degrees and points.

conformal projection. A map projection in which all angles around any point are correctly represented.

conic projection. A map projection in which the surface of a sphere or spheroid, such as the earth, is conceived as developed on one or more cones which are then spread out to form a plane.

constant error. A systematic error of unchanging magnitude and sign.

contour. A line connecting points of equal elevation or equal depth.

coordinate. One of a set of magnitudes defining a point in space.

correcting. The process of applying corrections, particularly compass corrections.

corrector. A magnet, piece of soft iron, or device used in the adjustment or compensation of a magnetic compass.

countercurrent. A secondary current flowing adjacent and in the opposite direction to another current.

course. The intended horizontal direction of travel. It is usually measured from 000° at the reference direction clockwise through 360°.

course angle. Course measured from 0° at the reference direction clockwise or counterclockwise through 90° or 180°.

course error. Angular difference between the course and the course made good.

course line. 1. A line extending in the direction of a given course. **2.** A line of position approximately parallel to the course.

course made good. The direction of a point of arrival from a point of departure.

course of advance. The course expected to be made good over the ground.

course over the ground. The course actually made good over the ground.

cross bearings. Two or more bearings used as intersecting lines of position for fixing the position of a vessel.

cumulonimbus. A massive cloud with great vertical development, the summits of which rise in the form of mountains or towers, the upper parts often spreading out in the form of an anvil.

cumulus. A dense cloud with vertical development, having a horizontal base and dome-shaped upper surface, exhibiting protuberances.

current. 1. Water in essentially horizontal motion. **2.** A hypothetical horizontal motion of such set and drift as to account for the difference between a dead reckoning position and a fix at the same time.

current chart. A chart on which current data are graphically depicted.

current diagram. A graph showing the average speeds of flood and ebb currents throughout the current cycle for a considerable part of a tidal waterway.

current difference. The difference between the time of slack water or strength of current at a subordinate station and at its reference station.

current direction. The direction *toward* which a current is flowing.

current rips. Small waves formed on the surface of water by the meeting of opposing ocean currents.

cyclone. An approximately circular portion of the atmosphere, having relatively low atmospheric pressure and winds which blow counterclockwise around the center in the northern hemisphere and clockwise in the southern hemisphere.

cylindrical buoy. Can buoy.

cylindrical projection. A map projection in which the surface of a sphere or spheroid, such as the earth, is conceived as developed on a tangent cylinder, which is then spread out to form a plane.

danger angle. The maximum or minimum angle between two points (separated either horizontally or vertically), as observed from a vessel, indicating the limit of safe approach to an off-lying danger.

danger bearing. The maximum or minimum bearing of a point for safe passage past an off-lying danger.

danger buoy. A buoy marking an isolated danger to navigation.

danger line. A line drawn on a chart, to indicate the limits of safe navigation for a vessel of specific draft.

danger sounding. A minimum sounding chosen for a vessel of specific draft in a given area to indicate the limit of safe navigation.

datum. The base value, level, direction, or position from which any quantity is measured.

daybeacon. An unlighted beacon.

daymark. A distinctive structure serving as an aid to navigation during daylight, whether or not the structure has a light.

day's run. The distance traveled by a vessel in one day, usually reckoned from noon to noon.

dead ahead. Bearing 000° relative.

dead astern. Bearing 180° relative.

dead reckoning. Determination of position by advancing a previous position for courses and distances.

dead reckoning plot. A plot of the movements of a craft as determined by dead reckoning.

dead reckoning position. A position determined by dead reckoning.

dead reckoning track. A line representing successive dead reckoning positions of a craft.

deck log. A written record of the movements of a vessel with regard to courses, speeds, positions, and other navigational information, and important events aboard the vessel.

deep. An unmarked fathom point on a lead line.

deep sea lead (lĕd). A heavy sounding lead (about 30 to 100 pounds), usually having a line 100 fathoms or more in length.

departure. 1. The distance between two meridians at any given parallel of latitude, expressed in linear units, or the distance to the east or west made good by a vessel in proceeding from one point to another. **2.** Act of departing or leaving.

depth. Vertical distance from a given water level to the bottom.

depth contour. A contour connecting points of equal depth.

destination. The point of intended arrival.

deviation. The angle between the magnetic meridian and the axis of a compass card.

deviation table. A table of the deviation of a magnetic compass on various headings.

dew point. The temperature to which air must be cooled at constant pressure and constant water vapor content to reach saturation.

diaphone. A device for producing a distinctive fog signal by means of a slotted reciprocating piston actuated by compressed air.

difference of latitude. The shorter arc of any meridian between the parallels of two places, expressed in angular measure.

difference of longitude. The smaller angle at the pole or the shorter arc of a parallel between the meridians of two places, expressed in angular measure.

dip. 1. The vertical angle, at the eye of an observer, between the horizontal and the line of sight to the visible horizon. **2.** The angle between the horizontal and the lines of force of the earth's magnetic field.

direct current. An electric current which flows continuously in the same direction.

direction. The position of one point in space relative to another without reference to the distance between them.

direction of current. The direction *toward* which a current is flowing.

direction of wind. The direction *from* which a wind is blowing.

directive force. The force tending to cause the directive element of a compass to line up with the reference direction.

distance finding station. A radiobeam with a synchronized sound signal.

distance marker. A device indicating distance, particularly one on a radar indicator.

diurnal. Having a period of, occurring in, or related to a day.

diurnal current. Tidal current having one flood current and one ebb current each tidal day.

diurnal inequality. The difference between the heights of the two high tides or two low tides during the tidal day, or the difference in speed between the two flood currents or the two ebb currents during a tidal day.

diurnal tide. Tide having one high tide and one low tide each tidal day.

dividers. An instrument consisting in its simple form of two pointed legs joined by a pivot, used principally for measuring distances or coordinates.

double tide. A high tide consisting of two maxima of nearly the same height separated by a relatively small depression, or a low tide consisting of two minima separated by a relatively small elevation.

doubling the angle on the bow. A method of obtaining a running fix by measuring the distance a vessel travels while the relative bearing (right or left) of a fixed object doubles.

draft. The depth to which a vessel is submerged.

drafting machine. An instrument consisting essentially of a protractor and one or more arms attached to a parallel motion device.

drift. 1. The speed of a current. **2.** The distance a vessel is moved by current and wind. **3.** Downwind or downcurrent motion due to wind or current.

ebb current. Tidal current moving away from land or down a tidal stream.

echo sounder. An instrument used for echo sounding.

echo sounding. Determination of the depth of water by measuring the time interval between emission of a sonic or ultrasonic signal and the return of its echo from the bottom.

electronic navigation. Navigation by means of electronic equipment.

engine revolution counter. An instrument for registering the number of revolutions of a propeller shaft.

equator. The primary great circle of the earth, or a similar body, perpendicular to the polar axis.

equatorial tides. The tides that occur when the moon is near the celestial equator, when the difference in height between consecutive high or low tides is a minimum.

estimated position. The most probable position of a craft, determined from incomplete data or data of questionable accuracy.

Fahrenheit temperature. Temperature based upon a scale in which, under standard atmospheric pressure, water freezes at 32° and boils at 212°.

fata morgana. A complex mirage, characterized by marked distortion, generally in the vertical.

fathom. A unit of length equal to six feet.

fathom curve, fathom line. A depth contour with depth measured in fathoms.

fictitious latitude, fictitious longitude. Coordinates based upon a set of fictitious parallels and fictitious meridians similar to the geographical graticule, but offset from it. These are usually used with a transverse or oblique map projection, or with a navigational grid.

fictitious rhumb line. A line making the same oblique angle with all fictitious meridians.

fix. A relatively accurate position determined without reference to any former position.

fixed and flashing light. A fixed light varied at regular intervals by one or more flashes of greater brilliance.

fixed and group flashing light. A fixed light varied at regular intervals by a group of two or more flashes of greater brilliance.

fixed light. A light having constant luminous intensity.

flashing. The process of reducing the amount of permanent magnetism in a vessel by placing a single coil horizontally around the vessel and energizing the coil.

flashing light. A light showing one or more flashes at regular intervals, the duration of light being less than that of darkness.

Flinders bar. A bar of soft unmagnetized iron placed in a vertical position near a magnetic compass to counteract deviation caused by magnetic induction in vertical soft iron of the craft.

flood current. Tidal current moving toward land or up a tidal stream.

fog. A visible assemblage of numerous tiny droplets of water, or ice crystals formed by condensation of water vapor in the air, with the base at the surface of the earth.

fog signal. A warning signal transmitted by a vessel or aid to navigation during periods of low visibility.

form line. An approximation of a contour without a definite elevation value.

front. The intersection of a frontal surface and a horizontal plane.

frontal surface. The thin zone of discontinuity between two air masses.

general chart. A nautical chart intended for offshore coastwise navigation.

geodesic line. The shortest line, on a mathematically derived surface, between two points on that surface.

geodetic survey. A survey which takes into account the size and shape of the earth.

geographical mile. The length of one minute of arc of the equator, or 6087.090 feet (on the Clarke spheroid of 1866).

geographic range. The extreme distance at which an object or light can be seen when limited by the curvature of the earth and the heights of the object and the observer.

geomagnetic electrokinetograph. A device for measurement of the lateral component of the speed of an ocean current by means of two pairs of electrodes towed astern.

geomagnetic equator. That terrestrial great circle everywhere 90° from the geomagnetic poles.

geomagnetic pole. Either of two points marking the intersection of the earth's surface with the extended axis of a hypothetical bar magnet at the center of the earth and approximating the source of the actual magnetic field of the earth.

geomagnetism. The magnetism of the earth.

geometric projection. Perspective projection.

gimbals. A device for supporting anything, such as an instrument, in such a manner that it remains essentially horizontal when the support tilts.

gnomonic projection. A map projection in which points on the surface of a sphere or spheroid, such as the earth, are conceived as projected by radials from the center to a tangent plane.

gradient. The change of any quantity with distance in any given direction.

graph. A diagram indicating the relationship between two or more variables.

graticule. The network of lines representing parallels and meridians on a map, chart, or plotting sheet.

great circle. The intersection of a sphere and a plane through its center.

great-circle chart. A chart on which a great circle appears as a straight line or approximately so, particularly a chart on the gnomonic projection.

great-circle distance. The length of the shorter arc of the great circle joining two points.

great-circle sailing. Any method of solving the various problems involving courses, distances, etc., as they relate to a great-circle track.

great-circle track. The track of a craft following a great circle, or a great circle which it is intended a craft will follow approximately.

greater ebb. The stronger of two ebb currents occurring during a tidal day.

greater flood. The stronger of two flood currents occurring during a tidal day.

grid. 1. A series of lines, usually straight and parallel, superimposed on a chart or plotting sheet to serve as a directional reference for navigation. 2. Two sets of mutually perpendicular lines dividing a map or chart into squares or rectangles to permit location of any point by a system of rectangular coordinates.

grid navigation. Navigation by the use of grid directions.

grid north. An arbitrary reference direction used with grid navigation.

grid variation. The angular difference between magnetic north and grid north.

grivation. Grid variation.

grounding. The touching of the bottom by a vessel.

group flashing light. A light showing groups of flashes at regular intervals, the duration of light being less than that of darkness.

group occulting light. A light having groups of eclipses at regular intervals, the duration of light being equal to or greater than that of darkness.

gyro compass. A compass having one or more gyroscopes as the directive element, and tending to indicate true north.

hachures. Short lines on maps or charts, to indicate the slope of the ground.

half-tide level. The level midway between mean high water and mean low water.

hand lead (lĕd). A light sounding lead (7 to 14 pounds), usually having a line of not more than 25 fathoms.

harbor chart. A nautical chart intended for navigation and anchorage in harbors and smaller waterways.

hard iron. Iron or steel which is not readily magnetized by induction, but which retains a high percentage of the magnetism acquired.

haze. Fine dust or salt particles in the air, too small to be individually apparent but in sufficient number to reduce visibility and cast a bluish or yellowish veil over the landscape, subduing its colors.

heading. The horizontal direction in which a craft is pointed. It is usually measured from 000° at the reference direction clockwise through 360°.

heading angle. Heading measured from 0° at the reference direction clockwise or counterclockwise through 90° or 180°.

heading line. A line extending in the direction of a heading.

headway. Motion in a forward direction.

heel. Lateral inclination, as of a vessel during a roll or when listed.

height of tide. Vertical distance from the tidal datum to the level of the water at any time.

higher high water. The higher of two high tides occurring during a tidal day.

higher low water. The higher of two low tides occurring during a tidal day.

high tide. The maximum height reached by a rising tide.

high water. High tide.

high water full and change. The average interval of time between the transit (upper or lower) of the full or new moon and the next high water.

high water inequality. The difference between the height of the two high tides during a tidal day.

high water lunitidal interval. The interval of time between the transit (upper or lower) of the moon and the next high water at a place.

humidity. The amount of water vapor in the air.

hunting. Fluctuation about a mid-point, due to instability, as oscillation of the needle of an instrument about the zero point.

hydrographic survey. A survey of a water area.

hydrography. That science which deals with the measurement of the physical features of waters and their marginal land areas, with special reference to the elements that affect safe navigation, and the publication of such information in a form suitable for use of navigators.

hygrometer. An instrument for measuring the humidity of the air.

induced magnetism. Magnetism acquired by a piece of magnetic material while it is in a magnetic field.

inshore. In or near the shore.

instrument error. The inaccuracy of an instrument due to imperfections within the instrument.

intercardinal point. Northeast, southeast, southwest, or northwest.

international nautical mile. The nautical mile, of 1,852 meters.

interpolation. The process of determining intermediate values between given values in accordance with some known or assumed rate or system of change.

interrupted quick flashing light. A light showing quick flashes for several seconds, followed by a period of darkness.

inverse Mercator projection. Transverse Mercator projection.

isobar. A line connecting points having the same atmospheric pressure reduced to a common datum.

isoclinal. A line connecting points of equal magnetic dip.

isoclinal chart. A chart showing isoclinals.

isogonic. A line connecting points of equal magnetic variation.

isogonic chart. A chart showing isogonics.

isomagnetic. A line connecting points of equality in some magnetic element.

isomagnetic chart. A chart showing isomagnetics.

junction buoy. A buoy marking the junction of two channels or two parts of a channel, when proceeding from seaward.

Kelvin temperature. Temperature based upon a scale starting at absolute zero ($-273°.15$ C) and using Celsius degrees.

kilometer. One thousand meters (about 0.54 nautical mile).

knot. A unit of speed equal to one nautical mile per hour.

Lambert conformal projection. A conformal conic map projection in which the surface of a sphere or spheroid, such as the earth, is conceived as developed on a cone which intersects the sphere or spheroid at two standard parallels.

landfall. The first sighting of land when approached from seaward.

landmark. A conspicuous object on land, serving as an indicator for guidance or warning.

land mile. Statute mile.

land navigation. Navigation across the surface of land or ice.

large scale. A scale involving a relatively small reduction in size.

latitude. Angular distance north or south of the equator; the arc of a meridian between the equator and a point on the surface of the earth, measured northward or southward from the equator through 90°, and labeled N or S to indicate the direction of measurement.

latitude line. A line of position extending in a generally east-west direction.

lead (lĕd). A weight attached to a line.

lead line. The line attached to a sounding lead.

lee. That side toward which the wind blows.

leeway. The leeward motion of a vessel, due to wind, expressed as distance, speed, or an angle.

leg. One part of a track, consisting of a single course line.

legend. A title or explanation on a chart, diagram, illustration, etc.

lesser ebb. The weaker of two ebb currents occurring during a tidal day.

lesser flood. The weaker of two flood currents occurring during a tidal day.

light. A lighted aid to navigation, or its luminous energy.

lighthouse. A distinctive structure exhibiting a major navigational light.

light list. A publication tabulating navigational lights and related information.

light sector. A sector in which a navigational light is visible or has a distinctive color.

lightship. A distinctively marked vessel anchored or moored at a charted point, to serve as an aid to navigation. It has a characteristic light or lights, and usually other aids.

line of position. A line on some point of which a vessel may be presumed to be located, as a result of observation or measurement.

line of soundings. A series of soundings obtained by a vessel underway, usually at regular intervals.

local attraction. Local magnetic disturbance.

local magnetic disturbance. An anomaly of the magnetic field of the earth, extending over a relatively small area, due to local magnetic influences.

log. 1. An instrument for measuring the speed or distance, or both, traveled by a vessel. **2.** Deck log.

longitude. Angular distance east or west of the prime meridian; the arc of a parallel, or the angle at the pole, between the prime meridian and the meridian of a point on the earth, measured eastward or westward from the prime meridian through 180°, and labeled E or W to indicate the direction of measurement.

longitude line. A line of position extending in a generally north-south direction.

loom. The glow of a light which is below the horizon, caused by reflection by solid particles in the air.

loran. An electronic navigational system by which hyperbolic lines of position are determined by measuring the difference in the time of reception of synchronized pulse signals.

lower branch. That half of a meridian or celestial meridian from pole to pole which passes through the antipode or nadir of a place.

lower high water. The lower of two high tides occurring during a tidal day.

lower low water. The lower of two low tides occurring during a tidal day.

low tide. The minimum height reached by a falling tide.

low water. Low tide.

low water inequality. The difference between the heights of the two low tides during a tidal day.

low water lunitidal interval. The interval of time between the transit (upper or lower) of the moon and the next low water at a place.

loxodrome. Rhumb line.

lubber's line. A reference line on any direction-indicating instrument, marking the reading which coincides with the heading.

luminous range. The extreme distance at which a light can be seen when limited only by the intensity of the light, clearness of the atmosphere, and sensitiveness of the observer's eyes.

lunar tide. That part of the tide due solely to the tide-producing force of the moon.

lunitidal interval. The interval of time between the transit (upper or lower) of the moon and the next high water or low water at a place.

magnetic bearing. Bearing relative to magnetic north.

magnetic chart. A chart showing magnetic information.

magnetic compass. A compass depending for its directive force upon the attraction of the magnetism of the earth for a magnet free to turn in any horizontal direction.

magnetic compass table. Deviation table.

magnetic course. Course relative to magnetic north.

magnetic declination. Variation.

magnetic dip. The angle between the horizontal and lines of force of the earth's magnetic field.

magnetic equator. That line on the surface of the earth connecting all points at which the magnetic dip is zero.

magnetic field. The space in which a magnetic influence exists.

magnetic heading. Heading relative to magnetic north.

magnetic meridian. A line of horizontal magnetic force of the earth.

magnetic north. The direction north as indicated by the earth's magnetic lines of force.

magnetic pole. Either of the two places on the surface of the earth where the magnetic dip is $90°$.

magnetic variation. Variation.

maneuvering board. A polar coordinate plotting sheet devised to facilitate solution of problems involving relative movement.

map. A representation, usually on a plane surface, of all or part of the surface of the earth, celestial sphere, or other area; showing relative size and position, according to a given projection, of the various features represented.

map projection. A representation or method of representing all or part of the surface of a sphere or spheroid, such as the earth, upon a plane surface.

marine navigation. The navigation of water craft.

maximum ebb. The greatest speed of an ebb current.

maximum flood. The greatest speed of a flood current.

mean sea level. The average height of the surface of the sea for all stages of the tide, usually determined from hourly readings.

mean tide level. Half-tide level.

measured mile. A length of one nautical mile, the limits of which have been accurately measured and are indicated by ranges ashore.

Mercator projection. A conformal cylindrical map projection in which the surface of a sphere or spheroid, such as the earth, is conceived as developed on a cylinder tangent along the equator, with the expansion of the meridians being equal to that of the parallels.

Mercator sailing. A method of solving the various problems involving course, distance, difference of latitude, difference of longitude, and departure by considering them in the relation in which they are plotted on a Mercator chart.

mercurial barometer. An instrument which determines atmospheric pressure by measuring the height of a column of mercury which the atmosphere will support.

meridian. A great circle through the geographical poles of the earth or a similar body.

meridional difference. The difference between the meridional parts of any two given parallels.

meridional parts. The length of the arc of a meridian between the equator and a given parallel on a Mercator chart, expressed in units of 1' of longitude at the equator.

meteorology. The science of the atmosphere.

middle latitude. Half the arithmetical sum of the latitudes of two places on the same side of the equator.

middle-latitude sailing. A method of converting departure into difference of longitude, or vice versa, when the course is not 090° or 270°, by assuming that such a course is steered at the middle latitude.

mid latitude. Middle latitude.

millibar. A unit of pressure equal to 1,000 dynes per square centimeter.

mist. Thin fog of relatively large particles, or very fine rain.

mixed current. A type of tidal current characterized by a conspicuous difference in speed between the two flood currents or two ebb currents usually occurring each tidal day.

mixed tide. A type of tide having a large inequality in the heights of either the two high tides or the two low tides usually occurring each tidal day.

modified Lambert conformal projection. A modification of the Lambert conformal projection for use in polar regions, the higher standard parallel being almost at the pole, and the parallels being expanded slightly to form complete concentric circles.

most probable position. That position of a craft judged to be most accurate when the exact position is not known.

natural scale. The ratio between the linear dimensions of a chart, drawing, etc., and the actual dimensions represented, expressed as a proportion.

nautical chart. A chart intended primarily for marine navigation.

nautical mile. A unit of distance equal to 1,852 meters (6,076.11549 U.S. feet, approximately). This is equal approximately to the length of 1′ of latitude.

navigation. The process of directing the movement of a craft from one point to another.

navigational aid. An instrument, device, chart, method, etc., intended to assist in the navigation of a craft.

neap tides. The tides occurring near the times of first and last quarter of the moon, when the range of tide tends to decrease.

Ney's projection. Modified Lambert conformal projection.

nightmark. An object of distinctive characteristics serving as an aid to navigation during darkness.

nimbostratus. A dark, low, shapeless cloud layer (mean upper level below 6,500 ft.) usually nearly uniform; the typical rain cloud.

nimbus. A characteristic rain cloud.

nun buoy. A buoy the above water part of which is in the shape of a cone or a truncated cone.

oblique Mercator projection. A conformal cylindrical map projection in which points on the surface of a sphere or spheroid, such as the earth, are conceived as developed by Mercator principles on a cylinder tangent along an oblique great circle.

occluded front. The front formed when a cold front overtakes a warm front.

occulting light. A light totally eclipsed at intervals, the duration of light being equal to or greater than that of darkness.

oceanography. The application of the sciences to the phenomena of the oceans.

oersted. The centimeter-gram-second electromagnetic unit of magnetic intensity.

offshore. Away from the shore.

off soundings. In an area where the depth of water cannot be measured by an ordinary sounding lead, generally considered to be beyond the 100-fathom line.

on soundings. In an area where the depth of water can be measured by ordinary sounding lead, generally considered to be within the 100-fathom line.

on the beam. Bearing approximately 090° relative ("on the starboard beam") or 270° relative ("on the port beam").

on the bow. Bearing approximately 045° relative ("on the starboard bow") or 315° relative ("on the port bow").

on the quarter. Bearing approximately 135° relative ("on the starboard quarter") 225° realtive ("on the port quarter").

orthographic projection. A perspective azimuthal projection in which the projecting lines, emanating from a point at infinity, are perpendicular to a tangent plane.

orthomorphic projection. A projection in which very small shapes are correctly represented.

parallel. A circle on the surface of the earth, or a similar body, parallel to the plane of the equator and connecting all points of equal latitude, or a closed curve resembling or approximating such a circle.

parallel of latitude. 1. Parallel. **2.** A circle of the celestial sphere, parallel to the ecliptic, and connecting points of equal celestial latitude.

parallel rulers. An instrument for transferring a line parallel to itself.

parallel sailing. A method of converting departure into difference of longitude, or vice versa, when the true course is 090° or 270°.

pelorus. A dumb compass, or a compass card without a directive element, suitably mounted to provide means for measuring bearings.

perigean tides. Tides of increased range occurring when the moon is near perigee.

perigee. That orbital point nearest the earth when the earth is the center of attraction (as in the case of the moon).

permanent magnetism. Magnetism which is retained for long periods without appreciable reduction, unless the magnet is subjected to a demagnetizing force.

perspective projection. The representation of a figure on a surface by means of projecting lines emanating from a single point.

pilot chart. A chart giving information on ocean currents, weather, and other items of interest to a navigator.

piloting. Navigation involving frequent or continuous determination of position or a line of position relative to geographical points, to a high order of accuracy.

pilot waters. 1. Areas in which the services of a pilot are desirable. **2.** Waters in which navigation is by piloting.

Pitot tube. A tube with an open end pointed toward a moving stream of fluid. It is usually associated with a coaxial or nearly parallel tube having holes in its side to permit measurement of static pressure.

plane sailing. A method of solving the various problems involving course, distance, difference of latitude, and departure, in which the earth or a small part of it is considered a plane.

plot. A drawing consisting of lines and points graphically representing certain conditions, as the progress of a craft.

plotter. An instrument for plotting lines and measuring angles on a chart or plotting sheet.

plotting chart. A chart designed primarily for plotting dead reckoning, lines of position from celestial observations, or radio aids, etc.

plotting sheet. A blank chart showing only the graticule and one or more compass roses, so that the plotting sheet can be used for any longitude.

polar navigation. Navigation in polar regions.

polar projection. A map projection centered on a pole.

pole. 1. Either of the two points of intersection of the surface of the earth or similar body and its axis. **2.** A magnetic pole.

polyconic projection. A conic map projection in which the surface of a sphere or spheriod, such as the earth, is conceived as developed on a series of tangent cones, which are then spread out to form a plane.

position. A point defined by stated or implied coordinates, particularly one on the surface of the earth.

prime meridian. The meridian of longitude 0°, used as the origin for the measurement of longitude.

profile. A graph showing elevation or distribution of some property along a line; as the graphic record made by a recording echo sounder while a vessel is underway.

protractor. An instrument for measuring angles on a surface; an angular scale.

psychrometer. An instrument consisting of suitably mounted dry-bulb and wet-bulb thermometers for determining relative humidity and dew point.

quick flashing light. A light showing short flashes at the rate of not less than 60 per minute.

radar. A system of determining distance of an object by measuring the time interval between transmission of a pulse signal and reception of a signal returned as an echo or by a transmitter triggered by the outgoing signal. The bearing of the object can be determined by noting the orientation of the directional antenna.

radio aid to navigation. An aid to navigation transmitting information by radio waves.

radiobeacon. A radio transmitter emitting a characteristic signal to permit a craft with suitable equipment to determine its direction, distance, or position relative to the beacon.

radio bearing. The bearing of a radio transmitter from a receiver, as determined by a radio direction finder.

radio direction finder. Radio receiving equipment which determines the direction of arrival of a signal by measuring the orientation of the wave front, using a loop antenna.

radio direction finder station. A radio station provided with equipment for obtaining radio bearings, particularly such a station on the shore.

radio navigation. Navigation by means of radio.

radius of visibility. The radius of a circle limiting the area in which an objective can be seen under specified conditions.

range. 1. Two or more objects in line. 2. The extreme distance at which an object or light can be seen, or a radio signal can be used.

range finder. An optical instrument for measuring the distance to an object.

range lights. Two or more lights in the same horizontal direction, particularly those lights so placed as navigational aids to mark any line of importance to vessels, as a channel.

range of tide. The difference in height between consecutive high and low tides at a place.

range of visibility. The extreme distance at which an object or light can be seen.

Rankine temperature. Temperature based upon a scale starting at absolute zero ($-459°.67$ F) and using Fahrenheit degrees.

Réaumur temperature. Temperature based upon a scale in which, under standard atmospheric pressure, water freezes at $0°$ and boils at $80°$ above zero.

red magnetism. The magnetism of the north-seeking end of a freely suspended magnet.

red sector. A sector of the circle of visibility of a navigational light in which a red light is exhibited.

reference station. A place for which independent daily predictions are given in the tide or tidal current tables, from which corresponding predictions are obtained for other stations by means of differences or factors.

refraction. The change in direction of motion of a ray of radiant energy as it passes obliquely from one medium into another in which the speed of propagation is different.

relative bearing. Bearing relative to heading or to the craft.

relative humidity. The percentage of saturation of the air.

relative movement. Motion of one object or body relative to another.

relief. Inequalities in the elevations of the terrain, or their representation on a chart.

repeater. A device for repeating at a distance the indications of an instrument or device.

residual deviation. Deviation of a magnetic compass after adjustment or compensation.

retired line of position. A line of position which has been moved backward to correspond with a time previous to that for which the line was established.

rhumb line. A line on the surface of the earth making the same oblique angle with all meridians.

rise of tide. Vertical distance from the chart datum to a high water datum, such as mean high water.

rotary current. A tidal current which changes direction progressively through 360° during a tidal-day cycle, without coming to slack water.

running fix. A position determined by crossing lines of position with an appreciable time difference between them and advanced or retired to a common time.

sailing chart. A small-scale nautical chart for offshore navigation.

sailing directions. A descriptive book for the use of mariners, containing detailed information of coastal waters, harbor facilities, etc., of an area, particularly along coasts other than those of the United States.

scale. 1. A series of marks or graduations at definite intervals. **2.** The ratio between the linear dimensions of a chart, map, drawing, etc., and the actual dimensions represented.

seamark. A conspicuous object in the water, serving as an indicator for guidance or warning of a craft.

sector. Part of a circle bounded by two radii and an arc.

sectored light. A light having sectors of different colors or the same color in specific sectors separated by dark sectors.

secular. Of or pertaining to a long period of time.

semicircular deviation. Deviation which changes sign (E or W) approximately each 180° change of heading.

semidiurnal. Having a period of, occurring in, or related to approximately half a day.

semidiurnal current. Tidal current having two flood currents and two ebb currents each tidal day.

semidiurnal tide. Tide having two high tides and two low tides each tidal day.

set. The direction toward which a current flows.

seven-eighths rule. A rule of thumb which states that the approximate distance to an object broad on the beam equals ⅞ of the distance traveled while the relative bearing (right or left) changes from 30° to 60° or from 120° to 150°.

seven-tenths rule. A rule of thumb which states that the approximate distance to an object broad on the beam equals ⁷⁄₁₀ of the distance traveled while the relative bearing (right or left) changes from 22°5 to 45° or from 135° to 157°5.

seven-thirds rule. A rule of thumb which states that the approximate distance to an object on the beam equals ⅞ of the distance traveled while the relative bearing (right or left) changes from 22°5 to 26°5, 67°5 to 90°, 90° to 112°5, or 153°5 to 157°5.

short-long flashing light. A light showing a short flash of about 0.4 second, and a long flash of four times that duration, this combination recurring about six to eight times per minute.

slack water. The condition when the speed of a tidal current is zero.

small circle. The intersection of a sphere and a plane which does not pass through its center.

small scale. A scale involving a relatively large reduction in size.

smog. A mixture of smoke and fog.

soft iron. Iron or steel which is easily magnetized by induction, but loses its magnetism when the magnetic field is removed.

solar tide. That part of the tide due solely to the tide-producing force of the sun.

sonar. A system of determining distance of an underwater object by measuring the interval of time between transmission of an underwater sonic or ultrasonic signal and return of its echo.

sonic depth finder. An echo sounder operating in the audible range of signals.

sonic navigation. Navigation by means of sound waves whether or not they are within the audible range.

sound buoy. A buoy equipped with a characteristic sound signal.

sounding. Measured or charted depth of water, or the measurement of such depth.

sounding lead (lĕd). A lead used for determining depth of water.

sounding line. The line attached to a sounding lead.

sounding machine. An instrument for measuring depth of water by lowering a recording device.

sounding wire. The wire attached to the recording device of a sounding machine.

spar buoy. A buoy made of a tapered log or of metal similarly shaped.

speed of advance. The speed expected to be made good over the ground.

speed over the ground. The speed actually made good over the ground.

spheroid. An ellipsoid.

spring range. The mean semidiurnal range of tide when spring tides are occurring.

spring tides. The tides occurring near the times of full moon and new moon, when the range of tide tends to increase.

stadimeter. An instrument for determining the distance to an object of known height by measuring the angle subtended at the observer by the object.

stand. The condition at high tide or low tide when there is no change in the height of the water.

standard compass. A compass designated as the standard for a vessel.

standard parallel. A parallel on a map projection, along which the scale is as stated.

station buoy. A buoy used to mark the approximate station of an important buoy or a lightship.

station error. The difference between the direction of gravity and the perpendicular (normal) to the reference spheroid representing the earth.

statute mile. A unit of distance equal to 5,280 feet in the United States; a land mile.

steering compass. A compass by which a craft is steered.

stereographic projection. A perspective, conformal, azimuthal map projection in which points on the surface of a sphere or spheroid, such as the earth, are conceived as projected by radial lines from any point on the surface to a plane tangent to that point opposite the point of projection.

stratocumulus. Low clouds (mean upper level below 6,500 ft.) composed of a layer or patches of globular masses or rolls.

stratus. A low cloud (mean upper level below 6,500 ft.) in a uniform layer, resembling fog but not resting on the surface.

strength of current. The phase of a tidal current at which the speed is a maximum, or the speed at this time.

surface navigation. Navigation of a vessel on the surface of the earth.

synoptic chart. A chart showing the distribution of meteorological conditions over an area at a given time. Popularly called a "weather map."

taffrail log. A log consisting essentially of a rotor towed through the water by a line attached to a distance-registering device secured at the taffrail.

temperature error. That instrument error due to nonstandard temperature.

thermometer. An instrument for measuring temperature.

tidal current. Current due to tidal action.

tidal current tables. Tables listing predictions of the times and speeds of tidal currents at various places, and other pertinent information.

tidal datum. A level of the sea, defined by some phase of the tide, from which water depths and heights of tide are reckoned.

tidal day. The period of the daily cycle of the tides, averaging about 24^h50^m in length.

tidal difference. The difference between the time or height of tides at a subordinate station and its reference station.

tide. The periodic rise and fall of the water surfaces of the earth due principally to the gravitational attraction of the moon and sun.

tide rips. Small waves formed by the meeting of opposing tidal currents or by a tidal current crossing an irregular bottom.

tide tables. Tables listing predictions of the times and heights of tides.

track. The horizontal component of the path followed or expected to be followed by a vessel or a storm center.

292 · BOWDITCH FOR YACHTSMEN: Piloting

transfer. The distance a vessel moves perpendicular to its initial direction of motion in making a turn.

transverse Mercator projection. A map projection similar to a Mercator projection but with the cylinder rotated through 90°, so that it is tangent along a meridian.

traverse sailing. A method of determining the equivalent course and distance made good by a vessel following a track consisting of a series of rhumb lines.

traverse table. A table giving relative values of various parts of plane right triangles, for use in solving such triangles.

tropical cyclone. A violent cyclone originating in the tropics.

tropical range. The difference in height between tropic higher high water and tropic lower low water.

tropic tides. The tides that occur when the moon is near its maximum declination, when the diurnal range tends to increase.

true bearing. Bearing relative to true north.

true course. Course relative to true north.

true heading. Heading relative to true north.

true north. The direction of the north geographical pole.

true wind. Wind relative to a fixed point on the earth.

turning buoy. A buoy marking a turn, as in a channel.

ultrasonic depth finder. An echo sounder operating at a frequency above the audible range.

uncorrecting. The process of converting true direction to magnetic, compass, or gyro direction, or magnetic direction to compass direction.

upper branch. That half of a meridian or celestial meridian from pole to pole which passes through a place or its zenith.

variation. The angle between the magnetic and geographical meridians.

vector. A straight line representing both direction and magnitude.

vector diagram. A diagram of more than one vector drawn to the same scale and reference direction, and in correct position relative to each other.

vector quantity. A quantity having both magnitude and direction.

veer. Of the wind, (a) to change direction clockwise in the northern hemisphere and counterclockwise in the southern hemisphere, or (b) to shift aft.

velocity. Rate of motion in a given direction.

velocity ratio. The ratio of the speed of tidal currents at a subordinate station and its reference station.

visibility. The extreme horizontal distance at which prominent objects can be seen and identified by the unaided eye.

visible horizon. That line where earth and sky appear to meet.

vulgar establishment. The average interval of time between the transit (upper or lower) of the full or new moon and the next high water.

warm air mass. An air mass that is warmer than surrounding air, and usually warmer than the surface over which it is moving.

warm front. That line of discontinuity, at the earth's surface or at a horizontal plane aloft, where the forward edge of an advancing warm air mass is replacing a colder air mass.

warm sector. An area at the earth's surface bounded by the warm and cold fronts of a cyclone.

watch buoy. Station buoy.

weather map. Synoptic chart.

weather signal. A visual signal displayed to indicate a weather forecast.

weather vane. A device to indicate the direction from which the wind blows.

wind. Moving air, especially a mass of air having a common direction of motion.

wind current. A current created by the action of wind.

wind direction. The direction *from* which wind blows.

wind rose. A diagram showing the relative frequency and sometimes the average speed of the winds blowing from different directions in a specified region.

wind vane. A device to indicate wind direction.

wire drag. A buoyed wire towed at a given depth to determine whether any isolated rocks, small shoals, etc., extended above that depth, or for determining the least depth of an area.

zenithal projection. Azimuthal projection.

zone time. The local mean time of a reference or zone meridian whose time is kept throughout a designated zone.

Index